will chang...
your life'
Richard Branson

The Virgin
Travellers'
Handbook

**The definitive guide for students and
career gap travellers planning a gapyear**

Tom Griffiths

This edition first published in 2002 by
Virgin Books Ltd
Thames Wharf Studios
Rainville Road
London
W6 9HA

First published in Great Britain in 1999
by Virgin Publishing Ltd (as *The Virgin
Student Travellers' Handbook*)

A catalogue record for this title is available from
the British Library.

ISBN 0 7535 0633 5

Maps supplied by Draughtsman Ltd
maps@atlas.co.uk

Talk 21 screens used with kind permission of BT.

Designed by Dominic Cooper
Styled and typeset by Cooling Brown

Printed and bound in Great Britain
by Creative Print and Design (Wales),
Ebbw Vale

A disclaimer from Tom: a disclaimer is here for a purpose.
It allows me to say that what I have written is for you to take
on board in a sane and sensible manner. These are not the
two best words in the world to describe myself, so I know
what I'm on about. All the information has been thoroughly
researched and is based on my own experiences, but
neither my publisher nor I can take responsibility for any
consequences arising from the use of this book.

Foreword by Sir Richard Branson

As we move into the new millennium, the concept of taking time out – taking a 'gapyear' – is booming.

At eighteen, school-leavers (including my own daughter, Holly) are readily taking up the challenge of making the most of their year between school and university, part of which invariably involves some travel. As a result, universities now encourage a 'pre-university gap', citing maturity, confidence and a broader mind amongst the positive attributes of these young gappers.

The 'pre- and post-university gaps' have never been more popular and, with employers placing a high value on the life skills developed by these gappers, it is often the first topic of conversation in an interview. With major graduate schemes now receiving 50–200 times the number of applications for each place offered, what will make you stand out from the rest?

Last but not least, the infamous 'career gap' has now become the topic of conversation amongst many 25–35-year-olds. Increasingly the search for more than just a successful nine-to-five job, car and house lead many to head off overseas, usually with the blessing of employers eager not to lose valuable employees suffering from the fatigue from life's never-ending treadmill.

Whatever stage you are at if you decide to take a 'gap', it will change your life. Tom's message is clear – nothing is ever achieved by staying at home and it's up to you to shape your own future. This book will certainly help you achieve that. His energy and enthusiasm is infectious and, being of the same age as his readers, my hope is that his 'if I can do it, you can' attitude will tempt many of you to pluck up the courage and take that final step.

So…live your dreams, do everything you have ever wanted to do, or go somewhere where you can really make a difference. You will only realise how young you are when you're too old to do anything about it! Most importantly, no matter what you do, enjoy it, as you are about to form memories that will stay with you forever. Have fun…

Sir Richard Branson

This book is dedicated to

Mum and Dad (again!). I know it's not easy to watch me go through it all, but I'm getting there. Mat and Rob for the constant support, advice and encouragement. Carolyn for always being there and always laughing no matter what. Jack, for being a wicked little nephew...and for being a messier eater even than Carolyn! Steph Lee, for reminding me 'what it is all about'. Tony – it all started with you matey. And Peter, for sharing the dream and who will make someone a great wife someday...!

The lessons I've learned...

Faith   you have to have it and show it...to be given it back.
Belief   if you don't believe in yourself, no one will believe in you.
Trust   trust others and they will trust you.

LIFE IS SHORT

You will soon notice that this is a theme running through this book. Recently 'Granjo', a grandmother we all adored, suddenly passed away. We were all devastated. I miss her terribly and think about her a lot.

Steph Lee (mentioned above) also passed away tragically recently whilst out volunteering in Thailand. She was 21. Following her gapyear to Southeast Asia at eighteen, she took an interest in the Karenni people on the Thai/Burmese border, and quietly raised over £28,000 to fund a refugee camp there. No one asked her to help, she just did it because it needed to be done. Her motto? *'I know that one person can't change the world...but I can change the world for one person.'* Over 4,000 people, including Karenni heads of state, attended her funeral in Thailand.

Both Granjo and Steph constantly remind me that *life really is short*, so short in fact that we often forget to live it! We worry about things that are irrelevant, forget to make time for the important things in life (or the people we care about most) and completely miss the point about why we are here...*to live our lives to the full and enjoy every minute.*

The world is one big mutha of an amazing place...

Go and see it.

Contents

Introduction

So why have I written this book?

For every 10,000 who take a gapyear and go off travelling the world, over 40,000 don't. Fact. Whilst the 'gapyear' is booming, the 'I bottled it' figures are going ballistic. Why?... because our generation has lost something. We lack drive, energy and enthusiasm, but most importantly the ambition and motivation to push ahead, live our lives and achieve our goals. Any excuse **not** to do something difficult...and we'll grab it!

This book will help those with a definite plan, but also guide those trying to 'get over the hurdles', by answering the questions that lead to the anxiety and nervousness that put us off finally 'going for it'...

Questions like :
- How do I pack a backpack for a year? What do I take?
- How am I going to afford it? Can I afford it?
- What are my parents going to say? How can I deal with a negative response?
- Will I be safe? Is travel dangerous?
- Who should I go with? Can I go by myself? Should I ask a mate?
- Can I find work over there?
- What if I get into trouble? What if I don't enjoy it?
- Where should I go?
- Can I really have a break in my career already?

...and then the big one...

WHERE DO I START?

Why me?
Well, over the past couple of years I have devoted my life to doing this kind of stuff via my first book, talks, articles, website (**www.gapyear.com**) and interviews in the media. At the time of writing, I'm 24. If I've 'done it', why can't you?

Why this book is different
I want you to read it, write in it, use and abuse it, and then give it to mum to keep by the phone. The *Back Section* – if you fill it in properly – will have everything they'll need to keep in touch and use should anything crop up. *Keep mum happy!*

Make sure you read:

● *How to...use the internet* – teaching you both how to use email properly whilst you're away **(the most essential way to keep in touch).**

● *Parents* – your parents are forced to accept silence and worry, **so wise up.** They worry about you, so worry about them – read this section carefully and take note.

I'm not afraid to scare you with home truths or be thought-provoking, in fact I want to make you think about your life for the first time ever...no, I mean **really think about your life in a way that will surprise you.** This all starts from getting stuff down in black and white, so, if a section needs to be filled in...get a pen and do it! Unfortunately, the book is useless if you wimp-out and don't go for it, which is why I want to get you thinking about what you are going to do. So ask yourself...

'Why do hundreds of thousands of 18–30-year-olds travel the world each year?'

We all have different reasons...

● **The ultimate way of 'finding' yourself**
Learning to appreciate others and who you are is a great thing (is this what they call 'growing up'?).

● **The challenge**
For me it was to go 'round the world' at eighteen and to hitch-hike solo across Canada at 21. Whilst others bus across America or cycle to Thailand, David Parker (a 24-year-old diabetic), walked across Australia in a world record 69 days! See *Travelling with diabetes* for David's advice.

Why did David cross Australia?   **'Because it was there!'**
Why travel?   **'Because you can!'**

● **'Been there done that' travellers**
Sitting on top of Ayers Rock, the Empire State Building, the Eiffel Tower – the sense of achievement as you tick another one off your mental check-list.

● **To meet people – 'Hi, I'm Tom...mind if I join you...?'**
If a stranger came up to you at home and said this, you'd probably tell them to 'sod off'. We're an anti-social bunch...sticking to our groups...**and then you go travelling.** In hostels and bars, you simply fit in – sitting around a table chatting about who you are, where you're from, and where you've been. Although from different countries, everyone is young and in the same boat.

● **Everyone else seems to be doing it...so I thought I'd give it a go!**
Say this and I'll kick your butt. Do it for the right reasons – your reasons, and don't let anyone shoot you down.

● To escape or change your life direction

For those stuck in a rut or in a job going nowhere, taking time out or a career gap can often be the solution to the problem of a life 'going nowhere'. Life always looks different when you are sitting up a mountain thousands of miles from here!

Whatever your reasons, the only question you'll find yourself asking is 'Why travel?' Hopefully your answer will be 'Why not?'

At the end of the day, you don't have to justify yourself to anyone…except you. As long as you are going travelling for the right reasons, then good for you.

As the concept of 'taking a gap' or time out embeds itself into **our** culture, more and more of us are disappearing off overseas to experience **other** cultures. We return with broader minds, self confidence and a fresh outlook on life that makes parents, family and friends double-take on impact. Like a good cheese, you have matured…your life has truly begun!

The bottom line?

You either live life, or exist. There's no in-between. You will never be totally happy in life until you are fully satisfied within…

Feedback

I am always interested in feedback, whether good or bad. So if you love or hate the book, please email me and let me know at **info@gapyear.com**.

If you want us to cover your trip, contact **editor@gapyear.com**…we are always looking for articles and, with the use of email, can cover you from virtually anywhere on the planet!

Good luck, enjoy the book…but most importantly, have fun. It is the most amazing experience you will ever have.

1: Getting started ▶

From my own findings, **out of every five people** aged 18–24 who talk seriously about going travelling, taking a gapyear, or doing something positive, **only one** ever does. For those approaching thirty, this figure is probably even higher. Just think about this for a second. Statistics tell us that that one person...**probably won't be you.** You think I'm joking don't you? **I'm not.** Don't be another statistic...and just so you don't forget, I'll keep reminding you as we go along. The moral of this statistic?

Descending the ladder of life

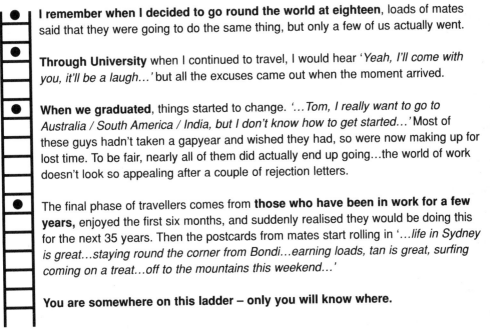

I remember when I decided to go round the world at eighteen, loads of mates said that they were going to do the same thing, but only a few of us actually went.

Through University when I continued to travel, I would hear '*Yeah, I'll come with you, it'll be a laugh...*' but all the excuses came out when the moment arrived.

When we graduated, things started to change. '*...Tom, I really want to go to Australia / South America / India, but I don't know how to get started...*' Most of these guys hadn't taken a gapyear and wished they had, so were now making up for lost time. To be fair, nearly all of them did actually end up going...the world of work doesn't look so appealing after a couple of rejection letters.

The final phase of travellers comes from **those who have been in work for a few years,** enjoyed the first six months, and suddenly realised they would be doing this for the next 35 years. Then the postcards from mates start rolling in '*...life in Sydney is great...staying round the corner from Bondi...earning loads, tan is great, surfing coming on a treat...off to the mountains this weekend...*'

You are somewhere on this ladder – only you will know where.

The fact that you're reading this now indicates that you are seriously thinking about travelling. For some reason, the bug has hit. You know deep in your heart that one day you will go. So why bottle out now?

My wise old brother Mat once said...**There are 'Doers' and 'Talkers' in this world.** I can't remember why, but he was spot on. **So which are you?**

Are you a 'Doer'?
Do you decide to do something and then get up and do it? Do you achieve and then look back on what you've done with pride?

Or are you a 'Talker'?

For a start, if you are, you won't admit it.

'Talkers' will always talk about what they want to do, when and where they are going to do it. They will then come up with a reasonably believable excuse about why they aren't going to do it this time, but what they intend to do next time. This is a bad habit to get into. It's your life, and as an adult it is up to you to take responsibility for it. Do you want to end up retiring and then realise you've missed out?

We've established that you are a 'Doer', so it's time to get started. Which means that it's time to make a list. No time like the present, so get your pen out! This stuff really works, so don't be shy.

Step One ❶

I'm going to ask you a question, which I want you to answer honestly. If you answer it honestly and fill in the stuff down below, you'll probably open up a whole load of thoughts you've never ever had before.

'If you had fifteen months to live and I gave you £50,000...where would you go?'

I know it may seem a bit sad filling this in, but, trust me, if you give it a couple of minutes' thought and do it properly, you'll surprise yourself. My suggestion is that if you're not going to do this seriously at this stage, wait until you are. Don't write just anything down.

The top ten countries I would like to visit ✏

1.
2.
3.
4.
5.
6.
7.
8.
9.
10.

The top ten things I would like to see (Ayers Rock, Taj Mahal etc) ✏

1.
2.
3.
4.
5.
6.
7.
8.
9.
10.

The top ten things I would love to do (bungee jumping, rafting etc) ✐

1.
2.
3.
4.
5.
6.
7.
8.
9.
10.

Now, in one sentence, write down your life's ambition ✐
Before I die I want to…

You now have a 'wish list'. Let's just pause here for a second and reflect on what you've just said. If you have taken the above questions seriously then the lists you have written, no matter how absurd they may seem to you right now, are what you want to do.

This is my way of getting you to look at what your dreams and ambitions are. Anyone can dream, but to have them written down and staring back at you, makes a helluva lot of difference.

Great…we're ready to start! ▶

Step Two ❶

Time scales ie. **when are you going to go?** This obviously depends on whether you're at school, University or have already joined the world of work.

FINAL YEAR AT SCHOOL

June	Finish exams
August	Get results
October	Uni / college academic year begins
Next October	**Your** Uni / college academic year begins

Options

1.	**WORK**	work from July to December (six months)
	TRAVEL	leave in January, when the air fares fall
		eight months' travel to August
	HOME	two months to prepare for Uni

2.	**WORK**	work from July to December (six months)
	TRAVEL	leave in January, when the air fares fall
		six months' travel to June
	WORK	get a job, work the summer, earn money for Uni

3.	**TRAVEL**	leave in September (before air fares rocket in the run-up to Christmas)
	CHRISTMAS	away from home. Ten months' travel to June, twelve months' travel to August
	HOME	month of September to prepare for Uni

NB. for this last one you will have to have enough money to go away with by September, or you have enough money for the flight and a bit extra, and have decided to go and find work out there – Sydney being the favourite place (see *How to...find work abroad*).

A couple of points

● **Although you have fifteen months,** you are still fairly 'time dependent'. Air fares rise and fall either side of Christmas, so waiting until February could save you loads.

● **You could work for a year,** using the holiday breaks to spend the money you're earning travelling overseas...a month over Christmas + a month over Easter + three months over the summer break = **five months away.**

POST UNIVERSITY

May / June	Finish exams
Results	June / July
Summer	Chill out? Work?

You then have two choices:

EITHER: Get a real job! **OR:** 6–18 months of the most amazing experiences
EITHER: Exist **OR:** Get a life, have a life, live a life

If you work for eight months from June to January, you can easily earn money to leave in the New Year (when the fares fall).

At this point in your life, 'the world literally is your oyster'.
- You can go wherever you want, whenever, and stay for however long you want.
- If you love a country, or find good work, stay for a bit.
- You are now 'qualified' (your degree) and so can go for thousands of jobs you were previously barred from. You may be an engineer, but finding it difficult to get a job at home. Maybe there's a shortage of engineers in Australia or South Africa? How do you find out? *Contact the international recruitment companies:*

TMP Worldwide 020 7806 8600 **www.tmpw.co.uk**
Robert Walters International 020 7379 3333 **www.robertwalters.com**

…ring them up, have a chat, and you never know, you may end up landing a job for when you arrive. **Imagine it – a job lined up for you in Sydney in June, giving you from January to June to travel to, say, Southeast Asia on the way.**

CAREER GAP

You know your timescales, you just need to make a firm decision, right? Some mates of mine decided to plan and save for a year, take time to make all the arrangements and bugger off to Australia. Others took two weeks to make the move! Some travelled for a month; others stayed for two years. It's your call! **Spend a weekend asking yourself what you want to achieve from your career gap.** Many companies will happily give you unpaid leave, guaranteeing your job when you return. Have you asked yours yet?

Before you move on to the next step, get a basic plan in your head along the lines of:

'I want to travel for six months, visiting America, the Pacific Islands, Australia, New Zealand and coming back through Southeast Asia, leaving in January, arriving back around June.'

Having done this, you can now contact a travel agent…

Step Three ❸

Hundreds of young people walk into student travel companies, all fired up, with one thing on their mind…'I want to go around the world!' Unfortunately, they don't know exactly where. Come on guys, help the sales consultants out, have a think first!

I hope you are aware that there are specialist student travel agencies out there. With the growth of student travel, companies like STA Travel, Trailfinders and Bridge the World have grown in line with demand. They specialise in the 18–24-year-old market. Trailfinders and Bridge the World cater more for the post-University market, but also give competitive prices. There are also loads of small independent travel agencies around, but, to be honest, **you're better off using the specialists.**

STA Travel ✕

STA Travel basically has the youth travel market sewn up in the UK. If you are a student or 26 and under, you can access cheap or discounted fares through them. They cater for your needs, as the staff are generally young people who have travelled and so understand what you are after. So use them! They have branches in the majority of student towns in the UK.

Before you call for a quote, get a basic plan sorted out first
Where do you want to go? Obviously a good place to start would be your list on page 10. If you need a bit more info then head to the **Top Fifty Backpacking Destinations** in this book and then to **gapyear.com**, where we have piles of articles about countries all over the world written by people like you who have 'been there, done that'.

In fact, a good weekend on the internet is highly recommended to find out more about the countries you are interested in going to and others you may never have thought about visiting. Surf to your heart's content taking notes as you go, bookmarking good websites you find on the way that you'll want to come back to.

Time to get a quote
The easiest way to do this part is to ring all the companies up in one go, tell them your plan / an intended route and write down what they say to compare, remembering to ask for any offers, specials, cheap days to fly out on, advice on when best to go, etc. To help you out with this, there is a box on the next page where you can write the quotes down along with notes and the name of the sales consultant (it's always easier not to have to repeat yourself).

When you tell them your rough plan (you don't need to have it finalised to ring for a quote), they will have a look to see what is on offer. Sometimes they will come up with real beauties such as the Air New Zealand deal, where you can stop off at a number of Pacific Islands for free:

'...you can then land in Christchurch, overland to the North Island and fly out of Auckland into Sydney. After Australia, fly on to Bali, overland to Bangkok and then home. Overlanding through New Zealand is extremely easy, as is the Bali to Bangkok route, taking you through Indonesia, Singapore, Malaysia and Thailand. You mentioned that you would like to go to Vietnam...we can book you a separate flight from Bangkok to Ho Chi Minh City, or failing that, you can get one when you are out there. So, prices...I'll put in a nominal departure date for 11 January and a date to return for 30 July. OK, that is going to cost you...'

They will then search around for other options or deals – we got an absolute stonker with Qantas – **three free flights within Australia** (so we were able to see the whole country). If you have specific ideas that are potentially difficult to pull off, now is the time to discuss them. Anything is possible with a combination of airlines, but breaking away from a basic 'round-the-world package' will cost you more. What do I mean? Such a package takes you to Los Angeles (a gateway city to the Pacific Islands), the Pacific

Islands, New Zealand and Australia and then back through Southeast Asia…or vice versa if you want to start in Southeast Asia. Adding stops in Africa, China or the North Pole breaks away from this route.

Ring for a quote:
STA Travel   020 7361 6129

Try to call in the mid-afternoon or evening when they will be less busy.

Would you prefer to go into a branch?

Call the number above and find out the nearest branch to you.

…or the information super-highway?

www.bridgetheworld.co.uk
www.statravel.co.uk
www.trailfinders.co.uk

Others worth a look are **www.austravel.co.uk** (as they often have great offers to Australia – the lowest I have ever seen at £299 once, yes £299!), **www.bargain-holidays.com**, **www.cheapflights.co.uk** and **www.lastminute.com**.

You are now ready to start planning your trip. Again, let's get this down on paper:

Where am I going to go?

Departing   **Returning**

Roughly how much is it going to cost? It's always advisable to get more than the one quote. Phone up the others, tell them your quote and ask them to beat it:

Quote 1 ✎
Company   STA Travel   ☎ 020 7361 6129
Name of sales consultant
Price
Notes

Quote 2 ✎
Company   ☎
Name of sales consultant
Price
Notes

Quote 3 ✎

Company

Name of sales consultant ☎

Price

Notes

INSURANCE

You need it, and it's not free. You can buy it from loads of places, so shop around. Beware of sharks, don't skimp and find a good deal where you are fully covered for everything you are likely to do on your trip, ie. adventure sports, scuba-diving, riding mopeds, etc. **Please** spend some time looking into this and don't leave it to the last minute like most people do.

Get a quote
Just like getting quotes for your flights, make sure you get a minimum of three. For a quote from insureyourgap either head to **www.insureyourgap.com** or call 0870 241 6703 and use this quote as a basis for the rest.

Need more advice?

● Have a look at Max's chapter on **Insurance**.
● Check out my 'Guide to buying insurance' on **gapyear.com**.

A quick word about round-the-world tickets

They are one of the safest bets for travelling the world. They are extremely flexible and don't tie you down. If you want to stay longer or move on earlier, you can phone, up to 24 hours before the flight, and change your departure date. You may have to pay a bit extra, but with STA Travel this is FREE from certain destinations (policies differ, so make sure you ask, and get it in writing). The good news is, as demand increases steadily from year to year, round-the-world ticket prices are falling. Three recent quotes from STA Travel and for travel from the UK are as follows:

London – Kuala Lumpur – surface – Singapore – Perth – Sydney – Auckland – Los Angeles – London – **from £660 + tax**

London – Singapore – Bali – Darwin – Cairns – surface – Sydney – Jo'burg – surface – Cape Town – London – **from £710 + tax**

London – Delhi – surface – Bombay – Sydney – Bangkok – London – **from £807 + tax**

These routes and prices are only a guide – please don't quote them!

NB: Tax will be £45–£60.

Personally, I don't recommend buying singles around the world, as you may get stuck in the arse end of nowhere with no ticket or money to get home. However, real bargains are always worth considering, especially if you intend to stay for a while.

Three points to consider

1. Here in the UK, flights are cheaper than in most other countries.

2. A round-the-world ticket is proof at borders that you're passing through their country and not planning to stay indefinitely.

3. If you are flying 10,000 miles to the other side of the world, why not see the rest of it? Stop-overs can be dead cheap and amazingly cool, so bear it in mind. NB: My mates Jason and Dave have bought singles out to Australia via the States, South America and a couple of Pacific Islands. They have worked a while in the UK, will find work in Australia and intend to stay for a bit. For them buying singles was the best thing to do.

 Round-the-world tickets: the big thumbs-up, especially for your first time.

PAYING FOR IT

Travel isn't free...but it is affordable. Every penny is important. **Save, save, save,** should constantly be on your mind – so not paying for rent and food is a bonus if you've got understanding/generous parents. If you're responsible for bills, food, rent etc. the onus is on you to earn, economise and save the shekels!

Need a job? The best ones are hard to find, so get writing to companies now. The fact that you need to save money for travel is a bonus as **they know that you'll work long hours.**

Tips on finding work

- Do it early, before everyone else (be a step ahead).

- Hammer home the fact that you need to earn loads of money fast and that you'll take all the hours given (and more!). *You need that money so you'll work for it.*

- Make your application smart, sharp and efficient.

- In an interview, be confident, be smart, but be yourself. Never be apologetic for being there (they wouldn't have asked you if they weren't interested). *Leave your 'smart arse' at home.*

They want to see a young person with a plan, so have one, and tell them about it. Working over Christmas and Easter in your final year will always help the bank balance, but don't let your studies suffer. You won't get a suntan re-taking exams! Study first, play later. You'll always regret a bad exam result.

Wanting to travel is also the best incentive in the world to study hard. Travelling with great grades can be the sweetest thing. Imagine sitting on the top of a volcano in Bali, on a beach in Bondi or trekking in Borneo with absolutely no weight on your shoulders, safe in the knowledge that…

1. **You can do anything you want** for the year because you have a place booked at the University of your choice.

2. **You can stay out for as long as you want** because you have the qualifications necessary to get a decent job when you get home, or anywhere else in the world.

NEED MORE ADVICE?

- 'Budgeting' is the next chapter!
- Read 'How to organise your finances'.
- Check out the 'Guide to Raising Money' on **gapyear.com**.

YOU'VE DONE ALL THE HARD WORK, IT'S TIME TO MOVE FORWARD. You know how much it's going to cost, when you're going, and you have a plan for your year. You are now halfway there…**SO PUT YOUR MONEY WHERE YOUR MOUTH IS! DO IT!**

Buy early

…a great way to start and ensure you're not going to bottle out. You are about to spend a lot of money and do something which, if we are honest with one another, is scaring the hell out of you (remember, we've all been there!). STA Travel are aware of this, and so have a **'buy early option' for £50** (acts as a deposit on flights which are provisionally booked for you)…you then pay the balance later. Should you change your mind, you will only lose the £50 deposit.

The benefits of booking early? You have a date to aim at.

In other words:

"I am going on 11 January. The round-the-world ticket will cost me £950. Insurance will cost me £85. By 11 January I am going to need to earn and save about £3,000 to have enough money to live off, because on the 12th, I'll be in India!"

Sum it up, Tom!

Great planning and all the donkey work involved with deciding where to go, getting quotes, finding a job, earning the money…**all count for nothing if you bottle out and don't go.** If at this stage you are wondering whether it's still a good idea…don't. Worried about the cost? Don't be. Thousands of people do it every year, so can you. Most importantly, if everything goes wrong, you can always change your flights and hotfoot it home. It's as simple as that. You've got nothing to lose, so give it a go. **Keep a cool head and you'll be fine.**

2: Budgeting

The Big Question – can you afford it?

Well…can you?

We're talking money here, everybody's least-favourite subject, apart from, perhaps, the Sultan of Brunei. This whole chapter subtly builds up to the fact that you're going to have to get your pen, calculator and brain in gear to do a bit of simple maths, so go and get them now – you need your money to last the whole time you're away!

'So, how much does it cost to go around the world?'
Let's break it down. For a six-month round-the-world trip…upwards of £700 for the ticket, £100 for the insurance and a bit more for backpacks, clothes, living expenses, transport etc. £1,000?, £2,000?, £3,000?

History says that if you put a load of money in our hands, we'll spend it. When you travel, there are thousands of opportunities…swimming with dolphins, scuba-diving, trekking, climbing volcanoes, bungee-jumping, rafting, pot-holing, paragliding…your money can, and will disappear.

You could end up overspending and be forced to come home early. It happens. It happened to me (more to do with the fact that I didn't have the money in the first place) and it could happen to you. Why go halfway around the world to do things, only to find that when you get there, you can't afford to do it anyway!!?

The only person to stop you doing this is you. Think about this right away. If you are on a really tight budget, look back at the 'wish list' you made, and look at the top three things that you want to do. For me it was bungee-jumping, rafting and sky-diving. No matter what happened, I was going to do these and nothing on earth was going to stop me. I therefore left £500 at home so I could stick them on my credit card when the time came, and get my mum to pay the bill using the money I'd put aside. I'm so glad I did, having now bungeed, rafted, sky- and scuba-dived my arse off! Class. You will only get one shot at most of these things whilst you are away, so start thinking about budgeting for them now.

Until you know how much all of this could cost, nothing else matters. To earn money, you need a job. No money, no travel. Here comes the moment of truth, so get your pen ready. It's time to create a balance sheet.

My Balance Sheet ✐

A: My stash
How much do I earn per day (after tax)? ....
How many working days is it until I leave? ....
What is the maximum amount of money that I can earn before I leave? ....
Do I have any savings? ....
Am I due a tax rebate before I leave (don't know? find out!)? ....
GRAND TOTAL for **My stash** ....

B: National Insurance
How much do I pay per week? ....
How much will I pay before I leave? ....
GRAND TOTAL for **National Insurance** ....

C: Whilst still at home
Rent (per week) ....
How much will I pay before I leave? ....
SUB TOTAL for *Rent* ....
Living expenses (per week)
Food ....
Electricity/Gas/Water/Council tax ....
Phone ....
Total amount before I leave? ....
SUB TOTAL for *Living expenses* ....

GRAND TOTAL (*Rent + living expenses*) for **Whilst still at home** ....

D: Extras (per week)
Socialising (beer, fast food, cinema, clubbing etc.) ....
Sports ....
Bits and pieces (music, clothes, videos etc.) ....
Total amount before I leave? ....
GRAND TOTAL for **Extras** ....

Add the GRAND TOTALS for B, C, D and take the sum away from 'My Stash' (the GRAND TOTAL in A).

How much do you have left?
This is the total amount of money you have to play with.
(let's call this '**My Wodge**')

To organise yourself for travelling you need to know what it's all going to cost.

So here we go...! ▶

E: Ticket + insurance

How much is your ticket? ----------------
How much is insurance? ----------------
GRAND TOTAL for **Ticket + insurance** ----------------

F: Things I need to buy

Backpack ----------------
Sleeping bag ----------------
Tent ----------------
First Aid kit ----------------
Clothes ----------------
Shoes ----------------
Other goodies ----------------
GRAND TOTAL for **Things I need to buy** ----------------

G: Accommodation and Food

As a very rough average, work on a cost of $20 per day. (MULTIPLY this by the approximate number of days you are going to need to pay for accommodation while you're away…don't panic, it's only an estimate!)
GRAND TOTAL for **Accommodation and Food** ----------------

H: Other transport

What other major transport will I have to pay for (internal flights, trains, buses etc)?
(Use guidebooks, travel agents and the internet for this one)
ROUGH TOTAL for **Other transport** ----------------

I: Socialising

Drinking, clubbing, fast food etc. – this is impossible to judge, as in some countries it will be dead cheap, and others, not…you may be going out all the time or not really have the chance or the time. To be on the safe side, add about $20 a week. This will even out. Be sensible. If you know that it's dead cheap where you're going add less…if you know that you drink like a fish or are visiting Sweden…be honest and multiply up.
GRAND TOTAL for **Socialising** ----------------

J: Adventure and other expenses (not yet included in lists above)

Bungee jumps ----------------
Rafting ----------------
Sky-diving ----------------
Sports ----------------
Others ----------------
GRAND TOTAL for **Adventure and other expenses** ----------------

Now add up the GRAND / ROUGH TOTALS FROM E to J. This will give you a rough idea of how much your experience is going to cost you. How much is this? (Let's call this the 'Travel Fund'!)

Now take the '**Travel Fund**' away from '**My Wodge**'.

If the 'Travel Fund' is bigger than 'My Wodge', this is what's known as negative accounting, meaning that you may have to live off lentils whilst you're away, not actually be able to afford to do **ANYTHING** whilst you're there (pain in arse) and maybe have to come home early (bummer!) **OR** You're going to need another job – one that pays better – a lottery win, or hope a rich relative you're not too keen on snuffs it! Think about this very carefully for a second.

DON'T at this point be put off by the fact that you think that you can't afford it. I may have scared you a bit, but don't use this as an excuse to do a runner. There is always a way round it. THINK. You may have to work for a bit longer and have less time away. You may have to find work overseas (see *How to...find work abroad*). Don't bottle it, beat it.

Tax

As the famous saying goes... *'**There are only two things you can be certain of in life, death and taxes!**'*...and only one of these can be avoided!

Tax is something that you're going to love to hate. The thing is, you may not need to pay it. There are loads of different tax brackets, so it's up to you to get it right. Watch out that you don't pay too much and that you sign the right forms. If you are a full-time student in the UK you are not obliged to pay tax, so sign a P38S form. If you earn below about £4,535 (at the time of writing), you are below the tax threshold. If you earn shedloads, you will be taxed. Most importantly, never agree to being on an emergency code with the promise of a rebate later as by the time your cheque comes through you'll be halfway up a mountain in Nepal. Of course, if you sign your account over to your parents, you'll be fine (see *How to...organise your finances*). If you do pay emergency tax, the Inland Revenue can pay it back into your account when you are away. Make sure you ask them how to arrange this. I prefer 'You've earned it, you take it, you spend it' – that £100+ won't get you far back home, but will give you a month in Vietnam!

National Insurance

You will have to pay this if you earn over about £60/week. The more you earn, the more you pay, and it's automatically taken from your pay packet. In the balance sheet above you can see that this soon adds up.

Any queries about tax, get in touch with your local tax office, which can be found in your local phone directory. Some of them are actually quite nice!! Give them a ring and have a chat. Tell them your plans and ask their advice.

Earning money

If you work your butt off, you can afford it. It's as simple as that. The hard graft now giving you an amazing trip, an 'achieved goal' and something good on your CV.

So how can you earn the money?

Any way possible. Get a job? Sponsored events – the London Marathon, shave your head, walk across the country? Wash cars, tidy gardens – cash in hand! Busk! – I do, with my didgeridoos (as long as you entertain and can draw a crowd, you can earn). However you do it, be proud of what you're doing and stick at it. The work may be mind-numbing, but, if you know that in 'x' months you'll be up a mountain, in the jungle or in a village in the middle of nowhere…what better incentive can you have? Time will go dead fast and before you know it, you'll be on the plane.

From the 'balance sheet' above, you know how much you have to earn. Your goal is in sight. Don't waste your cash now you know what you're saving for!

Sum it up, Tom!

'How much does it cost?'
I will always be asked this question. If I had a £1 for every time I'd been asked it, I'd be a millionaire by now. The thing is, having filled in the pages above properly, you'll soon realise that it's not a question of 'How much does it cost?', but **'How much can I afford?'**. If I stuck a price of £4,000 on a round-the-world trip, half of you would simply think 'sod it' and give up. This defeats the whole objective of a gapyear. However, if you know what the bare costs are going to be, work from there…the rest is up to you. If your mate can spend eight months away and you only three, so what?…you'll have the best three months of your life! It's not the length of time you're away that's important, it's what you do with it.

So get off the price tag issue
The only price you should be concerned with is the one you can afford. Work, earn and save. Save, save, save, save, save! Every £10 you save now will be two days' board and lodging next to an amazing beach in Thailand, a bungalow in the mountains in Nepal or in the middle of a game park in the depths of Africa. Just think about it for a second. £10 here in the UK won't even buy me a CD. It will, however, buy a few pints on a night out, or three McDonald's meals. Spend £50 on a decent shirt, pair of jeans or shoes OR have 10 days chilling in the most amazing surroundings in Vietnam. I know what I'd rather do, and I think you do too.

Worried about money? Don't be
Everyone else can do it, so why not you? Think around the problem, and if all else fails…find work out there. What I don't want to hear is that you have given up on the idea because you couldn't afford it. I worked in McDonald's to fund mine. Anyone can get a job at McDonald's.

The bottom line
Earning the money is down to you and you alone. If you need it, earn it. If you can't be arsed, fine, but don't whinge at me. I've held down three jobs at a time. I know others who have had more.

That's it.

'Nuff said!

3: Who to go with?

Who do you go with? With your mate? With the love of your life? On your own? Will you be lonely? Will you get fed up with them? There are loads of advantages and disadvantages to both. If you are by yourself, I think you get a lot more out of travel. Each day is completely new; you go where you want, with whom you want, and learn a lot about yourself. It's amazing just who you can be when there are no links to home peering over your shoulder...*that's right...you can be yourself!*

Occasionally though, it's great when you get to a place late at night, to just sit with your mate and chill over a beer. Sometimes you just can't be arsed to go through the 'meeting people' saga – all you want to do is relax with a bit of familiar company. Finding accommodation, queuing for food, haggling with taxis, getting photos with you in them and dealing with problems is **always** easier if there is someone else around. Sometimes it's great to share experiences with others. Sometimes your mate/partner, quite simply, gets on your @**!ing nerves!

If you do decide to travel solo, you hook up with others anyway, so you'll never be by yourself unless you go to really remote areas and make no effort to meet people. The good friends you make will become 'life-long', always putting them up on your couch, sending Christmas cards etc.

Below, I'll take you through both options, solo travel and going with mates. Mates can get on your nerves and solo travel does need a bit of thinking about. Whatever you do, you'll be fine. Travelling is safe and easy. The only problem you'll have is convincing mum that to go off by yourself is a good idea, especially if it involves a country that has been hitting the headlines recently for all the wrong reasons.

SOLO TRAVEL ✗

'Will I get lonely?' 'Am I going to meet people?'
If you are not a naturally confident person, then you'll probably never think about travelling solo anyway. However, I met Ed, one of the shyest people on earth, who'd decided to travel solo as a character-building exercise. We finally met him in Oz – he was brimming with confidence and bloody amusing. He carried a guitar with him...

A quick note about guitars – they're great for breaking the ice, making friends and, if you are any good, making you impossible to forget. They are bulky and get knocked about a bit (so take a cheap one), but all who carry them say that they are well worth the trouble.

The beauty of travelling solo

You are your own person. You can go where you want and stay until you decide to go. You can hook up with people you like (and travel with them for a bit), avoid those you don't, or leave them and hook up later with others. You have total freedom.

Will I get lonely?   **No.**
Am I going to meet people?   **Yes.**

Of course, if you don't make any effort, you'll be left out, but as I mentioned earlier, it's easy to meet and make friends. Hostels are usually staffed by travellers or friendly people, and everyone is in the same boat anyway. You can't help meeting people.

Having time to yourself...to reflect on life

It's good every once in a while to have a bit of time to yourself. Some of the most special moments in my life have been when I was travelling alone. **One day you'll have a 'special moment' which will probably change your life.**

My 'special moment'

Sitting on a rock on the side of Lake Superior was unique and amazing. I had just proved to all my doubters that I could hitch-hike solo across Canada, and had met some amazing people, heard some incredible stories and learnt a lot about life and people's kindness. I was sharing a tent space with Stu and Wendy Sutherland, a couple of strangers who had picked me up in one of the worst hitching spots in the world. They showed me the most incredible kindness. As the sun set **it suddenly hit me...life is short.** I realised that it was important to get a good degree and make sure I always did things in my life that I enjoyed and believed in (which seemed to be the 'secret to a successful life' from the people I met). I decided to work for myself, answer to no-one and have a laugh doing it.

...and here I am!

This all stemmed from a bit of space and freedom, the chance to be alone with my thoughts and have a major think about my life. When I am in an amazing place, I just take it in for a minute...and feel great to be alive. You only get this by escaping from your home environment and your mates. This is what I got out of travelling solo.

The disadvantages of solo travel

Fending for yourself, asking others to take photos of you, guarding your own stuff when looking for accommodation etc.

For the next section I have asked 'Cousin Helena' (who is a very experienced traveller) to take you through women travelling alone.

Girls Solo – Women Travelling Alone by Helena Sampson ✈

What's Stopping You?

There is absolutely no reason why a girl shouldn't travel alone. I admit it's not for everybody, and you do need a certain amount of confidence and determination to go for it, but the rewards are rich, mainly in amazing experiences and the wonderful people you may meet. Whether you're 17 or 71, in India, Indiana or Indonesia, you are at a distinct advantage, **because everyone – local and tourist alike – wants to be sure that you are safe and comfortable.** People go out of their way to help you...booking trains, finding accommodation etc.

I spent four amazing days staying in the Golden Triangle in Thailand with a Thai family I met when hitching a lift. After an hour of curious introductions, sharing snapshots of my family and giving their five-year-old daughter a few balloons and bottle of magic bubbles that I had brought with me from England, there was no way that they would allow me to find a hotel and explore the area alone...I saw a side of Thailand that most travellers and tourists never have the opportunity to experience.

Risk Minimisation

Your safety is paramount, so always be hyper-aware of everything that is going on around you. Act in a confident manner and have eyes in the back of your head. Your instinct and gut-feel is often justified, so act on it.

A few tips for hassle-free travelling: Always prepare your journey, even if it's just around the corner. Try to remember your route. If you need to re-consult a map, be discreet. If all else fails, ask a local shopkeeper/restaurant owner for directions. **Avoiding attention is good...**

... unless you are already being hassled – in which case drawing attention to yourself is a good thing.* Carry an alarm to attract attention (if threatened), and use your lungs and feet. **Never try to fight your way out of a threatening situation, as travellers' cheques, watches and backpacks can be replaced...you, however, cannot.**

I was accosted in Peru when trying to change travellers' cheques on the black market. My aggressor was a teenage lad, brandishing a knife. I lost a fake watch, my 'decoy' wallet (containing about $10) and my travellers' cheques. Within two hours, I had a full set of replacement cheques from American Express. **In such a situation, hand your decoy wallet over and avoid taking anything with you that can't be replaced.**

If you get lost, try to look as if you know where you are going. A confident walk may deter a potential harasser. Be aware at all times.

On local transport, sit near the driver and if you have to share a seat, sit next to another woman. In Rajasthan, I was unpleasantly groped by a harmless local drunk on an overnight

* There is a brilliant personal alarm in the **gapyearshop.com** which also converts into a door and luggage alarm.

WHO TO GO WITH?

bus journey. Because I was very loud and affronted (although wanting to blub my eyes out), the local women on the bus had him thrown off, and couldn't do enough to mother me (equally terrifying!). *Avoid these situations by choosing your neighbour with care.*

Call home and/or email regularly. This will give your parents peace of mind. Arrange when you will contact them, and stick to it. Bear in mind that in some countries where telecommunications are less advanced, you may queue for ages for a phone and then for an available line to the UK.

Politically unstable countries. Report your presence to your embassy. Within hours of our arriving in Jordan in 1990 (the same day Mr Hussein decided to lay claim to Kuwait), the British Embassy had organised security passes for us through the West Bank into Israel. Now that's what I call customer service!

'Fitting in' is key to a safe trip…and will open doors you never dreamed of. **In Muslim countries** shoulders and heads should be covered at all times – respect for this custom will grant a greater chance of acceptance. **Dressing inappropriately** will offend the women, and be seen as 'available' by the men (whose perception of western women comes from snapshot views of satellite TV porn). **NB: local attire is also suited to the climate** – covering heads and shoulders avoids sunburn, heat stroke and insect bites.

Handy hints for a suitable Girl Solo dress code:

THE most essential item is a **decent-sized sarong**, for wrapping around the waist as a skirt (below the knee), over the shoulders when visiting religious monuments, for covering the head, as both towel and beach towel, and for dressing speedily in an emergency.

A smart outfit (preferably crease-free) for 'smart' occasions, 'impressing' (eg. applying for visas at sensitive borders) or for work.

A fake wedding ring is also great to deter potential hassles and would-be-husbands! It lends respectability in countries where it is not considered acceptable for young women to travel alone, and if in a fix, simply suggest that your husband is joining you today/tomorrow.

Do remember to **take plenty of sanitary protection** if you plan to visit under-developed countries, especially the rural areas. You can get most things in most big cities nowadays, but may pay a huge premium.

Looking back, *the major problem that I encountered as Girl Solo was the 'limpet fellow-traveller'.* As a solo female traveller, there are always plenty of people happy to hook up with you…beware of trust in other travellers.

Overview
You can choose to travel for portions of your trip with like-minded people who you meet *en route*. *At times you need a blunt, honest approach to unwelcome company.* You alone make the decisions, you alone are responsible for yourself. It's your adventure.

If you are prepared to go for it and use it wisely and with judgement, it is surely the most free a person will ever be.

You will have more ups and downs when you're solo, but you'll learn a lot more. With no-one to rely on, you are forced to cope. Your confidence rockets as you become adept at making friends and getting involved (rather than waiting for stuff to happen to you). You will meet like-minded people and hook up with them as travel partners. Whenever you seek solitude, you'll find it. Travelling solo gives you a chance to reflect and focus on what's important in life.

Safe? Male or female?
Yes. Look after yourself, avoid dodgy situations and think on your feet...like any other traveller. You can always be around other people should the need arise. **If you are contemplating it, just go for it. You will be fine and you can always come home!**

Need more advice?
Head to the 'Gapgirls' section on gapyear.com to meet others in the same boat or to get advice from girls who have been there, done that.
Boys – there is a similar 'Gaplads' section for you.

TRAVELLING WITH A FRIEND   ♙

There is no doubt that travelling with a friend or a partner can be a great idea...amazing experiences are often doubled if shared with another person.

Convenience
One sits with your gear while the other searches for a place to stay, haggles for taxis, waits in queues, checks out, organises things etc.

Companionship
You will never get lonely, as there is always someone there. The late beer with undemanding company, sharing the burden of difficult decisions.

Lots to think about
I have met loads of people who started the trip with someone else (girlfriend, boyfriend, best mate or Uni friend) and ended up going their separate ways, causing bitterness and resentment of *'it was all their fault'*. This wrecks friendships and can ruin your trip (especially if one goes home). If you are considering travelling with someone else, I want to give you food for thought and a few ideas on how to have a good time, and return without having killed each other.

Your best mate
Your buddy, 'the girls', 'the duo', 'the team'...you've known each other for so long that you've got photos of them aged five with no pants! You've 'been there done that' – and never been caught! There's nothing you wouldn't do for them. Your parents know each other and are happier that you are going off with them and not 'Mental Mat' from Angelsea Road! So, how are you going to get on? Fine.

...or are you?

You usually sort out grumbles with a quick 'Don't be an idiot!'. By the time you end the trip, the bond between you will be even stronger. Even so, ask yourself…

Your travelling partner
- How well do you know them?
- Is there something about them that annoys the hell out of you?
- Do you have the same budgets?
- Whose idea was it to travel in the first place?
- Are they 'attached to you' under the title of 'girl/boyfriend'?
- Is one, or both of you, gay?
- Do either of you have a disability?
- Who is the more confident?
- Who is the more talkative?

Is there anything about the above list which, when you look at it now, strikes you as uncomfortable?
- Is there an annoying laugh?
- Is he a bit sexist?
- Does she exaggerate the whole time?
- Are his jokes repetitive/crap, yet he thinks they are great!
- Does she get really embarrassing after a few beers?

You're about to spend 24 hours a day with this person!
Irritating habits, back home, can be laughed off and ignored. While you are away, minor irritations can easily become major aggravations. The two of you are sitting there with a group of new people, and that laugh appears…

There might be things about you that they find irritating, but as mates, they never say – so a bit of give and take is essential here. Spending so much time together, best mates or not, is going to take its toll on anyone.

IT IS VITAL YOU HAVE AN HONEST DISCUSSION BEFORE YOU HEAD OFF

Go for a beer…and have a chat about your impending trip. Should you decide that you need to have a break from each other for a little bit, why not meet up further down the road? If you're a bit nervous and think 'It's easy for you to say that Tom!' – don't worry. *Have the conversation and then see when you get out there.*

You also need to agree that, should anything happen, you get it out in the open. Never bottle anything up when travelling, as it only gets worse. Bring things up and then, most importantly, *always agree to find a solution or end to the argument.* You guys are going to have to work these things out – people split up for all sorts of reasons – please don't let this happen to you.

If you're thinking '**…nah, we're cool about this…we've been mates for years…**', good…then it'll be easier for you to have this conversation and keep it in the back of your mind throughout the trip. ***Should things start to go wrong, nip it in the bud as soon as possible.***

Planning the trip together
'Together' means together. Don't settle for being happy to let the other make the decisions, **it's your trip too you know**, so make sure you get what you want. You should both write down your preferred trip and then compare notes. A few extra hours of thought and research to find a common ground may save you going to a place you shouldn't have gone to, or missing out on others.

Push each other to get organised
By planning the trip together you can encourage each other to get yourselves organised and off… stopping stupid spending, checking savings and setting targets for buying the ticket.

Travelling with your man / woman   ♈

Romantic walks along deserted beaches? Cuddling up in a hammock under the stars? …may seem like a good idea when you are at home working your butt off to earn the cash. However, when the row that has been following you around all evening finally hits (just you two alone in the room except for two Japanese, three Italians, a German, a Canadian and a Swiss guy called Hans)…the romantic bubble bursts faster than a balloon in a pin factory. They all know, you know that they know, and they all know that you know that they know! Tension? No shit!

Ask yourself the question… **'is this the first long period alone together?'**

Like anything in life, sometimes it works, and sometimes it doesn't. I don't want to put you off travelling with your partner as I know of a few who have done it with great success, but then I've also met loads of 'ex-couples' who had a mare!

Breaking up is a nightmare at the best of times, so imagine being thousands of miles away from home and the usual support mechanism of mum, dad, mates and chocolate! Serious point though. It is tragic when one of you ends up coming home alone, early.

Leaving your other half at home
You've been planning the trip for ages. 7 August, D-Day, you are going Round the World. One month to go, at a party…a god/goddess walks through the door. You fall in love. You start to date, you both know that you're leaving in a few weeks. What do you do? Whether you have been going out for four weeks or four years, it's a dilemma!

At the start of Uni loads of my mates tried to continue long-distance relationships, 99% lasted a month. There were tears, broken hearts and mountains of chocolate eaten…and that was just the lads! Advice? Can't give any…it's up to you. You know what your relationship is like, just bear in mind that from the age of 18–24, relationships do come and go.

WHO TO GO WITH?

For those of you approaching thirty, or at a stage where things are getting a little serious, you obviously have your reasons for leaving and know how your partner fits in, if at all. If you are reading this and are still unsure, all I can say is good luck. Take your time and remember…life is short and things happen for a reason…

There is a happy ending to this one…I have known many couples who have been split up by travel, but, when the partner returned, have got back together. So it can work. May I suggest investing in one of the cheap international calling cards and have a serious read of *How to…keep in touch*.

Going away as a group

This will either work really well, or be a complete disaster. No middle ground.

How well do you know each other?
You can get away with not knowing each other, loads of 'combinations' to keep the peace – unless there is one person everyone hates – 'nice one sunshine!' Cockney Paul…gets a bit much sometimes! **A clash of egos can get very messy** if a couple of you like to play the starring role, but with a few of you, this can usually be sorted out quickly. If there are three of you, and two are quite similar, don't get 'cliquey' and leave the other out – be considerate.

IT IS VITAL that you all sit down and chat the trip through before you go away. If there are going to be tensions, it's best to find out sooner rather than later, and nip them in the bud. It is important not to be selfish. If you are not enjoying something, don't make life hell for the others. It's their trip too (you may end up being left behind somewhere!). **Remember, the last person to realise that you are the problem is you**, so take criticism on the chin like an adult and adapt. Don't get bogged down in petty arguments. You are out there for a laugh. Have one.

Advantages of travelling with someone else

The accommodation search etc. Also, by sharing your room and combining your budget, you can save money; buy food to cook between you; changing money together to save on commission. Most importantly, there's always someone around for companionship, security and sharing unique moments.

Making new friends
With a friend, or in a lively group, you will draw people to you (including those crowds of solo travellers). Make a hostel lively and its reputation will spread (the guys running the hostels know this and may be willing to keep you there).

Someone else to help carry the tent!
Taking a tent can save a lot of money, as you pay for the pitch, not the number of people in it. A tent is also a great way to meet some really cool local people (see *How to…camp*).

And the disadvantages?

There aren't all that many…if things go wrong you are sort of bound by this *invisible rope,* making it difficult to get a bit of space to think things through (problems can fester and boil – even long-standing friends may need a bit of space). If one of you has the budget of a wealthy Arab state and the other of a skint student, this may cause problems. Show a little consideration, but don't be dissuaded from doing things just because your partner can't afford it…*consideration swings both ways, you know*.

Think about love and what it has done/is doing for you. **It is better to leave 'the other half' at home, than have them come with you and be looking at their watch all the time wondering when they can leave!** This is not the way to travel.

Sum it up, Tom!

Travelling with a mate, or a group of friends, can be one of the best things in the world. Sharing this amazing experience can bring you even closer together. But when something happens or trouble erupts from nowhere, things can go wrong. People feel constricted by being with each other for 24 hours a day, and things can explode. Trust me, it happens. Talk to each other and sort your stuff out. Leave all egos, stubbornness and temperamental behaviour at home. If they comment on your behaviour, take note. Trust their judgement and they'll trust yours.

Your bloke/woman. Young love can be cruel. Many people cancel their plans and their trip to stay at home with their 'loved one', only to find that around the corner they walk into 'Dump City' (in either direction). **If it is meant to work, it will**. For practical reasons, safety, the loneliness factor and the overall sharing of the whole experience, it can't be beaten. But please, don't argue about things which will mean nothing in a day's time…and come back home together!

How romantic. I'm starting to get a warm, tingly feeling inside!

4: Being safe

'There is always someone bigger and harder than you out there.' Fact.
If you don't think so, you're a prat and one day you'll meet them. Grow up.

Being safe is something which, at the end of the day, is up to you. If you go around doing stupid things and getting involved in disputes which are nothing to do with you…then it's your fault, your responsibility and you are the only person to blame. Every once in a while something happens to a backpacker that excites a media frenzy. Splashed all over the headlines: **'BACKPACKER KILLED IN…', 'MY SON DIED BACKPACKING', 'DEATH ON THE BACKPACKER TRAIL!'**

For anyone to lose someone they love is a terrible thing, and for a person to lose their life at such a young age is a tragedy. Unfortunately a very cruel paradox is drawn. You have to live life to the full, but that may mean taking risks, especially if you are planning to go off travelling and seeing the world. I hear a lot of parents saying…**'I'm not going to let my son/daughter go off travelling…it's not safe'…NOT SAFE! NOT SAFE!**

Pick up the papers! Have a look at what's happening in your own back yard. It's a bad world out there. You're actually 'safer' overseas than you are in familiar surroundings that you see every day (to the point that you don't notice them). You are so relaxed at home that, without knowing it, you take risks every day. However, when you travel, you are hyper-aware of your surroundings…**Who's that guy? What does she want? Why is he talking to me?** Dark alleys look dark and dangerous, short cuts are never taken and you'll always be exceptionally careful when you take money out or handle it in the street. When you handle cash at home, what precautions do you take?

News, bad news, worse news… Whenever there is a blue moon and something happens to a backpacker, the media pick up on it. There was a feature quite recently about a young guy who died overseas, on a brief trip before he went to University. Unfortunately it appeared that he died of a 'freak' medical complaint that could've struck anywhere in the world. Had he died of the same thing in Birmingham, this article would not have been run. 'My son died backpacking' appeared on the front page where it was read by thousands of parents. I spoke to a few parents to see what they thought – the general opinion was that it was their worst nightmare and so, naturally, unsettling. Articles like this don't help the backpacker cause.

…I rarely see articles about how many backpackers there are out there having an amazing time, with follow-up articles by those who, as a result of their time away and a chance to become broader minded and more confident, have cruised into University or stormed into the jobs and careers of their choice. The news never ends with a quip about the tens of thousands of female backpackers out there who are safe and having the most incredibly fulfilling time of their life!

So, we choose to generalise and form opinions on something we know nothing about. **BACKPACKING IS DANGEROUS. WHY? BECAUSE I'VE READ ARTICLES IN THE PAPER AND I'VE HEARD STORIES. I REFUSE TO LET MY SON/DAUGHTER GO.** This is what many of your parents may think. This is maybe a good time to check out the *Parents* and *How to...keep in touch* sections. Be aware of your parents' worries and try and calm their fears. Find a good method of keeping in touch, and use it!

How should you keep safe?   ❶

Think about the country/countries you are going to. Are they safe, or more importantly, are they considered safe? The Foreign Office has a website – **www.fco.gov.uk** and a page on Ceefax (470) where you can access this information (for more info and numbers see *Embassies, passports and visas*). In many unstable countries (African nations in particular) people tend to pick up guns and charge toward the capital when the politics go wrong. This is the sort of stuff you don't want to get involved in! War zones – don't even think about it. Drought, volcanoes, hurricanes, tornadoes, avalanches – a little research will tell you what is happening and where to avoid. If you are in an area when a hurricane or tornado hits, make sure you know what to do.

Being Mugged
Unless you have been mugged, you may think you know how you are going to deal with the situation, but you don't. When I was sixteen, I was mugged in France. I got chatting to a couple of cool blokes...the next minute a knife the size of a sword was produced! It would have been great to produce a rocket launcher from my pants and say '...tell you what asshole, why don't *I* take *your* money?...' and then stroll casually into the nearest bar, sit down next to a gorgeous girl...dreams eh!?

In reality, I was stunned. I stood there thinking '...this isn't happening to me, this isn't happening to me, this isn't happening to me, this isn't happening to me, this isn't happening to me...'. I was petrified and ashamed at being caught out. But there I was in a very dark street with a guy, a knife and a wallet full of cash that he'd noticed when I'd bought a drink earlier. He was being aggressive, I was being mugged. I let him have the money, he ran off. I was in shock. It had happened so quickly, I didn't have time to think.

When I got back to school after that summer, the word went round...I had comments like *'...why didn't you hit him?...you should have chased after him...I'd have told him to @**! off!...'* ...sure you would, boys! It's all very well being smart and hard from afar.

Should it happen to you, think...*Is my life worth what I have in my pocket or on my person?* If your answer is (obviously) 'NO!', then why fight someone with a weapon for it? Just give it to them. I lost £40. Big deal. Even if I was carrying the Crown Jewels, I would still not give up my life. Full stop. Why? Because I like living too much...

Are they in control of the situation? Assess their mental state. People mug for a reason, quite often due to drugs. More than likely they will be off their face and – if 'tooled up' – dangerous. In this situation, stay calm and hand over the money, or whatever... promptly. They will soon disappear to get the next fix anyway. If they are nervous, and you're not backed into a corner or down an alley and are **sure** that there are other people about – do a runner! Distract them with 'POLICE!' as you point over their shoulder, and as they turn away, run in the opposite direction (it works!). If you have a bag, push it into them to put them on the back foot and then peg it. They're unlikely to chase you as they'd have to rugby tackle you and wrestle money from you. They'll always find someone else.

Final thoughts on muggings It will all be over in a minute, except it will seem even quicker. You will never see that person again. Put it behind you and learn from it.

Hand over a 'dummy wallet' (containing a bit of cash and nothing else). If you have your main wallet, keep your head, take control of the situation, open it up and take all the money out. Give it to them. Don't give them all the stuff inside that is of value to you.

Be alert...if you sense a situation developing, avoid it (you may misread an innocent situation, so what? It's better to be safe than sorry). Having been mugged, I'm determined that it won't happen again. In Manchester with my girlfriend, I spotted two guys coming towards us on the dark side of a street, hoods pulled down, checking me out, looking to see if anyone was around. My sixth sense went into overdrive. I put my arm around my girlfriend and forcefully led her into the middle of the road. The two guys stopped, bemused, watching us pass them in the middle of the road. They had a quick chat and continued on their way. They were going to try it on, I was sure of that. Situation averted.

If someone grabs your bag (with everything in it) and runs, think about giving chase. Try and keep tabs on where they go. If they grab your pack, definitely give chase as they'll have a hernia within fifty yards and they'll think 'sod this!' and drop it. Beware, never chase them into quiet areas, things could get worse. Use your judgement.

THE BOTTOM LINE: **DON'T FIGHT, JUST HAND STUFF OVER. IF YOU GET STABBED, SLASHED, BEATEN UP OR KILLED, YOU'LL REGRET IT! PUT IT DOWN TO A BAD EXPERIENCE AND TRY NOT TO LET IT HAPPEN AGAIN.**

KEY POINTS ON KEEPING SAFE

Trouble in the street – nothing to do with you – don't get involved. Look after yourself and those around you, but do a runner if it gets hairy.

Don't look like a tourist! Blend in with the crowd, stay in busy areas and keep your valuables hidden. By taking plain white plastic bags with you when you go out you can pass as a local. Holding maps and pointing at monuments makes you stick out. Be discreet when you're lost, because when you're lost, you're vulnerable.

In the hostels ✦

There are always assholes who decide to help themselves. You're unlikely to find them and get your stuff back (it's also easy for locals to 'blend in'). Just make sure that they don't get the opportunity in the first place.

👍 The chain on my backpack (see **How to...pack**) secures it to the bed or immovable fitting in the room.* 'Saklocks' stop people rooting around. A locked door (not possible in most dormitories) stops people getting in. Most hostels have safes, but if they don't, keep your valuables with you. Most backpackers look out for each other, so introduce yourself, be nice and get to know others in the dormitory, so they notice if someone is messing around with your stuff. Valuables in your pillow or at the bottom of your sleeping bag when you sleep are impossible to nick.

👍 **Don't trust anyone** '...*excuse me, I'm just popping out for five minutes, could you just watch my cash, passport and credit cards for me?...*' '...*Si señor!...*' Know them first and ask yourself '...If someone walked off with this right now, how would I feel?...' If the answer is 'Crap', don't take the chance.

👍 **Be security-conscious.** If there are a couple of you travelling, why not get a twin room and keep it locked? Tony and I did this in Sydney, whilst staying in Kings Cross (which can be a dodgy area). We were able to sightsee without worrying about our stuff. In hot countries, hostels leave the windows open for a breeze. There are usually beds next to windows and fire escapes on the other side. I shall say no more.

👍 **Be choosy.** Anyone can open a hostel and many will pack everyone in with no concerns for safety. You may have a key to the room, but then so may every thief in the block! If you don't feel safe, find somewhere else.

EXTREMELY IMPORTANT NOTE
The Childers Hostel fire, which killed a number of backpackers, is a very good warning to check the hostel out before you stay there and **don't** be afraid of going elsewhere and telling the owners why. Some hostels are dangerous as owners pack backpackers in. Read page 263 for more advice.

Sum it up, Tom!

Being safe and looking after yourself and your belongings is something that is up to you. You will develop this sixth sense, which will help you avoid certain situations and deal with others. Travelling is safe and easy. It is very rare that any of the above will happen, however, it is essential that you are aware that it could happen, and that if it does, you are the only one who can deal with it while you are away. If it happens, it will be scary, occasionally dangerous / potentially life-threatening, but as long as you stay cool, you'll be fine. Don't let it ruin your trip. Learn from it. It happened, but life goes on.

---

* **gapyearshop.com** has a pile of safety gadgets and advice on how to use them.

5: Mum and Dad...parents!

Before I start, an important point. *This book is designed to be given to your parents when you leave (or a close friend or relative). There is a section at the back which you should fill in anyway, so that you both have a record of your travellers' cheques, passport, insurance etc, which you will find invaluable if anything goes wrong as your parents can sort it out from home...(easier, quicker and will save you a fortune in time and money). Make photocopies of these pages and take them with you. Your parents will have everything in one place, details of changes in your itinerary etc.* It's essential that you fill these pages in and give them to your parents anyway...an assurance that you will be fine and that, if anything happens, you (and they) will be able to deal with it.

I know that both 'kids' and 'parents' will be reading this section, so I'm going to try and split it up to give you both food for thought. This is a very personal section for me. I have made many mistakes and learned from them, so have a lot of good advice 'for the kids'. However, I have also seen the different viewpoint of many parents who have asked my advice on the gapyear dilemma. It all boils down to the question of letting them go. But it's not easy.

What you guys need to do right now is talk

If you are 'The Kid' reading this, and wondering what all the hassle is about, I want you to start taking a more mature view about what you are about to do...*have you told your parents that you are about to go overseas or around the world for a while?...* **No?** Just nip out and tell them and see what their reaction is! **Oh...and...Good Luck!**

If you are 'The Parent', 'The Enforcer of all Rules', occasionally 'The Embarrasser of your Offspring' please read this section with an open mind. Taking a gapyear, or indeed travel of any sort, is one of the most amazingly beneficial things your son or daughter can do. If you don't know why, have a quick read of the last part of '*Back to reality!*' about employers and University.

Parents worry, because it is their job to worry. They have 'reared' you up until this point. They put your absurd irrationality down to puberty and have forgiven you for your outrageous behaviour, ridiculous clothes, attitudes and opinions, and they know not to push it because they were young once...

And, for the girls out there...exactly why didn't your dad let you out when you were in your teens? **BECAUSE HE REMEMBERS WHAT HE WAS LIKE!**...a quick splash of the old Brut...flares so wide that there were certain streets he just couldn't go down!!...

'I'll tell you why you can't go out dressed up like that…that's not a skirt, it's a belt, and I don't care what everyone else is wearing nowadays…when you're old enough to earn a decent living, have a mortgage and pay your own way, you can do what you please…but whilst you're living under my roof, you do as I say…this is our home, not a hotel… **I WAS A YOUNG MAN ONCE, AND I KNOW WHAT THEY'RE LIKE!!!…end of chat!**'

Parents are parents because they had you! If you are the eldest in the family or an only child, this is going to be new ground for them. It's not their fault, they've never been in this situation before. **OK, you have this situation, you are there now – deal with it.**

At eighteen you are classed as an adult by law. If you do silly things, you can now end up in prison. You can vote, smoke your life away, drink yourself to death, run off in a moment of madness, marry someone completely unsuitable, get divorced. No-one can stop you. Dangerous thought eh!? You may not fully appreciate this, but your parents do. Until now they have been in control, bringing you as best they can to this point, to send you out into the world 'well equipped' to be a decent member of society, and make them proud.

A new relationship?

BE THAT ADULT. Work with your parents on this one, not against them. After years of trying to break away from them, you will now witness a kind of 'coming back'. Getting to know them better, many 'kids' now see their parents more as friends and advisors.

What do your parents want to know?
Basically that you are taking the decision for the right reasons and that you have thought it through. You are about to go miles from home and their protection. Calm their fears.

What do they want to hear?
Where you are going to go, who with and when, how much it is going to cost, where you are going to buy your ticket and how you propose to afford all of this. When are you going to return, and what you are going to do when you return.

What they don't want to hear.
Cock and bull stories of make-believe about what you are going to do ie. follow your dreams, find your inner self and get an amazing suntan…they've heard it all before, remember – you wanted to be a doctor, then a brain surgeon, then an architect?

Pre-University

You are about to take an infamous 'gapyear', so you'd better have a bloody good plan. You have a lot to think about and a lot to do. Time to do a bit of 'research' – make a few phone calls and get some information sent to you, so you can start building your case.

"

You >   I'm taking a gapyear and going around the world…

Parents >   No you're not, you're going off to University like everyone else. You've got plenty of time to do all that afterwards.

You >   Actually, I'm young for my year (my reasoning) and I'd like to go now. Can we talk about it please?

Parents >   OK.

You >   STA Travel specialise in student travel…they have round-the-world tickets that cost as little as £700. This ticket will take me to Los Angeles, Hawaii, Fiji, New Zealand, Australia, Indonesia, Singapore, Malaysia, Thailand and back home.

Parents >   And how do you propose to pay for it?…I'm not paying you know!

You >   I've got an interview for a job next week. I'm going to have to earn about £x,xxx as I've got to buy insurance, a backpack, etc, etc, etc.

Parents >   You're not going by yourself, are you?

You >   No, I'm going with Pete…his parents are OK with the idea…he's already got a job and…(justify the rest).

Or

You >   I am actually. At this point: a) refer to someone you know who has been travelling by themselves, preferably where you want to go, b) show them an article by a young male or female traveller that you can show them, c) get them to read the section on ***Solo Travel.***

Parents >   What about your University place?

You >   I can defer it. Universities actually encourage gapyears. I have spoken to the Admissions Tutor and they are happy for me to defer my place. All I have to do is to say that I am going to defer my entry on my UCAS form, which my Careers teacher is going to help me do.

Parents >   Silence…**or**…possibly considering it…**or**…disapproval written all over their faces.

You > (killer punch) …look, it will help me get into University to do the course I want at the place I want to go to. When I eventually go for a job, it will give me loads of experiences to talk about…it will make me different and put me well ahead of all the rest. Basically, I really want to do this, I've thought about it a lot, and looked into it, so I'm not going into it blind. I want to do this with your support. It is going to be the most amazing year of my life and I want your help…

"

You need to have this conversation, so have it on your terms…, especially if you know your parents are completely against you going on the grounds that you are too young, irresponsible, or that you have to do what they say. Have all the facts and use this to prove that you are an adult, and that you are taking your first major decision to do something positive with your life. Prove to them, but more importantly, prove to yourself that you can do it. It's not easy.

When I first broached the subject of taking a gapyear and going round the world my dad was actually quite receptive to the idea, but soon changed his mind. He still had the perception that going travelling meant joining the hippy trail and dropping out, like so many of his contemporaries did in the sixties. But things have changed. Millions of people have trodden those trails since, and yes, a few do drop out. But to the majority, a gapyear is only half about going away and doing your stuff…the rest is about coming home and getting on with your life, making the most out of your time away. Those that don't, in my opinion, are just a waste of space. If that's you, then that's your problem and you have to deal with it in your own way.

My personal experience

This is a personal note from me that really comes from my heart. I have been there, made the mistakes and hope that you can learn from them like I never did.

Exams came and went, followed by the 'summer of discontent' in the lead-up to the results. The relationship with my dad soured as it was pretty obvious that I had every intention of going travelling. Unfortunately my results were not the three Bs I needed, so I entered the Clearing Process. In a desperate bid to get somewhere, I rang round, and got rejections left, right and centre. I finally phoned Manchester University – again, a rejection. Feeling a bit dejected, I decided to ring back for some advice (the woman I spoke to sounded really sympathetic). The phone was answered by the Admissions Tutor for the course who offered me one of the last places! **I accepted. I had a place!**

I waited half an hour, and then rang up to ask their opinion on deferring. They said it was possible once you have a place…so I immediately deferred my place. I then rang dad and told him that I had a place at Manchester University to read Economics. He was thrilled. I said I should head up to Manchester the next day to sort out my accommodation.

Manchester, the next day.

I did actually go through the motions of trying to find accommodation. The advice I had was to find the biggest mixed hall and have an amazing laugh. In Manchester, this was Owens Park – but there were no rooms left. Having checked that my deferred entry was secure, I rang dad, discussed the genuine lack of accommodation and said that I had discussed with the Admissions Tutor the possibility of deferring…(deep breath). Hurriedly I said that I had a plan (to continue working at McDonalds until Christmas and then to leave in January with Tony). To be fair, and I know it can't have been easy for him, dad had a think about it, rang me back and agreed to the gapyear.

'…we'll discuss this when you get home!…'

It was as if a massive weight had been lifted off my shoulders – and for a few precious hours I looked round Manchester, eating the biggest (cheapest) kebab in the whole world, drinking the nicest (and cheapest) pint I had ever had and basking in one of the only sunny days I was ever to witness there…I was the happiest person alive…**my life had truly begun.**

In hindsight, I realise my immaturity.

This is the first time that my dad will know the full story, but a lot of water has gone under the bridge since then. Our relationship has gone up and down and broken both our hearts. I have resented him for not allowing me to live my life and do things my way, and I'm sure he has resented me for having a carefree attitude when it comes to making important decisions and possibly throwing away a valuable education which he has worked extremely hard to pay for.

I will be the first to admit that I was immature, not fully understanding that, like myself, my dad had a game plan for life. As far as he was concerned, 1995 was to be the year when he had done his bit and he was going to graduate with honours from the school of 'Paying For His Sons'. Therefore, news of my gapyear was simply **YET ANOTHER YEAR LONGER** for Pops, cutting into any plans for retirement, slowing down work etc. Did I think about this? Did I hell!

This is the way not to do it. Please learn from my mistakes.

'Do you care what your parents think?'

Deep down you do, but peer pressure dictates that we puff out our chests and deny all allegiance to our parents, who have, up until now, given us everything they possibly can. Time to grow up and make them proud and happy that they have done a good job.

You are about to 'leave the nest', but by taking a gapyear you will be leaving it unconventionally, breaking away from the

School – A Levels – University – Career Route

So…let's prove to them that we are ready to do it. Let's work with them on this one. Let's get it right! It'll be worth it in the long run, but, if it gets tricky, make sure you stick to your guns and do what you want to do. It's your life…**so, what are they going to say?**

• The 'Victorian' attitude

Life is about qualifications, a job, a career and becoming a fully paid up member of 'The Rat Race'. They won't agree with the gapyear…why don't you continue your education and get a job like everyone else's children? You will have to fight to prove that it is a good thing. An ultimatum may be drawn, along the lines of… *'If you can earn the money and prove to me that travelling is a good thing, then I will let you go'.*

If not, what's been good for the world since time began will be good for you in the next few years (University, job, career).

> **They say**　*A gapyear is a wasted year in your life!*
>
> **I say**　*What's the difference between working 39 years and working 40 years?*

• Victorian attitudes with a hint of modern awareness

Many, as employers, have seen the benefit of the gapyear. 'I'm neither for them or against them', a father once said to me. 'As an employer I can see the benefit, and I travelled a lot, years ago, when I was in the army…however, I don't think it is right for him to go right now…he has plenty of time.' Remember the one in five statistic? (the number who don't bottle)…this father had just claimed number four!

> **They say**　*I think gapyears can be a good thing, it's just not right for him/her at the moment.*
>
> **I say**　*Why don't you ask him/her what they actually want to do for a change?*

• Free-spirited 'sixties kids', now parents, aware of all the options

Social commentators have put the rise in the popularity of the gapyear down to this generation of 'hippies' coming through the ranks – now with kids of their own aged 18–24 – who they want to encourage to become 'worldly-wise', well travelled, and more broad-minded, rounded individuals.

• Anxious parents who try too hard

It is essential to get your parents involved in your plans, but anxious parents can be a hindrance. I have seen parents who do all the preparation, buy the tickets, pack the bags, read the guidebooks and send the kids off into the unknown. This can only be a bad thing! You need to be mentally and physically prepared yourself, because when you're out there, you'll be on your own. You'll never learn unless you do it yourself. Make a stand.

We are all different, it's up to you

Only you will know what your parents are like and if/how your relationship is about to change. People react to every situation in different ways. 'Suck it and see.' Be aware that your parents have a life and plans as well. Be an adult. It is your gapyear, and a valuable 'life-learning' experience. Parents will worry, and your decision to go may not be taken lightly. Most importantly, I think you should be adult enough to realise this as well.

Point to note: announcing that you are going to tour the world with 'Mad Baz' could be unwise. **Choose your travel partner well or face the consequences.**

A quick word to any parent reading this

I can feel you looking at this section with great disapproval. If you're reading this thinking that I'm inciting rebellion…then I guess your son or daughter wants to travel and you disapprove.

- What do I know about being a parent? **Nothing.**
- What do I know about responsibility of raising children? **Nothing.**
- What do I know about the fears you have of things happening to them? **Nothing.**

I don't make any assumptions about parent-child relationships, everyone is different.

What can I offer you? I hope that I can offer you some sort of assurance of why travel is a good, safe, thing.

Why is a gapyear / travel a good thing?   ❷

It can help you get into University. It puts you a step ahead of the rest when it comes to finding work. It broadens your mind, builds your character and gives you confidence *and* as far as I'm concerned, it makes you a better person…I have rarely seen a negative effect.

Is it safe?   ❷

If it wasn't, thousands of people wouldn't be doing it and I wouldn't promote it. Everyone looks after each other. Organised gapyears have to be safe. Media stories play on our imagination and paint a bad picture, **it is just not like that out there!** What is safe? Occasionally things happen, I don't deny it. But more things happen to us right here on our doorstep than when we are travelling. When you travel, you are alert and more aware of your surroundings, making you safer than in familiar surroundings at home.

Let them go!   ❶

Most parents are happy to do it so long as they are confident that, upon leaving the nest, the kids don't hot-rod it straight to the floor. **Force your children to prove to you that they can pull this one off**. At eighteen, we are adults. Accept this fact. From my experience, failure to do so will only have negative consequences.

Read the *How to…keep in touch* carefully and think seriously about sorting out the best ways of staying in contact:

1. **email**
2. **voicemail**
3. **phone cards**
4. *poste restante*

Make sure they leave with:

1. **a good first-aid kit**
2. **a sterilised needle kit**
3. **full insurance**
4. **a free email address**
5. **an international calling card**
6. **a good backpack**

and you'll have given them a great start.

Sum it up, Tom!

At the end of the day you are going to be faced with a situation that only you know how to deal with. If you have been reading this section wondering what all the fuss is about, then you obviously have a good relationship with your parents, and a lot of support for your impending trip. The thing is, you are unique and you are lucky.

For those that don't have this kind of support, please stick at it, although it can seem very lonely and frustrating at times. In hindsight, you'll realise that your parents are only looking after your interests, attempting to continue to guide you on the right path. It's time to sit down and talk this through. Hear each other out and come armed with a great plan to cover every angle.

Prove it.
Prove that you are an adult, that you can make, take and carry through a major decision.

Succeed. They will be proud, have no doubt about that, even though some have a funny way of showing it.

If you are stuck and need some advice, please email me at **helpme@gapyear.com.**

6: The airport experience

Do you remember your first visit to an airport? Wasn't it great? Looking at the planes, getting on one, 'belting up', free sweets, the fast take-off, going up to see the pilot, the holiday abroad, being told off...I loved it. And now?...the magic has gone. **Obviously I still mess around on the trolleys, get told off and go and visit the pilot...but it's not the same any more!**

Delayed plane
No worries. This is when your day bag comes into its own (see **How to...pack**). Find a comfortable spot and 'dig in'. Airports are uncomfortable, and moulded seats are impossible to lie on. However, your towel makes a handy cushion. Catch up on some reading, play a card game, or just sleep. Don't pay the extortionate prices for the refreshments, bring your own...or wait to be fed on the plane. Above all, don't get stressed. When the plane is ready, you go...it's as simple as that!

The check-in
Two hours prior to departure for long-haul and an hour for short-haul or domestic. **By getting there early, you get the pick of the seats** – leg room? window seat? aisle? *Chat up the check-in staff and ask for the good seats.*

Ideally, on a full plane, grab a window seat by the emergency exit halfway up a section. This seat will have leg room and a wall to lean against. You will need to sleep, which is where a window seat, a pillow against the wall and a half-turned body buried into it does the job perfectly. If you are exceptionally tall it is regarded as a disability and will get you a good seat. Never accept a middle seat, unless you are sitting next to a mate who you can go to sleep on, or the only other choice is missing the flight!

❶ *On an empty plane, you have a duty to get this right!*
Book night flights to save a night's accommodation. The best seats are the penultimate seats at the back (the back seats don't recline properly). Get the middle four. Put all the armrests up, use the blankets to form a mattress (jam the cushions down any cracks to even them up), and lie out across all four seats. Make this area yours – spread your stuff all over it. You are on an empty plane, so you're not being selfish. On take-off and landing you can sit in a vacant window seat for the view...and for the film – move closer to the screen, unless you have a screen on the back of the seat in front of you.

✍° **Food on board**...is getting better and better. The secret is to ask for 'spare' food, as food not eaten gets binned. Politely ask for more – eat what you can and then carry the rest of the sealed stuff away with you.

Ψ **Drink on board**…is usually free on long-haul and scheduled flights, but be careful about drinking too much alcohol on planes – as the air pressure can cause you to become dehydrated much more quickly…this can give you a stonker of a hangover.

Deep vein thrombosis…been in the news a lot recently. Basically, if you are inactive for a period of time, blood clots can form in your legs and get pushed around your body. This can be fatal. What can you do, then? Get up and walk around. Do feet exercises every hour (they usually show you some now before you take off – circle your feet, go from heel to toe, etc. for a couple of minutes). It is advisable to take an aspirin just before take-off, as this thins the blood. There are socks available to help, but exercises will probably do the trick.

Short-haul and domestic flights
The problem with the 'hour before' rule is that delays in traffic mean missed flights. Many check-ins now close half an hour before the flight, so make sure you get there on time. Also, go to the right airport! I had to cancel a talk in Glasgow because I went to the wrong airport to catch my plane. The title of my talk? *'How to prepare for travel.'* Arse!

Important point: **when a flight says it's departing at 9.30am, it actually takes off at 9.30am!** We tend to forget this. Many miss flights because they think that they have more time than they really do, especially at some of the larger airports like Heathrow and Gatwick, where you face massive walks or a monorail ride to a satellite terminal at the other side of the airport!

Departure Lounge madness!
'Proceed to Gate 85' comes up on screen, the cue for 150 people to prepare for battle. It is 8.30am, the plane leaves at 9.30am, they reach Gate 85 at 8.31am, queue to get into the waiting room and then scrum for the seat nearest the exit to the plane! At 9.10am the alert ones sense 'boarding' and start to queue. Others see this, grab the kids and follow suit.

Meanwhile…others like myself (of which I hope you will be one), sit quietly reading the papers. Well aware of the nine-hour flight, our allocated seats and the ten-minute wait to get us through the gate…there is clearly no hurry.

Landing
Before you land, you may have to fill in a visa/immigration form…you'll learn to have a pen handy and know your passport number! It asks where you intend to stay. If you are too honest, you could encounter problems…I left it blank once and to my joy was hauled into a room where I waited for half an hour for someone to ask me where I was intending to stay. I said I didn't know. I proved that I was a backpacker with a return ticket and he let me go. Just choose a hostel out of the guides and use their address. Basically, immigration are after 'illegals'. Don't get caught by red tape. Fill in the forms completely, but not falsely (a criminal offence).

Immigration

Back in the UK, the queue for non-EU passport holders will be five miles long! The EU queue has someone on it who gives you a quick glance as you walk past waving your passport, and only stops the odd person. **Any problems**, be patient and calm. Keep an eye on your passport and documents. If you get seriously hassled, call your embassy.

Customs – what are you allowed to take in?

Generally your Duty Free allowance is a couple of hundred cigarettes or equivalent, a couple of litres of wine, a bottle of spirits, a couple of bottles of perfume. It's up to you to find out what you are allowed and what you're not.

Weapons, explosives, obscene material, fakes, animals, birds, endangered species (dead or alive, includes fur, ivory or leather taken from an endangered species), meat and poultry (especially if raw), certain plants and CB radio transmitters, are all prohibited from coming into the UK from outside the EU, so this should give you an idea of what you're not allowed to carry between countries. Other countries like Australia, New Zealand and the US have an even more rigorous policy on food. Restrictions are there to stop the spread of disease, so be a 'caring' traveller and abide by the rules.

Smuggling   ❶

There are two types of smuggling. *The petty stuff:* a couple of watches here, a bottle or two of spirits, clothes etc. **If you get caught then you'll pay charges on the full value of them**. To avoid this, take all the price tags and labels off new clothes, scrunch them up, and make sure that they don't look new. If you get a new suit made up in Asia, for example, don't leave it in the wrapping.

The serious stuff: **if you do this, then you're a bigger idiot than you realise!** Drugs, clothes, cigarettes, alcohol – if you take the law into your own hands, you pay the penalty when you get caught...Read up on the section about drugs if you're thinking about becoming a runner, and take note especially of the bit about 'The Death Penalty'.

The Red Channel: 'You have things to declare.' You have brought ten pairs of Levi's and are over the limit. By declaring them you will simply pay the duty on them. They will still be a lot cheaper than you can buy them at home. If you aren't sure, go through and ask. I bought a samurai sword back for my brother from Indonesia. I went through and declared it. They didn't want to let me keep it, but my case that it was a present and that I had brought it all this way was strong enough, so fair play to them – they let me keep it.

The Green Channel: By going through, you are stating that you have 'nothing to declare'. So if you do have 'something to declare' and are knowingly going through the wrong channel, then you are, what they term...'breaking the law'! Be aware that this can mean fines and prison sentences for arrestable offences.

The EU Channel: The funky little blue lane with the yellow stars for any EU citizen going from one EU country to another. No borders, no barriers, no customs. However, if you think that you aren't being watched, then you're a little greener than you realise. Again, if you have something to declare, go through the Red Channel.

A backpacker in customs

Rumours say that backpackers are hauled over, searched and given a rectal examination before you can say 'pass me the vaseline Jack!' Now, you should already know what I think about that. If you have long greasy hair, look a mess, stink, and walk though cool as a cucumber because you have nothing to hide, you'll be fine. If you are dead smart, in a suit, carrying only a brief case...and you have something to hide, **chances are, you will be pulled over**. Why? Customs guys are there for a reason, and they are very good at what they do. They know what to look for...but if you're doing nothing wrong, you've got nothing to worry about...right?...that having been said, it's always good to help your cause. Smarten up. Get a shower and a shave. Make your hair look presentable and your belongings clean. If your backpack converts into a holdall, convert it!

If you are pulled over for a search, especially in countries known for their (as I pull on my 'diplomatic hat')...**'interesting views and interpretations on how their legal system works'...be alert**. If you are asked to empty your bag, **MAKE SURE <u>YOU</u> DO IT**. Take out the contents piece by piece and don't let anyone crowd round. I'm playing on your paranoia here; the chances of you being stopped are minimal and in any event you should be fine, once you have shown that you have nothing to hide. Any problems, get in touch with your local embassy immediately.

✌ Airport departure tax

A real bastard of a tax, it creeps up on you at the worst possible time – just when you've spent all your local currency and are ready to fly out. Occasionally they want US dollars, but they are all different. The best bet is to ask at the hostel the day before you leave, or check it out at the airport when you arrive.

⑤ Changing money

Airports will always have a place where you can change money...you may not get the best rate, but they are always there and very convenient. If you have arrived with no local currency and you need to get a bus or taxi from the airport, you are going to need it. Get small denominations, as it is easier for you to deal with and also stops you getting ripped off by the bus or taxi 'not having change'.

In the wake of 11 September 2001, security at airports has obviously increased, so make allowances. If you get caught out, remember that it's for your own protection. Check-in may take longer (so allow plenty of time), and if you try to take **anything** that could be a weapon on a plane, it will be confiscated (penknives, tweezers etc.), so pack them in your luggage to go in the hold. The good news is that it's theoretically never been safer to travel by air.

7: Your first night

Your first night in any place is going to feel a bit strange, but the very first night of your round-the-world trip in a dive in Delhi is also going to be a culture-shock. Unfortunately, you will go away with preconceived ideas and dreams. If, in the first few days and nights, all is not what it is cracked up to be, don't panic.

You're on the plane…it takes off. You sit back. This amazing sense of achievement sweeps over you, and then it dawns on you…I'm on my own! (in my case, Tony was there, so *we* were on *our* own!). We kept toasting 'our trip' and having a laugh. We couldn't wait to get to Los Angeles, where we'd been told accommodation was really easy to find. Neither of us slept. We watched all the films, ate all the food and drank loads (not all alcoholic I must add!). LA for us was literally a stopping-off place, en route to the Pacific Islands, so we were only going to spend a few days here, seeing Venice Beach (Baywatch was big at the time!), Hollywood etc.

We arrived and collected our baggage. '**…OK, what do we do now?…**' A bloke walked up behind us and whispered '**…*you boys looking for some accommodation?…*'** Now, since about the age of two, we have been told not to talk to strangers. We'd been warned in the run-up to our departure about people trying to con us into this, that and the other. We knew this guy was dodgy…it wasn't right, the approach, the way he talked…what accommodation? Would we end up in the boot of a car? Or maybe at the bottom of the river? We just couldn't be sure of his intentions '**…yup, we sure are!…**'

He was actually on the level (the discreet approach being down to the fact that touting was illegal at the airport) and took us to a backpackers' right on Venice Beach like he said. Apart from the worst rain for six years, Venice Beach gave us time to get used to the idea that we were now 'backpackers' and to taste the hostel experience…**this was the start of our trip.**

In terms of 'starts', it was quite a kind one. Had we landed first in Delhi or Bangkok, I'm sure things would have been different. It can be pretty scary…arriving with a pack on your back and attracting all the usual hassle and attention from touts.

This will be a new experience for you, **so what should you do if faced with more hustle and bustle that you can cope with? Chill out!** You are in no hurry, you are perfectly safe. Take this chance to get used to the country and the people. At this point it's a good idea to remind you to try and ensure that you arrive either in the morning or early afternoon. In the mornings there will be fewer people about so you should be able to get yourself to your first night's accommodation relatively easily. Once you are there…chill…big time!

When you arrive at your accommodation

Get yourself comfortable, make sure your belongings are safe and then go for a wander. Don't go far and take with you your bare essentials, and your most valuable valuables. Mooch around at a nice slow pace, see what makes the place tick. Whether you are in a developed English-speaking country or the arse end of nowhere, get a card for the hostel or backpackers' you are staying in (or a clearly written address)…so if you get lost, locals (or police) will always be able to help you get back to where your stuff is.

By the end of the first day, you should be relaxed. Get a good meal inside you (even if you're paying over the odds). Go for a beer. Try and meet a few people.

A few pointers ▶

If you end up sitting there thinking 'shit, what've I done; shit, what've I done!' then you are panicking. Calm down. On your first night you are going to be nervous. Everyone you meet is going to be confident, well travelled and look a lot older and more tanned than you. Give it a month and you'll be the same! Do not go back to the airport and fly home! (Some do!)

Get a good night's sleep. It may be odd sleeping in a dormitory with a bunch of strangers (or you may love the experience, who knows) and in the morning, get some food inside you and go for another wander. The day is yours. If the weather is a bit shitty, stay inside and read a book – take the day to relax and acclimatise (you may still be suffering from jet lag). Give it time to settle in and you'll be fine.

Sum it up, Tom!

Your first night is an amazing experience. Pumped up with adrenaline, nervous as hell, and possibly scared out of your wits. Don't be embarrassed by this – there are four people at home (one in five remember?) who haven't made it this far. If you're worried about starting in 'difficult' countries like India and Morocco, why not go to easy-backpacking, English-speaking countries first, before moving on to the harder stuff of Asia, Africa and South America?

Also, many parents are prepared to pay for a nice hotel for the first couple of nights. This is actually a good idea, so don't turn it down if offered. If you are with someone else, you should be able to explore and settle OK. **If you are by yourself, find some company. At the airport, before you get on the plane, see if there are any other backpackers around and have a chat with them**. Find out what they know, where they are going and if you can join them. If you explain that it is your first night, they'll more than likely look after you and help you acclimatise.

The bottom line. It's a marathon, not a sprint. If it takes you a week to adjust and get into it, so what? Go at your own pace and you'll be fine.

8: Back to reality!

'Announcing the arrival of Qantas flight QA284 from Bangkok'... you're home!

The general feeling of disorientation and boredom when you arrive back home is incredible. It may be hard to believe, but you'll see. It affects us all in different ways. Some come back and go straight to Uni, others into a job. Many struggle to readjust. Whilst you've been away, life has continued to tick by and you've missed out. People and places have changed. The job market is different. You're seeing life through different eyes now, and occasionally you don't like what you see. **Me?...I got bored and went to France**.

I thought returning home was going to be a re-enactment of a glorious black and white movie – you know, soldiers marching through the streets, crowds shouting, kids cheering, strangers running to kiss you, tears streaming down your cheeks...you've done it, you've achieved...you're back!

Heathrow. 5.30 am. Wednesday morning. You pass through the arrivals gate. Your mum (who has been up since 3am) spots you, spots your hair, spots your clothes... hmmm...She drives you home. Everything seems to be different, faster. By the time you get home you get an ordered history of everything that's happened in the last year, in its greatest detail. Dad counts on his new industrial-strength shower to nuke your hair into a presentable state and maybe, just maybe, get rid of that strange smell (the result of a mad dash from the Full Moon party on Ko Phangan to your flight from Bangkok – three days without a wash). However, he's happy to have you back and hopes you'll get a job soon.

Your first morning. You wake up in your own bed, the soft duvet, the warmth, the feeling of security again. Nothing to do all day except chill out and get used to home again. The first cup of tea...nice...You walk around the house feeling a bit awkward – carpet under your feet feels really bizarre...a fridge, stocked with food, not a plastic bag in sight, simply saying...'help yourself!'. So you do...but it still feels odd. 'What shall I do, I'm bored...'

So you're on the phone to the mates, *'wahaaay, I'm back!...yeah this morning, 5.30...yeah, mum picked me up...didn't like my hair much...yeah, wait till you see it!!...so, what's happening tonight?...pubbing it?...OK...The Shark Bar?...where the hell's that?...ahhhh-hhh, used to be The Oyster Sheds...OK, see you at 8...yeah, tell them I'm back!...cool!'*

A small cheer as you walk in, hand-shakes, hugs, kisses, pisstake of your hair, weight (lack of or extra), tan, unsent post cards, invisible presents etc....and you love it, because, let's face it, you've missed it. Your first pint with the guys goes down, bringing with it the euphoria of an old taste, an old feeling, you can't quite put your finger on it...what is it? That's right...YOU'RE BACK!

'So...you had a good time then?'
'Yeah...amazing!'
'Cool...where was the best place?'
'Hard to say really, Australia was pretty special.'
'Cool...so...errrrmmmm.................. did anyone see the football last night?'

If you haven't been, it's impossible to talk about it. You won't believe me now, but that's the way it is, especially if you've been in less developed countries, or working on projects where you actually make a difference to other people's lives, community or general well being. Everything back home will sound, and seem, extremely trivial and unimportant.

So how do you deal with this?

Be aware of what might happen and get on with your life. Those who sit on their backsides, decide not to bother going to University (*because maaan, I've like, eeermm, got out of the studying thing maaaan*), or give up finding work after a couple of rejections, are just wasters. Don't throw away a perfectly good University place because you can't be arsed to go. If you want to, you will get back into the studying routine. Thousands do each year. If you're lazy, that's your problem.

There is one danger which must be avoided at all cost. **Being a 'travel bore'.** Whether you like it or not, someone, somewhere, will find you boring. Michael Palin once commented that he could be in a room full of people with no-one to talk to – after all, what do you say to someone who has just been around the world, when the furthest you have ever been is to Disneyland with your folks!!

So be careful about the number of stories you tell and photos you show. You'll generally notice the tell-tale signs, the glazing over of eyes, tears, desperately held-back yawns, people leaving the room (subtly, obviously, or Linford Christie style)...
'...Tom?...Do me a favour fella?...'
'...Yes mate?...'
'...Shut the #*@$ up!!...'

Look at it from another angle

Do you remember at the start of the book I reckoned that out of every five who are seriously interested in taking time off, only one ever does? Well, you're soon going to find out who those other four are! It's easier to label someone a 'travel bore' and to make them feel guilty about doing something with their life, than to face up to the fact that they've done what you never had the guts to do in the first place. But they always have the nagging feeling of **'If only...'**

'**If only** I had gone through with deferring my place on the UCAS form.'
'**If only** I had sat down with my parents and chatted the whole gapyear thing through.'
'**If only** I had gone to STA Travel with the other lads...I could have afforded it...they're living and working in Sydney now...I'm temping, doing nothing of any importance, and of no relevance to my career. Thinking about it...what career??'
'**If only I'd gone with them!**'

So, they haven't done it, but they can always 'do it later' right? Wrong. The problem is, when their mates come back, all the regrets come flooding out. Unfortunately the only way to deal with it is to take the piss.

Jealousy. That's all it is. Don't feel awkward about what you have done just because a few saddos are jealous of you living your life. Don't hide away, hide your photos, or avoid the subject, virtually pretending it never happened. Be proud of what you've done and move on. You now have a head start and are a cut above the rest. What you do with it is up to you.

The next step   ❶

Even though I have split the following into 'Getting into University' and 'Getting a job', there is stuff in both that will be relevant to all of you, so don't just skip through. Pay attention!

GETTING INTO UNIVERSITY   ▢
Thinking about deferring your University place and taking a gapyear? Fantastic – fifteen months of the most amazing experiences…if you get it right. Planning and using it wisely when you get back are the key things here. I have, of course, covered this in more detail earlier on in the book, so you should know what I'm talking about by now.

So, how do you 'get it right'? On the back of the UCAS form there is the 'Personal Statement', that I like to call 'Why should I let you come to my University?'. At seventeen or eighteen we have this amazing belief that we're invincible! Unfortunately your UCAS masterpiece gets scrutinised by someone, usually in their forties or fifties, who doesn't know you, but is fully aware that it is getting late (hence the bad mood) and this is the two hundredth smart arse of the day. Impress them, make them smile.

What have you got to tell them? '…I am going to defer my year, take a gapyear, do x, y and z, and then come back to study Economics. This is what I'm going to do and this is what I'm going to get out of it.' Bingo.

Remember, they don't have to take you, they have hundreds of applications from others of equal ability and almost everyone has been a prefect. Sell yourself and believe in yourself – if you don't, no-one else will – bullshit is normally obvious, and if you get found out, you're history!

Read what you've written – would *you* offer *you* a place?

…really?

We may all think that we're bloody amazing and worth the top money that all the best jobs seem to be offering. Hey, guess what! You know all those people that left school at the same time as you, maybe graduated with you, who grew up with you, random people that you see in the street, at football matches, in the parks?...**they're all competition!**

A little example: applying for a graduate position

You get ten Grade A GCSEs, three Grade As at A Level and a first class degree. You're pretty bloody impressed with yourself, and so you should be. It's time the world had the privilege of having you enter the workforce. You're more than worth your weight in gold, and you can breeze into anything you want, right? So you apply and they send you an application form. You secretly sweat a little as you realise that the questions are a little more complicated than you had anticipated. Nevertheless, you complete the form, address the envelope, pop on a stamp, take it to the post box, give it a good luck kiss, and send it on its way.

Let's just hold it there a second and contemplate the situation...

The Blue Chip company you have applied to has probably advertised thirty jobs. Therefore......AT THAT EXACT MOMENT IN TIME, A MINIMUM OF 5,000 OTHER PEOPLE, LIKE YOU, ARE GOING TO APPLY...

So, ask yourself: are – you – going – to – get – that – job?

If the answer's still 'yes', then, to be honest, you're a bit arrogant, and the chances are you won't get it. **This question should worry you**...you are allowed to be confident *and* worried, you know. Right now, the ones who will get the jobs will be taking this in and thinking about it – their CVs, their interests, what they want to do and with whom. If you're not, wise up, or get a rude awakening.

Unfortunately, bragging about your GCSEs and A Levels goes out of the window on this one, and if you're relying on them at this stage, you'd better have a good think about your life. A degree will count up to a point, but as everyone says that they're going to get a 2.1 nowadays, you're going to need something more.

What employers want to know from your application form is that you are somebody. You don't have to have won a Nobel Prize, indeed, it's very rare at our age to have done a hell of a lot. So ask yourself the questions that they're going to ask you...

1. **Why am I different...what have I got, or what have I done, which is different?**
2. **Exactly what is it about me that makes me employable?**
3. **WHY WILL THEY EMPLOY ME? (as opposed to the other 5,000?)**

SELL YOURSELF

On the application form there is this little section called 'hobbies and interests', something to that effect, or in other words 'Tell me about yourself'. Tell me about you...and I might just give you an amazing job.

So, what do we write to impress these guys? The following are the top four statements on graduate application forms:

'I like to read.' 'I play sport.' 'I like to socialise.' 'I'm ambitious.'

Well, congratulations, Mr Griffiths, you are now officially a member of the human race! You can almost hear the inaudible 'swishhhh' as your application wings its way deftly to the bin. Quite often a 'junior' will sift through the massive piles – turning straight away to the 'hobbies and interests' section and giving it a two-second flick through. If he/she likes what they see, it stays; if not, 'Bin City'!

'I went around the world at eighteen…I hitch-hiked across Canada when I was twenty…I have travelled through Southeast Asia…When I was working in a school in China…We bought a jeep and decided to head east, sixth months later we ended up in Cape Town!'

THIS IS WHAT THEY WANT TO HEAR… TURN ME ON. EXCITE ME!

This one statement proves that you have character, confidence, you've made a decision at an early age, you've decided to do something and you've achieved your goal. What's more you've proved yourself in so far as financial planning, project management and getting off your arse and doing something with your life goes…and you've even matured and developed a broader mind as a result!

I know who I'd rather interview.

Sum it up, Tom!

When you get back, revel in the fact that you've been away. Don't be shy, but don't be a bore. No doubt you will have caught the 'travel bug', and will be going off again soon. Good for you.

1. **Gapyears can help you get into University.**

2. **Travel and mind-broadening experiences can help you get a job.**

3. **'Talkers' stay at home. Ignore them and live your life.**

9: Drugs by Max Andrews

General

Drugs are available the world over. While you are away there is a good chance that you'll be offered some illicit substance or other, as favourite travellers' haunts attract the young, and the young at heart, searching for an illegal high. An array of drugs is usually available to meet this demand, and, whatever your attitude towards them, it is better to be both aware, and prepared, for any situations which could arise.

Substances such as cannabis, opiates, cocaine and amphetamines are just as illegal as they are at home, but while you're away this can easily slip to the back of your mind. Travelling is essentially a carefree existence, where you experience situations utterly different from back home, and where, seemingly, anything goes. Travellers fearful of heights may find themselves at the end of a 300ft bungee rope, likewise some may decide to try drugs, having had little experience or inclination before. If you feel tempted to experiment with illicit substances, remember the many possible implications of your actions. **If, however, you genuinely have no interest, there is no reason for you, or your worried parents, to think you'll be enticed into any involvement with them.** Keep your wits about you and you should experience few, if any, problems.

Being offered drugs

Being offered drugs is a fact of life, but if you're not interested there is little to worry about. Abroad, small-time drug peddlers are usually discreet in their approaches, to avoid drawing attention to themselves. If you are offered drugs at a beach party or night club, a simple but firm 'no' should be enough to discourage sellers, as they won't want to waste time on those who are obviously not interested. Don't even feign interest, or strike up a conversation, as they will only spend more time badgering you into buying. Generally speaking, no-one is ever forced into taking drugs, so if you don't want to get involved you can easily stay out of it.

If you do dabble

If you do envisage yourself dabbling, the obvious possible entanglement with the law is not the only complication which could arise. Medically, you are in a far more precarious position. If you have a bad reaction to manufactured amphetamines at some remote beach party, an ambulance won't be there to rush you to hospital. The same rules apply as at home: think about the content of the substances you are imbibing, and if what you are offered appears dodgy, don't bother. Also, be discreet. Destinations once famed for the availability and open smoking of, say, cannabis have altered recently. The attitude of the authorities in some beach resorts, Goa for example, has become more severe in light of the greater lure of money from the mainstream tourist sector. Where once a more liberal attitude was prevalent, drug 'problems' are now seen as unattractive, and the police are cracking down on travellers.

Smuggling

Attempting to smuggle drugs between countries whether across land borders or through airports **IS BOTH DANGEROUS AND COMPLETELY IDIOTIC**. Nothing, no amount of money or free drugs, is worth the risk, which in some countries is, quite literally, deadly. To knowingly get involved in drug transportation is to demonstrate serious signs of insanity. The word is, DON'T!

Perhaps of more concern, to first-time travellers in particular, is inadvertently carrying illegal drugs, either through being duped by a 'friend' or acquaintance, or having them planted in your luggage. This is easily avoided. **With care and vigilance, it should be extremely difficult for anyone to plant drugs in your rucksack.** Your baggage holds all your belongings, so needs to be constantly looked after anyway. Ensure that you alone pack your bag every time you travel into a new country and, if you have used drugs, clear out the pockets so that no tiny amounts are left to be discovered at a later and far more unfortunate date. Once packed, keep an eye on your rucksack at all times, and, especially around ports and airports, do not leave it anywhere unattended.

In reality, why would anyone want to plant drugs on a stranger, with the inherent difficulty of recovering them later? Drug traffickers would far more likely want to 'recruit' a known person to transport the stuff. This could be an unwitting carrier, who, unaware of their illegal cargo, would not demonstrate signs of nerves to alert customs officials. With this in mind, it is extremely unwise to carry anything not packed by yourself through customs, or to drive other people's vehicles across borders. Even if fellow travellers ask you to transport an innocent-looking package or parcel through customs, think: **'why do they want me to do this?'** and usually your natural suspicions will tell you to say no. After all, if you are caught, a lame excuse about being duped will get you nowhere.

Penalties

Penalties for drugs offences in most countries are extremely severe. Smuggling is generally a far more serious offence than possession, and the punishments reflect this. Countries such as Malaysia, Thailand and the Philippines, among others, do enforce the death penalty for trafficking, while many others which are favourite among travellers carry long prison sentences for possession. If you are caught with a small amount of, say, cannabis, it is possible to pay your way out of a tricky situation. Police officers have been known to demand payments to 'forget' the offence, and if you are offered a deal it may well be in your best interests to cough up. Be exceedingly careful, however, as it is not unknown for officials to be corrupt, even deliberately selling drugs only to demand large sums upon revealing their identity.

What then?

If you face an official drugs charge, you will very likely be held awaiting trial. Insist on seeing someone from your embassy or consulate. They will know the procedures and be able to contact your relatives. They cannot, however, get you out of prison. The judicial process can be very slow, so it could be up to a couple of years before your case is heard. In such serious situations there are charitable bodies with whom contact can be made. **Prisoners Abroad (☎ 020 7561 6820, www.prisonersabroad.org.uk)** offers advice and information for Britons held overseas; acting as an intermediary between those in prison and family back home, as well as keeping relatives informed about judicial procedure in the relevant country. An extended spell in a foreign prison would seriously take the gloss off your travels. Be sensible and do not allow such a situation to arise.

Other things to bear in mind
Problems with drugs extend beyond the classic image of westerners being caught with small amounts of dope. There have been cases of travellers robbed after being drugged on trains and even in hotel rooms, having eaten food laced with sleep-inducing substances. Especially when travelling alone, beware of kindly offers of food and drink, which may hold more than you bargained for. And be aware of the recent cases of date-rape drugs, particularly in the US. In drinks they can be undetectable as they are colourless. Also, remember that Muslim countries can impose stiff penalties for drinking alcohol, particularly in the Middle East.

DRUGS

10: Embassies, passports and visas

For this whole section I will use the example of how the British system works. For all you Aussies, Canadians, Americans etc. out there, please use this as a guide for your own country.

How do embassies work? ❷

Embassy/High Commission/Consulate

British Consuls are there to help you if you get into trouble or need help or assistance overseas. The main Consulate in any country is usually part of the Embassy or High Commission in the capital city. But there are often smaller Consular Offices, including Honorary Consulates, in other cities and towns. I recommend you carry a list of British Consular Offices in the countries you plan to visit. We have listed embassies in the Address books of all our *Top Fifty Destinations*.

In the UK, this information is also available from...

The Foreign and Commonwealth Office: ☎ 020 7270 1500 – for a 24-hour first contact number. Website: **http://www.fco.gov.uk.**

The Foreign and Commonwealth Office's Travel Advice Unit: ☎ 020 7008 0232/3, **www.fco.gov.uk/travel.**

Most British Consulates operate an answerphone service giving details of office hours and arrangements for handling emergencies at other times.

Before you leave home, find out the address and telephone number of the Embassy, High Commission or Consulate in the country or countries that you are visiting. Consulates exist to help their citizens abroad to help themselves, but their resources are limited.

For a list of embassies worldwide, have a look at 'The Travel Zone' on **www.gapyear.com.**

What a UK Consul can do

- Issue emergency passports.
- Contact relatives and friends and ask them to help you with money or tickets.
- Advise on how to transfer funds.
- At most posts (in an emergency) advance money against a sterling cheque for £50 supported by a bankers card.
- As a last resort, provided certain strict criteria are met, make a repayable loan for repatriation to the UK. There is no law that says the Consul must do this and he/she will need to be satisfied that there is absolutely no-one else you know that can help.
- Provide a list of local lawyers, interpreters and doctors.
- Arrange for next of kin to be informed of an accident or a death and advise on procedures.
- Contact British nationals who are arrested or in prison and, in certain circumstances, arrange for messages to be given to relatives or friends.
- Give guidance on organisations experienced in tracing missing persons.

What a Consul cannot do

- Pay your hotel, medical or any other bills.
- Pay for travel tickets for you except in very special circumstances.
- Undertake work usually done by travel representatives, airlines, banks or motoring organisations.
- Get better treatment for you in hospital (or prison) than is provided for local nationals.
- Give legal advice, instigate court proceedings on your behalf, or interfere in local court procedures to get you out of prison.
- Investigate a crime.
- Formerly assist dual nationals in a country of their second nationality.
- Obtain a work permit for you.

Your passport

Passport enquiries: ☎ 0870 521 0410, www.passport.gov.uk. If you don't have a passport, order one well in advance, as it can take time for your application to be processed. If you have a passport, check it is up to date, signed and valid for the whole time you are abroad (beware that some countries won't let you in unless your passport has at least six months to run, so make sure you aren't caught out). If your passport expires, or you lose it, go to the nearest British Embassy. They can issue you with an emergency passport, but they might not be able to do it immediately...and without a passport, you're not going anywhere!

At the end of the day, if you lose everything and are left only with your passport, you will be able to get home. If you have everything and you lose only your passport, you ain't going nowhere! Look after it. It's your property, which is why, theoretically, you don't have to hand it over to any official. Sure they can look inside, as you keep hold of it and show them the different pages...but if you are in a dodgy situation where you can't trust the officials in front of you...don't hand it over, and then get in touch with the embassy if it looks like it's all going a bit wrong. Beware to tread the fine line between diplomacy and rudeness, as if they are genuine and you refuse, you may end up in trouble.

A stamp from the 'wrong' country

…could mean hassles and/or refusal to allow you into some countries (eg. the problem of getting into an Arab country with an Israeli stamp). Ask, politely, for a temporary stamp, which can be put on a separate piece of paper and stapled into your passport.

Your passport photo

Make it smart, clean, professional and presentable. This will help you at borders and with all other officials. Make sure you take at least six passport photos with you, stored in a dry place with paper in between them to stop them sticking.

If, like a mate of mine Chris W, it was taken when you were about ten with a particularly fetching haircut and eyes popping out of his head, you might want to get it changed…as an immigration guy, who may well not speak your language, will look at the photo, laugh, look back at you…and decide it isn't you. Beards, different colour hair, a hat on, or, for comical effect, Sooty peeking over your shoulder – may also cause problems.

Dual nationality

You are extremely, extremely, lucky. You will be able to zip in and out of immigration quicker than a Queen's messenger, simply by using the different passports to beat the different queues. However, remember to make sure that, should you be given an entry visa, you use the same passport to exit the country, so that it is properly registered that you have been 'in' and 'out'.

Visas

Trying to find whether you need a visa and how you are meant to get one can be a very frustrating and time-consuming experience. Most embassies now have these annoying pre-recorded message systems…**'for visa information, press 1', 'for information about information, press 2', 'and if you'd like to speak to an operator…tough, and press 3 for further options!'**

They give out general information about how to join queues and not get very far. The thing is, most of them have to deal with thousands of people and this is the only way. There are a few that do actually answer the phones in person, but their opening hours are normally very restricted.

✍ So, what's the best solution?

Look at the *Top Fifty Destinations* for information on embassies and visas. All countries are different and you are best to check with all the embassies of the places you are intending to visit well in advance to find out what is required. Ask at your travel agent, as many have visa services which you can use, especially now that it is possible to get many visas immediately through your travel agent. When we were researching the *Top Fifty Destinations* section we found that most governments now have websites (some of them quite funky), where you can get all the info you require about the country, embassies, visa requirements etc.

Working visas

If you want to work whilst you are away, you may need a working visa, especially in Australia, the most popular working destination. The Australian authorities issue twelve-month working visas valid from the moment you enter the country. You may have to prove that you have sufficient funds or a ticket out of the country. Most of this red-tape stuff can be got around with a bit of cunning thought. Evidence of money in your account?...borrow some, stick it in a couple of weeks before and photocopy the evidence that it is there...and then pay the person back. To be honest, they're not really concerned with you...as long as you're not intending to stay there and live illegally, collect money off their state, or make a nuisance of yourself, you're fine (my excuse for the little white lies). If you are overlanding it through a country, your return tickets are proof that you're going to leave (a round-the-world ticket is proof that you are going home). Evidence of a job at home or the fact that you're going to University may also do the trick.

Don't be denied a visa on stupid grounds...think around the problem.

...but also be aware that in some countries overstaying your visa is an offence which carries a huge fine and sometimes prison. A bit of careful preparation and thought will help you to avoid this.

11: Etiquette by Max Andrews

One of the pleasures of jetting off to distant shores is the opportunity to experience cultures inherently different to our own. This does, however, present innumerable scenarios for western sensibilities to conflict with the cultural etiquette of a country. Primarily, this can be avoided by a little common sense and sensitivity. Yet there are a number of social niceties to be observed, adherence to which will ingratiate you to the locals you meet and, in some cases, prevent you from getting into trouble with the law. In the larger, more westernised cities you visit, many of these conventions will seem less apparent. Again use common sense to judge how far the particular code of etiquette needs to be observed. But as a general rule, in the more remote areas of any country, adherence to traditional mores is more strict, and you should temper your behaviour accordingly. Remember, your conduct will affect the overall impression the locals have, **so everyone has a certain responsibility to create a good atmosphere for future travellers**.

General Conduct

Impatience
Try and show patience at all times whilst abroad. Travelling can be tiresome in the face of, say, apparently slow and complicated bureaucracy, but showing annoyance is unlikely to enhance your chances of overcoming difficult situations. This is particularly the case in Southeast Asia and the Far East (especially Indonesia, Malaysia, Thailand, Japan and those surrounding), but also applies to many other countries. In such cultures visible impatience or anger shows a lack of control, and creates embarrassment for the other person.

Social laws
There are specific anomalous social laws in individual cities and countries, ie.
Singapore – bans the chewing of gum or spitting in the street.
Thailand – locals offended by licking of stamps bearing the king's head.
Japan – disgust at blowing your nose in public.

Invest a little time reading up on these kinds of social mores in the places you intend to visit, it will help you to avoid causing unintentional upset.

Pointing ☞
Pointing is seen as rude in many cultures. Travellers to Malaysia and Indonesia, and other southern Asian countries are advised to indicate directions using their thumb rather than finger, and in general to try not to point in the manner you would back home.

Head and feet

Throughout Asian countries there are certain codes regarding the head and feet. Patting young children on the head as a sign of affection is frowned upon, as the head is seen as the seat of the soul. Similarly, the feet are deemed both literally and spiritually the lowest part of the body, and thus, in certain social situations, such as dining at a low table seated on the floor, it is inappropriate to point the soles of your feet in anyone else's direction.

Eating

As well as not taking food with the left hand (see below) there are other niceties of eating to observe. In hot climates where hygiene is at a premium, it is generally accepted that everyone should wash their hands before a meal. There are other civilities observed in individual countries, too numerous to list here. In Thailand, for instance, you eat with a spoon, not a fork, and start the meal with a mouthful of plain rice, before tucking into the dish wholesale. Putting a fork in your mouth can cause offence in the same way as licking a knife in Britain.

Photographs

If you wish to take photographs of strangers, it is common courtesy to ask their permission first. In the Middle East, this is particularly important, as it causes offence if you don't, and photographing local women is largely out of the question. Similar 'rules' apply in African nations, where small payments are expected by the prospective 'model'. Also, avoid photographing anything with military establishments in the background as you can be arrested on security grounds.

Religion

Remember that temples and mosques are religious buildings, not just sights on the tourist trail. In most (mosques, Hindu, Sikh and Buddhist temples), you will be asked to remove your shoes and don a cloth covering for your feet. Similarly, mosques and Buddhist temples require you to wear long trousers and cover the upper arms.

Muslim countries

As the Muslim religion is prevalent over such a wide area of the planet, from Northern Africa to Indonesia, the rules regarding entrance to mosques differs between regions. Strictly speaking, non-Muslims are denied entrance (women in particular), and in Oman and Saudi Arabia this is stringently applied. In other areas, for example Indonesia, both sexes may visit mosques as long as they are clothed appropriately.

Ramadan, the period of Muslim fasting, requires particular note. It lasts for a lunar month, but the timing varies so check if you intend to travel to a Muslim country. All Muslims are expected to go without food between dawn and dusk, and in deference to the religious festival, it is deemed polite for foreigners to refrain from eating, drinking or smoking in public during daylight hours.

Alcohol is banned under the Muslim faith. Although in the more tourist-friendly Turkey boozing is permitted, it can lead to punishment for non-Muslims in some countries, such as Saudi Arabia. In others, eg. Pakistan, licences proving your non-Muslim identity must be sought before you drink.

ETIQUETTE

The left hand

Across Africa and Asia in both Muslim and Hindu countries there is a certain etiquette applied to the left hand. For the sake of hygiene there are particular tasks assigned to each hand, and the left is generally used for washing oneself after using the toilet. For this reason it is deemed unclean, and should not be used for eating and shaking hands, or making contact with others.

Etiquette – A tale of two cities

The importance of remaining calm and polite when facing difficulties while abroad:

A: I arrived in Agra with three travelling companions, skint. Banks etc were shut until Monday, but a five-star hotel had its own exchange facility. **'Sorry, you are not guests.'** *'Leave this to me, lads,'* said Mark and, full of charm, turned to the cashier. *'...and realising that this is the finest hotel in Agra we thought this would be the only place to exchange some travellers' cheques at this time of day.'* Immediately the attitude softened...if we purchased some drinks from the bar this would grant us patron status. A result, even if the four cokes were ridiculously over-priced.   **10/10**

B: Kathmandu, a couple of months later. A Tamil watering hole popular among travellers. After a few rounds we decided to settle up. The previous night we had sensed a slight discrepancy with the bill, but had put that down to our inebriated state. This time we were sure. We were adamant, the barman was resolute. The discussion became heated, an assorted gathering of local men surrounded our table. Finally I used my ace card, picked up from bartering with Indian rickshaw drivers – **'Are you a thief?!'** – he was **supposed** to back down. A terrific cry went up, 'We are Nepalese!' We were showered with drinks (thrown). One threatened repeatedly to kill us. We were quite relieved to fly out of Kathmandu unharmed.   **0/10**

12: Food and diet

Two important points ❶

- If you can't cook it or peel it, don't eat it!
- Reheated food? Bacteria City. Don't do it!

The hostel cooking experience – fight for those pots and pans!
At home, you have cupboards, a fridge, freezer, plenty of cutlery, plates and cooking utensils. When you're travelling, you don't. It's as simple as that! Keeping yourself fed can sometimes be a hassle and a chore, especially when you have to fight for the frying pan with Klaus from Switzerland and wait for Claudia from Sweden to finish with the saucepan…the unwritten rule of…**YOU USE IT, YOU WASH IT!**…doesn't seem to apply to some countries. With all the nationalities in the kitchen, it has been known for NATO **and** the UN to send in peace-keepers for breakfast, lunch and dinner!

Fast food…the saver of my soul!!
With all this hassle, 'fast food' may seem appealing. Hot dogs and burgers are cheap and easy, but not particularly healthy.

You are going to have to cook for yourself…
Cooking is actually very easy, it's all about timing and basic food with a bit of flavour. **Noodles…**a life-saver, there is nothing you can't do with them. Cheap, quick, easy and a good base for any meal. They come in loads of flavours – just add boiling water.

Keep healthy. Eat well and eat wisely.
When you're hauling your ass round the world and have no fixed abode, this can be a bit tricky. Does it matter? – yes, it does. *So, what should you watch out for in your diet?* **A few pointers from Susan, my Scottish dietician.**
Basically, you need three essential food groups:

1. Carbohydrates
…in pasta, rice, spuds, bread and breakfast cereals = energy. Sugar is a carbohydrate, giving a really quick energy fix – but it wears off just as fast. These guys are slower, but the benefits last longer.

2. Protein

Gives you energy and feeds your muscles. How do you get it? Either hunt animals that go 'moo', 'oink' and 'cluck' or, for you veggies out there, eggs and dairy products do the same job. Lentils are easier to stalk, can be found in obvious hiding-places (next to the tinned tomatoes) and won't put up a fight when you try to wrestle them into your trolley!

3. Fat

...everybody thinks that this is an extra that you can do without, but you can't. It is good for energy, and is the only source of essential fatty acids and fat soluble vitamins. We all need it, but don't go overboard...**'Who ate all the pies'** is a great song, but not when it's aimed at you!

The secret? Let me spell it out for you...**b.a.l.a.n.c.e.d...d.i.e.t.**

The best method to achieve a balanced diet is to split foods into the following five groups:

1. Large portion   **fruit and veg**: vitamins, minerals and fibre
2. Large portion   **bread, cereals and potatoes**: carbohydrates, fibre and vitamins
3. Smaller portion   **meat, fish and alternatives**: protein and iron
4. Smaller portion   **milk and dairy products**: protein and calcium
5. Smaller portion   **fatty and sugary foods**: fat and sugar

The most important issues are:
- Choose a **variety of foods** from the different food groups.
- **Adequate fluid intake**: make sure you get plenty of drinkable water down you, especially in hot countries.
- **Food safety** – cutting raw meat on a separate board to the veggies, to avoid food poisoning etc.

Important points

➡ **Girls** – ensure you have plenty of iron and vitamin C, especially during periods.
➡ **If you are ill** – take in plenty of vitamin C and zinc (available in tablets).
➡ **Three regular meals a day** – cereal in the morning, bread and salad for lunch, meat and vegetables for dinner, with plenty of water and orange juice.

You've heard about all the vitamins and minerals that you are meant to have and take. Well...**What are they, why do you need them and where are they found?** Check it all out on the following chart.

To sum up, for your vitamins:
🍴 **Eat** – meats (if not vegetarian), green vegetables, fish, dairy food, eggs, cereals
🍷 **Drink** – water, orange juice and milk

It might be worth taking a general multi-vitamin and mineral supplement with you if you are worried that you won't get enough of any particular thing. Talk to your doctor about this when you go for your check-up.

Name	What they do	When you don't have enough	Found in
Calcium	Forms the structure of bones and teeth, muscle contraction.	Infected gums, aches and pains, cramps, muscle spasms etc.	Milk, milk products, dark green veg, canned fish.
Phosphorus	Bone development and energy release from foods.	Anorexia, weakness, lethargy, bone pain.	All plant and animal cells.
Magnesium	Skeletal development, muscle and nerve, metabolism.	Loss of appetite, nausea, vomiting, fatigue, diarrhoea, cramps, constipation, dizziness.	Green veg, meats, fish, dairy food and hard water.
Sodium	Maintains extra cellular fluid volume and acid base balance.	Muscular cramps, vertigo, nausea, reduced appetite.	Ham, bacon and processed foods, condiments and mineral waters.
Iron	Important to carry oxygen in the blood. Absorption improved by presence of Vitamin C.	Tiredness, muscle fatigue, dizziness, headache, insomnia, brittle nails, sore tongue, difficulty swallowing.	Red meats and offal, dark green veg.
Thiamin (Vitamin B1)	Energy metabolism and normal appetite.	Irritability, loss of appetite, fatigue, muscle tenderness. Severe deficiency results in beri beri.	Pork, poultry, fish, beans.
Riboflavin	Normal vision and healthy skin.	Mouth lesions, skin rash.	Meat, eggs, green veg, offal.
Niacin	Energy, healthy skin, intestine.	Dermatitis, diarrhoea, disorientation and fatigue.	Meat, fish, dairy food, peanuts, yeast extract.
Pyridoxine	Protein metabolism, sensory nerve function.	Dermatitis, convulsions, muscle weakness, anaemia.	Wholegrains, fish, meats, nuts.
Folate	Essential for cell growth.	Anaemia, cracked lips.	Liver, yeast extract, green leafy veg.
Vitamin B12	New cell synthesis, nerves.	Nervousness, fatigue, brain degeneration.	All animal products, algae.
Pantothenic acid	Energy release from food.	Headache, dizziness, muscle cramps, fatigue, weakness.	Yeast, meats, wholegrain, veg.

FOOD AND DIET

Name	What they do	When you don't have enough	Found in
Biotin	Protein metabolism.	Nausea, vomiting, depression, hair loss, dermatitis.	Cereals, grains.
Zinc	Metabolism.	Wound healing, eczema, acne, fight infection, diarrhoea.	Red meats, unrefined cereals.
Copper	Healthy skin, hair, red blood cells.	Metabolic and muscle problems (rare), less resistance to infection.	Nuts, offal, oysters, veg.
Iodine	Metabolic rate.	Tiredness, muscle weakness, breast pain, weight gain.	Sea foods, dried seaweed, milk.
Manganese	Bone and tendon growth.	Depression, weakness, leg cramps.	Green veg, nuts, cereal.
Fluoride	Healthy teeth.	Tooth decay, soft bones.	Seafood (bony fish), drinking water, tea.
Chromium	Energy metabolism.	Can't metabolise glucose.	Beer, meats, whole grain, nuts and veg.
Selenium	Anti-oxidant effect.	Muscular weakness.	Wholegrain, cereal, meats, fish.
Vitamin A	Vision, bone, teeth, tissue repair.	Night blindness, painful joints, fatigue.	Dairy foods, liver, fish liver oils, carrots, yellow and green veg.
Vitamin C	Promotes immunity collagen forming and wound healing.	Swollen/bleeding gums, scurvy, slow healing wounds, bruising, fatigue, depression, muscle degeneration, painful joints.	Oranges, lemons, grapefruits, potatoes, tomatoes.
Vitamin D	Bones and teeth as promote absorption of calcium.	Bone problems.	Oily fish, egg yolks, offal, margarine, sunlight on skin.
Vitamin K	Blood clotting.	Blood clots slowly.	Dairy foods, green veg and cereal.
Vitamin E	Anti-oxidant and cellular respiration.	Anaemia, muscle wasting, nerve damage and reproductive failure.	Wheatgerms, eggs and vegetable oils.

Food – a few thoughts

- **Bread** Cheap and fills you up. Carbohydrate.
- **Chocolate** For energy, and apparently makes you happy...so not always bad. The idea that it gives you lousy skin is a myth invented by parents!
- **Doughnuts, muffins etc. I am Homer Simpson** when it comes to doughnuts. They provide the fat content in my diet, are cheap and fill me up. Great for long car/bus journeys, hiking, camping, or anything where you need energy or a quick snack.
- **Fruit** All fruit is good for you. Ensure the skin isn't pierced, it is washed in clean water and peeled before you tuck in. Juicy when you're thirsty and a great cheap snack. NB: always cut fruit in half before you eat...uninvited guests make you vom!
- **Marmite / Vegemite** I always carry a jar (wrapped up, 'cos if it breaks your stuff will stink). Great on fresh bread, it also contains vitamin B.
- **Muesli bars** Tasty. Come in all sorts of flavours, good for you and easy to carry around. Buy in bulk.
- **Porridge** The perfect brekkie. Comes in all sorts of flavours – just add water. Tasty, good for you, and sticks to your ribs. Add chopped fruit for variation.
- **Rice, pasta, potatoes and cereals** Rice and pasta can be kept in your backpack (tie tightly to avoid escapees). Potatoes are bulky, but a nice change from the others (and also contain vitamin C).
- **Salads** Smother in dressing for a tasty snack. Ensure it's been washed properly in clean water. You only find out about the dodgy water after a sprint to the toilet at 3am!
- **Vegetables** An essential part of any diet. Wash properly. They take about seven minutes to cook when boiled (broccoli, cabbage etc) – and are 'done' when a sharp knife passes through comfortably. Healthier eaten raw, as boiling takes away all the good stuff.

What to drink?

Water

Is good for your skin and good for you, especially in the mountains near a 'source'. Eating loads of fruit at the same time can rid your bod of toxins.

- **Bottled water** If the water, H_2O, is better described as $Na(CH)_3Mg_4Sn_2OH$...don't drink it! Bottled water is everywhere nowadays. Always check the seal – any sign of tampering (ie. filled up by tap) – look elsewhere.
- **Carbonated water** Choose carbonated over still water every time – more difficult to tamper with.
- **Water purification tablets** Where there is no bottled water – and you have been advised not to drink the water – be careful (see *Travel health* for more details).
- **Drinking from streams / rivers / sea** Not advised unless you are a fish, hippo or bear...and even then, be careful. Streams, especially, may look pure and inviting... unfortunately, two miles upstream, on the edge of the mountain, a flock of sheep use the stream as their pool when they get hot, and are the envy of all the other flocks of sheep in the area with their free flowing, fast moving toilet.
- **Ice cubes and ice cream**...contain water! Enough said.

Orange juice I drink it at every opportunity. Vitamin C does loads for you – fighting infection being number one.

Coca Cola (and other carbonated drinks) Should come in a bottle or can that is opened in front of you (prevents watering down). Beware, also, that there is a deposit on the glass bottles (a little Thai chap chased me down the street when I walked out of the restaurant, bottle in hand). Coke is dead cheap all around the world...is safe to drink (rigorous standards) and is good for rehydration (when flat) after a bout of 'Delhi belly'...it replaces all the stuff your body has lost, and is even recommended by doctors.

If you are continually on the go, it is impossible to buy food for the week ahead. But in many developing countries, you will probably find it affordable to eat out. In most of the family-run places you can buy food in the reception/eating area. And in the States? *Fast food heaven!*

Staying in one place. If there are fridges and freezers, use them. Communal fridges have an air of distrust about them...worry that anything you put in them will somehow just disappear into the Bermuda Triangle! Generally, though, backpackers are quite good about not nicking each other's food.

The Bottom Line...have a healthy diet. Watch what you eat. Your body is used to being fed three meals a day...if meals are regular, so are you! This all goes out the window on your travels, with meals at odd times and in various shapes and forms. Recovery from illness may take time and is not a bundle of laughs. You may be really hot and uncomfortable and, if not treated properly, you may get worse. *Everyone gets 'The Trots' when they are away, it is virtually unavoidable. What is avoidable is picking up every bug under the sun as your immune system, being run down, can't cope.*

Sum it up, Tom!

You have to look after yourself when you are away, because no one else will. Have a think, now, while you are still at home, about **what you eat** and **what you *should* eat**. If you can't cook...learn. Get plenty of vegetables, fruit and protein down you and you'll be fine. **On the dehydration front – by the time you feel thirsty, you are already dehydrated.** Water? You know the risks by now...the jokes have been made. Be careful, even when brushing your teeth.

Eat well, stay well.

13: Travel health

We have all suffered the odd scrape and graze since childhood. The only difference is that, overseas, in different climates and conditions, cuts can become septic, bruises may be fractures and what may seem like a small ear infection may spread into a full-on painful condition needing to be treated. Here in the UK you can nip down to casualty or your local doctor and get it seen to. When you are travelling, it is not as easy. In the US, for example, to be treated you need money, or evidence that someone, somewhere, is going to foot the bill. If you fall ill in India, have a temperature in Thailand, malaria in Madagascar, or 'The Trots' in Timbuctoo – you're going to have to sort it out for yourself. **The main thing is to learn to look after 'Number One'**, which means allowing yourself to recover fully from illness…or you'll suffer even more.

I'm a traveller and a writer – and an accident-prone one at that (the '*pièce de résistance*' being the head in the ceiling fan trick while it was doing Warp 9!). I'm therefore probably not the best person to be giving you advice on keeping healthy whilst away, which is why I have handed this section over to the experts.

But first, a few notes from me:

Go to see your doctor at least three months before your trip
Make sure you have a check-up. You have to have a check-up and if you are going to need jabs, you will have to find out which ones you need, and when you should have them. With hepatitis jabs, for example, you have a booster a month after the initial injection, so make sure you give yourself enough time.

While you are there…ask all the questions that are on your mind that you're worried about. All doctors are highly confidential, even if they are a friend of your mum and dad. If you want advice about the Pill or any other contraception, now's the time to ask. Family planning clinics are another option. If you are a bit nervous, why not go with a mate? If you are on any other medication, your doctor is likely to know about it. Have a chat, and ask their advice.

Special medication
Friends of mine have had to take special medication away with them, epilepsy pills for example. You are going to need a good supply, so what happens if they run out whilst you're away? How can you get some more? Careful planning could prevent having to come back early. Sending stuff in the post, or taking certain medications with you may require a **Special Export Licence**, especially if they are prescribed drugs. If your drug is controlled, ask your doctor about the quantity and dosage. You may well need a licence, if so, and for more advice, call the Drugs Office ☎ 020 7273 3806.

❶ Make sure you get a doctor's note about any medication you take with you for borders and nosy officials. ❶

If you don't ask your doctor about things now, you may not know what to do if things go wrong, or you may get yourself into a situation easily avoided with a ten-minute chat.

Also go to see your dentist for a check-up – they might catch and clear up a potential future problem. On the subject of oral hygiene, brushing your teeth twice a day is a habit worth getting in to. Dental floss – loads of gunk gets caught in between your teeth, removed only by floss.

Looking after yourself!   *As I said, it's down to you...*

- **Keep your feet dry** to prevent fungal conditions.
- **Mouth ulcers or cuts and sores in the mouth**…rinse with hot salty water four times a day.
- See to **all scratches, cuts and bruises** – keep them clean and, if it's an open wound, be careful not to let it get infected.
- **The Trots?** Make sure you let it all out, as it is a bug…festering. Diarrhoea is due to your body fighting and trying to flush it out. **So let it out.** Suffer it for a day, and then think about blocking it up. **The most important thing then is to rehydrate to replace all the minerals and fluids you have now lost.** Flat Coke or rehydration powder do the job ('Electrolade', found in all pharmacies, is a good, flavoured version).

The sun
Yes, it can give you skin cancer. Yes it does burn. Yes it can give you a tan.
NOMAD go through this in a minute, but a quick note from me:

The secret to tanning: Don't burn. Low protection sun cream and 'tanning oil' (with no protection) will fry the skin; **factor 15** applied regularly (especially after you've been in the water) will give you a long-lasting tan. In hot countries, you will tan anyway just walking around, especially if you are away for anything over a couple of weeks, so don't rush it. Cover eyes, ears and nose with loads of cream. Be aware that you can burn through cloud and from the reflection on water.

Sunglasses. The cheap ones may make you look cool, but they are sod all help. The good ones have UVA and UVB protection. Look into it.

The bottom line for looking after yourself: My philosophy. If I were ill in a country where I couldn't speak the language and where I found myself in a situation important enough to warrant a visit to a doctor – I'd go to the Embassy (they have doctors they use themselves). Who do the guys who run the hostel use?

Whatever the situation, think on your feet and think round it as best you can.

And now…the important stuff…

The following information has come from the Travel Health Centre on **gapyear.com** provided to us by Nomad Travel Clinics. My thanks to Jason Gibbs (MRPharmS) and Sarah Mann (RCN) for putting it together.

Founded in 1990, Nomad Travel Clinics have become leaders in preparing travellers. The Nomad teams have in-depth knowledge of travel and the medical staff – specifically trained in travel health – to ensure the right medical advice preparation for a safe and successful trip.

As specialists in their market, Nomad Travel Clinics often give lectures around the country for independent groups, conferences and exhibitions, shops, clinics and colleges – so you may bump into them! Their expertise has also led to the creation of the Nomad Medical range of travelproof equipment, all tried and tested in the field. These can all be found in the **gapyearshop.com**.

Travel Health Info Line: 09068 633414 – *calls cost 60p per min / office hours only* This line is answered by one of their medical staff who you can speak to on a one-to-one basis and get all the advice you need. (Note: if it clicks into an answerphone message, leave your name and number and they will call you back free of charge!)

Vaccination Appointments can be made on 020 8889 7014 (North London), 020 7833 4114 (Central London) or 0117 922 6567 (Bristol).

Before you go

The key to a successful and fulfilling experience during your time away, whether it is a short duration backpacking trip, or a full year's travelling taking in some conservation work, diving as well as backpacking, is **preparation**. It's impossible to prepare for all possible situations, but if you have all the basics in place it makes those tough situations seem a little easier to handle.

Health checks

Don't forget to visit your GP well in advance of your expected date of departure for a medical and your dentist to ensure that you have no loose fillings and that you don't require any new ones. Most cities will be able to provide good dental services, but be prepared to check that all the equipment they use is sterile, and therefore the risk of contracting Hepatitis B or even HIV through a minor procedure is zero.

Existing conditions

If you have any pre-existing medical conditions that require regular medication, ensure that you have sufficient for your entire trip. When travelling, it's always a good idea to divide your medication between your hand luggage and backpack just in case it gets lost or stolen. Some GPs may be a little reluctant to prescribe an entire year's worth of medication on the NHS, so be prepared to pay for some of it on a private prescription. It's also a good idea, if you know where you will be for an extended period, to investigate availability of your medication at your destination. Always make sure you know both the brand name and the generic name (chemical name) of the drugs you are using, in case you need to obtain a supply whilst abroad. Finally, try to get your GP to write you a covering letter explaining the nature of your illness and the medication/dosage being used. This may prevent any difficulties when travelling through customs and it may help in an emergency.

Known allergies
Be aware of any allergies to drugs that you have encountered in the past and if the allergy is severe, such as anaphylaxis due to penicillin, you should consider wearing a necklace or bracelet explaining this fact. Your local pharmacy will be able to put you in contact with one of the many companies that provide these items.

Blood group
It is not essential that you know this prior to departure, but it may come in handy in an emergency. Your GP should know this, or you could always become a blood donor well in advance of your first vaccinations, since this option may well be ruled out for some time following the administration of certain vaccines or tropical travel.

Medical kit
A fairly comprehensive medical kit can make life a lot easier when you're in some of the more remote areas of the globe, since it gives you a degree of self-sufficiency as well as peace of mind. It's always advisable to carry your own set of sterile equipment when outside of Western Europe, North America and Australia/New Zealand, just in case you find yourself in a situation that requires medical intervention. Many countries believe in giving injections just for the sake of it. These often contain nothing more than salty water, so ensure that an injection is truly necessary and then ensure that they use your equipment. The most common ailments that travellers encounter are caused by accident. Serious accidents will be covered by your insurance but general first aid is essential as well as medications to treat insect bites and travellers' diarrhoea, the two most common problems reported by travellers.

Vaccinations

A full vaccination schedule should be started eight weeks prior to departure. Not every disease can be vaccinated against, so knowledge of the problems you're likely to encounter and how to avoid them is paramount.

Immunisations and diseases
Before commencing overseas travel it is important to obtain the relevant vaccines. We are not going to provide a list of recommendations here, but instead we will provide you with some information about some of the diseases that you can catch overseas. In order to decide whether you need vaccines and malaria tablets for your trip, you should talk to a qualified healthcare professional. They will perform a 'risk assessment' of your trip, looking at the destination, length of trip, intended activities, standard of accommodation, etc. They will then tell you what vaccines you may need and what other health precautions you should take whilst you are away.

Some Diseases Explained

Cholera

Transmission – via food and water contaminated with faeces. **Disease** – an acute diarrhoeal illness. **Symptoms** – sudden onset of profuse watery diarrhoea, known as rice water stools. Dehydration, circulatory collapse and death can occur. **Treatment** – rehydration with either intravenous or oral fluids and antibiotic therapy. **Prevention** – scrupulous attention to food and water hygiene. This disease is fairly rare in travellers and tourists. **Vaccine** – not available in the UK and not recommended for travellers. The World Health Organisation states that a cholera vaccination is no longer an official entry requirement into any foreign country.

Dengue Fever

Transmission – via mosquitoes. **Disease** – a severe flu-like illness usually lasting less than seven days. Sometimes the more serious form can occur – Dengue Haemorrhagic fever – leading to bleeding, shock and possibly death. **Symptoms** – rash, headache, high fever, painful joints and muscles. **Treatment** – there is no treatment for the actual disease, only management of the symptoms with paracetamol, rest and plenty of fluids. For the more serious form of the disease, hospitalisation would be necessary. **Prevention** – bite avoidance. The mosquitoes that transmit Dengue tend to bite during the daytime. **Vaccine** – none available.

Diphtheria

Transmission – airborne via respiratory droplets or less commonly by direct transfer of secretions from an infected person, eg. through skin wounds. **Disease** – a bacterial infection affecting the upper airways from nose to throat and occasionally the skin. This is complicated by the development of a membrane that can obstruct the airways, causing difficulties in breathing. **Symptoms** – sore throat, neck swelling, greyish coloured membrane in affected area. **Treatment** – infected persons would need to attend a hospital for treatment. **Prevention** – immunisation. **Vaccine** – Diphtheria is given as part of our childhood immunisation programme and, as of 1994, school children aged fifteen should have received a combined tetanus/diphtheria booster. Immunisation lasts for ten years.

Hepatitis A

Transmission – through ingestion of infected faeces. Usually from person to person but can also be through contaminated food and water. **Disease** – a viral disease of the liver. **Symptoms** – lethargy, lack of appetite, generally feeling unwell. Whites of the eyes or skin may become yellow (jaundice), stools pale and urine dark. **Treatment** – symptomatic. Sufferers can take a long time to fully recover and during this recovery there may be a complete ban on alcohol. **Prevention** – immunisation. Avoiding contaminated food and water and oral/anal sex. **Vaccine** – one vaccine offers protection for up to a year – if this is then boosted with a second injection within six to twelve months then ten years' protection is conferred. Ideally you should have this vaccine fourteen days before travel.

Hepatitis B

Transmission – through contact with contaminated blood or bodily fluids. **Disease** – a viral disease of the liver. **Symptoms** – lack of appetite, vague abdominal discomfort, nausea and vomiting. **Treatment** – specialised medical treatment needed. **Prevention** – immunisation. Avoidance of risk activities such as unprotected sexual intercourse. **Vaccine** – three injections are given over a six-month period. For those with less time prior to departure, there are two more rapid schedules available – one over two months and one over three weeks but both these require boosters after twelve months.

Japanese Encephalitis

Transmission – via mosquitoes. Only occurs in Central and Southeast Asia. **Disease** – a viral encephalitis (inflammation of the brain). **Symptoms** – headache, severe flu-like illness, confusion, although some cases have no symptoms. **Treatment** – none for the disease itself, only for relief of symptoms. **Prevention** – bite avoidance. Immunisation for those at risk. **Vaccine** – a vaccine is available but should only be used by those genuinely at risk of contracting the disease. A course of three injections over thirty days or two injections at a seven-day interval. Either course should be completed ten days before travel in case of any adverse reactions to the vaccine.

Malaria

Transmission – via mosquitoes. **Disease** – a parasitic disease affecting the red blood cells. There are four different strains of the disease. The worst type (falciparum) can cause multiple organ failure including cerebral damage and sometimes death. **Symptoms** – headache, diarrhoea, high fever, generally feeling unwell or coma. These can take up to one year to occur for certain strains. **Treatment** – anyone exhibiting symptoms who has travelled to a malarial area in the past year should seek medical help. Prompt treatment is essential in order to preserve life. For travellers who are getting well away from medical facilities in malarial areas, it could be prudent to carry a 'standby treatment kit'. This enables you to start treatment whilst getting to medical help where they can check you do actually have malaria, and not some other nasty! **Prevention** – there is a multi-pronged approach as no malaria tablet alone is one hundred per cent effective. Find out where the malaria risks are on your trip. Follow the bite avoidance advice and use an anti-malarial tablet that is appropriate to your area of travel. Guidelines for anti-malarials change regularly, so make sure you get your information from an up-to-date source rather than relying on friends. Completing your course of tablets post-travel is very important, as the parasite can be in the liver up to ten days post-bite. Once it is released into the red blood cells, it could take a further week for any symptoms to begin (ie. two weeks after the bite), so if you have stopped taking your pills, you would be susceptible to full-blown malaria. **Vaccine** – none available yet.

Meningitis

Transmission – airborne, via respiratory droplets. **Disease** – a bacterial infection affecting the lining of the brain and spinal cord. It can also present as an infection of the blood stream and major organs (septicaemia). **Symptoms** – fever with headaches, neck stiffness, photophobia, blotchy rash. **Treatment** – specialised medical treatment needed.

Prevention – immunisation. Avoiding crowded areas or contact with infected persons. **Vaccine** – Meningitis C is given for those living in the UK. For travel, other strains are more common. The combined A and C vaccine is most commonly given. For religious pilgrims to Mecca, a four-strain vaccination certificate is required covering A, C, W135 and Y. This situation is subject to change as the strains that predominate may change. Vaccination should be taken at least two weeks prior to travel.

Poliomyelitis (polio)

Transmission – through ingestion of infected faeces (most commonly in contaminated food and water). **Disease** – a viral infection. Severity of illness varies from an asymptomatic one to infection of the motor neurons leading to limb paralysis and breathing problems. **Symptoms** – headache, gastric disturbance, neck stiffness and malaise. **Treatment** – specialised medical treatment needed. **Prevention** – avoiding contaminated food and water. Immunisation. **Vaccine** – polio vaccine is part of the childhood vaccine programme with the final dose being at age fourteen to fifteen. Boosters are then required every ten years. The Polio virus has been eradicated from much of the world now and efforts continue to rid the whole world of this disease within the next five years.

Rabies

Transmission – through a bite, scratch or lick on an open wound from an infected animal. **Disease** – an acute viral infection that is almost always fatal. **Symptoms** – initially fever, headache and tiredness followed by spasms, mental state changes and coma. **Treatment** – if a person is thought to have been in contact with a rabid animal, the wound should be thoroughly washed with soap and water to remove as much of the virus as they can. They should then seek medical help as soon as they can. Persons bitten need 'post-exposure' treatment, which consists of an injection of rabies immunoglobulin followed by a series of five further vaccines. This immunoglobulin is in short supply in much of the developing world. **Prevention** – avoiding contact with warm-blooded animals in countries that are known to have rabies. Immunisation pre-travel is available. **Vaccine** – a course of three injections given over 28 days prior to travel is available. This is called 'pre-exposure' rabies. It does not make travellers immune to the disease, but in the event of a bite it will reduce the treatment needed to only two vaccines, completely negating the need for the immunoglobulin. This also buys the traveller a little more time in which to find the post-exposure treatment.

Tetanus

Transmission – through tetanus spores that are present in soil entering the body through a cut or wound. **Disease** – an acute disease with muscular rigidity and painful contractions. **Symptoms** – severe and painful muscles, breathing problems. **Treatment** – specialised medical treatment needed. **Prevention** – immunisation. **Vaccine** - tetanus vaccine is part of the childhood vaccine programme with the final dose being at age fourteen to fifteen. Boosters are then only required after a tetanus cut or injury if the time lapsed since the last booster is greater than ten years. Travellers should consider being up-to-date with tetanus in preparation for travel.

Tick-Borne Encephalitis (European)

Transmission – through the bite of a tick. Occurs only in central and eastern Europe. **Disease** – a viral illness causing swelling of the brain. **Symptoms** – headache, neck stiffness, confusion. **Treatment** – symptomatic relief only. **Prevention** – avoidance of tick bites. Immunisation. **Vaccine** – a vaccine is available. Two doses are given at a four- to twelve-week interval.

Tuberculosis (TB)

Transmission – airborne. **Disease** – TB can affect any part of the body but is mostly seen in its respiratory form. **Symptoms** – weight loss, night sweats, cough, fever. **Treatment** – specialised medical treatment needed. **Prevention** – avoid overcrowded places and contact with infected persons. Avoid drinking unpasteurised milk. Immunisation. **Vaccine** – BCG vaccine available in the UK. If travellers have not been immunised in their life and are at risk then immunisation needs to be taken about two to three months prior to departure.

Typhoid

Transmission – through consuming contaminated food and water. **Disease** – a bacterial infection of the intestine. **Symptoms** – prolonged feverish illness with lethargy, stomach pains, constipation and headaches. **Treatment** – with antibiotics. **Prevention** – good food and water hygiene. Immunisation. **Vaccine** – vaccination lasts for three years. It should be taken at least two weeks prior to travel.

Yellow Fever

Transmission – via mosquito bites. **Disease** – a viral haemorrhagic fever. **Symptoms** – flu-like illness, jaundice. **Treatment** – specialised medical treatment needed. **Prevention** – bite avoidance. Immunisation. **Vaccine** – a single vaccine gives protection for ten years. For entry to certain countries, a certificate of vaccination is compulsory. Vaccination takes ten days to become effective.

There is still a long list of diseases that can be acquired whilst you are away. Reading our advice about how to prevent these diseases will enable you to keep healthy whilst you are away.

Staying Healthy

Most common serious ailments that affect travellers are contracted either from the bite of an infected animal or insect, by ingestion of contaminated food or water or by close contact with infected individuals. The last of these three is very difficult to avoid, so those at specific risk should be vaccinated where appropriate, but certain measures can be taken to avoid contracting an illness transmitted by the first two routes.

Bite avoidance

The most commonly contracted mosquito-borne disease is malaria. It is certainly not the only one and therefore good bite avoidance knowledge is essential and should be employed by day, but especially at night when a majority of malaria-carrying mosquitoes bite.

- Reduce the amount of exposed skin by wearing a long-sleeved shirt, trousers and socks. Baggy clothing made of closely woven cotton seems to be the most comfortable and effective.
- In high-risk areas, this clothing can be impregnated with permethrin which is a type of insecticide (harmless to humans) available as Bugproof™.
- Application of a good insect repellent to all exposed skin. Those containing an excess of twenty per cent DEET provide the best protection.
- Wrist and/or ankle bands impregnated with one hundred per cent DEET can give added protection.
- Always sleep in a mosquito net impregnated with permethrin, ensuring that that there are no tears and that it is tucked in properly.
- If you have electricity, use one of the plug-in units that release insecticide while you sleep.
- Spray your room with a knockdown spray prior to retiring.
- Air-conditioned rooms often prevent mosquitoes entering, but only if you never open the windows!

Ticks can cause several very serious diseases and generally live in low-growing vegetation and scrub. If you think you may be at risk because of trekking, wear long trousers tucked into your socks and, if possible, apply a DEET-based insect repellent to both. You must also check yourself regularly, at least once every evening. Ticks tend to head for the groin before starting to feed and the longer they are there, the deeper they become attached and therefore the harder they are to remove. They should be removed gently by holding behind the head with tweezers or fingers and rocking patiently until they release their grip. Be careful not to leave the head or mouth-parts imbedded as this may lead to infection. Apply antiseptic and wash your hands. If a rash or fever develops, seek medical attention.

Food and drink
Contaminated food and drink can lead to a multitude of ailments from uncomplicated travellers' diarrhoea to a variety of worms and parasites. It will always be a temptation to eat as the locals do, or from street stalls serving enticing meals. Always ask yourself if the food has been prepared from fresh ingredients and is well cooked. There is an old adage that will serve you well if applied at all times: **'Peel it, cook it, boil it or forget it.'** Here are a few extra tips that may help you remain healthy whilst away:

- Ensure your food is well cooked, piping hot and freshly prepared from fresh ingredients.
- Avoid salads and vegetables unless they have been thoroughly washed in water containing iodine or chlorine.
- Avoid fish and shellfish whenever possible.
- Peel all fruit.
- Avoid dairy products and ice cream unless from a known reliable source (branded).
- Ensure that your cutlery is clean.
- Eat nothing from buffets or food that may have been lying around for any reason.

TRAVEL HEALTH

- Avoid 'fried rice' that may be made from leftovers.
- Avoid ice in your drinks.
- Ensure that your drinking water is safe.

The last point mentioned here is of vital importance and bottled water should be used where possible. That said, there is a growing trade in 'fake' bottled water which may even have a suitable seal on it, so if there is any doubt drink fizzy water (too expensive to fake), chemically treat your water (see below) or boil it. Water brought to a rolling boil and kept there for five minutes at any altitude will be safe, but is expensive in terms of fuel and may not always be a viable option. Chemically treating your water using one of the following methods may, therefore, be the best option.

- **Iodine** tincture or tablets may be the most reliable methods of purification, since at higher concentrations these will remove even giardia or amoebic cysts. By using a neutraliser, the colour and taste imparted by this chemical can be removed.
- **Chlorine** tablets are very effective for all but the most contaminated water, however the taste can only be disguised and not removed.
- **Silver** is very good for water storage, but not as good as chlorine or iodine when used for purification. It does however have the advantage of not imparting any taste or change of colour to your water.
- **Purifiers and filters** can be expensive to purchase and maintain over a long period of time, but they do provide immediate drinking water. There are a wide variety available – if you wish to purchase a filter or purifier, check with the retailer that they meet your requirements

NB: Don't forget to clean your teeth using safe water.

Travellers' diarrhoea
Should you apply all of the above tips and still become ill, management of travellers' diarrhoea is very important. The first thing to do is to maintain a good level of hydration by frequently drinking freshly prepared rehydration solutions (available from any pharmacy so get some before you leave). If these are not available, a suitable alternative can be made by dissolving eight level teaspoons of sugar and one level teaspoon of salt in a litre of drinking water. At least one glass after each loose stool should prevent any severe dehydration from occurring. The use of loperamide and other 'blockers' should not be a matter of course, as they will only decrease the frequency but not necessarily the volume of your diarrhoea, and may even make it worse in the long run. They do however have an important role to play when travelling on a bus or train where there may be many, many people sharing one toilet. Once you have reached your destination, however, their use should be discontinued.

Danger signs would include blood or mucus in the stool, fever or prolonged severe diarrhoea (more than twelve loose stools per day) and under these circumstances medical attention should be sought.

Antibiotics can sometimes be used to treat severe travellers' diarrhoea. These may be available locally, or they can sometimes be prescribed by your GP or travel health consultant prior to departure, providing you are confident about when they should be used.

Motion sickness

Some people are more susceptible than others to becoming nauseous whilst travelling. Sitting in the front seat of a car or towards the front of a plane may help, likewise being in the middle of a ship. Never attempt to read whilst experiencing motion sickness. There are many brands of 'travel sickness' tablets on the market and your pharmacist will be able to advise you on the one most suitable for you. Alternatively ginger tablets or capsules seem to provide some relief, as do wristbands that work on acupuncture points. Both will be available through local pharmacies.

Jet lag

There are many tales around about how to prevent jet lag, but very few have any proof attached to them. There is much talk of melatonin (a hormone released by the brain just before sleep), but it is currently unavailable in the UK. There are a few tips that may make the transition to a new time zone easier:

- It is always best to avoid alcohol on flights and maintain a good fluid intake of water and fruit juices.
- Change your watch to the time at your destination as soon as you board the plane.
- Get some sun (sensibly) as soon as you get to your destination. This will suppress natural melatonin production and help your body to adjust.
- Adopt local time as soon as you arrive: even if you are not tired, go through the motions of going to bed at night to get a new rhythm as soon as possible.

Safety in the sun

When first arriving in a tropical climate, the high temperatures and humidity may well seem quite oppressive and you will sweat profusely. This can lead to dehydration and lethargy. It will take about three weeks for you to adapt to your new environment, therefore during this settling-in period it is advisable not to overexert yourself and to maintain a high intake of safe drinking water. Throughout your stay there are a number of other points that should help you stay healthy in the sun:

- Avoid sunbathing or spending excessive time in the sun when it is at its strongest between 11am and 3pm.
- Always wear a wide-brimmed hat to protect your face and neck.
- When purchasing the clothes for your trip, check on the UV protection rating. Closely woven cotton is comfortable and protective, but some of the newer, lighter fibres are also very effective.
- **Always** wear at least a factor 15 sunscreen that protects against UVA (burns and ages skin) and UVB (burns only), and if applying insect repellent as well, don't forget to put this on **after** your sunscreen.

Altitude

When travelling to altitudes above 3,000 metres, it is imperative that the ascent is made slowly, with time to acclimatise below this level. If this is not possible, most individuals will experience breathlessness on even the most minor exertion, possibly with headache and nausea. Paracetamol should relieve the headache, but if it is too severe, and combined with nausea, medical attention should be sought. At least three days should be allowed for acclimatisation at this level before strenuous activity, but if this is not possible

TRAVEL HEALTH

there is a drug called acetazolamide that may be of help in some circumstances. It is available on prescription only and must therefore be discussed with your GP or travel health professional before you go. To limit the effects of altitude sickness:

- Avoid alcohol on the plane if flying directly to altitudes above 3,000 metres to prevent dehydration.
- Rest as soon as you can when you arrive at your destination, and take it easy for at least 24 hours.
- Local remedies such as coca tea are of dubious effectiveness. They shouldn't be relied upon but are culturally important.
- Altitude sickness is potentially very serious, and therefore if the headache and nausea do not resolve, medical attention should be sought.

Safe sex
Condoms – taking a good supply of condoms is always advisable. Before travel, most people would say that there is no chance of them having sex whilst travelling – it's too risky. However, it is a fact that in a relaxed atmosphere, after a few drinks, the unexpected will often occur. It is always better to be prepared than to run the risk of pregnancy and sexually transmitted diseases, not least HIV. You may think that the partner you have chosen seems a nice bloke/girl, but the last person that they slept with may not have been! Condoms also come in handy should your oral contraceptive pill be made ineffective due to diarrhoea or vomiting. Condoms may be in short supply in many countries throughout the world and those that are available may be of poor quality due to bad storage or old age.

The Pill – probably the preferred method of contraception amongst the younger age groups in the UK. Under normal circumstances, it offers a very high level of protection, but its absorption may be decreased by profuse diarrhoea or vomiting within three hours of taking the pill. Certain antibiotics may also decrease its activity and theoretically doxycycline (a commonly used antimalarial) may come into this category, so alternative forms of contraception should be used for the first couple of weeks of such an antimalarial course. When crossing time zones, try to continue taking your pill every 24 hours, whatever the time may be. In order to change your daily time always take your pill **before** it is due, ie. less than every 24 hours.

IUD (IntraUterine Device) – very effective method of contraception but provides no cover against STDs.

Injectable contraceptives – effective but provide no STD cover. Have the advantage of reducing menstruation.

Whatever your choice of contraceptive, you should still carry some condoms, and, if you wish to change your method of contraception before you go, this should be done in plenty of time to allow several cycles to pass to check for side effects or difficulties.

Post-Coital Contraceptives (morning after pill) – Effective for up to 72 hours following unprotected sex, this should be used in emergencies only. It will only be available through your GP prior to travel and even then since you have no need of it right now, it may be difficult to convince him that it is necessary.

Further advice on all contraceptive matters should be sought from your GP or local family planning clinic.

Women's health

Menstruation – tampons may be very difficult or virtually impossible to find in many places, and where available they may be of an inferior standard to what you use at home. Therefore it is advisable to take sufficient to cover you for your entire trip if at all possible. In very rural areas disposal of used sanitary towels can also pose a few problems, since they cannot be flushed into a safe sewer system, nor will the dustman collect them, so follow local advice or do the best you can to dispose of them in a responsible manner. For short trips, several packets of pills can be run in together to prevent menstruation, but this is not a good idea for longer travels.

Thrush – is very common is hot humid environments, and your chances of getting it may be increased if you are taking doxycycline as your antimalarial. It is therefore a good idea to take a treatment with you if you're spending any time in a tropical area. There are a variety of treatments available through your local pharmacy including a single oral tablet. If using this, it is imperative that you are not pregnant and that you are well hydrated before taking it (an antifungal cream used at the same time will also help to reduce symptoms immediately).

Cystitis – this is characterised by an extreme desire to urinate frequently, but very little urine is produced, often accompanied by a burning sensation caused by an infection of the urinary tract, bladder and in severe cases the kidneys can become involved. It is often made worse by dehydration: another good reason to keep up your fluid intake. It can by managed by drinking lots of water (about a pint per hour), but if the symptoms do not resolve within about 24 hours or there is blood or fever present, medical attention and antibiotic treatment must be sought. If you are prone to cystitis, then it may be worth taking a course with you – see your GP prior to travel.

Need more advice?
If you have any questions that aren't answered here or need some further information and advice, head to the Travel Health Centre in the Travel Zone on **www.gapyear.com**.

14: Travelling with diabetes

by David Parker

I've handed this section over to **David Parker, who holds the world record for walking across Australia**, and happens to be a diabetic…it's all yours Dave…

I manage my diabetes, rather than it managing me, and I'm determined it will never get the better of me, or stop me doing what I want to do. With careful management and a healthy lifestyle, it is possible to do anything you want.

By the age of 25, this attitude had helped me travel around the world three times, break an endurance world record, and allowed me to see more spectacular sights and scenery than your average person would in a lifetime.

My world record! ☆

I firmly believe there is nothing that a diabetic cannot accomplish. **To prove my point, I walked 2,600 miles across Australia from Perth to Sydney.** By walking an average of 40 miles a day and completing in 69 days (assisted by a back-up support vehicle), I achieved a new world record, breaking the previous record by eight days. People always ask 'Why?' **I did it to prove to diabetics that, if you want to, you can do it!**

Parents' reaction to my travels

Although understandably concerned about me travelling with diabetes, they were very supportive of my ambitions, and were reassured by my travelling with a friend who was aware of the potential complications. We all agreed that I understood and managed my condition well, so why should I have any problems just because I wasn't in the UK? My parents' worst fear – of a hypo occuring while I was away – were calmed by showing Alan (my travel partner) how to use the Hypostop kit, and his assurance that *he would actually use it*, should he ever need to. Fortunately, he never did. **Their attitude was simple:** 'If you're going to do it, now is the time.'

Each trip has taught me an improved way of managing my diabetes

- The discovery of a new carrying case for my medicine.
- Experimenting with carrying mini chocolate bars (small, compact, convenient).
- Carrying/wearing ID that explains I have diabetes, the details of my treatment and a contact address in case of emergency. These can be small and discreet, and medical staff will always look for a necklace or bracelet…saving valuable time.

Travelling with a friend

Make them aware of:

- how to deal with a 'hypo'.
- the symptoms of a drop in blood sugar to dangerous levels.
- what to do if I get to this stage (especially the importance of staying calm enough to rectify the situation). It is imperative for me to feel that I can rely on a friend should such a situation occur, as much as it is important for us both to feel comfortable.

Travelling in isolated locations / trekking

- Inform people of your condition before you set off.
- Take vast quantities of high-sugar items and slow-releasing carbohydrates like pasta, rice, cereals and bread, if it's a long trek.
- Test your blood-sugar levels up to once every two hours.

INSULIN ✚

Because of our inevitable isolation from towns and villages during my world-record attempt, I made a point of taking twice the quantity of insulin with me. There are loads of carrying cases on the market and I have never had a problem storing insulin:

- **hostels and hotels always have fridges.**
- on long journeys **a silver carrying case with an ice block** does the job. I prefer a silver case (the size of a small make-up bag) and an ice block – in direct sunlight for an hour…the temperature only rises by one degree!
- **even in very hot countries with no access to a fridge, insulin can last for up to six months, so don't be alarmed.**

But if, for whatever reason, your supplies do run low, be aware that **different countries have different names and packaging for their products**. I found this out to my cost once in Australia, but after a long discussion with a local doctor we agreed on a close alternative and a slightly different regime until I returned home to the UK.

Another option is to have items such as blood-testing sticks posted out to you…to ensure that you stay with a familiar medicine. However, a freezing cargo hold/sweltering warehouse makes me wonder what condition the items will be in when (and if!) they arrive. Also, my local doctor once refused me a prescription, knowing that I was abroad at the time, on the grounds that I was not covered under his budget. So ideally, have an adequate supply of medicines to cover your trip, or get advice from Diabetes UK (see below) on the services available in the countries you intend to visit.

Hot or cold climates affect the way you manage your condition.

Hot climates

I was convinced in Thailand (constantly 90°F) that my blood sugar was decreasing much faster than I was used to – so to avoid hypos I tested my blood more frequently, and adjusted my diet and insulin requirements accordingly. With a high blood sugar in hot climates, it's easy to feel sluggish and lethargic – added to the very real chance of becoming dehydrated. Ensure plenty of sugar-free fluids are available, and that exercise can be taken regularly.

Cold climates

The opposite occurs as insulin is absorbed more slowly – so I spread the intake of food over a longer period to prevent a rapid increase in blood sugar.

For long journeys, whether by car, coach or plane – pack plenty of high-carbohydrate foods, plus insulin or tablets in your hand luggage. My blood sugar often increases if I remain inactive for long periods, so test your levels more frequently and adjust your food intake accordingly.

FLYING ✗

- Airlines don't usually inform you prior to a meal being served (even though they say they will!).
- Always ask a member of the cabin crew how many meals are going to be served and when.
- Specific diabetic meals (if pre-ordered) will be given first, sometimes up to twenty minutes before the other passengers, which is a bonus.
- Although diabetic meals do meet the requirements, I usually find insufficient carbohydrate (hence the extra food in my hand luggage) – airline staff will always find extra fruit, bread or snacks if you ask.

Time zones

Time zones are confusing so plan ahead. For example, on a recent evening flight from Canada to London (six hours) we took off at 8pm and were given an evening meal in the first hour. Five hours later, one hour from arrival (with my body-clock telling me it was 1am – but the real time being 6am), we were served breakfast. I knew this was going to happen, and worried about eating breakfast five hours after my evening meal, instead of the usual thirteen! To save overlapping the insulin still digesting dinner, I left breakfast and ate three hours after landing. **Confused?...read it again!** Throughout the day I gradually decreased the fluctuated times at which my normal meals were consumed.

- You may want to adjust your intake if your sleep-cycles and insulin levels are affected.
- If schedules are confusing or cause concern, take advice from your doctor/diabetes specialist.
- Remain flexible about your control, and never aim for your control to be perfect whilst travelling.
- Plan well in advance – find out flight times, length of flights and local time of arrival – be prepared for delays.
- Do plenty of blood tests during, and up to 24 hours after, the journey.

FOOD

I have never found food to be a problem whilst travelling:
- Rice and starchy food is the basic ingredient in most countries.
- Meals are easily found in restaurants and bars in towns and cities.
- I always carry my obligatory loaf of bread with me at all times, whether walking about town, up a hill, or lazing on a beach.

NB: Beware of sweetened tea on Pacific Islands, and remember that although 'diet' isn't on the can, 'light' means the same thing.

ALCOHOL   ♀

I always eat a light meal before alcohol, and **have plenty of water to avoid dehydration**. There is no problem with beer, but watch the alcohol content, especially with obscure, unknown labels! Also, **avoid low carbohydrate beers**, as these can be higher in alcohol and calories too.

✍ To sum up

Nothing is beyond your capabilities because of having the condition. I, and many others, have proved it. Doctors/diabetic specialists will advise you on any aspects of travelling that may be a concern, to ensure that you are fully confident to be able to get as much as possible from your time away.

- **A health check-up prior to leaving is essential**.
- **Planning ahead**, and considering a course of action for a 'worst-case-scenario', is advisable.
- **A doctor's letter is essential** (+ copies) to confirm your diabetes, and to please any curious 'officials' who enquire about your needles – saves time, hassle and problems.

If there is an adventure you fancy attempting...try it. If there is a country you want to experience...go for it! Above all, be confident in what you believe you can achieve, and give travelling your best shot. You'll love it! If you want any motivation, contact me through Tom at **gapyear.com**.

For advice and literature on travelling with diabetes:
Diabetes UK in London have a detailed knowledge of all sorts of medical items available in the most frequently visited countries. They have booklets packed with useful information and relevant phrases for travellers that I can't recommend highly enough.

Diabetes UK
10 Queen Anne Street
London   W1M 0BD
☎ 020 7323 1531   Fax 020 7637 3644

Diabetes UK Careline   ☎ 020 7636 6112

www.diabetes.org.uk

careline@diabetes.org.uk

TRAVELLING WITH DIABETES

15: Insurance by Max Andrews

Check that the level of insurance cover is sufficient for your needs, and includes emergency medical attention and repatriation (which can cost thousands). Travel agents offer all sorts of schemes – some are 'free' (ie. included in the price of your ticket), **but many may not give adequate cover**.

EU residents are entitled to emergency medical care throughout the EU, simply by getting an E111 (from the Post Office). There are many other reciprocal arrangements worldwide (eg. between the UK and Australia) – find out locally, but still ensure that you are suitably covered.

General

In the excitement of planning routes and choosing destinations it is easy to leave travel insurance until the last minute…don't! Allow plenty of time to shop around. National newspapers carry the numbers of a selection of insurance brokers who can quote prices over the phone. The travel agent who sold you your tickets may also try to sell you their insurance. Beware that many use the opportunity to almost force you to buy from them, inferring that you **must** buy insurance from them. This is illegal. By all means get a quote, but compare it with others before you buy.

What policy best suits your needs? If you intend to partake in 'dangerous sports', from skiing to scuba-diving (see below), individual insurers will offer varying standards of cover for such activities. **It may be wise to opt for the best and most comprehensive policy, even if it is not the cheapest.**

The quality of the cover depends greatly on what you are willing to pay. Although most policies provide adequate cover for major incidents, eg. hospitalisation, it is frustrating to discover that a minor theft or medical matter is hardly worth claiming for once the excess is deducted, all for saving £30 or £40 on the price of your insurance.

The kind of things decent travel insurance should provide:

Medical / illness ✚
A good standard of medical cover **is the most important aspect of any policy**. It should cover any medical bills that you incur during your travels, from a course of injections to hospitalisation, bearing in mind that you will probably have to pay for even the most minor treatment. There will be a certain amount of excess before the insurance policy comes into effect, usually around £30 to £50, so don't expect to be compensated

for every minor scrape or ailment. Ensure that the policy offers an efficient means of returning you home if medically required ('repatriation'). It's reassuring to know that, should you fall very ill, **your policy provides an air ambulance service to fly you home**, with the possibility of a friend or relative to travel with, or fly out to meet you, should a doctor deem it necessary.

Most policies will offer a discount for those travelling solely within the EU (due to reciprocal medical agreements).

Prospective insurance companies will want to know of any pre-existing medical conditions before they sell you the policy. **An untruthful answer could nullify a medical claim, so don't even think about it.**

Repatriation
Should the worst come to the worst, it is vital that your insurance policy specifically covers your repatriation: the euphemistic term given to flying the body home. It can be very expensive, so is a vital part of any policy. Don't get scared, just get the best and forget about it. Funeral expenses abroad should also be covered.

Cancellation and curtailment
A decent policy will compensate you for travel and accommodation costs should you have to cancel or cut short your trip for any reason. Some insurers even offer cover against the need to re-sit exams, worth considering if you're not too sure of any results!

Baggage
If you are unfortunate enough to have a claim on your insurance, it will more than likely be a result of the theft or loss of some personal effects. Small electrical items, particularly cameras, are easy prey for the opportunistic thief, and because of the relative frequency of claims on baggage insurance, the excess applied usually negates most of the compensation for less expensive items. Indeed, insurers offer incentives to waive baggage cover, which may be an option if you are taking nothing of value, but could leave you in the lurch if your whole backpack goes missing. If you have a valuable camera or similar equipment with you, choose your insurance carefully. Better policies will pay out larger amounts, both for single items and overall, and it would be foolish to have insufficient cover for the value of any individual items you take with you. Some also offer compensation for emergency purchases if your luggage is delayed.

Travel documents
Losing tickets and documents is particularly annoying whilst abroad. Western passports are a valuable commodity in many countries, and liable to be stolen if you don't take proper care of them. Getting replacements eats into your time. A good policy will cover the price of replacement documents, and any enforced travel and related accommodation expenses.

Hazardous sports
Trekking, bungee-jumping and rafting (amongst others) are a regular part of the backpacker search for excitement. Unfortunately they all carry a risk of injury, or worse,

INSURANCE

so you need full coverage. **Most 'backpacker' policies claim to cover for many 'dangerous activities', yet upon closer inspection...they don't:** motorcycle and moped riding are typical examples. Read the policies carefully to see what exactly is covered; if in any doubt, phone the insurance company. Some policies have an optional 'Hazardous Sports' add-on, providing extra security. Even if you don't see yourself abseiling down Everest or rafting the Amazon, you'll be surprised what you get up to whilst abroad, and it is well worth being covered. *Also be aware that before you partake in many of these activities, the companies make you sign a disclaimer, putting all responsibility upon you.*

Personal liability

...is definitely worth considering, especially for the US. It covers you for injuries to other persons or damage to property.

Small print

Read it before setting off – once something has occurred it's too late to realise you are not covered. It gives details about the excess (the initial amount you must pay towards any claim), and specific activities and circumstances excluded under the policy. Some of these exclusions will seem idiotic, designed to exclude exactly the scenarios in which you are likely to have to claim. But it is better to know the extent to which you are covered, even if you have gambled and taken a less than comprehensive policy. If you don't understand any of the small print, ask the insurance provider to explain it.

Claiming

The small print also tells you how to claim. Some policies allow you to leave the processing of the claim until you arrive home, or up to a certain amount of time after policy end date. Others, however, may require preliminary notification within 28 days, usually by phone. Whatever the nature of your claim, ensure that you get the correct official documentation to support your story. In the event of a fire, obtain a copy of the fire report. In the case of theft or loss of belongings, inform the police at the first opportunity, as some policies have a time-limit on this. They should make out a written report detailing the date and nature of the incident and value of anything taken (the reason you should fill in the details of your valuables in the *Back Section*, together with receipts for your parents to keep – to aid any claims). Also, if your policy covers you for the theft of a certain amount of cash, keep your receipt from the last time you cashed a traveller's cheque. If you change $100 and all your is money stolen the next day, you can prove that there was probably a substantial amount left.

Final important points
1. Think about everything you may need cover for before getting a quote – riding mopeds, skiing, bungee-jumping, etc.
2. 'Unlimited medical cover' is a sales gimmick. The largest ever claim was for £750,000. £3 million minimum will do the job. After all, how much would it cost to rent a 747 from Sydney?
3. The E111 doesn't give full medical cover, so you still need insurance in Europe.

4. If you travel without insurance, you could rack up a £50,000 to £250,000 bill. **For the sake of saving a few quid here, you could bankrupt your parents/friends who may have to pay to save your life.** It's as simple as that. Don't be selfish.

5. For more advice and information, head to the 'Guide to buying insurance' on gapyear.com and also the Foreign Office website – **www.fco.gov.uk/knowbeforeyougo**. Got an immediate question? Call 0870 241 6703 for advice or log on to **www.insureyourgap.com**.

Himalayan hold-up / Nepali nightmare

Having arrived in Pokhara, Nepal, a few days before, Simon, Ian and I turned our thoughts to trekking. Our plans evaporated at 3am one night, when we were rudely awoken by a shadowy figure at the bathroom door, making a 'hushed-lip' sign. An accomplice emerged brandishing a silver magnum-style handgun – realisation dawned.

The smaller one waved his firearm in an alarming fashion, whilst the other, brandishing an 18-inch Gurkha knife, searched our rucksacks. We meekly met their wishes. They made off with around $10,000 in traveller's cheques, two passports, cash and a host of credit cards. They warned that 'friends' would exact mortal revenge if we informed the law. For a bizarre finale, the knife-wielding accomplice apologised explaining that: 'You are rich, we are poor,' and wished us 'good-night'!

Despite their chilling threats, we reported the matter. Our confidence was lifted by Pokhara's finest. The Chief of Police listened intently, and we filled out crime reports which he then signed officially, an essential formality to authenticate our claims. Insurance and traveller's cheque companies demand this. For the rest of the morning we were whisked around the town with no fewer than half a dozen uniformed officers in tow as we telephoned parents, cancelled credit cards and traveller's cheques – and received a general lecture in being 'a man' from our hotel proprietor, berating us for not attempting to overpower the thieves!

Our troubles hadn't ended. We had to go to the capital, Kathmandu, to start replacing passports and traveller's cheques. The process took nearly two weeks, so goodbye trekking and rafting. The British Consulate was excellent in dealing with the passport applications, but it took several visits. **It helped that I had photocopies of the relevant pages, and other photo-bearing ID.**

Replacing traveller's cheques was a nightmare. Seven visits over nine days to get a full refund. I wasn't even offered a preliminary settlement to tide me over (guaranteed in the small-print, but I hadn't noticed). Unfortunately, the Kathmandu office of a well-known traveller's cheque provider was only a 'representative' and all authorisation had to be sought from Delhi by phone. **Believe me, replacement traveller's cheques are not hand-delivered while you sit by the pool sipping cocktails!**

As regards the insurance claim, there was further disappointment. I had, through my parents, informed my insurer of my claim the morning after the robbery. Armed with police report, receipts for travel to, and accommodation in Kathmandu, I anticipated a decent amount of compensation. **In the small-print (unread), however, much of the claim was excluded**, eg £30 worth of telephone calls to 'free' credit card cancellation lines (the phone booth owners in Pokhara insisted on payment), and once the excess had been removed against the cost of the passport etc, it was hardly worth claiming, leaving me with some unique experiences but little else.

The moral of this tale? Make sure you are fully insured, know how to claim, what you can claim and gather all the evidence needed to make the claim go through. Fill in the *'Back Section'* of this book, leave it with someone in the UK and photocopies of policies, receipts, etc.

16: How to...organise your finances ⑤

When at last you have the cash, what do you do with it? How do you carry it around the world? How do you access it when you're halfway up a mountain in Kathmandu when your donkey has stopped and it needs another fifty rupees' worth of carrots before it takes another step? What about when you are trekking in northern Thailand, rafting the Zambezi, or watching polar bears in Alaska? Surely you don't take it all with you?

Traveller's cheques? International debit cards? Western Union and Moneygram? Thomas Cook? Dollars? Rupees? Mastercard? Visa? American Express? The good old British pound sterling?

So many options. What do you use? How do you do it? Hopefully, I've got all the answers. ❷

Traveller's cheques

Many say that traveller's cheques could soon be a thing of the past, as the world gets 'smaller' through technology. But there are millions out there who don't think so. Traveller's cheques are useful, safe and acceptable in even the most undeveloped countries (there are always banks [or private 'money changers'] in the capital cities that can cash them for you at a price).

Remember...keep the carbon copy and a note of the serial numbers separately. Leave a note of the numbers at home in a safe place, where they can be found easily should you need them (when everything 'hits the fan'). Fill in the **Back Section** so your parents can keep a record while you're away. **I can't emphasise enough how important this is.** It will take two minutes...and if there's a problem while you're away, it can be dealt with swiftly and smoothly. As a safe way of carrying large amounts of money around the world with you, this has got to be up there with hiring a personal bodyguard and a pitbull called Rex.

Currencies go up and down daily, so which currency to take?...I always opt for US dollars (US$), as they are the most widely accepted. Flash dollars around in many less developed or inflation-ridden countries and you get somewhere. It's definitely the safe option, but you can always check with your bank as to what they would advise.

Think about it!
Currencies fluctuate in value and you get the rate at the exact second of purchase. So watch what the currency is doing and decide when to buy to get the best rate. The way the markets change, it could make you a few bob, so get in the habit of looking now. There is a funky little website called '**The Cheat Sheet for Travellers**' found at

www.oanda.com/converter/travel, which is a currency converter (it is 'time specific' so you can check out the rate over time to see if there is a rising, falling or stable trend). Again, your bank can advise on this. Make sure you allow a week in case they have to order traveller's cheques in.

American Express Traveller's Cheques. Amex offers loads of additional services and will (reputedly) replace lost or stolen traveller's cheques instantly (but see Max's problems in the chapter on *Insurance*). They also offer a postal service (similar to *poste restante*) which is free to their clients and can be used to receive mail (see *How to... keep in touch*). Amex issues a booklet which tells you where their offices are and if they offer this service, so ask for one when you buy your traveller's cheques.

Watch out for...commission

If you have to pay it, make sure you don't pay too much. Thomas Cook and Amex will cash their own-brand cheques for FREE if you go into their branches overseas. Thomas Cook have 1,000 branches worldwide and relationships with a further 4,200 'financial institutions' in over 188 countries (at the time of writing) – so you should always find somewhere to change money. Amex also have a huge number. In the *Top Fifty Destinations* we list the addresses for Thomas Cook and Amex in the main cities. However, rather than charging around wasting money on buses etc trying to find the right office, think about going to a *bureau de change* closer to where you are staying, and pay that little bit of extra commission – it could work out cheaper in the end.

If you go home with unused traveller's cheques, they can also be changed back for free. However, I would advise spending the lot, and having a blow-out on your last few nights away!!

Also watch out for 'fixed rate' and 'percentage' commission, and be aware of what's best for you at the time; usually this will depend on how much you are exchanging.

Fixed rates If there is a fixed rate, change as much as you can to make it more worthwhile (don't end up paying $5 just to change $20!). Join up with mates or travel partners you can trust ie. 'I'll get $100 for us now, you do it in a couple of days.'

Percentage rates...may surprise you. Basically they take a percentage (usually 1.5%) of everything, so the more *you* change, the more *they* get! On a blank bit of paper write down: '$100 to you, how much to me?'... get it written down so that there is no mistake. But bear in mind that percentage rates are usually a better option if you only want to change small amounts, say, $50.

Signing cheques

You will sign the cheques originally at the bank, and then countersign them when you want to cash them. You must countersign the cheque only when you are presenting it, not before, or it becomes invalid. Should you make a mistake, simply explain the situation and have proof of your identity.

I always get small denomination traveller's cheques: Walking into a money-changer with a cheque big enough to be mistaken for their country's national debt (or using it as 'cash') may draw unwanted attention to you, and may be difficult to exchange in out-of-the-way places.

Important points

- If you are only in Thailand for two days before moving on to Malaysia, don't get loads of Thai currency; you'll only have to change it again and pay more commission. Yes, you get a better rate for cash, but what would you feel safer carrying round?

- Watch the commission, it soon adds up, so make sure you get the best service. As pointed out, Amex have a *poste restante* system. ***Does your traveller's cheque provider offer any other services you could use?***

Traveller's cheques make budgeting easy – when the number of cheques goes down, the alarm bells start to ring. However, the trusty old hole-in-the-wall spits out money with no moral judgement and no regrets, leaving you at the mercy of yourself, draining your account and being none the wiser...

International debit cards

How do you get one? Simple. Ask your bank to change your normal cash card into an international debit card ie. paint a couple more logos on it. It's free, so make sure you get this done in plenty of time before you leave. Most of you will have used one of these without even knowing it. Your cash card or switch card actually has a lot more to it – **Cirrus and Maestro**.

Cirrus 'C' is for Cirrus which is for cash. If you see the following symbol, and it's on your card,

you can take cash out of that machine by entering your PIN number like you would with your bank. You can draw up to £250 per day in local currency from around 200,000 machines in more than sixty countries. You are offered the choice of different languages, so all the instructions on the machine can be in English. Your account will be debited within seven days and the transaction details will appear on your next current account statement.

The charge is about 2% (many are 2.25% – check with your bank before you leave) per transaction, with a minimum of £1.50 (at the time of writing). Ask at your bank for details of Cirrus availability in the countries you are going to visit.

Maestro With the Maestro symbol on your card

you can buy goods in department stores overseas with one swipe!

HOW TO...ORGANISE YOUR FINANCES

However, a couple of points to note: the money comes straight out of your account at home, the details of the transaction appearing on your next current account statement. You pay the minimum charge of £1.50 on every transaction (at the time of writing) or the percentage of 2.00–2.25% of the value of the transaction. The money comes straight out of your account at home – yes I did just repeat myself, for a good reason…**swipe, spend, swipe, spend, swipe, spend**…and your bank balance will go down faster than the *Titanic*. You will then be left with no money. It is a great way to organise your finances if you are a controlled type who budgets well, but beware if you are prone to massive spending sprees.

International debit cards have some massive advantages, but there are also some obvious drawbacks:

- Countries without cash machines.
- No cash in your account, and the card is useless.
- If you lose your card it will have to be reissued at home and sent to you. Character-building if you are trekking in Nepal…!

Credit cards

You need them, so get them…it's as simple as that. The time may come when you need to have access to a large amount of money quickly. BANG, credit card on table, situation dealt with. For example, a relative goes into hospital and you need to come back. Credit cards will give you that instant purchase so you can buy the tickets and return home.

How to get them?
This might be difficult, as they are issued on a credit-check basis. But if you or your family are not considered a credit risk, you should be fine.

- **Your parents could get you a supplementary card in their name.** There is a lot of trust involved here, as they have to pay the bill (or cancel their own if it gets lost or stolen). If you want to stay alive, or ensure they don't move house whilst you are away, I suggest you use it for emergency or agreed purposes only.

- **Your parents could be a guarantee for you** – putting their account down as a kind of collateral on your card. Worth thinking about if the folks have a good relationship with the bank.

- **Shop around** – you can get a card from any bank and loads of companies offer cards free of charge to students, so get one! They can be used in cash machines if the Visa, MasterCard etc. signs are showing, *but you'll be charged interest on that cash straight away.* **Make sure you remember to take your PIN number with you and keep it well away from where you keep your card. Better still, memorise the number, or at least write it in code like a phone number or a birthday.**

Security ❶

- We can be very blasé about these fellas – **guard them like a hawk** – they can be worth literally thousands to the guy who has nicked them and is busy buying a car! They are your emergency back-up. If they have to be cancelled, you will face a load of hassle and it may even cost you money. Should they go walkabout, report it straight away. **Remember to write a note of the emergency numbers for lost/stolen credit cards in the *Back Section* and take a photocopy with you!** Credit cards are easy to nick and use. Your statements come through to your home address, so you may not realise until it's too late. Keep an eye on it, and get someone at home to monitor your bill.

- When you sign for things, ***check carefully that all the boxes have been filled in correctly***, and make sure you keep the carbon copy (the middle bit, usually pink or yellow), otherwise zeros may be added or the currency changed (1,000 baht suddenly becomes $1,000!).

A final point: *if your card is a bit knackered,* **get a new one issued.** *Overused cards may have damaged tape, and not swipe properly. If the signature and/or numbers are faded it may not be accepted. It's free, so request a new one in plenty of time before you leave.*

Cash

You get a better rate of exchange for cash but if it gets nicked, you've had it. Don't chance it! Max was robbed in Nepal and lost the equivalent of $10,000 (in traveller's cheques). They were reimbursed, and he continued for the next eighteen months! Had it been cash, he would've had to come home.

- **Don't accept torn and manky bank notes.** They may be refused by shops and other places.

- **Fake/counterfeit money** – you are an easy target, so be vigilant.

- **Having a few dollars in cash can be very handy** to get a good rate of exchange. In some places dollars are worth a lot of money…hard cash. I am, of course, talking about…
The Black Market…which is illegal…so get caught and pay the price. You'll get a great rate with no extra charges. Beware of an intermediary taking your money off to 'someone' to change it…he may not return. Beware of 'doing the deal' down a side alley away from prying eyes. Chances are, you'll be mugged. It happens all the time…keep on your toes.

- Handling money in public? Cash machines at night or in dark/quiet areas? Flashing cash in a bar when buying a drink? That's how I got mugged, and how you will be mugged. Take only a small amount of money out with you, hide the rest in your backpack or put it in the hostel safe.

- **'Muggers' money'** Carrying a dummy wallet or purse is a great thing to do. Get a knackered old wallet, put a bit of cash in it and always carry it with you. In a bad situation, you just hand it over. Inside they'll find a bit of cash and sod all else.

Managing your bank account while you are away

Think about adding your parents or a trusted friend as signatories to your account: sounds like a loony thing to do, but smacks of common sense. If there are any problems they can be dealt with straight away, rather than being left to fester until you get home. Banks cannot do anything on any account unless they are dealing with an authorised signatory. It does mean that your parents can access your balance, so if that's a problem for you, think twice…but it also means you can leave money in the account to pay for credit card bills, etc which is important.

In emergencies it could make all the difference: you lose your international debit card, or it gets nicked while you are up a mountain in Pakistan. Your parents can authorise a new one and get it posted to you. OK, problem: your new, unsigned, card could be intercepted *en route*. It's a risk you are going to have to take. The safest option is to go to the capital city, find the biggest, most impressive bank you can, find someone in authority who speaks English and explain the situation. Ask them if your bank can send the card to you via them, find out how much they will charge for this, etc. It is important to get the full details of the bank ie. name, address, sort codes and anything else your bank will need. Be extra polite to the person you are dealing with abroad, and ask if you can use him/her as a contact.

Hopefully, your problem will be solved.

Emergency money transfer

Western Union ☎ 0800 833 833 and **Money Gram ☎ 0800 894 887** – the 'money in minutes' guys. They are mostly used by travellers in an emergency, but can obviously be used at any time to get cash to you when you are abroad. How does it work? Simple!

There are thousands of agent locations worldwide. Call to find which ones are near to your parents and near to wherever you are. If you are in the middle of nowhere, you may have to head to a major town or capital city. Once your parents (or whoever is sending the money) find their local branch, they simply fill in the forms, hand over the money, take the receipt and look after the Control Number they'll be given. They inform you of the transfer, and all you do is head off to your nearest agent, show some ID and pick up the money.

The money is converted at the exchange rate current at the time the transaction goes through. All the operators speak English, so there should be no hassles and, because everything is done by computers, phone line and carrier pigeon, it is practically instantaneous. Western Union and Money Gram agents are found literally everywhere.

The best thing is that most agents are in places like chemists or 24-hour shops, so you're not stuck with the Monday–Friday nine to five regime.

Security

To ensure a secure transfer, why not attach a question to the transfer ie. names of relatives, maiden names, birthdays, defining calculus etc (this would be something that my brothers would do for a laugh – I'd turn up, desperate for cash, show my ID and be asked the terminal velocity of a fully-laden sparrow in flight!).

Other money transfer

…through the normal banking system. **Local banks can act as a recipient for money to be sent over.** All you have to do is show some ID to pick the money up, and pay any charges. (Use the same routine as above with sending a debit card out to you…go to the capital, find the biggest bank etc).

Opening an account abroad

If you get a good job abroad, you will need a bank account to get paid. With money coming in, most banks will be happy to oblige! Tony and I did this, transferring our money to the Westpac Bank in Sydney, which waited for us to pick it up. On our first day in Sydney we went to the head office of The Westpac, showed our ID and opened up our accounts (your bank will explain how this works – there are two charges, both of which you pay back at home at the time when the arrangement is set up). This worked really well. We couldn't touch that money until we got there, helping us to budget on the way out. In Australia we had a bank account with a cash card, so we could use the cash machines, and have wages paid in. The only worry was overspending, as it's all too easy to access your cash.

Sum it up, Tom!

- **Traveller's cheques** are still the best form of organising your cash.

- **International debit cards** are funky little dudes that make practically every cash machine in the world your best friend – ready cash, local currency, charges paid.

- Look after your **credit cards** as they are your emergency back-up and, if nicked, will cost you precious time and money.

Looking after your finances is actually quite simple, **it's the budgeting, not the spending which is the most difficult thing**. A mix of traveller's cheques and an international debit card, backed up with a credit card and your account signed over to mum and dad seems to be the best recipe for success. Banks are there to advise as well, so use them.

17: How to...keep in touch

This is the key to travelling, and will help you deal with worried parents, family and friends.
I am as guilty as the next for not keeping in touch properly, something which I grew out of pretty damn quick. We've all heard the expressions '**Keep in touch!**' and '**Send me a postcard!**', laughed off as the common joke for when anyone goes overseas. Why laugh? In this day and age there is no excuse for not being able to keep in touch properly.

The internet has now reached just about everywhere...**a free email account being as essential to the travellers of the new millennium as fresh pants and spare toothpaste**. There are 'internet cafes' everywhere where you can link up to the rest of the world. So, even for those technophobes out there (who, like me, have only just mastered massive technological advances like the microwave and video recorders), mastering the internet is a must before you get on the plane. See **How to...use the internet** for a few pointers.

Again, learn from my mistakes!
When I went round the world with Tony, he kept in touch with his family with the regularity of an Olympic athlete on a diet of fibre flakes and cabbage – phone calls, cards and letters. Due to the problems I was having with my dad, the last thing I wanted to do was to talk to my parents. Unfortunately my poor old mum bore the brunt. In my opinion, they didn't care what I was up to, so sod them. I was off having fun, so why ruin the time of my life? This all changed after my run-in with a ceiling fan (see below). My mum was dead pleased to hear from me – worried that the subtle messages via Tony's parents of 'Is he still with Tony? in Australia? alive?' hadn't quite got through!

As long as I'm OK, what do I care?
To be honest, I was having such an amazing time that I didn't really give a shit about anything or anybody else...as long as Tom Griffiths was all right, what did I care? In hindsight, to think that I was over 10,000 miles from home and my parents didn't even know where I was, what I was up to, or where I was going next, is a crazy thing to consider now. I have learned from this...so now when I go away and I say that I'll be in touch, I hope that my parents know that I will be.

'Hi mum, look, ermmm, I'm afraid I've had a bit of an accident!...'
Not exactly the best way to resume contact with an anxious parent...I was feeling a bit sorry for myself, having just had a ceiling fan extracted from my head after a run-in with an ant. These hard little bastards seem to make a point of following me on my travels, and one night in Airlie Beach, Australia, having discovered that my room was full of them, I decided to fight back. With full body protection, armed with my shoe, and with not a

thought for my own safety, I took them on. Brave? – well, I thought so. You'll be pleased to know that I got them all, suffering very little injury, only slightly scuffing my finger on the wall a couple of times. However, there was one left – sneaking away at the very top of the wall, using the height advantage. Being an ant, he obviously hadn't worked out the principle of 'the bunk bed'. I jumped on the top bunk and, with a resounding 'thud', I sent his teeth through his arse!

With a victorious 'YESSSS', I swung round, raising my hand in victory, only to be knocked over to the far side of the room as I stuck my head in the ceiling fan...which was doing roughly Warp 7. With blood everywhere (it had actually dented my skull – apologies if you're squeamish) I was dazed, concussed and ended up with five stitches. Had I swung round even more, I probably would have lost an eye!

So, here I was telling my mum, Dr Griffiths, that I'd had a 'bit of an accident'. A BIT OF AN ACCIDENT! It nearly took my sodding head off. Obviously my mum wasn't too impressed, worried sick more like. Obviously she now thought I would only contact them when I was in serious trouble and so she would dread the phone ringing! Now I always send postcards (it gives them something to collect), plus making the odd phone call. They always like to know where I am and what I'm up to and that, if ever I'm in trouble, I'll let them know…

There's no excuse. Keeping in touch is important, so what are the best ways to do it? I've got four on my shortlist: email, voicemail, cheap international call companies and letters (the '*poste restante*' system).

1. Email ✉

With a **free email address** used on a 'regular basis' (daily, weekly or monthly) you can always be contacted, no matter what...anytime, anyplace, anywhere. You need to get one of these to keep in touch with family, friends and other travellers. '**...the internet never sleeps!...**', so messages will always get through. **www.cybercafes.com** will tell you where the internet cafes are around the world.

The Internet See *How to...use the internet* for a full section on this, parents especially.

2. Voicemail ☎

Approved by parents with daughters who are travelling solo around the world (and also sons). It is simply your own personal answerphone that you can access and control from any telephone in the world. **You can leave a message for your parents to hear, telling them where you are and what you're doing and, if the need arises, collect important messages.** It makes sense to access your voicemail through a chargecard to keep costs down, or you can email your parents to tell them where you can be contacted.

How does it work? You have a phone number, usually based in your home capital city...either a national or freephone number. You set your own PIN number which enables you to access the number and change/pick-up messages, etc from anywhere in the world. As you have to use a touch-tone phone, you will have to buy a keypad before you leave (usually around £10) in case you end up staying somewhere remote with old-style phones.

Ideal messages to leave 'Hi there, I've now arrived in Mexico. I am staying in Veracruz at the xxxxxxx hostel. The phone number is xxxxxxxxxxx, but their English isn't great! I will be in Mexico for about a month – email me on xxxxxxxxxxx@hotmail.com. I'm having an amazing time, the weather is gorgeous. **Please don't leave a message unless it's urgent as I can't afford to pick them all up.** Oh, and by the way, I hope it's raining in England!'

Potential problems...note the last bit of my message above about '**...please don't leave a message unless it's urgent...**' here's why: *You access your message from a payphone in Kathmandu:*

'**You have 22 messages...first message**......wayhaaay, oi boys, it's Tom!...what do you mean where?...on the phone you pillock...naaaah...It's his answerphone...come and say something to him...hang on mate...oi, behave...careful...Hi Tom, it's Lynds how are y...**end of message**...**to repeat this message press 4**...**to delete this message press 7**...**to save this message press 9**...*BEEP*...**message deleted**...**next message**... ....wayhaaaaay, it's us again, sorry, we've been in the pub all evening and Dani just dropped the phone...what mate, no I'm not ringing abroad, it's a London number...shut up fella, it's a local call...anyway, hope you're OK and things are going well...Jane wants to speak to you and tell you about something...see ya mate...och ai hellooooo Tom (Jane's Scottish by the way)...you'll never guess what happened the other day......'

The most important point in the whole world, listen up! It is a cheap call for all those back home, but for you it will cost a fortune to get through all the messages, and you may miss something really important amongst the dross.

My advice is to get voicemail for one reason only: for family and friends to track you as you go around the world and for important messages to be left. Link it up to a chargecard and don't let it clog up with messages, or you'll end up ditching it as it becomes useless.

'**Wow, I've made it to Sydney. Write to me at Post Restante, GPO, 159 Pitt Street, Sydney NSW 2000, Australia. The number at my hostel is xxxxxxxx**'...works wonders.

Warning. Like all the other methods here, be careful of the regularity thing. If your parents get used to you changing your voicemail every week, and then it remains the same for two weeks, they may worry.

VOICEMAIL IN THE UK
Alpha Telecom   ☎ 0800 279 0000

3. By phone ☎

A ten-second phone call...to say 'Hi, I'm fine' from anywhere in the world will cost next to nothing and is one of the biggest reassurances your parents and those close to you can ever have. To hear the sound of your voice is worth over one hundred postcards (postcards say that at the time of writing you were in that particular area of the world, with at least one limb to write with and at least one eye to see the damn thing!).

International pre-paid phone cards
The cheapest method of calling to, and from, abroad. These have exploded over the last couple of years, and save you loads. Parents always like to hear your voice...so get a couple of accounts (one for you to take with you and one for your parents at home).

So how do they work? Dead simple. You ring them up and pay up-front for a line of credit (say £20). You are then given a PIN number which you type into a touch-tone phone. You then make the call. Rates are good, and you don't need to mess around with coins, local currencies and payphone instructions you don't understand. Your initial £20 will give you over six hours of calls from a UK residential phone to Australia for example! **But be aware that there are differing rates depending on whether you access your account through a free phone number or a local number.** Some also have an initial connection charge. It will always be cheaper than making a normal international call, but make sure you check first.

Examples of international call companies
Alpha Telecom ☎ 0800 279 0000 www.alphatelecom.com
(also offers a free voicemail service)
One-Tel ☎ 0800 957 0700 www.onetel.co.uk
Planet Talk ☎ 0800 036 2195 www.planet-talk.co.uk
Primus ☎ 0800 036 0020 www.primus.co.uk
World Telecom ☎ 0870 101 0101 www.worldtelecom.co.uk

BT (and other) chargecards
Advertised as 'the card you can't leave home without', what they forget to mention is that, should you decide to use it whilst you are 'away', it's going to cost you an arm and a leg. Yes, they are expensive, however, if used properly, they can be extremely useful. Link it up with one of the voicemail services so you can call your voicemail from anywhere in the world. Your parents are in control (as they pay the bill) and you will always be able to use the phone.

Dispel the myths! Worried parents fear that as soon as Pedro and his group of Banditos see that you have a calling card they'll nick it and chalk up thousands of pounds' worth of calls. *If you do get a chargecard make sure that it only works for one phone number*...your parents'. And those gangs who use video cameras and binoculars to see your PIN number? There are a lot of digits and I generally tap them in faster than a hyperactive squirrel. But again, if it's set up so that it can only dial your home number, what's the problem?

Don't have a chargecard where you can call any number (sorry BT!), unless there is a trust thing going where you won't use it excessively. Also, remember, it's expensive and could be nicked.

Reverse-charge calls

To discover the national debt of a South American country on your phone bill may shock some. Reverse-charge calls are bloody expensive, but can be a life-saver if used properly. If you need to call home and have no money, ring up the international operator and ask to do a reverse-charge call.

A great tip is to chat to the operator. Generally you will be talking to someone who has one of the most mind-numbing jobs in the world. Your call is free if from a pay phone, so you have all the time in the world. How a reverse-charge call works is that the operator will call the number, you will then hear the person answer, for example your dad. The operator will then say:

'...I have a reverse-charge call coming through from a Tom Griffiths, will you accept the call?...' Provided they don't say *'...no, tell him to sod off...!!'*, it'll work.

Now, by getting the operators to help me (explain to them nicely about any situation you're in) I have got directions, found out where mates are (in Vancouver one chatted to the mother of one of my Canadian buddies for me!) and, the best – on finding myself in a dangerous part of town at 3am, guided me to a safe place for the night.

Mail ✉

Postcards

...in the world of postage are the lowest of the low. Postmen all over the world throw, kick, maul and, I'm sure in some places, eat them. **Advantages?** They have lovely little piccies on the front to show all those at home just what it is they're missing out on. **Disadvantages?** They don't always arrive. Beware, as always, of the regularity issue. If your parents get used to receiving postcards every week/fortnight and then one gets lost – they will have to wait about a month for the next one. They will worry. Think about it. If you want to ensure that your postcards will get there, put them in an envelope.

Letters

Pre-paid airmail letters...write it, seal it and send it. Letters are great...you can pack loads in, therefore probably making up for about three postcards. However, the best thing about letters is that they are great to receive whilst on the road.

Before Claire B left to go around the world, she sent an itinerary of her trip to all of her friends, telling everyone where she would be and where to send letters to. Claire really went to town, armed with a voicemail, hotmail and a load of *post restante* addresses. A load of what addresses?

Poste restante
(Don't skip over this bit. Get used to the phrase, it's really important.)

What is it?
A worldwide postal system that allows you to have letters sent to General Post Offices (and other places) around the world...which will sit there and wait for you to turn up. If they are not collected within a specific time period (anywhere from one to six months), they are returned to sender.

Many believe that with the growth of the internet this little sucker has about as much chance of surviving the next few years as my neighbour's parrot, 'Banjo'. Emails are fine, quick, convenient and cheap...but, at the end of the day, a hand-written letter, with something from home enclosed, always goes down really well.

How does it work?

I know that Tim will be visiting Bangkok, so I address the envelope as follows :

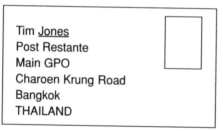

Tim <u>Jones</u>
Post Restante
Main GPO
Charoen Krung Road
Bangkok
THAILAND

This letter zips to the main Post Office in Bangkok and stays there for the next 'few' months – this can be anything from one to six. Check in your Lonely Planet/Rough Guide, or when you get there (and then email friends with your address). In an ideal world (where beer is free and women fall at my feet)...Tim could forecast that he will be in Bangkok in May or June (but could arrive in July – plans change). I would therefore send his letter in the last week of April, to arrive at the beginning of May. It would then stay there for up to six months (or whatever their time limit is). All Tim has to do is get his lazy butt off to Bangkok's main Post Office to get my literary masterpiece (and having read this book so far, you may be justified at laughing at that one!)...present his passport and pick up his mail. If the letter is not picked up it will be returned to sender. SIMPLE!
[NB: in the US it is called 'General Delivery' and internal mail is only kept for ten days]

'Backpacker meccas' like Sydney, which now have more letters than the Russian alphabet in their *post restante* system, publish daily lists (and now only keep letters for a month). Keep in touch via email to see when to send letters and to where, as dodgy photos, comical newspaper cuttings, beer mats...and anything to remind you of home are always gratefully received.

A few hints
My name is Tom Griffiths, born Thomas Peter Griffiths. I prefer Tom, hence the name on the front of the book! My friends would write to Tom Griffiths, parents and relatives to

Thomas Griffiths, my French friends to Griffiths Tom (bless the French eh!), others to T.P. Griffiths and, if any of my mates were trying to be funny, they would address it to 'xxxxxx' – one of my many nick-names – which they seem to find amusing and which I don't intend to share with you at this point!! They are all filed in different areas, so ask everyone to address the letters the same.

Underline the last name and get people to write in capital letters. They will be unused to western names overseas, so make sure you look under other letters for misplaced post ie. 'I' and 'L' , 'M' and 'N', and under 'M' if they put Mr or Miss!

Bright letters are always easy to pick out of a pile, especially in the smaller post offices in less developed countries, where the letters will more than likely be stored in a box in the corner! (Security can be dodgy, so don't enclose cash, credit cards and expensive Y-fronts.)

If your name is John Smith or Joe Bloggs ie. **a really common name**, beware that you could open or walk off with someone else's post (a polite way of saying that someone could open yours). The sender's name on the back should sort this out. On the subject of lost post – if anyone knows who nicked my brother's parcel from Fiji...do get in touch.

Still on *poste restante*...If you find a mate's letter...a small note on the back of it saying where you are and until when seems to work well. However, refrain from making rude jokes at the expense of his/her family. Funny 'down the pub' is not (as I found to my cost in Thailand) funny when 'return to sender' takes it back to their mum!! Oops!

Check out the Poste Restante department at the main Post Office when you arrive somewhere. Leave messages for other travellers by writing a letter, stamping it and asking to put it in with the other *poste restante* letters. It works well.

American Express have their own postal service similar to *post restante*, where post is held for up to three months (some of their outlets are in the ***Top Fifty Destinations***).

Contact points   ☆

Relatives or friends overseas can be a great place to send stuff to. If you know that you will definitely be working somewhere, then you have the ideal contact point. However, family and friends? A bit of food for thought...

'I tell you what, while you're in Australia, why don't you stop off and see my second cousin's husband's brother...I met him a few years back when he was over at a party. He was a nice enough chap and lives near Brisbane...said that if we were ever in the area to call in...you're going to Brisbane...why don't we get in touch and ask if we can use him as a point of contact?...'

It happens... Let's stop it there for a second, rewind...

Play…*'I tell you what, while you're in Australia…'* Said like 'Tell you what, whilst you're at the shop…' Australia is a massive country. Leaving the main route could mean an expensive detour.

…*'why don't you stop off…'* built on the massive assumption that you will be going past their doorstep.

…*'my second cousin's husband's brother'*…said in the same tone of 'I was at school and University with him and we have been best friends ever since'. Only, he is absolutely no relation and will vaguely remember your mum…at the party everyone was fascinated that he came from Australia, he was drunk, issued loads of invitations and has since, along with all his other English contacts, hosted a whole bunch of snotty British people who treat his pad like a hotel!

…*'he lives near Brisbane'*…see above behaviour at party and add the fact that whenever you say that you're from Waggabalong, people look at you blankly! So you say you're from Brisbane (the nearest recognisable city, 100 miles away!).

…*'Aaaaaaah, Brisbane, I hear it's lovely out there!'*…so, you trek out to the arse-end-of-nowhere to pick up a jumper, fresh pants and two letters off a complete stranger with vague/no family ties. People can be very kind, but don't take advantage of it.

Tapes 🎞

We are living in the age of technology, so why not use it? **Tape yourself:** This can be done in a number of ways:

Cassette tapes: normal size or the mini dictaphone ones are small, cheap and easy to send. 'Talk' to family and friends or record your trip. If you have a dictaphone, why not take it? Imagine sitting on the top of Ayers Rock, seeing the sunrise. You look out – all you can see is the red earth and a vast expanse of absolutely nothing. The Olgas on one side, Mount Connor on the other. The feeling is amazing. Never have you seen such beauty, you are in your own little world. You start the dictaphone…

'Hi mum, dad…it's now 6am and I'm sitting on the top of Ayers Rock. I can see for hundreds of miles and the most amazing sunrise has just happened. This is what I have been dreaming of – I just can't believe I'm here.'

Video tape: don't take a camcorder with you, but you can always hire or blag one. A brief video diary? A birthday/Christmas message to make someone's day?

Also, you can now send photos and even moving film through the internet. So why not email photos/film of yourself? There are webcams all over the world. If you get your timing right with your friends via email, you can tell them to have a look at http://www.xxxxxxxx.com at 3pm on Tuesday…and wave at them. It's a funky little thing you can do for a laugh.

Sum it up, Tom!

Keeping in touch is one of the most important aspects of travel. It's easy to go away, have the time of your life and forget about others you have left at home. You may be sitting here thinking, **'Well Tom, I am an adult, I think we've gone past this stage.'** If you are, then I think you should have a big think about things. Your parents have done a lot for you, so let's just spare them a thought eh? Hearing a voice or seeing familiar writing can make the world of difference to you and your parents. **'There is nothing worse than silence.'**

When you are away you don't tend to get lonely because so many things are happening. With so many different and new experiences, time will fly, and the last thing you think about is home. However, every once in a while, a little reminder of home sneaks up on you…great moments, that make you appreciate where you come from.

The thing is, at home, nothing has changed. Life goes on as normal. The only difference is that you're not there, which makes it a lot easier for people at home to miss you.

Letters. I've been going on about making sure you think of others whilst you are away BUT, make sure they think about you. Claire B's letter to me contained all the approximate dates and destinations of her trip. It also contained threats that if we didn't write then she'd (a) kill us (b) haunt us (c) come and see us when she got back to make us feel guilty. (a) and (b) I could obviously handle, having had plenty of experience with some of my ex-girlfriends in the past. However, having Claire come round and talk non- stop at me for anything more than ten minutes, well…let's just say that I got in contact!!

Why not head to the search engines – **www.google.com** is a good one – type in 'webcam' for a listing of them around the world.

18: How to...use the internet

by Richard Mortimer

The following chapter is of use to everyone. I have joined forces with Richard M, a mate of mine who answers to the nickname of 'Oof' (a long story). On his travels, he was 'email king'.

This guide is for adventurous parents/email virgins who want a basic guide, others who want to know more and for email/internet boffins who are after ideas, cool sites and something a bit different.

We've all heard of the three Ws but of what use are they to the average gapyear traveller, I hear you cry. Let me enlighten you. For those of the computer generation, feel free to skip this bit, but for all you technophobes out there, here follows: *Oof's guide to the internet.*

The number one most useful facility is email, but the internet itself can be useful for all sorts of other stuff...you can book low-cost flights, accommodation, tours, check sports results, read newspapers on-line, apply for jobs or even delve into the thousands of pages of travel info. At the end of the day, the opportunities are endless. The technology and information is there, its just whether you can be bothered to make the most of it.

What is the internet?

In simple terms the internet is just an enormous library. Imagine walking down the street and you see the sign 'Library' over the door of a building...except, the building is the size of Luxembourg...and it has every possible book, magazine and newspaper in the world! There are no library cards, so anyone can access it, but instead of walking in through the door and taking books out, you access it through a computer.

When you walk into the foyer of this massive library, you find yourself in front of an enormous map of the entire building. You are looking for information on travel, so you find the section named 'Travel' on the map, and are given directions to the Travel Area. You walk there and then begin your search for the book you are after. Having found the book, you use the index to find the information you are after within the book. You flick to it.

On the internet, this process is done by a 'search engine'.

Search engines – The big guys:

www.altavista.com
www.ask.co.uk
www.excite.com
www.google.com
www.hotbot.com

www.infoseek.com
www.lycos.com
www.msn.com
www.webcrawler.com.
www.yahoo.com

UK-based search engines:
www.mirago.co.uk is a great one out that is UK-specific, but doesn't just list the co.uk names. It registers all UK-related sites .net .com .org etc.
Also check out www.scoot.co.uk www.ukplus.co.uk www.yell.co.uk

How do they work?
Simply type their address into the box at the top of the internet screen. They will then appear. These search engines work by you typing into 'the **Search Box**' exactly what you want to find. For example, to find the website for a hotel in Newquay, England, you would type 'Hotel, Newquay, Cornwall, UK' into the search box, and then press 'Go' or 'Search' (or whatever they use). If it is a company, an object, a sector of industry, or whatever, **make sure you are as specific as possible so as to get a good match**. Beware that if you enter something like 'gapyear', you will get about 365,000 responses, as it will match everything with the word 'Gap', and everything with the word 'Year' in it! So be specific. Remember, you are dealing with a worldwide source here, **so if it's in the UK, say so!**

If you know the site address, simply type in its address, for example **www.gapyear.com** (the address our gapyear website). These addresses come in many forms, most starting with www. and ending with the country of origin. 'co.uk' illustrates that it is a UK-based site, similarly world or American sites end in 'com', Australian with 'au' etc etc.

At the end of the day, the best way to understand it is to try it yourself, as it really is very easy when you grasp the basics. Access to the internet now comes in a variety of forms and a whole host of options: work, home computers, universities, schools, internet cafés that are popping up on every street corner…and even local libraries.

What is email? ✉
For those of you not in the know, the easiest way to describe email is to compare it to your own postal address at home. Somebody writes you a letter and on the envelope puts your name, address and postcode (which is like a unique identifier). A couple of days later, the letter arrives on your doorstep – easy? Email is even easier, providing exactly the same function but in an electronic form, with the letter going from computer to computer with not a postman in sight. Instead of a postal address you have an email address like oof@talk21.com to send the letter to, which incidentally, you still have to write yourself!

For the technophobes out there, here is _your email address explained:_ it takes the form of: (any name you want) @ (the company who provides it).(the postcode)

For example, my address is oof@talk21.com (a fake one, by the way!)

Let's break it down:

(any name you want) I have 'Oof', my nickname. You can have literally anything you want, richardmortimer, rmortimer, richardm, or a company name. Your name is the best, as people can remember it. Nicknames are fun, but difficult to remember. It is best to choose a name that you will always keep, even if you change to a different email provider. If you have a 'common name' like John Smith, you'll have to think up something good. If you have an unusual/difficult to spell name like Jorganowitz, you can have any variation you want, so think about shortening it to Jorgi or something (the shorter the address, the better).

@ This is the bit that signifies that it is an email and tells the internet where to send it. For my address above, it simply says 'put this in the post box of "Oof" which is looked after by Hotmail'.

(the company who provides it) I use Talk21, provided by BT. There are hundreds of companies who provide free email worldwide. To be honest they are all just as good as each other (see below for more).

Other free email providers to check out are: www.excite.com   www.hotmail.com
www.pmail.net   www.talk21.com   www.tripod.co.uk   www.yahoo.com

www.iname.com is quite a funky one, but you have to pay. You can have: oof@myoffice, oof@home, oof@work, etc for about $30/year.

Setting up your own email

Setting up your own email is easy, free and ready for use immediately. It takes five minutes and involves filling in a registration form and choosing a personal address like traveller@talk21.co.uk. Not only can you send emails to anyone with an address but you can also receive them from friends, family and fellow-travellers.

So for all you email virgins, here comes a step by step guide to getting your free email. I'll use Talk21.com as an example as it's the email that I have, so I know the format best.

Screen 1

Step 1 – Type www.talk21.com

Step 2 – Press 'Enter'

Step 3 – Click on 'Register for your free Talk21 email account'

Step 4 – Click on 'Agreement'

Step 5 – Fill in 'Personal Details' including chosen address e.g. jo.bloggs@talk21.com, password etc. If someone has already chosen your name, you will be told, and usually offered alternatives. If jo.bloggs has gone, try jbloggs, bloggsj, jobloggs, j.bloggs etc. And the password? **Try and choose one you won't forget!**

Step 6 – You're off

Most providers will immediately send you a Welcoming Email saying thanks, which allows you to get to know what you're doing as far as reading, writing, sending and storing mail.

You are now ready to email!
Get back out of the system by clicking on the 'x' in the very top right-hand corner. Once you are out, get back onto the internet and type in www.talk21.com.

When faced with **Screen 1**: click on the 'Username' box and type in the name you use (in my case 'oof').

A quick tip – make sure everything is copied exactly as it is written, usually lower case ie. no capital letters.

Next type in your password in the box below, and then click on 'Enter'.

You will then move through to **Screen 2**:

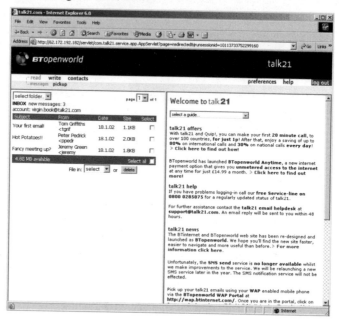

INBOX is where your incoming messages will be shown. To read one of the messages, for example my first one is from Tom Griffiths (some idiot I know!), subject 'Your first email', I simply click on his name. The message will then appear on the next screen (**Screen 3**).

Screen 3

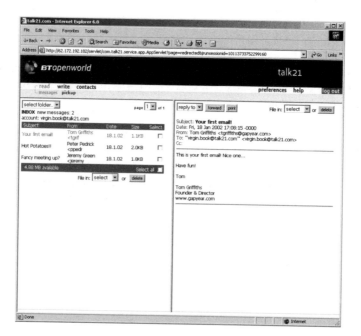

HOW TO...USE THE INTERNET

The message now appears underneath. Whilst you are on this screen, you are given options ie. whether you want to reply, delete, print, forward or move the message to a folder. I will delete this message, as I always delete messages from Tom!

If I want to send a message, I click on the button that says 'Back' in the top left-hand corner, which takes me back to Screen 2. I then click on 'Write' in the bar above the 'INBOX', and a new screen will appear. You will be offered an address box. Simply type in the email address of the person you are sending it to in the 'to:' bit and, under 'subject', give your message a title. It can say anything...this is the bit which they will see when they see that they have a new message ie. 'Your first email'.

The thing is, you need to get in there and have a little play around. Get used to sending and receiving the messages. Make use of the folders and address books. They are easy to use and pretty self-explanatory.

You are now fully functional! Your email account can be accessed from any computer in the world that is connected to the internet: all you do is type in the address, your login name and your password and you're off. This is the best way to stay in touch with those back at home, and likewise for them to keep tabs on how and where you are. At the end of the day, receiving email while travelling is as good as receiving a letter and what's more, ten times easier, quicker and more reliable.

Additionally, email offers us travellers a great way of staying in touch with our own kind. Whether it's meeting up with them again a few miles down the coast, 'Lucia, I'm at Byron Bay, Arts Factory, Room 3, come and see me when you get here', or simply remaining in touch with old travel friends who live all over the world.

Final pointers... If you need to find out about something, the chances are you'll find it on the web (if you look hard enough). If you're looking for anything use the search engines – see above about refining your search.

A word of warning: treat your email as something personal, and be selective as to who you give your address to, or you'll end up with continual emails from people you'd really rather forget about.

An example of how useful the web can be: last year I was travelling around Southeast Asia at the time of the civil uprisings in Timor and, more particularly, Java. I was naturally a bit worried about visiting Jakarta so I looked on the web for reassurance. Within minutes I'd located the British Embassy site in Jakarta which gave detailed advice on the subject, even down to particular streets to avoid – useful hey!

There really is more info on the web than you can ever read in a lifetime, some of which has been hinted at before. When I was travelling I used it mainly for three things: sending emails, receiving emails and checking Ipswich Town Football results – yes, I'm a fan too!

You really can use it as you please, but here is a list of some potentially useful sites that you might find interesting.

www.cybercafes.com is a must for you to have a look at when you are overseas. It tells you where all the 'netcafés' are around the world. So have a look and get a few down for places where you are going.

Some useful sites
www.gapyear.com   - everything to do with gapyears

Student bodies
www.istc.org   - International Student Travel
                                                     Confederation...global student discounts
www.iyhf.org   - International Youth Hostel Federation

Huge travel sites!
www.lonelyplanet.com   - destinations worldwide; travellers' tales;
                                                     latest travel news
www.roughguides.com   - 4000+ destinations; quarterly travel
                                                     newsletter

Cheap flights and holidays
Find and book cheap flights and last-minute travel deals via these internet sites:
www.cheapflights.co.uk   www.lastminute.com
www.flightfinder.co.uk   www.travelweb.com
www.itsnet.co.uk

Travel companies
www.austravel.co.uk
www.statravel.co.uk   www.travelcuts.com

Travel-relevant
www.embassyworld.com   - embassies around the world
www.hostels.com   - a growing list of hostels worldwide
www.intellicast.com/LocalWeather/World/   - world weather forecasts
www.journeywomen.com   - for 'gals' on the road!
www.theglobe.com   - global newspaper (and everything else!)
www.sydneycity.net   - everything that's happening in Sydney
www.tagish.co.uk/embassy   - any embassy...every embassy
www.timeout.co.uk   - what's on in all the big cities worldwide
www.towd.com   - Tourism Offices Worldwide Directory
www.travelhealthcentre.org   - independent travel health advice

News

www.bbc.co.uk	- BBC
www.cnn.com	- CNN
www.economist.com	- The *Economist*
www.ft.com	- The *Financial Times*
www.guardian.co.uk	- The *Guardian*
www.independent.co.uk	- The *Independent*
www.mirror.co.uk	- The *Mirror*
www.nytimes.com	- The *New York Times*
www.radio-directory.com	- lists radio stations
www.the-times.co.uk	- The *Times* and *Sunday Times*
www.usatoday.com	- *USA Today*
www.virginradio.co.uk	- Virgin Radio

Sport

www.golf.com	- golf coverage
www.nba.com	- everything basketball
www.scrum.com	- rugby coverage
www.soccernet.com	- everything football
www.wsc.co.uk/wsc	- *When Saturday Comes* football fanzine

Others

www.fco.gov.uk/travel	- The Foreign and Commonwealth Office advice on safe travel.
www.travelmag.co.uk	- *Travelmag* (independent travel magazine)
www.who.ch	- World Health Organisation

Other Tips ❶

Just about every medium/large company in the world has a website, invariably featuring recruitment information. Many recruitment agencies now work on-line as it's much quicker than using traditional post – CVs received electronically are much easier to manipulate and store.

Try to scan some photos. This is a great one for family and friends to show them what you've been up to, I mean, what could be better than sending them a photo of yourself in some exotic location? It really is a great idea, and most internet cafés will offer the service relatively cheaply, so just ask.

19: How to...pack

Your backpack

Me, a grown up, teaching you, a grown up, how to pack your backpack? Ridiculous eh? Well, no, not really. Packing a backpack is actually an art. I remember the advice Tony and I were given when we first went away at 18: **'...make sure you turn up to the airport with a half-full bag...'** Why?...because you'll fill it twice over (and you won't use everything, so why bring it?). I heeded this advice, but Tony forgot, poor old boy wheeling it in on a trolley! Within a couple of months mine was chocka and I was even carrying a didgeridoo around as well!

How to choose your backpack You are a backpacker, you put a 'pack' on your 'back'. A good one is essential. If the thing falls apart on you, or damages your back because it is the wrong shape, you will only have yourself to blame. You can get a good one for about £50, so it's well worth the investment.

More about backpacks If you've not used a backpack before, take note. When we first went, we didn't have a clue. Luckily the guy in the shop took pity on us and went through all the different makes; what they do, how to pack them and, most importantly, how to wear/carry the sodding thing! **It has to be comfortable and the right size for you.**

Finding one that suits you I am, let's say, 'vertically challenged'. Due to my stocky frame, mine sits comfortably on my back as we balance each other out. If you are 6ft 2in with the nickname Beanpole, a heavy backpack not in tune with your centre of gravity (around your waist) will kill your back.

Choosing the right backpack There are loads of them in the shops...does one attract you? It's not a fashion thing, but you need to like looking at it! Grab an assistant and get some help. Try the packs on. See what they feel like. They all feel comfortable when you are fully clothed and they are empty, so put stuff in, make it heavy and bulky. Does it feel right for you? Cheap may be best, or indeed worst...they are all different. Look out for zips and pockets. I like big, long, deep side pockets, and also ones at the very top to access things quickly.

Backpacks that convert into holdalls There is now a trend for backpacks that can be zipped up and made to look like a holdall (have a look in **gapyearshop.com** for examples and further advice). They are useful if ever you want not to look like a backpacker, simply zipping the straps away, turning it on its side and carrying it like a holdall. Most also come with a small backpack zipped to the front, which can either be used as a compartment to the pack, or unzipped and used as a separate day bag. *But once you take the 10-litre day bag off, a 65-litre backpack would be reduced to 55 litres – is this going to be enough for you?* I generally take my trusty 65-litre knackered old backpack plus a 10-litre day bag, which is about right for me.

Backpacks are sized in 'litres' – 55, 65, 75 and 85 are the ones to look at. If you fill an 85 you won't move it! Even 75 is a bit of a beast. 65 is about right – again, a heavy bastard if filled! It's dangerous to go 'one stage up to be sure' as you'll only end up filling it up anyway.

Things to look out for:

Adjustable back systems Cost a bit more but allow the pack to slide up and down until you are comfortable. Whatever your build you can still carry big packs and heavy loads without killing yourself.

Some backpacks now have **bum bags** attached to them as extras. Not the best to wear, but great to put stuff in when you're out and about.

Solid back supports (missing in some of the 'holdall' packs). They make the pack stronger and stop a full pack bulging against your back (more than a tad uncomfortable).

Stitching Is it strong and tight? Airports and Indian buses can do a bit of damage. If it's going to leak, this is the place (through weak stitching).

Waterproofing A cheap backpack could let in more water than the *Titanic*. You need one that is impregnable to everything except bomb blasts and mad cow disease. You can add waterproofing yourself, or get a pack with its own rain cover (stored at the top or bottom). You'll only see the value of these at 11.30pm, when you're cold, looking for a backpackers' and ten tons of monsoon rain lands on you.

Zips with holes...wide enough to take a small padlock to secure the zips together to 'lock' the pockets. Yes, they can be broken, but act as a deterrent and always stop opportunist thieves who, if given the chance, will be in there...they won't mess around with padlocks in full view of everyone.

Sum it up, Tom!

The backpack is the most important item you will take with you. Forget your dad's 1962 green-issue Scoutmaster Alpha 2 – canvas, heavy, small and full of rivets. You're a backpacker, not a rambler. Get the professionals and/or the guys in the shops to take you through what your choices are and the differences between them. If it turns out to be wrong, take it back and exchange it while you have time. **It's about to become your home, so choose a goodie.** Check out backpack reviews at **gapyearshop.com**.

What to take

Sleeping bag There are sleeping bags for all climates nowadays, two- three- and four-season ie. light, medium and 'hibernation'! As time goes on, they seem to be getting smaller, thinner and warmer. The ideal one would pack into a match-box and keep you warm and snug in the Arctic. Synthetic 'caravan' ones are basic, cold and pack down to an area the size of Belgium. Don't you dare! **Top of the range** – 'all-seasons', pack down to 'sod all' and are expensive. I have a two-season, which packs away to nothing, but I freeze! When it's hot, you sleep on top of it (or just in your sleeping sheet) anyway, so, final advice?**...go warm, but not bulky**.

Sleeping sheet...simply a cotton bed-sheet sewn up into a sleeping bag. It can be another layer in your sleeping bag (easy to wash so you don't have to wash your sleeping bag so often). Many hostels insist on sleeping sheets on the beds, to stop travellers who sleep rough on beaches/outdoors spreading bugs and making everything filthy. So, get one...or make one (stitch three sides of a double sheet – good quality cotton is best). Why not take two? Northern Dave uses a duvet cover in hot countries...not a bad idea. Available in cotton or silk (better but more expensive).

Synthetic drawstring bags Invaluable. Take a few away with you. Waterproof and ideal for separating underwear, dirty washing and toiletries.

Towels Handy when you're wet! Leave a wet towel in your backpack for long and it develops an attitude, so air at every opportunity. A medium-sized one will do – the big ones just fill your pack up. Don't use it on the beach as it gets too dirty too soon (that's when you need your sarong). Also think about a **'pack towel'**. They are dead small (about the size of a hand towel), very compact but have the water retention capacity of a dehydrated camel (superb!). Even when sopping wet, give them a squeeze, hang them out of the window (they have a little strap) and they'll dry in about ten minutes. Too small to wrap around you though, so use a sarong or take as a supplement to your main towel. A **hand towel** is also essential, always carried in your day bag – great for airport delays, bandaging your head when you stick it in a ceiling fan or using as a pillow.

Peg-free washing line A great, dead simple, invention. *Essential.* It's a length of elastic with a hook on each end which is twisted in the middle. The twists form little holes to trap your clothes in. You can hang it anywhere. There is nothing more idyllic than lying in a hammock outside your bungalow, by the beach...the hot sun, crashing waves***...and your pants, slung between two impressive palms, fresh and clean, flying free and drying in the breeze. Magnificent!***

Sarong Seen by the males amongst us as a skirt and obviously a bit of a wussie thing to wear. Basically, it is a big bit of highly-decorated cloth with a million different uses from beach towel, drying-up cloth, bed sheet, sling, towel, pillow case and of course – 'wrap'. In many countries it is essential to cover all 'pink bits', especially if entering temples. They cost you next-to-nothing overseas, and, like the towel, keep it clean. **You have to have one, so get one!**

Toiletries Toothpaste, toothbrushes, deodorant etc can be found everywhere. For deodorant, get the stuff that works (like Right Guard Double Protection), not that makes you smell nice! Other useful things are nail clippers (which can be used for just about anything), tweezers (with a sharp end) and a small scrubbing brush. A decent toiletries bag is also important – waterproof, strong, and preferably with a loop on the top so you can hang it up in the shower. NB: Remember that airport security will confiscate sharp objects from your hand luggage, so think about what you take on the plane!

Medicines and first-aid kit ✚

Most first-aid kits contain: plasters, bandages, scissors, antiseptic cream, safety pins, gauze. You need to get a decent one (check out **gapyearshop.com)**.

Essential extras which you should get include:

Anti-diarrhoea treatment   Pills, capsules, powders – Imodium is the best-known brand. If you are on a bus or train for ten hours, in the middle of India, and the horses are about to get loose, you may need to pop a couple of these to shut the gate! However, with a really nasty bug, you ideally need to let it out first, so it doesn't sit inside your gut and fester. **An important point...**I know of someone in India who, at the first sign of diarrhoea, blocked it all up tighter than a Russian steelworker with a 1,500 ton press! By not letting it out, it got worse...she nearly died, but was flown back to England in the nick of time. So be careful and have a think about what you're about to do.

Antibiotics   Ask your doctor for a 'broad spectrum antibiotic' (the hard bastard of the pill world – kills all bugs)...if you get a rattly chest infection, or if a coral cut goes septic...this will clear it up before you have to go to hospital.

Bandage tape   Will stick anything to anything. Comes on a roll so you can cut it to any length.

Bilharzia pills   When you go for your jabs, find out whether Bilharzia is rife anywhere you are going. If it is...think seriously about taking the pills.

Calamine lotion cools sunburn or normal burns.

Condoms – let's be responsible.

Emergency eye wash

E45 cream for dried areas, irritations and rashes.

Iodine (bottle with a pipette) to make water safe to drink and sterilise wounds – tastes disgusting and dyes you yellow as well, but very effective!

Lip-salve   for dry areas, chapped lips and sunburnt ears!

Painkillers for headaches and pains.

An important note about painkillers (eg. Paracetamol, Aspirin, Ibuprofen, Codeine)

Aspirin	can help to reduce a temperature.
Aspirin and Ibuprofen	are anti-inflammatory (and painkillers) but may precipitate an asthma attack (if you're asthmatic!).
Codeine	can make you drowsy/constipated.
Paracetamol	a really good painkiller.

All of the above are sold under different brand names like Nurofen, Brufen, Panadol, Hedex, Anadin etc, which is why you have to be careful about mixing. **The bottom line...is to read the instructions and to follow them.** They are there for a reason. It is possible to overdose accidentally, so whatever you do:
- don't exceed the recommended dose.
- don't take with alcohol.
- don't take combinations (as many will contain the same drugs).

A quick warning to emphasise my point...four sachets of Lemsip (the maximum dose in 24 hours) – add any more, or combine a couple of sachets with another couple of Paracetamol, and you're in serious trouble. *I really can't emphasise this enough. You can overdose on Lemsip. It happens. Follow the advice carefully.*

Rehydration sachets restore all the good things your body has lost during an attack of diarrhoea.

Sting relieving spray/stick takes the sting out of bites. There is also a wicked little gadget around which gives you a tiny electric shock on the bite for instant relief.

Sterilised needle kit

Essential, especially in less developed areas with limited resources, or places with a high risk of AIDS. I know this is the scary word but GET ONE. It's a little pack containing sterilised needles and all the bits and pieces that could be used by a hospital in an emergency.

Three reasons why you should take one of these fellas:
1. You can be sure equipment used will be properly sterilised.
2. Some countries have limited resources, so don't use them up.
3. Someone else might need it.

These kits are clearly marked and recognised worldwide, so you won't have problems at airports. If drug-users nick them (very unlikely)...it's a sealed sterilised kit, so you'll know if anyone has been inside without an invitation.

Note: Max is the only person I know who has used his – stitches in his chin after coming off a moped – but don't be blasé, the day anything happens, you'll need it. There is also no use in having it if you don't use the damn thing when needed...so keep it in an accessible place and make sure you're travelling partner knows where it is.

Extras for the girls:

'The pill' – if you are on the pill, take enough to last for the length of your trip (see the notes on travelling and the pill in the chapter on **Travel health**).

Sanitary towels – bulky! If you have a favourite variety, stock up (in that super dry place in your pack). Should the worst come to the worst, there's always the local stuff.

Tampons – stock up, remove from the boxes and put into a waterproof (water-tight even better) bag. Carolyn forgot, and swam across a river with her pack. Two weeks later she discovered 'Tampon City' quietly expanding towards Botswana…

In developing countries they can cost a fortune – plan accordingly. Stock up prior to departure and restock before heading into more remote areas. (Local varieties may be a bit more bulky, but still do the job.)

Essential points

- **Keep your first-aid kit in an accessible place (the side pocket is ideal).**
- **Prescriptions and medicines should always be accompanied by a letter from your doctor as proof to show nosy officials.**
- **In some of the less developed countries you may be offered all sorts of drugs (legal ones) that you can buy over the counter. Unless you are a doctor or medically trained, please be careful.**

Insect repellents

Many of the sprays, creams, lotions and stick-repellents currently available are DEET-based (diethyltoluamide for the chemists amongst you). These are pretty effective, but because DEET dissolves plastics, you have to be careful about storage. Insecticide vapourisers are good for de-bugging a whole room before you turn in for the night. Mosquito coils, repellent strips and candles are less effective, and forget about electronic buzzers – they don't work.

Knifeforkandspoon set Get the ones you can separate…saves wrestling with Big Helga for the last fork in the hostel (and useful in restaurants with suspect hygiene – but be subtle!).

'Leatherman tool' In a league of its own as a combination gadget knife where the blades actually lock out. They're not cheap, but if you intend to trek, camp or do any rigorous stuff whilst you are away or in the future, then you should get one.

Mosquito nets – there are all sorts of nets out there – the best ones are permethrin-impregnated. There is advice on these in **gapyearshop.com**.

Sewing kit…a long story set in Hawaii, ten crazy Americans, a dark camp site, a camp fire and a jerk dancing around with a burning stick…he was pissed, our tent was dark green…one big hole. **Can you sew? We couldn't! Result? Leaky tent.** You only need a small sewing kit – nothing flash (if it makes your granny go '…ooooooooh!…' then you've gone overboard!). If you're really inept, you'll always find someone to give you a hand.

Small 'sealable' plastic bags Very handy for jewellery, camera film, leaky sun cream, tickets or passes, anything that might leak or must be kept dry. Almost every backpacker has an amusing story about things that have leaked…mine was a bottle of coconut oil. Get some.

Swiss army knife An essential bit of kit. Invest in one, or get one from Santa Claus. Its multiple blades and 'things' come in handy at the weirdest of times. Learn to use the can-opener and cork screw properly – sharpen all blades before you leave.

Tissues, toilet roll (or as 'Fat Jerry' likes to call it – 'poo tickets'!), **wipes** et al. Keep a plentiful supply in a larger plastic bag. Wipes are great for refreshing yourself, also, if left in the fridge over night, can calm a 'ring of fire' better than a snowball.

Travel alarm clock Those with time zones are the best. Mine has an alarm loud enough to wake me whatever…essential for those early morning flights. Get one with a lid or a protective 'shell' of some sort. A cheap one will fall apart on you, and the alarm may fail… the one time you need this to work will be for that early bus or plane, so get a good 'un.

Travel wash Fantastic stuff…concentrated washing liquid in a tube. All you need is a sink or bucket, fresh water (hot or cold), a small blob of this…and then hand wash your little heart out! Pants and socks, T-shirts and jeans – it does the lot. Test it at home. With a tube of this and a peg-free washing line, you can canoe up the Amazon with confidence!

Shaving equipment

For the girls – take a supply of disposable razors with you. Don't take ones with a specific head which may be hard to replace. Another option to consider is waxing, which lasts about six weeks, and in most places you can get it done very cheaply.

For the boys – shaving is a bit of a hassle and razors and foam can be quite expensive. You could grow a beard to please your mum! (A 'goatee' needs small scissors to keep it neat.) A battery shaver is ideal if you aren't too hairy – no socket or power problems. For the hairy ones amongst us, wet shaving is the only answer. There's the (expensive) Gillette Sensor series, and Wilkinson Sword have some sharp little numbers… disposables aren't as good.

Shaving oil is amazing. All you need is a few drops. It works really well, especially if you aren't too hairy. A couple of small bottles will last your whole trip! I have friends who swear by it. Haven't tried it yet? Give it a go!

Shorts Be bold, be baggy! Be sad...be bright! You only really need a couple of pairs. Solid cotton ones will last and won't chafe 'your bits'. 'Tailored' or smart shorts are handy when you need to look presentable, or when it's too hot for jeans. *The Lads* – swimming shorts are a great invention, especially if you're by the sea, as you can practically live in them. Rinse in fresh water as often as possible. *The Lasses* – really short shorts are absolutely fine with me, but can be deemed offensive in many countries.

T-shirts *Girls* – take a big unsexy white cotton one – the sexy little cut-off numbers may look good in Ibiza but (a) in certain strictly religious countries – play by the rules and (b) when your skin is blocking the plug-hole in the shower, the last thing you want is more sun on your burnt bits. *Boys* – 'Vest' tops give plenty of room around shoulders and arms when it's really hot and sweaty – but your shoulders may get burnt, so watch it. NB: T-shirts with stuff on them – University name, football team, your home town or things you have done on your travels – bungee-jumping, skydiving, etc. are great conversation-starters.

Long-sleeved T-shirt New research has concluded that you are more likely to get bitten if you are sexy – it's the pheromones! My research has concluded that, quite simply, 'mossies are bastards'. Long sleeves, especially in the evenings, are essential...a warm night, you're all sitting round a table out under the stars playing Monopoly...the Mortimers, a mosquito family from Mauritius...out on the town, survey the group of international travellers...and then I wake up with a million bites all over me. Everyone else – not a scratch! Mind you, that must mean that I'm extremely sexy! Long sleeves do the job.

Long-sleeved cotton shirt Again, good for mossies and sunburnt shoulders. When it gets really hot, they are cool, but also manage to keep you warm when it is a bit cold! Perhaps take one knackered one and another smart one.

One smart outfit
Chaps...
- Smart shirt – preferably non-iron
- Tie – not too loud if you're going for a serious job
- Smart trousers
- Smart black shoes – that you can shine
- Good socks – black, to go with the shoes
- Black and whites – for work in bars/restaurants/hotels (maybe your smart trousers are black). A black bow tie may also come in handy

...and for the ladies...
- 'Little black number' – with lycra for non-iron (always does it for me!)
- Good sandals – that look good with the 'black number' and for going out in
- White shirt and black skirt – for bar/restaurant/hotel work and interviews

Swimming things For the boys – swimming shorts. Trunks are fine for posing on the Côte d'Azur, but not for looking round an Indian market. Likewise, girls – if you wear the g-string, leopard-print tiny bra number in a country where bare knees cause weak hearts and old ladies will chastise you…you won't find trouble – **trouble will find you!** Find something sensible to wear. Going topless may offend, lads included. You are a guest, obey the rules.

Jeans For going out purposes. If wet, they take ages to dry and are easy to catch hypothermia from if you're out trekking or somewhere where it is impossible to strip off and get warm. Light coloured jeans get really dirty very easily, black 'appear to be clean' for longer, can get hot, but chances are you'll only wear them after the sun has gone down…

'Beach pants' Remember the pyjama bottoms that they wore in the film *Karate Kid?* They may seem a bit arty-farty, but they are light, comfortable and ideal for travelling. However, '**…what the !**@ are you wearing!!!!**' when you arrive home means you may well have to change.

Pants and socks Pants to me is the archetypal, stereotypical English word. I love it. (For North American guys reading this, in England 'pants' means 'jocks', underwear.) How many pairs to take? Whether you change your underwear daily, every two days, weekly – or, I suppose, whether you wear it at all? – obviously affects how many you take. I rarely wear socks in hot countries, so only take five normal pairs and maybe one thick pair…in case it gets cold or I find work. Pants, on the other hand, I like to take two weeks' worth. My view is that although fourteen pairs do take up a bit of room, it cuts washing down to once a fortnight.

Shoes Whatever you take, wear them in. Old trainers are my favourites, comfortable and should last. Desert boots (from Nomad) are really popular and robust. Think about ankle-high shoes to support dodgy ankles. If it's really hot, you won't want big heavy Cats or hiking boots as you'll sweat like crazy. Dock-siders/deck shoes are also a good option for hot places, especially as some of them are washable, and most don't mind getting wet.

If you intend to go hiking, you will be able to buy or hire stuff there. Don't hump massive boots round the world for two weeks' use. In cold countries, make sure you have boots with a bit of insulation – in Russia, at –20°, my insulated boots with a thick pair of socks kept my toes warm (whilst the hairs froze in my nose!). Make sure they are waterproofed properly, especially if going to wet or snowy areas.

Sandals …not as worn by Jesus or your physics teacher, nor with socks, unless you are English and my dad! Most brands do some classy little numbers with rubber soles, velcro straps etc. Perfect for swimming in rocky areas, then rinsing down and going to the market. Should you end up in a place with the temperature as hot as the surface of Mars…you'll be glad you have them. Very important to get a good fit as they'll kill you when you're carrying your backpack/walking long distances.

Your 'day bag'   🎧 ✉ ⑤ 📄

It is essential that you carry a day bag with you. It's one of your most valuable bits of kit. It's my personal safe and I never let it out of my sight unless I know that it's secure.

Think of a worst-case scenario: **Your pack gets nicked, lost on transfer between countries or spontaneously combusts…**hopefully you have your day bag with you, in which you will have your passport, identification, traveller's cheques, credit cards and all other important bits and pieces – enough to start again – with a credit card you can buy a new backpack and clothes.

Whereas your backpack is a bit of a heavy bugger to whip and do a runner with, your day bag is smaller, lighter and could quite easily be lifted or ripped out of your hands. It is always worth splitting your valuables between the two. Keep a credit card, some ID and a bit of money hidden in your backpack so you will always have something to start from scratch again.

● **What sort of day bag should I take?**
The small 'mini backpacks' are perfect.

● **Can it be secured?**
Mini padlocks, whether key or combination, do the job.

● **Do you need hundreds of outside pockets?**
No. On a crowded bus or train, it's dead easy for someone to quietly unzip one of the outside pockets and have a free delve around. One major opening, and maybe one side pocket, both of which can be padlocked, is all you really need.

● **What should I have in my day bag?**
I like to carry a 'bum bag' or a money belt inside my day bag where I can put all my traveller's cheques, credit cards, passport, driver's licence, tickets, insurance, ID and any other important things that need to be kept together. This is my safe within a safe. If ever I go out and I'm not sure, I take them with me.

Money belts / 'bum bags' If worn around your waist under your T-shirt it can all get a bit sweaty and itchy in a hot country. 'Bum bags' (or 'fanny packs' as they are known in the US), draw attention to the fact that you are a tourist and are very easy to nick. The best bet is to hold onto them when you are out and about (wrap the straps around your hand). And be careful not to put it down anywhere and forget about it!

Useful stuff for when you are hanging around without your backpack
A small hand-towel and a few toiletries can make all the difference. Before any long flights, I put some soap, deodorant and a small toothbrush and toothpaste into a washbag. Spare undies, a jumper, jeans, some cards, a book and a walkman with a few tapes – and you're ready for a long delay, sudden changes in temperature, etc. Also food and drink, which is incredibly expensive at airports!

Handy extras:

Chain
Door locks
Gaffer tape
Hammock
Safe
Saklocks
Small torch (Maglite) and head torch
Water bottle

NEW OUT! Tropical quilt (in between a sleeping bag and sleeping sheet) – as used by the US troops in Vietnam (**gapyearshop.com** £30).

For everything you would ever need for your trip, but most importantly for advice, information and reviews of the travel kit you do and *don't* need, visit **gapyearshop.com**.

Checklist of what to pack

Essentials
Passport
Tickets
Money
Credit cards
Emergency numbers
Immunisation record
Insurance
Student identity cards
(ISIC = International Student Identity Card)
Passport-sized photos for visas etc. (minimum of six) – *when you want them, you want them now! Make sure you have enough.*

Camera
Diary
Film
First-aid kit
Glasses/contact lenses
Guidebooks
Hat/woolly hat
Medications
Moneybelt
Pens
Photocopies of documents
Poncho
Shampoo
Shaving stuff
T-shirt
Soap
Steri-kit
Sunglasses
Sun cream
Sweater
Toothpaste and brush
Traveller's cheques
Underwear

Hardware
Adapter plugs
Alarm clock
Batteries
Camera
Candles
Chain – link or wire
Padlocks
Personal alarm
Swiss army knife
Universal sink plug
Watch
Whistle
Walkman or CD player

Toiletries
Brush or comb
Condoms/contraceptives
Deodorant
Ear plugs
Flannel
Insect repellent
Lip salve
Safety pins – you can never have enough!
Shampoo
Sun cream
Tampons/sanitary towels
Tissues – leave the box at home!

Other
Binoculars
Dental floss
Eye shade
Manicure kit
Moisturiser
Travel iron
Wet wipes
Inflatable neck pillow

Camping / hiking
Immersion heater/hot pot
Roll mat
Stove
Tent
Water bottle
Compass
Head torch

Clothes
Beach pants
Belt
Cotton shirts
Jeans
Light waterproof top (windproof)
Long-sleeved shirts
Long-sleeved T-shirts
Sandals
Sarong
Scarf and gloves
Shoes – take a good strong pair
Shorts
Skirt
Swimming things
T-shirts
Thermal underwear
Underwear

Smart clothes
'Little black number'
Bow tie
Shirt
Skirt
Tie
Trousers
A smart pair of shoes
A smart pair of socks

Medical bits and pieces

Antibiotics
Anti-diarrhoea treatment
Anti-fungal foot powder
Bandages
First-aid kit
Medic Alert identification
Nail clippers
Pointed scissors
Sewing kit
Sharp-ended tweezers
Steri-kit
Thermometer
Throat lozenges
Travel sickness medication
Vitamins
Water purification tablets
Spare glasses/contact lenses (get a second pair free / very cheap) and prescription

General

Make a list of the following in the **Back Section** *for your parents, then photocopy it and make sure you take a copy with you:*

All emergency contact numbers
All insurance details
'Car breakdown club' card
Credit card numbers (and their emergency numbers)
Driving licence
Embassy addresses
Glasses/contact lens prescription
International driving licence
International Youth Hostel (and other) membership
Passport number and date issued
Serial numbers on valuables eg. cameras

Paperwork

Address book
Books
CV
Diary
Education certificates
Family photos
Job references
Pens
Phrasebook
Other useful items
Large black dustbin bag
A ball of string
Little things for kids

Identification tags for your backpack/day bag

...so that if they do get lost, they end up back at your parents' house (tell your parents about this – a knock at the door and a complete stranger handing your dad your backpack with '...I believe this belongs to your daughter!...' will not go down well). Keep the tag hidden inside your bag (so dodgy people can't start a conversation).

Money

Credit cards
International debit card
Foreign currency
Traveller's cheques + all relevant emergency numbers

Handy hints

- Buying clothes. They can often be bought at a fraction of the price overseas.
- Securing your backpack. Thin chain, bought from hardware stores, can be stretched across the front of the pack to secure it (and also used to chain it to beds, chairs etc.). Stories about putting chicken mesh inside to stop people slashing it and getting inside? 'Serious thieves' will always get in, so is it really worth it? Hide valuables with your dirty laundry. **Safety…think about it for a second.** People rarely nick backpacks – they are too heavy and usually have sod all of value in them. So, don't think that as soon as you go away the world and his dog are going to try and nick your backpack. They won't. Be vigilant.

Packing your backpack

You've looked at it, chosen it, played with it, worn it around the house, in bed and out with the lads…*now it's time to pack it*. Packing is an art. You can't just stuff everything in fast, and it won't pack itself. **The following is a guide which is best used when you are getting close to actually leaving:**

Step 1
Get out absolutely everything that you think you might have to take. Hair dryers, Sony Discmans, tumble dryer and sod it, why not, your mountain bike. Arrange everything into piles – **'have to takes'** (passport, first-aid kit), **'would like to takes'** (jumpers, girlfriend) and **'other'** – for 'stuff' you haven't got a clue about (check out the checklist).

Step 2
Be cruel. Remove everything you **'hoped you might have room for'** – slippers, dressing gown, girlfriend (apologise, offer flowers and chocolates). Has pile decreased? Will it really fit in? Start to pack. When the bloody thing is full up and you only have a quarter of your things in, kick it very hard, curse me for getting it wrong about what to pack, give up on travelling and break down in tears.

Step 3
Dry your eyes and re-read the bit above about not taking everything with you. Re-pack just the top things from each pile (the best T-shirt, pair of shorts, jeans, shoes etc.)…if you still have too much, you've got to be more severe. **You have to leave with a backpack three quarters full. I'm not joking.** Aim for this. If, on this pack, you are looking fairly confident, get serious and go to…

Step 4
The 'final pack'. Get your piles and make sure you have everything you think you will need.

START TO PACK...HOW?

Sleeping bag Needs to be easily accessible because you'll be getting it out every night: I put this in the bottom section of my pack (it has a separate zip and a string-drawn 'false bottom' which can be left open for one big deep pack, or drawn shut to split the pack into two compartments). I also keep the things I don't usually need, ie. jumpers, smart clothes etc. here as well.

Really important tip (dad taught me): **always pack to the corners, you'll gain crucial extra space.**

Pants and socks Either in a drawstring bag laid flat in a layer across the pack making them organised and easy to find or, as I do, stuffed into all the empty gaps here and there.

T-shirts Best rolled or packed flat as another layer. Fold the arms in (rectangle shape), fold in half across middle and half again (long, thin rectangle shape), turn and roll tightly from one end to the other to make a 'Swiss roll' shape (ideal for stuffing into holes like pants and socks). If rolled properly they will stay fairly crease-free.

Travel saucepan I always take one and put all the 'small stuff' in that I need to find in a hurry, keep dry, or that can be easily damaged...my knifeforkandspoon set, travel adapter, Swiss army knife, matches/lighter, Maglite, small pots of curry and chilli powder and spare pair of pants (emergency only).

A quick note to you at this point. If you think I'm being really sad in the way I pack my bag and organise my things...I'm not, so sod off. I soon learnt to get in a habit with packing, after hours spent finding T-shirts, sun cream, or annoying little things like a tiny tube of lip-salve. When you're in a hurry and have to be packed and 'outta there', the bloody thing will never close and you eventually leave panting and sweating picking up the bits and pieces that fall out en route. *'Been there, done that.'* By having layers in your backpack you take them out and put them back (like building a wall) in an organised fashion. *Have a go and find out what's best for you.*

The rolling and coiling technique: by creating a whole series of snake-like things, you can coil rolled jeans, shorts and shirts into your pack with ease. If done properly it does cut down on creases. **Camera film** Put the canisters into freezer bags, roll into a long snake and put anywhere in your pack (they'll be kept dry and protected). **Dresses/skirts** Place dresses or skirts into a stocking to create another long snake-like object. I am told it keeps 'smart/work outfits' crease-free, so give it a go.

Pack the area behind your back carefully to prevent things bulging and sticking into you. This can be extremely uncomfortable, so think about solid back supports.

Finally, over the top of everything else, I put my towel and sarong, which helps keep the contents inside the pack. If your towel is still wet and minging, or your sarong needs a damn good airing…you can whip it out as soon as you arrive at your next stop to minimise contamination of the rest of your pack.

So, where are we up to at this point? *If you're reading this thinking, 'I've got loads of time left, what do I care?'* fair enough.

However, when it comes to a week to go and you are still flapping around trying to sort your pack out…*give me a ring…so I can have a bloody good laugh at you!* Warning. Last-minute packing is something you do for a holiday…you can do without things for a week or two.

Unfortunately, this time – if you don't take it, you're going to have to buy it. Getting things sent out costs money and is unnecessary. You will also have to send heavy, useless stuff back, so don't take it!

Do take a bit of time to make sure that you pack properly. Have a dummy run in so far as filling the thing up and carrying it goes. **Once it is full and feeling a bit heavy, put it on.**

How to wear a backpack

(This is the way that works well for me and just about everyone else I know.) **The weight is not borne on your back** – your hips and shoulders should do the work. If it's a touch heavy (trust me, it will be), **never, ever, ever, ever, ever, ever pick it up with a bent back…**it is agony if you put your back out and it will ruin your trip.

So, how do you do it?
Lift the pack onto a high surface (with a bent back!) – a bed, table or chair. Balance it there, loosen all the straps, sit in front of it and slide your arms through the shoulder straps. Then, bending your knees, start to stand up, taking the weight onto your thighs. Don't stand up straight, keep leaning forward until you've done up the waist band sufficiently tight. Stand upright, transferring a bit of the weight on to your shoulders…

Now the crucial bit to the whole thing: lift the waist band whilst tightening so that it is sitting on the top of your hip bone and pull it really, really, tight. It should almost hurt. You know if you are doing it right as the backpack sort of lifts up and away from your shoulders. Sounds weird, but trust me on this one! Then grab the two cords at the sides and pull them down evenly together to tighten the straps around your shoulders. This will now feel more comfortable. Finally, pull the straps located behind the top of your shoulders to bring the top of the pack nearer your head. Then simply exit the plane, count to ten and pull the chute!

Only you will know what feels comfortable

Trial and error and intense fiddling to make it as comfortable as possible – combined with wearing it around the house (or on a long walk) a good week before you leave is the key.

Is it the best one for you? If not – change it for one that you're happy with. Make sure that you don't damage it, keep all the receipts and wrapping, take it back to the shop and find one you like. This is the most important item that you're going to take away with you (apart from your lucky pants).

Sum it up, Tom!

After what seems like a monster section, I think we've covered just about everything! At the end of the day, it's all down to common sense.

Pick the right backpack
If you don't like it, change it. Fashion? No-one gives a shit! Practical. Strong. Waterproof. Built to last.

Your day bag
Too many pockets that little hands can get in to, or having something which is impossible to lock up and secure is a waste of time.

Packing
You will get a shock when you find there is no space. Take only things you are going to need and use. Things like climbing boots and equipment can be hired out there. Going from a hot country to a cold one? Don't hump heavy clothes, buy them later or have them sent out.

Packing is an art you will acquire and develop
The method I have described above works for me. Others do it differently. Pack to the corners and use all the available space (you'll fit a lot more in).

Need more advice?
There is a 'Guide to buying, choosing and packing your backpack' on **gapyear.com**, complete with photos where I show you some of the techniques and ideas outlined above.

Last thought...If someone nicks your whole backpack, you are bloody unlucky. It rarely happens, so please...don't have nightmares!

20: How to...camp

Where to camp? – 'The Bush' vs Campsite

Campsites are more organised and usually have good facilities: showers, BBQs/cooking areas, flat ground, power points and, occasionally, swimming pools and other 'entertainment'. They will be managed well, with some security – always a good thing! If they are just camping areas, be very careful of your stuff, especially if it's quiet...your tent may be padlocked, but, given ten minutes and a sharp knife, anyone could do you over!

Camping in the bush or on a beach lacks the amenities of a campsite, but you do have it all to yourself. Find a comfortable spot, get your tent up, keep your stuff dry and cook yourself a good meal – there's nothing better!

When you get there   ❶

Building a fire
Everyone assumes that they can build a fire. Why? Match onto paper onto wood does not = roaring fire! So, how do you do it?

Step 1 collect the wood. You need tinder (bone-dry pencil-sized twigs). Collect loads, and as much dry, rotten wood lying around as you can (no leaves). Big logs/dead trees also give the fire substance. Pile it upwind of the fire.

Step 2 choose a flat area, preferably where a fire has been before. Create a bare circle of earth and put large stones around the outside to form a barrier (when hot you can put pots on them). Find a big, thin, flat bit of wood (like a large book); place this in the middle of the area, and place a big log behind it (as a wind-break)

Step 3 place scrunched up newspaper or a fire-lighter on top of the flat base of wood and next to the big log, ie. in a little 'alcove', and stack loads of tinder and twigs against the big log and over the fire-lighter or paper (leave a space to light it!).

Step 4 set light to the fire-lighter/paper. When the tinder catches light, add progressively larger bits of wood...stacking them against the big log...and keep building. Add the big stuff when there are decent flames. When it's 'roaring' add anything you want, wet or dry. Let it burn until it starts to die down. The main heat is generated from the red embers. Every once in a while feed it with more wood.

Key points
- Stay with, and in control of, the fire.
- Have water to hand, if poss, and a rake or strong stick to move bits down or out of the fire if necessary.
- To prevent fire spreading across the grass, clear a decent patch of earth. Fire can quickly get out of hand – don't laugh, it happens – think Forest Fire! If it gets out of control, deprive fire of oxygen and it'll go out…ie. smother it with a blanket or sleeping bag, but don't set yourself alight!
- If you do cause a fire, get help immediately.

What to cook and how?

Flames look good, but won't cook your dinner – you need HEAT. The fire should be really hot, but raked down ie. level the 'coals' out. Now put in a couple of large stones, close together, with the hottest spot of the fire in between. You are ready to cook, by balancing pots or trapping and turning the food (in a folding grill) on the stones.

Another idea: wrap food in heavy-duty foil (thin stuff just burns). Stick in potatoes, or something special – fish, salt and pepper and herbs and spices, and cook slowly. (NB: Put a bit of butter in to stop it sticking.) In Australia we caught our own fish and trapped a crab the size of a house…whacked them in the wok over the fire…beauty!

Cold night? Dig a hole (deep enough) and kick the stones from the fire into it to warm the sand below your sleeping bag.

Where to sleep?

Sleeping rough
- Choose your spot carefully…flat dry area, no rocks, upwind of the fire, look out for ant hills and crocodile nests! Mossie nets must be hung from a tree.
- Unroll your bed *only* when you get into it, or spend a cosy night with Sammy the Snake and Rolf the Redback Spider.
- Roll mats are not for comfort, but warmth (insulation from cold ground), so don't take a big fluffy effort…also handy to sit on, particularly if it's damp.

Pitching a tent
When Tony and I arrived in Hawaii, we had the scouting ability of a pair of disorientated ferrets. We opened up our tent for the very first time not knowing if all the bits were there, or even how to put the friggin' thing up! I learnt from this. I got a new tent before my Canadian trip and spent time putting it up, taking it down, packing it etc…still lost the pegs though!

What tent? There are loads of different tents out there that all do weird and wonderful things. As far as I'm concerned, the dome ones are best.

HOW TO…CAMP

They are light to carry and really easy to put up (collapsible poles – just throw it at the ground and it sort of puts itself up), easy to manoeuvre into position, and in strong winds they simply bend. You don't actually have to use the pegs, as the weight of your backpack and 'stuff' will keep it on the ground. Make sure your fly sheet doesn't touch the inner tent (the rain will soak through)…and you have the perfect home! However, for really windy areas of the world, it's worth getting the wedge-shaped ones…more aerodynamic than a jet, but with slightly less acceleration!

Any tent will do, as long as you know how to put it up, have all the bits and it doesn't weigh a ton. A two-man tent is sufficient for you, your backpack and a bit of space. You will probably only ever sleep in it, so you don't need adjoining rooms. Cheap ones are for kids in the garden, not for trekking in Nepal. If it has shiny animals painted inside…leave well alone.

Stuff to take with you for serious camping

Ground sheet Stick it under your tent, enclose all your belongings in it, put it outside and sit on it, or use it as a storm cover/roof. A really useful bit of kit!

Survival blanket The foil that you get when you finish the Marathon. Light, but warm when you need it.

Shower…with either a solid or soft container. Fill and leave out in the sun to heat up and then…use it!

Stove A fire's great, but for early morning tea or coffee a camping stove's the answer. Watch out – the gas bottle fittings are not always compatible from country to country.

Water container Fill it at every opportunity, but make sure you can carry it ie. keep it in the back of your car, or get a smaller one to carry amongst your group.

Esky or cool box Essential, especially in hot countries. Keeps food and drink cool and fresh. Fill up with ice at every petrol station you pass, or keep in the shade.

Woolly hat as your head will freeze at night.

Really good torch When you get back to the dark campsite at night, how do you find your dark green tent? A good Maglite does the job. I have one of the smaller ones which goes on my key ring, which I keep in my saucepan…so I always know where it is in an emergency.

Head torch Extremely useful for cooking (keep both hands free), walking around the camp, in caves, all the usual stuff.

Peg-free washing line (or big ball of string) plus two trees.

Mossie repellent Helps prevent arsey little bites and, on the odd occasion, malaria. Rub on arms, legs, neck and any other exposed bits. Or a spray, for you, your tent/mossie net. I usually break the little coils up into two-inch pieces, light them and stick them in the ground around me, giving a 'wall' of protection. Even though I have the mossie sheet down at the tent entrance, I always stick a couple in the ground in front of the flap. Lemon oil candles do the same job, smell nicer and give light.

A few golden rules:

● **Never have food in your tent.** Wildlife…that's a polite way of saying…BEARS!…love to come and investigate those lovely smells. Most campsites with wildlife around have a sodding great cage for you all to put your food in. If you're woken up at 6am by a hungry grizzly after your Weetabix…give it to him! In Botswana, Carolyn woke up to the tent caving in and a couple of warthogs getting stuck into her cornflakes and coffee, and this wasn't 'Pumbaa' from *The Lion King*, these had real tusks! Keep your food away from the tent!

● **Take a puncture repair/sewing kit** with you to fix the tent if you get holes.

● **Remember that if you have a light inside the tent**…everyone outside can see what's going on inside!

● **Learn to be neat and look after your tent.** A few extra minutes of careful folding, organising and separating in the tent bag each time you pack it up saves loads of hassle later.

● **Be careful where you pitch your tent**, especially in the dark. You may wake up in the morning in the middle of a market, or, as we once did…a bird sanctuary…all these gorgeous, colourful, fluffy, feathery little things…bellowing their lungs out at 5.30am. Cute? I thought so.

● **Don't wear shoes inside the tent**, leave them under the fly sheet outside…to avoid excess stones, sand and gravel kicking around and getting under you when you sleep and, worst of all, dirty water, which gets everywhere.

Sum it up, Tom !

Tents…the lighter, the stronger, the easier to put up…the better. Go in and have a look around, get advice from the experts. When you buy your tent, put it up in the garden and spend a night in it. Take it down and put it up again. A couple of hours' practice here will save you loads of hassles there. But most of all, have fun! It can be an amazing experience. Woken up by the sun, the sound of waves on the shore, birds in the forest…or the roar of the cars, as the place you thought was a campsite in the dark is, in fact, a roundabout! You can't beat it.

21: How to...buy a car

by Carolyn Martin

Over to Carolyn for some first-hand experience: In 1997 Carolyn drove around Australia in a Volvo Estate. Being the same age as her, with 120,000 miles on the clock when she bought it...170,000 miles when she sold it (the equivalent of driving around the world), there's nothing she doesn't know about a ton of Swedish metal and a greasy old spanner!! Below, she imparts her knowledge to all those interested in buying cars overseas. Enjoy.

Why do you want it? It was only over a few beers and a chat about disastrous organised tour experiences that I realised a car could work out cheaper in the long run than coach journeys and flights. It was the best decision we made.

So ask yourself:
- How far do you want to go in it?
- Do you need to sleep in it? ie. do you need a camper van?
- Are you going to need something that doesn't break down?
- Can you afford to get a banger? ie. can you repair it yourself?
- Can you afford to cut your losses (if it dies), sell it for scrap and still get to where you need to go?
- How much do you really know about cars? If it rattles and the engine is hot, would you know what to do? There's no room out there for smart arses, because if you pretend you're a hot shot, and you're not, it'll cost you a fortune.

Something worth doing
Work out your costs: compare the cost of buying, running and selling the car with savings on accommodation (by sleeping in it), other transport, and any other savings you think you may make. It'll probably work out the same or even cheaper. Combine this saving with complete freedom ie. being able to watch the sunset over Ayers Rock when all the tour buses have gone home...and it may prove the best decision you'll ever make. Living out of the car is a great laugh, as is picking up other backpackers and heading off to see things (a way to make the car pay for itself, or at least keep yourself in beers when you get there!).

What type of car?

If you want to sleep in it you need **a camper van, a stationwagon or an estate car**. Dalit and I slept in the back of our Volvo Estate (with the seats down!)...it was dead comfy. The lads camped outside...with the surfboard and windsurfer on the roof! It worked really well...arriving at deserted beaches in the middle of nowhere, chuck a ground sheet down, empty the boot onto the roof, crack open a couple of beers, and chill. The next morning you'd have a whole bath to yourself, shared only with a school of dolphins and a few multi-coloured fish in their coral reef jacuzzi! **Saloon** – make sure it has a big boot/trunk. **Soft top** – let's face it, you shouldn't be backpacking!

Petrol or diesel? Diesel is cheaper than petrol in most places and can take you further for your cash. There is less performance, but who cares.

Automatic or manual? If you're going to attempt to do maintenance yourself, don't get an automatic, and if you're going long distances you'll hardly change gear anyway.

The make? Get a well-known make, so you can pick up parts anywhere (breaker's yards will always have bits you need, saving you a fortune). If there is a good list of dealers (which is hopefully in the car), then any make will do. Failing that, you can always find dealers in the phone book.

Does size matter? Actually 'no'...should please a few of you out there! Larger cars are more expensive to run (petrol, oil, insurance etc), but you can fit more people in to help you pay for it. If you are travelling long distances, you might want to pay a bit more for room to spread out. Make sure it has a roof-rack. Personally I go for a big one every time! If you are going to use it as your house, go for a mansion, not a shed.

Where to look?   ❷

'Backpackers' noticeboard Usually the cars sold here are old bangers, but, despite having six million miles on the clock, they will have been round the continent several times and are likely to be able to do it again! Beware of dealers selling cars they can't get rid of. If they don't look like backpackers, don't trust them.

What backpackers will tell you
- What it takes to run and where they've been in it.
- Places to stay and things to see on the way.
- How and where to get it serviced and what to do in an emergency.
- About paperwork you'll need.

What they won't tell you
- If they've had a bit of a 'bump'.
- Where to go if it breaks down...as it'll sound like it already has.
- If bits don't work.
- That it'll go round the block on the test drive, but no further...

Local paper / notice boards at supermarkets etc Sold by 'locals'...so you know where they live, but, with the home advantage, they are in a better position to pull a fast one on you. The cars may be more expensive, but then you know that their ass hasn't been hauled round the country 58 times, and that they have been treated well. Beware 'one careful lady driver', but check it out – it may be true.

Used car auctions…for really cheap cars. You can pick up a real beauty here if you're lucky, so get a mechanic to come along with you (for cash) on the understanding that if you get a good one, he'll get a bonus (you might well be able to sell it later for more than you bought it for). Ask the locals where the best auctions are.

When buying, ask about:

- Handbooks – is there one? Has handy stuff about fuses, tyre pressures etc.
- Insurance – what type and how much?
- Mileage – see above.
- Registration – the car needs to be registered in your name so you are covered by your insurance.
- Roadworthy certificate – easier and cheaper to get in some states / areas of the country than the others. To find out, ask around and phone the different states…the difference could mean loads of $$$s to you!
- Service history – hopefully it'll have one and it'll be good.
- Tax – you have to be taxed by law. Is this included?

Looking over the car

If you know nothing about them, get a local mechanic. If you can't find one, here are a few easy things for you to check out. **See it during good daylight** – you'll never find holes with a torch! The only thing you can check in the dark are the lights.

General condition Look for rust around the doors…rusty bodywork may fail the roadworthy certificate, which means that you can't get insured. Look for dents. Mattresses or large boxes can cover a multitude of sins…a friend of mine bought a camper, and woke up soaked. There was a huge hole underneath the mattress. Fortunately he was able to find the guy who sold it to him and got a full refund. Oh no he didn't!

Leaks If the car's been sitting there for a while, check for damp patches on the ground: 1. *Oil* (sticky and shiny). 2. *Coolant* (white or rusty coloured). 3. *Fuel* (stinks and explodes when you drop your ciggy on it!). 4. *Water* (if there's a hole in the radiator, the car won't go very far).

Lights Get your mates to check they work (best at night). Don't forget the hazards.

Seat belts Are they all there, not frayed, and attached to the car?

Steering Does it turn fully and evenly to the left and right? Something to watch with old camper vans.

Tyres Look for damage, tread, bulges, cracks, foreign bodies and uneven wear.

Wheel nuts ...keep the wheel on (a good thing when travelling at speed). Make sure they're all there.

Take the car for a test drive and check:

Brakes Make sure the car doesn't pull to the left or right when braking. A vibration through the steering or the brake pedal means they are worn and need replacing.

Clutch Check it isn't jerky, and that it doesn't slip. This is a very expensive piece of kit to replace. Exit the car and do a runner.

Gears Go far enough and fast enough to check they all work smoothly, and do a three-point-turn to check reverse (some cars don't!).

Handbrake You may need it, plus it's important for parking on hills.

So...you want it

• **Don't look keen straight away** (gives you a chance to find out where they live, should you buy it and have problems later).

• **Don't be afraid to haggle**. If backpackers are going home soon, they'll be wanting to sell.

• **Offer cash for a better price**, then hope there's a Thomas Cook in town!

• **Get all tools, equipment and anything else included** to save you buying extras.

Extras to take
Water container, cool box (a couple of cheap polystyrene 'eskies'), spare fuel tank, oil, WD40 (cure all – if in doubt...spray it!), insulating tape, de-icer and scraper, spare fuses, luggage/elastic bungee (brilliant – enough said!), tyreweld. *And, if you're really keen:* bulbs, spark plugs, wire brush for the battery, Leatherman tool.

Before you leave home, get a mate to point out bits in the engine, as a basic knowledge will help you maintain any car whilst you are away. **Why not take a brief car maintenance course** if you are definitely going to get a car overseas?

You need to know... The **oil level** (how to measure it), **tyre pressure** (loads in the car: increase the pressure, if it's hot: let some out), **coolant level** (NEVER UNDO THE RADIATOR CAP WHEN THE ENGINE'S HOT, BECAUSE ALL THE WATER WILL BOIL OUT...and never let the car overheat), **brake fluid level** (don't let it go down too far...it's also poisonous and flammable), **fuses** (fuse boxes usually under the glove compartment or dash board), **wiring** (more loose wires than in a Russian Premier's head – leave well alone), **fan belt** (if it's slack it will squeal when accelerating), **brakes**, **bulbs** and **battery**.

And, most importantly, buy a note book When you stop for petrol, note down the mileage, amount of petrol you've put in, cash you've just spent, water used, parts and any work done. This will allow you to spot problems very quickly and help with sharing the running costs with others.

Selling it again

- Try selling it for what you bought it for.
- Put posters anywhere you think will work (including in the car window).
- See notes above about buying!

At the end of the day, you need to sell your car. If you don't, you're going to have to give it away or swap it for a beer. This may take time, so don't turn up two days before your flight home expecting to sell it and take the cash. Get there a good week or two before and give it time to sell. Get to a major entry point into the country, eg. Sydney, where there are loads of backpackers coming in looking for cars. Don't try and make a profit unless you've got an amazing car (a high price on it = people won't even come forward). '*Give me a reasonable price and it's yours*' and they'll come running.

If you bought it for $700, try to sell it for $700. If you have to get a certain amount of money for it, add on a couple of hundred dollars and then come down in price. If you eventually sell it for $600, nice one. Accept the fact that you've got shedloads of use out of it, that it's saved you more than that, and given you so much more in value...accept it.

So how did I sell mine?
We sold ours by parking it in the main street of Cairns, Australia, beside the seafront, with large colour posters over each window saying...**Must go! Make an offer!**...and then sunbathed next to it all morning in our bikinis...sold it in the afternoon to someone working at the Thomas Cook across the road! **Easy!**

Sum it up, Carolyn!

Buying a car was the best thing I did in Australia. It gave me total freedom to see everything I wanted, in the time-scale I wanted, with people I wanted to travel with. If you're going to buy one, be prepared for people trying to take advantage of you when you're buying, selling and maintaining it...and don't be shy about making sure that everyone pays their share...you're not a charity!

You're going to learn more about cars in a short period than you would ever have thought possible. It's a great experience, it has to be done...and if you're travelling long distances, be prepared for your bum to take on the shape of a well worn car seat. Good luck!

22: How to...hitch-hike

If you have never hitch-hiked, throw any preconceived ideas out of the window. There is an art to everything, and hitch-hiking is no exception. It's just common sense.

Warning!

Hitch-hiking has always been seen as dangerous. Why? The media. Every once in a while, something happens to a hitch-hiker. In 1991 some loon in Australia went around picking up hitch-hikers and killing them. In Israel a few years ago, a guy picked up a couple and shot them (killed one and severely injured the other). I've heard bad first-hand accounts too. To be honest, the media have got it right. As the 1990s progressed, hitch-hiking slowly became extinct. Hitchers are scared of getting picked up by a nutter, and drivers are scared of strangers. Hitch-hikers get a bad name from the few oddballs who hitch – you see them at the roadside – hat covering their face, dirty, slouched, thumb out – you say to yourself: '**...What is that?...no chance mate...!'**

I suppose I should say that hitch-hiking is dangerous. I certainly wouldn't recommend it to the females amongst you, in fact, the bottom line is – don't do it. I'm not being sexist ...I'm being serious. If there are nutters around when you hitch, a single female is going to attract them more. Blokes 'should' get away with it.

There are places where you can hitch safely. In New Zealand, Australia and some parts of South Africa, hitching is so easy it's untrue...backpackers have been invited in for meals and sometimes to stay the night. Ask other backpackers and the guys at the hostels if you want to know the score.

In 1995, aged 21, I hitch-hiked solo over 5,000 miles across and around Canada... successfully and with absolutely no problems. It was quick, cheap (well, free!) and convenient...and it was one of the best experiences I have ever had. Hitching in Oz and the UK had been easy, so I had a fair idea of what I was doing.

❶ *The bottom line – it is something I can't recommend, despite doing it myself. But, it is something that many of you will do, which is why it is essential that I give you the right advice so that you do it successfully and safely.*

Get your technique right

Hitch-hiking is not about standing at the side of the road and sticking your thumb out. For long distances you've got to get your act together. Ask yourself...**Would I pick myself up?** You may say 'Yes', because you know how nice you are. But when someone is driving along...**you have about eight seconds to persuade them they should take you in their car...**

Eight seconds...to persuade a total stranger, probably wary of hitch-hikers, to take you, a total stranger, in their car – their secure little area which can be kept protected by simply driving on. They'll forget about you in five minutes...*Why should they pick you up any-way?*

Who will pick you up?
- People who used to hitch when they were younger (on a nostalgia trip!).
- Other young people.
- Parents who see their 'son/daughter' in you.
- Businessmen, sales reps and people driving long distances. Journeys go a lot quicker when you are chatting to someone.
- Ex-pats – in my case English people living abroad. They're a great source of lifts. They love to talk about England, where you're from etc.

So, how do you get these rides?
Simple, cover all eventualities. Every time I got a ride in Canada I would ask the people '...**why did you pick me up?...**'.

They would say things like '...**because I knew where you were going...I could see your eyes...I knew you were English...etc...**'. Next time I would 'hone' my technique, adding in what I'd learnt...

Nowadays if I don't get picked up within fifteen minutes I ask myself what I am doing wrong. If I'm still there 20–30 minutes later, I try something new, or move on. Generally I get picked up in about ten minutes...my fastest was ten seconds (getting out of one car and hailing the car behind!).

What to wear
If you look OK you should get a ride. You need to be clean, presentable, and non-threatening. Be smart and, in hot countries, be cool. Wear shorts and a T-shirt – clean and 'smart' ie. not in shreds. Wear shoes with socks (people like this!) as sandals/bare feet = 'traveller' and/or 'hippy'! Wear 'as little as possible'...obvious that you have nothing hidden ie. a weapon.

What not to wear
- Sunglasses – even when really sunny...people like to see your eyes.
- A hat – they don't like your head being covered.
- Dark clothes – '**dark = dangerous**' – wear white (the 'harmless, pure' look).

Your hair

- If it's long – wash it, tie it back and make it neat. Apparently long hair = 'dangerous biker' or hippy.
- If it is short – avoid the skinhead-on-holiday or prisoner-on-the-run impression!
- Have a shave – look tidy. If you have a beard (ladies!), make it neat.

Your sign

- Write out in massive letters where you want to go.
- Write 'Please' on it in the local language.
- Have another large sign next to your backpack saying where you're off to next.
- To save writing loads of signs, plan your route and write the name of a major town en route or the name of the motorway you want to go on ie. M6 south, London.
- Find a decent-sized 'strong' cardboard box and rip off the edges (keep all the bits for later signs). Fill the whole space with your destination.

Get a flag!

- People instantly know where you are from.
- The world is full of ex-pats – the flag draws them to you.
- It shows you are genuine – nutters wouldn't bother!

Have your backpack in a visible place

You are a backpacker, you are harmless. Make it obvious, disassociate yourself from 'The Weird Bastard Club'!...drivers will take more notice of you. You are travelling, going from A to B – you have a reason for being there.

YOUR EIGHT SECONDS OF PERSUASION

What they should see first of all

First impressions are crucial. With me, they see a young guy, with a backpack clearly in view, wearing a pair of shorts, a T-shirt, shoes, standing straight (not slouching) right at the edge of the road and holding a sign clearly in view.

Their thought…   a backpacker hitching

As they get closer

They see my flag, a clearly-written sign with my destination (and the word 'please'), a clean-shaven young man, with a smile and a relaxed stance. Is he 'completely with it' (not on drugs) and harmless?

Their thought…   a British backpacker, off to xxxxxxx, seems harmless enough.

As they pass

They see the second sign by the backpack (in Canada it said 'EAST') – so they know I'm going somewhere/moving on after they drop me off. They see my face clearly – I smile at them and shrug my shoulders in a kind of 'Please?' gesture.

Most at that point either :

- shake their head to say 'No', smiling.
- shake their head roughly to say 'No…sod off scum!'
- point up ahead, which means they are turning off soon.
- put both hands in the air – 'Sorry…not this time'.
- drive past looking the other way: 'If I can't see you, I can't pick you up!'
- talk to you, unaware that you can't hear a sodding thing (so you smile and mouth words back at them!).
- wave, smile, honk the horn, point, laugh etc.

…I smile and wave back…'Cheers anyway, have a good one!' kind of a thing.

Their thought…he's harmless, he's going my way, he looks kinda fun, I'll pick him up!

…Bingo!

Enjoy it!
This is the key. If you look like you're having fun, you give off 'positive vibes', exuding an energy and enthusiasm they can almost feel. You can spot confidence a mile off, **and by smiling and waving to say 'thanks', many, at the last moment, have stopped after all**. Other times, people have seen me joking with the cars in front, and decided to pick me up!

Where to stand?
No matter how good you are, a car doing 70mph **can't** stop.

Positioning is the key
- the last traffic lights out of town.
- just past a roundabout.
- on the slip road down to the motorway/freeway/autoroute.
- at 'toll booths' on major roads.
- at the exit to a roadside café or petrol/gas station.

…a place where motorists are either stationary for a second, or driving at the speed of a snail, so they can check you out and pull over.

Make sure they can pull over
I passed a couple of students hitching on a major roundabout on the approach road to the M1. I nearly ran them over as I came flying round the corner. *'Novel approach!' I thought – getting knocked down for the sympathy bit!* I couldn't pull over, so drove up the motorway and back again to pick them up…and gave them a bollocking for standing there!

Traffic lights on a crossroads are great, especially with a hard shoulder close by where someone can pull over. Stand close to the lights and 'play' to the waiting cars.

Slip roads on to main roads tend to have big hard shoulders. Stand far enough down the slip road so the cars have time to turn the corner, adjust and spot you before accelerating (too near the main road and they'll be going too fast).

Roundabouts are great – the traffic is slowed (they have time to notice you). Drivers tend to look ahead, so position yourself where they can see you on the other side, or stand well round the corner in a place where they can stop.

Toll booths are good and bad. 'Close-quarter tactics' with stationary cars, but which lane do you pick? The people in the booths, security and police may not welcome you. You can't stand on the other side – so get between two lanes and work quickly. Be amusing, be helpful (push the button for them etc), but don't try too hard, as they may feel unsafe.

Road side petrol/gas station, stand by the exit, hopefully in a place where they can spot you as they are filling up or just about to leave. Easy hitching and great for snacks.

Road works In Montreal, I trekked for two hours through town, across a massive bridge (in the burning heat), to find the perfect hitching place to get to Quebec. When I got there…more cones than a bloody ice-cream van. Millions of them – I couldn't even see the road. I collapsed with exhaustion, had a rest and then moved the cones to make my own little lay-by! Two minutes later, I was picked up…perfect. NB: If you move cones, please put them back to avoid 'diverted' drivers crashing into big holes!

Get to the right position

This is important. Ask the locals where you should go (ask several so you get it right). If you have to take a bus or a long walk, do it. Trying to hitch from the middle of town just won't work. People are normally quite good about dropping you off at a good place to catch another ride. Talk to them, say where you are going next and the sort of place you need to be dropped of at (see above!). I have been dropped off in some bad places because the drivers thought they knew what was best…in the middle of nowhere or on the side of a busy road…you are going to struggle to leave (passing cars will think the previous ride threw you out)!

Food, drink and sun cream

Take plenty of water and snacks with you…it may be a long day. Standing out in the sun – dehydration, burning and sunstroke can be avoided with sun cream, regular drinks and a hat/shade. If you look, and feel, hot and shitty – you may not get a ride (on the other hand, someone may feel sorry for you).

Right / wrong timing

7am to 8am: those with long journeys may start early to avoid the morning traffic, or finish the journey before it gets too hot.
8am to 9am: people are heading to work/kids to school, don't go far, will not stop.
9am to 10am: the 'Sales reps' head off, company cars, air-conditioned, great rides – comfortable, occasionally you get fed on the company account (if you're nice enough!).
10am onwards: the long-distance guys who didn't leave at 7am, trucks appear, plus more sales reps.

5pm to 6pm: work traffic going home.

6pm: those with long journeys who like the empty evening roads, and in hot countries, the cooler time of day…don't hitch at night unless it is really light and you can easily give up and find a safe bed for the night.

Accepting a lift

If your technique is right, people will stop; so, be choosy about the ride, but not so choosy that you get stuck. **When someone pulls over, check them out…**luggage in the back, baby seats, tidy cars, air-conditioning, children, nuns, are all good signs. Have a brief chat with them – where you want to go, where they are going, how far they can take you, where they can drop you off. **If they say they are going on a long journey, look for signs that they are** ie. a pile of music, drinks, food etc…things people normally take. One guy seemed to be telling me too much about where he was going, a monster of a journey, to exactly the place on my sign – but the car was completely empty. *I didn't take the risk.*

Getting in…and out of the car: If you open the back door, put your bags in, close it and then open the front, a dodgy person could drive off with your stuff. *Keep the passenger door open while you put your bag in*, or take it out of, the back. Close the front door last. Always keep your day bag with you: if someone tries a fast one, you'll still have the important stuff.

In the car…be nice, *'…thanks for picking me up…'*, is a great start. Generally they are interested in what you're doing, where you're from, etc. (all the conversations end up the same!). Get your map out and let them know where you are going. Find out where they are from, what they do – it's a final way to check that they are OK. At rest stops, offer to get them something to eat or drink. They will appreciate the gesture and it may reap dividends later.

In Canada I was often invited in and given a meal and a bed, even invited to weddings and taken to parties. In the morning, after a massive brekkie, many took me to a great hitching spot too. If you are shown such kindness, do clear away, wash up, etc… prove you are not using them as a hotel. Never beg, nick, be rude or take the piss. Finally, get their names and addresses and send them a 'thank you' or Christmas card from home.

One guy took me past his turning for another hour to a place where I would get a great follow-on hitch. Why? Because I was doing something that he had always wanted to. He sent me a postcard to say 'Thanks!' (for making him realise that there was more to life than work). I was gobsmacked.

I asked one guy what he did. *'…I've just got out of prison after a thirty-year stretch!…'*

Thirty years!!!!! All I could think was **m.u.r.d.e.r.** In fact he'd robbed banks, played the prison service around…and woke up, aged fifty, with no life. Finally he got out, married his lawyer's daughter, had a baby and lived life. He took me for a meal, bought me beers, and told me some really interesting stories.

I had an amazing trip, met some incredibly kind people and learnt a lot of lessons. **'What goes around, comes around'** and I intend to always do for others what others have done for me.

Points to note

- You are talking to people, not cars.
- Hitching is illegal in some countries and on some motorways/freeways.
- Trucks are often unable to pick up hitchers due to their insurance – many still do for the company. Trucks are comfortable, but slow; always suss out the driver before you decide to get some kip.
- If you are going far, be brave and turn down short rides (unless you've been there for a while and are hoping for a better spot down the road).
- If you smell alcohol, beware. Accidents, aggression…tread carefully.
- Give up if it isn't happening. Get to a town and a safe bed for the night.
- Never sleep at the side of the road. You are unsafe and vulnerable.
- If desperate, wave your arms and flag anyone down. The best options are caravans / mobile homes (families, tourists or old people).
- Major cities cannot be hitched through. Get a lift that takes you round. Don't get dropped off on the outskirts of town or city – it can take ages and cost a fortune to get to the centre.
- Try hitching at home. Practice makes perfect you know!

Sum it up, Tom!

It's an amazing experience, enjoy it and have fun! If you treat it as a serious method of travel and put time-scales on it, people sense your urgency and are put off – lifts dry up and you get fed up. There are comedians everywhere…hanging out of the window with their thumbs in the air…or pulling over and then driving off again as you walk up. Forget it! You'll never see them again. It's actually quite amusing! If you get angry, the genuine people will feel the 'bad vibes', and pass you by.

Those who say that…'all hitchers are spongers'…'it's dangerous'… 'you'll never get picked up'…have obviously never done it themselves, or picked anyone up.

I've done both, all over the world. It's not dangerous if you take care of yourself and treat every situation with caution. You'll get picked up if you go about it properly. Often I can travel distances faster than on a bus or train. It is cheap/free and you meet some fantastic people. I learnt more about life in those 5,000 miles across Canada than I have anywhere else.

23: How to...find work abroad

You may need visas, you may not. You may be looking for a six-month placement or a two-week cash-in-hand bonus to your budget! Whatever your reason, you have to get there first. Anyone can find work, it's as simple as that. If you can't, think about what you're doing wrong.

Doing it off your own back
If you have 'a skill', then you should always be able to find work. *Get off your backside and find it...*

Hairdresser / 'bloke with clippers'
Your name should be put about in every hostel you stay in – a note on the noticeboard saying '...Hi, I'm Tom from England. I cut hair. I'm staying in room 21 if you fancy a chop!...'. Make it cheap and do loads.

Mechanic / know loads about cars
Read *How to...buy a car*. You will understand the dilemma of so many backpackers out there. Be the expert they all use. Again, notes on all the noticeboards and you could soon be making $50 a hit...and save other backpackers loads of money and heartache.

With all work like this... Advertise, advertise, advertise. Put the word about and get cash. Beers are always a good form of payment if cash is not forthcoming. If you have a skill which you think other backpackers could use, let them know.

Getting work is as easy as one, two, three...I'm going to use Australia as the example, as that's where I worked, and thousands out there are working now...so it's a great place to start.

Step 1
Get a Tax File Number straight away, by going to the nearest Tax Office and presenting your **working visa**. NB: you need to get a working visa issued by the Australian Embassy in your home country **before** you travel. By proving that you have money in your account, a reason for coming back (ie. Uni) and that you're a good citizen, you'll get one issued on the spot from Australia House.

NB: If you are under 31, you are entitled to one Australian working holiday visa in your life. My advice would be to use it wisely. Many people, like me, waste it at eighteen. My advice is – don't! Unless you are going to work in Australia constantly for over six months, save it, as you'll probably head back out there post-University and want to work.

Step 2 ♢

Go to an agency. Don't go to too many, keep to about five, max. Be smart, be keen, be employable. Remember, they make their money from placing you. If you can be placed easily in a job, you are easy money. They will take you on and get you a good job.

Step 3 ♢

Be available. Show a willingness to work. Look at noticeboards, be ready to work immediately (especially if they come into the hostels asking for volunteers)...first come, first served.

If you are going for a decent job, take decent clothes or a suit. Take a load of CVs with you. Take the CV on disk as well, there will always be places where you can pop it in a machine and print off more up-to-date copies. Take all references/paperwork with you too.

Look eager. Agencies don't normally see people face to face, but get seen. Some like backpackers, others don't...do you look like one? Make sure you don't!

What work is out there?

...loads. In Sydney, for example, you can find anything. If you have done any normal jobs at home, this will all count in your favour...nursing, accountancy, IT professionals, even me and good old McDonald's! Building work, telesales, labouring, removals, setting up conferences, bar work, waiting/waitressing, security, au pairing, packing boxes etc.

Seasonal work: fruit picking, farm work and road construction

You can earn a fortune and you often get cash in hand. But be careful not to get ripped off. Before you get taken out into the middle of nowhere to work your ass off, ask what you get, when and what hidden extras you have to pay back to them.

The hidden extras? Being charged for a picking licence, food, accommodation, picking shoes, sky insurance, anti mouse-bite protection, apple duty, the farmer's new fence and his son's bike. If it is taken out of your wages, there isn't a lot you can do about it. You have to play by their rules, and there are a hundred backpackers after you should you decide to leave. If they are ripping off backpackers, a threat to call, or indeed a call to the immigration department might be in order...but make sure your actions don't get backpackers deported for working without visas (as has happening in Oz recently). Ask all the questions before you go out there. If they are being vague or irritable, think twice, you are probably about to be ripped off.

Working out on a road in the middle of nowhere is also a good earner, a week or two with nothing to spend your money on. You need to be fit and a hard worker, or you won't survive.

Cash-in-hand ⑤

Don't ask for cash-in-hand with agencies, as this is illegal and you are likely to get deported if you do it. If you do get it and you don't get caught, it is obviously a bonus. Don't tell anyone about it, as it only takes one person to inform the authorities. Being deported will cost you thousands, so think about it carefully.

To conclude

Everyone I know who has tried to get work in Sydney has, and they have had fantastic lives out there, most staying for around eighteen months and never wanting to come home! There is always work around. If you are at a hostel, ask if there is any work there...these are some of the best jobs. Tim landed in Sydney, anxious to find work, hopped on the minibus to the hostel and chatting to the driver...another backpacker...

'...So, any work around?...'
'...Yeah, you can have this job if you like, I leave tomorrow!...'

                                    ...one of the sweetest jobs in Sydney!

Go to the 'job centres', read all the notices and see how their system works. Or be creative. As a didgeridoo player I have 'busked' in the past, and by dressing up smartly and having a decent act which draws crowds, I earn about ten times the wages I would in a bar.

Taxes

Not paying them is illegal, overpaying is stupid. You may have to open a bank account if you are earning (for the wages to be paid into). Be wary of pulling one over on employers ie. taking a six-month placement when you know you'll be there for two. I was outsmarted by one employer who ended up charging me 50% tax!!!

Three rules:
● Be smart, in all senses of the word.
● Be there first.
● Be confident...there is always something out there for you.

Need more advice? Head to the 'Finding Work' section on **gapyear.com**.

24: The gapyear...explained

We are now in the middle of some very exciting times. Even though the internet bubble with the 'dot coms' has burst, the application of this new media and the uptake among people around the world has lead to an irreversible change in life as we know it. We are now a generation of text messagers, email addicts and web gurus! It is only a matter of time until we have computers all over the house helping us with our day-to-day chores, a car that drives itself to where we want to go and shopping in shops becomes a thing of the past (or something like that).

At the same time, the fabric of our society is changing as the baby boomer generation (the guys born in the boom years after the War) now approaches retirement, leading to:

(a) A different attitude to life, changing from '*born, live, work, retire, die*' to '*born, live, work, live, retire, live, I'm never gonna die!!*'
(b) A growing acceptance amongst families that it is ok to 'take risks' like take a year off before University, a year out whilst at University, time off after University or even decide to change your job or career before the age of 35.
(c) A huge army of bungee-jumping grannies and 'Sagalouts' who now travel the world...which is awesome.

The next 'new age' has officially arrived!

...and with it, the explosion in the concept of taking time out.

The history of the 'gapyear'
In the 1960s, those pesky baby boomers were in their twenties. As young people / students, they started to change society with their different views and behaviour. The generation gap between themselves and their parents was immense and their experimentation with a whole different set of laws to live their life by often shocked their parents and peers. One result of those interesting times was the birth of the 'Hippy Trails', generally around India, the purpose of which could be summed up in five words... 'smoking pot and cultural enlightenment!' The reason you are therefore sitting here reading this book is because back in 1968 your folks went to India to smoke pot! Interesting thought, eh?

The '70s and '80s
The hippy trail continued to be popular during the '70s ('flower power' and all that!) but, along with the fashion statements, it died in the early '80s. The baby boomers were now

settling down to serious jobs, having children and being responsible citizens. Young people in the '80s were more interested in making money, big hair and trying to get on in life and those influencing them, ie. their parents, were still 'old school' and proud.

The '90s revival...
At the beginning of the 1990s, the baby boomers' children were now either starting University or well into it. However, different to the generation before, their influencers were now the inventors of the hippy trail who started to encourage a bit of mind-broadening travel before and after University. And so the boom in pre- and post-University gaps kicked off in the early 1990s...and has never looked back.

The millennium
...and the explosion continues. With more and more people taking gaps as the years go on, it becomes more of an accepted thing to do. As the parents become 'younger' in their attitudes to life it is now no longer a case of 'Should my children take a gapyear?' but 'They really *should* take a gapyear with a bit of travel to broaden their horizons and see a bit of the world.'

'Career gaps' and 'pre-retirement gaps'
The final chapter in the history of gapyears is now coming to fruition. The fastest growing gapyear at the time of writing is the career gap – 25–35-year-olds who have chosen the wrong career or have simply become bored of life and seek something new. Many, having not taken a gap pre- or post-University, are persuaded by friends and work colleagues who did, to make the bold move and take up to a year out from their working lives. In an effort not to lose good staff, many employers are now recognising this new form of sabbatical and will guarantee the job on return, many even handing out cash bonuses to spend whilst you are away. Walking the trails of Machu Picchu in the middle of a six-month tour of South America is never more appealing than having slogged your guts out for little or no reward in a job that has never challenged you or made you happy for the past five years of your life!

The pre-retirement gaps?
Yup – those bloody baby boomers again! The world has never seen so many fit, healthy, 60-year-olds who are certainly not 'sitting around, waiting to die'. Life is for living, right? For many people, retirement doesn't begin until past 70, so these guys take a nice long pre-retirement gap to reward themselves for 40 years of work, trekking, bungee-jumping and doing all the things they never did in their youth...and then come back to find a job they will enjoy for the next ten years!

So what does this all mean to you, reading this right now?
To some it will be an assurance that what you are doing is the right thing, that you are not alone and that there are thousands of others out there right now with the same thoughts as you in their heads. To others, especially the younger ones amongst you, life may seem pretty rosy now that you realise that life is actually just one long series of 'gaps'! How cool is that?

Hopefully to most of you it will reinforce the view that life is indeed short and that you need to make the most of it. We place such a huge emphasis on working and existing that we often forget to live. The opportunities you have to take time out at various points in your life, I believe, *are a crucial part of your life*, reminding you to make the most of the time available and the world at your fingertips.

The only shame is that so many people *don't* go through with it (remember the one in five statistic), many ending up with a life of regrets. It's also a shame that most people only think about living their life when faced with a life-threatening illness or situation, or who tragically lose someone close to them. Suddenly, nothing is important any more – work, debts, concerns that really mean nothing – and all that is important is striving to live life to the full.

Why wait for bad stuff to happen to realise this? Why not wake up every morning on a positive note, no matter what is going wrong in your life, and treat every day as your last?

I do…and it's a great way to live your life!

Make the most of your gapyear

Pre-University gap

You have fifteen months to have the most amazing year of your life. You finish exams in June and don't go to University until the following October. Fifteen months. Now, this is quite a long time and you can fit a helluva lot in. You also have the bonus of knowing that if you have a *constructive gapyear*, ie. one that you 'get something out of', whether it is an enhanced CV or simply a bit of direction and focus in your life, then Universities and employers really value it.

Universities

…recognise the importance of a gapyear and its ability to breed more mature, broader-minded students, who fit into University life more easily than those who have just escaped the clutches and watchful eye of 'mummy and daddy' for the first time.

Employers

…relish pre-University gapyear activities on CVs and application forms; proof of a motivated person with character, confidence and the ability to take a major decision and achieve a goal at such a young age. In any interview you will definitely talk about what you did, why you did it and what you got out of it. The fact that you have something worth talking about will, in many cases, guarantee you an interview (see **Back to reality!** for more thoughts…and take in the point about your slim chance of even making the interview stage for the best jobs).

Post-University gap

Much of what is written above about the employers' opinion of the pre-University gappers applies here. It is a widely recognised fact that the Milk Round broke down a few years ago. Over two thirds of the graduates going into jobs fail to stay in them for three years. Millions of pounds' worth of training down the drain! It is also recognised that there is a skills gap – a 'life skills gap' – between ending your student days and starting your first job. Add to this that it is now believed to take around two years for a graduate to find their chosen career path, and the post-University gap comes into its own.

Employers are after *life skills* – initiative, communication skills and decision-making skills being the top three above education and background. Who cares about your degree? No-one! (Sorry guys...) Employers are more interested in what your values are, how you will behave in the office environment and whether you would be a credit to the company. The rest, such as your day-to-day work, etc., you will pick up and learn quickly if you have enough initiative and ability.

Post-University gappers now, on average, spend over a year overseas, many now taking the opportunity to spend over eighteen months away, living and working in another country (usually Australia). Does it put them behind their peers? On the contrary, it puts them ahead, more attractive to the employers, jam-packed with life skills learned while working in Sydney, living on the beach in Bondi, trekking mountains in Nepal, dealing with the poverty and destruction of AIDS in Uganda or swimming with dolphins on the reef off Belize.

If you are considering a post-University gap right now and are concerned that it is a bad move – don't be. Just as long as you don't waste your time away, you'll love it. I have not met one person who regretted it. So go!

Career gaps

As a growing phenomenon this is a subject not many people know a lot about. It is rising, of that there is no doubt, but it is very difficult to measure as people tend to leave the workplace quietly, head off and then slip back into it again.

Why do people take career gaps? All sorts of reasons: burn out, stress, the wrong job, lack of challenges, too little money, too much money (yup!), redundancy, the fear of commitment (to either the job, a partner, debt or all three!)...but usually, because despite being the most successful / least successful / most ordinary person in the office, there is something missing in their life. Life experience. Your photos of the pool in Tenerife pale into insignificance beside John from Accounts' postcards from Machu Picchu, the Sydney Opera House, the Great Wall of China...

You may have a BMW, a nice house, dinner parties every fortnight, a wardrobe full of expensive clothes and a full social life...but have you ever cacked yourself doing 120mph through the air in a sky-dive over New Zealand? Have you ever seen a bear in the wild or dived with a shark, trekked to ruins thousands of years old, been in temperatures of −30 or +40 degrees? Have you ever spent six months having time to do whatever you wanted, wherever you wanted and, even better, whenever you wanted! No? If you had a year to live...what would you do?

Career gaps? We all know why you take them, unfortunately most people are scared to admit that they have suddenly woken up ten years later, two stone heavier but one hundred times wealthier than they were at eighteen...which only seems like yesterday...and they haven't really lived (but other bastards who they know, and despise, have!).

Do it while you are thinking about it, as you might not get the chance again.

Ideas for your gap?

Travelling is, in itself, extremely rewarding and fulfilling in many thousands of ways. But you need to make sure you make the most of your gap, so here's a few ideas to get you thinking about maybe doing something a bit different.

Give me some ideas!

ski instructor	IT	creative/design
archaeology	accountancy	pharmaceutical
drama courses	nursing	journalism
chef's courses		

Working in :

orphanages	care homes	conservation
hostels	'kids' camps	industry
schools	leisure	medicine

Doing?

TEFL	caring for others	farming
languages	adventure stuff	overlanding
projects	media	ANYTHING!

Working on/in:

sheep farms	environmental projects	disaster relief projects
cattle ranches	game parks	development projects
coral reefs	rainforests	self-development

Anywhere in...

Australasia	Asia	The Arctic
South America	Europe	Far East
Africa	North America	ANYWHERE!

THE GAPYEAR...EXPLAINED

All the mad stuff!

bungee-jumping
rafting
sky-diving
rap-jumping

pot-holing
rock-climbing
rock-jumping!
hang-gliding

elephant-trekking
shark-wrestling
crocodile-racing
piranha-farming

Then, of course, there's the stuff we dream about:

swimming with dolphins
whale-watching
cage-diving to see sharks

seeing turtles hatch
sunrise at the Taj Mahal
safaris

deserts
rafting the Grand Canyon
gorillas in the mist

Have all you post-University and career gappers reading this ever thought of the phrase, **'Have a skill, donate it'?** There are projects all over the world crying out for people with skills to get involved and add value. Been working in the IT industry for five years and bored? Why not find a project in a developing country that would love to have you on board?

Ever heard of the phrase **'If you want to do something, do it'?** I met a barman in Sydney who used to earn a fortune with one of the top five law firms, but was loving taking time out earning sod all doing the job he had always wanted to do! So follow that dream, even if it isn't going to be a permanent feature in your life. Be an artist for a year, a gamekeeper for six months or take a month to learn to be a chef...

What is a gapyear?

...you tell me!

The next step?

Really work out what *your* gapyear is. Take a bit of time to see what is available and try to find something which is perfect for you. Why settle for second best on something that you will remember as one of the best times of your life?

Time to head to www.gapyear.com

We have created the site for you to look for ideas, meet other people in the same boat and get a bit of guidance on how to finally go about doing what you want to do properly.

People seem to like it, we enjoy doing it, so please come along and help yourself.

We have created this thing for you, so if you have any ideas how we could improve it or would like to write about your experiences to help others like you, then let us know – **info@gapyear.com**.

Anything is possible, so follow that dream

...before it is too late.

TOP FIFTY
BACKPACKING DESTINATIONS

All prices in *Living costs* are given as US dollars.

All dialling codes in the *Address book* assume that you are phoning from outside the country – except for *'embassies/consulates at home'* where local dialling codes are given.

Important note – whilst we make all efforts to ensure that the information enclosed is up-to-date, I would advise you to double-check important info before relying on it, eg. visas, hotel and embassy addresses, etc. as these often go out of date. This book should be used as a guide to get you started. All up-to-date info can be found on **gapyear.com**. If you find any incorrect information, please email me – **tom@gapyear.com**.

Canada ✈

(–3hrs 30mins in East; –8hrs GMT in West) **Capital:** Ottawa

☎ **Country: 1**, Ottawa: 613, Vancouver: 604 💲 Canadian dollar

At opposite ends of the country, the oh-so trendy cities of Montréal and Vancouver are both beautiful, friendly and great places to hang out. Montréal has a mix of French and English cultures. There are good clubs, food, accommodation (cheapest is west of downtown area) and shopping all set near the majestic Mont Royal. Vancouver has a Californian vibe, with lovely views of the ocean and around the bays. Check out the Gastown area, Stanley Park and Wreck beach for starters. When it comes to wilderness, Canada has it in bucketloads. Best of all you've got the Rockies (and just because you've seen them in the USA that's no excuse for ducking out). Head to Jasper National Park for the most rugged terrain and the cheapest prices. You can swim, raft, cave, climb or trek – basically anything that takes lots of energy. The bus network in Canada is excellent, and is a cheap but time-consuming way of seeing a lot of the country. The Canadian train (if you have to go by train) goes from Vancouver to Toronto. If you've got the cash, consider hiring a car, which is easily the best way to travel around this phenomenally huge country.

👁 Banff and Jasper National Parks, canoeing and skiing, Cape Breton Island with the Cabot trail through its national park, the Great Lakes, Halifax, Montréal, National Hockey League game, Niagara Falls, Nova Scotia, the Prairies, Prince Edward Island of *Anne of Green Gables* fame, Quebec City, the Rockies, Toronto, Vancouver, and Vancouver Island.

Weather:

The west coast has warm and dry summers, but foggy and damp winters. The Rockies are cooler with more rain. Inland areas are mainly dry. Eastern Canada is a lot wetter and colder throughout the year. Summer in the south is the warmest in the country, but it gets freezing in the winter. The best time to visit is from May to July.

Languages:

English, French and 53 indigenous languages.

Religion:

Roman Catholic, Anglican and United Church.

Money:

Canadian dollar = 100 cents
Cirrus: fair for ATMs (machines in major tourist areas).
Maestro: not accepted.
MasterCard: excellent for retail, fair for ATMs.
Traveller's cheques: Canadian dollars.
Visa: good for retail and excellent for ATMs.

Electricity:

110V, 60Hz. American-style flat 2-pin plugs.

Living costs:

It's slightly more costly than the USA but if you're careful, you should be able to eat and rest your head for about $30 per day. Food is fairly cheap; your main expense will be pricey accommodation.

Health:

No major health risks.

ADDRESS BOOK

Amex 220 Laurier Avenue West, Ottawa, Ontario K1P 5Z9. ☎ (613) 563 0213.

Canadian Tourism Commission 8th Floor West, 235 Queen Street, Ottawa, ON K1A 0H6. ☎ (613) 946 1000. Website: http://www.travelcanada.ca

STA 568 Dunsmuir Street, Vancouver V6B 1Y4. ☎ (604) 806 4040 or (888) 427 5639. Fax: (604) 806 4044. Email: yvr@statravel.com

Your embassy/consulate in Canada:

Australian: 602–999 Canada Place, Vancouver BC. ☎ (604) 684 1177. Fax: (604) 684 1856. Website: http://www.ahc-ottawa.org/

British: 80 Elgin Street, Ottawa, Ontario K1P 5K7. ☎ (613) 237 1530. Fax: (613) 232 2533. Website: http://www.britain-in-canada.org/

Irish: 130 Albert Street, Ottawa, Ontario K1P 5G4. ☎ (613) 233 6281. Fax: (613) 233 5835. Email: emb.ireland@sympatico.ca

NZ: Metropolitan House, Suite 727, 99 Bank Street, Ottawa, Ontario K1P 6G3. ☎ (613) 238 5991. Fax: (613) 238 5707. Website: http://www.nzhcottawa.org

South African: 15 Sussex Drive, Ottawa, Ontario KIM 1M8. ☎ (613) 744 0330. Fax: (613) 711 1639. Email: rsafrica@sympatico.ca Website: http://www.docuweb.ca/SouthAfrica/

US: 100 Wellington Street, Ottawa, Ontario K1P 5T1. ☎ (613) 238 4470. Website: http://www.usembassycanada.gov

Canadian embassies/consulates at home:

Australia: Level 5, Quay West, 111 Harrington Street, Sydney NSW 2000. ☎ (02) 364 3050. Fax: (02) 364 4099. Website: www.dfait-maeci.gc.ca/australia/

Ireland: 4th Floor, 65/68 Saint Stephen's Green, Dublin 2. ☎ (01) 478 1988. Fax: (01) 478 1285. Email: dublin@dfait-maeci.gc.ca

NZ: 3rd Floor, 61 Molesworth Street, Thorndon, Wellington. ☎ (04) 473 9577. Fax: (04) 471 2082. Email: wlgtn@dfait-maeci.gc.ca Website: www.dfait-maeci.gc.ca/newzealand

South Africa: 1103 Arcadia Street, Hatfield 0083, Pretoria. ☎ (012) 422 3000. Fax: (012) 422 3052. Website: www.canada.co.za

UK: 38 Grosvenor Square, London W1X 0AB. ☎ (020) 7258 6600. Fax: (020) 7258 6333 Email: ldn@dfait-maeci.gc.ca Website: www.canada.org.uk

US: 501 Pennsylvania Avenue, NW, Washington DC 20001. ☎ (202) 682 1740. Fax: (202) 682 7726. Website: http://www.cdnemb-washdc.org

Accommodation:

HI-Centre International de Séjour de Québec 19 rue Ste-Ursule, Québec, Québec G1R 4E1. ☎ (418) 694 0755 . Fax: (418) 694-2278. Email: reservation@cisq.org. Website: http://www.cisq.org

HI-Ottawa International Hostel 75 Nicholas Street, Ottawa, Ontario K1N 7B9. ☎ (613) 235 2595. Fax: (613) 569 2131. Email: info@hostellingintl.on.ca Website: www.hostellingintl.on.ca

Auberge de Montréal 1030 Mackay St, Montréal, Québec, Canada, H3G 2H1. ☎ (514) 843 3317. Fax: (514) 934 3251. Website: http://www.hostellingmontreal.com

Poste restante:

A 'hold mail' service (for a minimum of two weeks) can be arranged at any post office.

Visas:

US citizens require proof of citizenship. South Africans need a visa, usually issued for 3–6 months, free of charge. Visas aren't required for nationals of Australia, Ireland, New Zealand, UK and the US.

USA

(–5hrs in East; –8hrs GMT on Pacific coast) **Capital:** Washington DC

☎ **Country: 1**, New York: 212, LA: 310, San Francisco: 415 💲 US dollar

New York's conventional attractions shouldn't be missed, but the best thing about it is the life, speed, diversity, people, delis, bars, taxis, skyscrapers, Broadway, Chinatown, Tiffany's, SoHo and Greenwich Village... Then there's the Met, MOMA and the Guggenheim. Next! Way south, see where the rich and famous live at Palm Beach, and Florida's Everglades are rather nice. Miami's Ocean Drive and the surrounding beaches are good areas for taking in perpetual sun. New Orleans' Mardi Gras festivities are a tad crazy, but not to be missed. A Mississippi cruise and dancing in the street to jazz are mandatory. San Francisco is America's alternative city, home of flower power, the beat generation and gay life. Chinatown and Fisherman's Wharf are both colourful, lively and a bit tacky. Castro is the centre of the gay community. Los Angeles is epitomised by fame-hungry wannabes and you'll either love it or hate it. If you like stalking film stars and steeping yourself in celluloid history, then you're in the right place. If you like real people and real life, stay away. If you're tired of city life, there's the Appalachian Mountains in the east and the Rockies to the west. The Grand Canyon in Arizona is yet another star attraction. The national parks of Yosemite in California and Yellowstone in Wyoming are cool, too.

👁 Appalachian Mountains, Arizona, Boston, California, Florida, the Grand Canyon's South Rim, Great Lakes, Las Vegas casinos, Los Angeles, Miami's Ocean Drive, National Parks of Yosemite and Yellowstone, New England, New Mexico, New Orleans, New York City, Palm Beach mansions, the Rockies, San Francisco, Seattle, and Washington DC.

Weather:

A wide range of climates depending on region. The north east is generally temperate with rainfall to match, but can get pretty warm during the summer months (May to September). The south east, from Washington down to Florida, is a lot hotter, but has increased rainfall which comes in the summer. The Midwest has hot, dry summers and freezing winters. The south, around Texas, is beautifully warm and sunny most of the year The Rockies can get very hot and dry in the desert areas, which contrasts with the much colder temperatures during winter.

Languages:

English. Many minority languages, and Spanish is rapidly becoming a main second language.

Religion:

Protestant, Roman Catholic, Jewish and several minorities.

Money:

US dollar = 100 cents
Cirrus: excellent for ATMs.
Maestro: very limited for ATMs.
MasterCard: excellent for retail and ATMs.

Traveller's cheques: US dollars.
Visa: excellent for retail and ATMs.

Living costs:

In the States you can spend as much or as little as you like. Hostels start from about $15 per night and food is relatively cheap – you can survive on $7 a day for food.

Health:

High standard of health care.

Visas:

Visas aren't required for EU nationals on visits under ninety days. Nationals of non-EU countries should check with the embassy or consulate before travelling.

Electricity:

110V, 60Hz

ADDRESS BOOK

Amex 420 Lexington Avenue, New York 10170.
☎ (212) 664 7798.
STA 10 Downing Street (6th Avenue and Bleeker), New York 10014. ☎ (212) 627 3111.

Your embassy/consulate in the US:

Australian: 1601 Massachusetts Avenue, NW, Washington DC 20036. ☎ (202) 797 3000.
Fax: (202) 797 3168. Website: http://www.austemb.org/
British: 3100 Massachusetts Avenue, NW, Washington DC 20008. ☎ (202) 588 6500. Fax: (202) 588 7850.
Website: http://www.britainusa.com/bis/embassy.stm
Canadian: 501 Pennsylvania Avenue, NW, Washington DC 20001. ☎ (202) 682 1740. Fax: (202) 682 7726.
Website: http://www.cdnemb-washdc.org/
Irish: 2234 Massachusetts Avenue, NW, Washington DC 20008. ☎ (202) 462 3939. Fax: (202) 232 5993.
Website: http://www.irelandemb.org/
NZ: 37 Observatory Circle, NW, Washington DC 20008. ☎ (202) 328 4848. Fax: (202) 667 5227.
Website: http://www.nzemb.org/
South African: 3051 Massachusetts Avenue, NW, Washington DC 20008. ☎ (202) 232 4400.
Fax: (202) 265 1607. Website: http://www.southafrica.net/

US embassies/consulates at home:

Australia: Moonah Place Yarralumla ACT 2600.
☎ (06) 270 5970. Fax: (06) 270 5970.
Website: http://usembassy-australia.state.gov/embassy
Canada: 100 Wellington Street, Ottawa, Ontario K1P 5T1. ☎ (613) 238 4470.
Website: http://www.usembassycanada.gov/
Ireland: 42 Elgin Road, Dublin 4. ☎ (01) 668 8777.
Fax: (01) 668 9946. Website: http://www.usembassy.ie/

NZ: 29 Fitzherbert Terrace, Thorndon, Wellington.
☎ (04) 472 2068.
Website: http://usembassy.state.gov/wellington/
South Africa: 877 Pretorius Street, Pretoria 0001.
☎ (012) 342 1048. Fax: (012) 342 2244.
Website: http://usembassy.state.gov/pretoria/
UK: 24 Grosvenor Square, London W1A 1AE.
☎ (020) 7499 9000. Fax: (020) 7894 0699
Website: http://www.usembassy.org.uk

Accommodation:

Banana Bungalow Hollywood 5533 Hollywood Blvd, Los Angeles, CA 90028. ☎ (323) 464 1131.
Fax: (323) 462 8171.
Website: http://bananabungalow.com
Hosteling International 891 Amsterdam Avenue, New York City, NY 10024. ☎ (212) 932 2300.
Fax: (212) 932 2574. Website: http://www.hinewyork.org

Poste restante:

Los Angeles – Send letters to: General Delivery, [name], Los Angeles CA 90086/9999.
Collect letters from: 760 North Main Street, Downtown. ☎ (213) 617 4421.
New York – Send letters to: General Delivery, [name], General Post Office, 421 Eighth Avenue, New York 10001. **Collect letters from:** General Post Office, 421 Eighth Avenue, New York 10001. ☎ (212) 330 3099.
San Francisco – Send letters to: General Delivery, [name], San Francisco CA 94142.
Collect letters from: 101 Hyde Street, Civic Center, San Francisco CA 94142.

Belize ✈

(–6hrs GMT) **Capital:** Belmopan

☎ **Country: 501**, Belize City: 2 ⟨$⟩ Belizean dollar

Belize City is totally missable, but you'll probably need to go there as it's the hub of the country's two (yes, two!) paved roads. The cheapest places to stay are in the North Front Street area of the city. Battlefield Park is the best area for buying stuff. Anyway, you're here for the Caribbean sea and the world's second biggest barrier reef. Beaches, and small, beautiful islands are definitely Belize's strong point. Caye (island) Caulker is a paradise place where a lot of the travellers hang out. Placencia has the atmosphere of a chill-out room, with scenery and beaches straight from a postcard. You can get overnight camping trips to some of the tiny islands from here, and also take a trip into the jungle interior. Also worth checking out is Mountain Pine Ridge, 300 square miles of fantastic forestry reserve and the Bermudian Landing Community Baboon Sanctuary where you can see some of your close relatives. Aaah. Planes and boats are the most popular forms of travel as the country's infrastructure consists of those two roads. Boats are your best bet for getting to the islands – where you should be spending most of your time anyway.

👁 Bermudian Landing Community Baboon Sanctuary, Caracol Mayan site, Caye Caulker, Cockscomb Basin Jaguar Reserve, Diving, Lamanai, Mountain Pine Ridge, Placencia, reef trip, San Ignacio, windsurfing, and Xunantunich ruin.

Weather:

Hot and humid climate all year round. The monsoon season is from June to September. Hurricanes can affect the coastal areas.

Languages:

English. Spanish is spoken by about half the population; also Maya and Garífuna.

Religion:

Roman Catholic and Protestant.

Money:

Belizean dollar = 100 cents.
Cirrus: not accepted.
Maestro: not accepted.
MasterCard: not accepted.
Traveller's cheques: US dollars or sterling.
Visa: not accepted.

Living costs:

Belize is one of the more costly places in Central America, but that doesn't make it bank-breaking. Allow about $15 per day for your food and board.

Visas:

Passports should be valid for a minimum of six months from your date of arrival. Visas are usually required, so check requirements before you go.

Electricity:

110–120V, 60Hz

Health:

A yellow fever certificate is required if you're travelling from infected areas. Cholera, dengue fever, hepatitis, malaria (outside the urban areas), polio, rabies and typhoid.

ADDRESS BOOK

Amex Belize Global Travel Services, 41 Albert Street, Belize City. ☎ (2) 77185.

Belize Tourism Board New Central Bank Building, Level 2, Gabourel Lane, P.O Box 325, Belize City. ☎ (2) 31969. Fax: (2) 31943.
Email: info@travelbelize.org
Website: http://www.travelbelize.org/ or
http://www.belizetourism.org/

Your embassy/consulate in Belize:

Australian: Bishop's Court Hill, Saint Michael, Bridgetown, Barbados. ☎ (1 246) 435 2834.
Fax: (1 246) 435 2896.

British: PO Box 91, Belmopan.
☎ (8) 22146/7. Fax (8) 22761.
Email: brithicom@btl.net

Canadian: 85 North Front Street, Belize City.
☎ (2) 33722. Fax: (2) 30060.

NZ: contact the British embassy/consulate: PO Box 91, Belmopan. ☎ (8) 22146/7. Fax (8) 22761.

US: 29 Gabourel Lane, PO Box 286, Belize City.
☎ (2) 77161. Fax: (2) 30802.
Email: embbelize@state.gov
Website: http://www.usemb-belize.gov/

Belizean embassies/consulates at home:

Canada: 1080 Côte du Beaver Hall, Montréal, Québec H2Z 1S8. ☎ (514) 871 4741. Fax: (514) 397 0816.

UK: 22 Harcourt House, 19 Cavendish Square, London W1M 9AD. ☎ (020) 7499 9728.
Fax: (020) 7491 4139.

US: 2535 Massachusetts Avenue, NW, Washington DC 20008. ☎ (202) 332 9636. Fax: (202) 332 6888.

Accommodation:

Deb & Dave's Last Resort Toadal Adventure
Pt. Placencia, Belize, Central America.
☎ (6) 23207. Fax: (6) 23334.
Email: debanddave@btl.net
Website: http://www.toadaladventure.com/

The Trek Shop Tino Penados, Susa Inc, San Jose Succotz, Cayo District. ☎ (9) 32265.
Email: susa@btl.net

Poste restante:

General Post Office Belmopan.

Guatemala ✈

(–6hrs GMT) **Capital:** Guatemala City

☎ **Country: 502** 💲 Quetzal

Leave Guatemala City as soon as possible and head for Antigua, thirty miles west. The old capital has beautiful colonial buildings that have somehow survived the country's many earthquakes. Antigua attracts foreign students, who come to learn Spanish at one of its many language schools. Head off for a dip in Lake Atitlan, an incredibly beautiful and tranquil stretch of water with a backdrop of twin volcanoes (dormant, so you can climb them). Panajachel is the place to stay – don't be put off by its nickname of Gringotenango – it's THE spot to indulge in hardcore relaxation therapy, and a good base from which to visit some of the authentic village life around this area. Catch the Sunday morning market at one of the Indian villages, such as Huehuetenango. In the same vein is Livingston on the Caribbean coast, a jungle hang-out with a comatose atmosphere. If you want to see a bit of the indigenous culture, the ruins of Tikal are probably the most magnificent of all Mayan sites. Alternatively, Santa Lucia Cotzumalguapa on the Pacific coastal strip has sugar cane plantations scattered with Mayan stone carvings. The bus system in Guatemala is fast and cheap and most places are accessible.

👁 Antigua, Flores, Fuentes Georginas, hot baths at Almolonga, Huehuetenango and Momostenango, Lake Atitlan, Livingston, markets in Chichicastenango, Quezaltenango, San Francisco el Alto, Santiago Atitlan, Tikal, and Todos Santos.

Weather:
June to October is the rainy season. The central plateau regions are cooler and drier than the lowlands. Best time to go is November to April.

Languages:
Spanish, English, Garífuna and about twenty indigenous languages.

Religion:
Roman Catholic, Pentecostal and Mayan-Catholic.

Money:
Quetzal = 100 centavos.
Cirrus: not accepted.
Maestro: not accepted.
MasterCard: fair for retail, no ATMs available.
Traveller's cheques: US dollars.
Visa: limited for retail and ATMs.

Living costs:
Eat and sleep for about $20 per day. Travel is also pretty cheap.

CENTRAL AMERICA

Visas:

No visa is required for UK or Republic of Ireland nationals on visits of up to ninety days – a tourist card is issued on arrival. Other nationals have restricted entry, and requirements are subject to change – so check with the embassy before you arrive.

Electricity:

110V, 60Hz

Health:

A yellow fever vaccination certificate is required if you're travelling from infected areas. Chagas' disease, cholera, dengue fever, hepatitis A, malaria, polio, rabies and typhoid. Dysentery and diarrhoeal diseases are also common. Altitude sickness can occur in the higher regions.

ADDRESS BOOK

Amex Clark Tours, Centro Gerencial Las Margarita, Guatemala City 01010. ☎ 339 2888.

Guatemala Tourism Institute

7a, Avenida 1–17, Zona 4, Apartado Postal 1020-A. ☎ (02) 331 1333; (1 888) 464 8281 toll-free USA-only. Fax: (02) 331 4416. Email: inguat@guate.net Websites: http://www.guatemala.travel.com.gt

Your embassy/consulate in Guatemala:

Australian: represented by the Australian embassy/consulate in Mexico: Ruben Dario 55, Col. Polanco, Mexico DF 11560. ☎ (5) 395 9988. Fax: (5) 395 7870.

British: Edificio Centro Financiero, 7th Floor, Torre 2, 7a Avenida 5–10, Zona 4, Guatemala City. ☎ (02) 367 5425. Fax: 367 5430. Email: embassy@infovia.com.gt

Canadian: The Canadian Embassy, P. O. Box 400, Guatemala C.A, Guatemala City. ☎ 333 6102. Fax: 333 6161. Email: gtmla@dfait-maeci.gc.ca

Irish: contact the British embassy: Edificio Centro Financiero, 7th Floor, Torre 2, 7a Avenida 5–10, Zona 4, Guatemala City. ☎ (02) 367 5425. Fax: 367 5430. Email: embassy@infovia.com.gt

NZ: represented by the New Zealand embassy in Mexico: Embajada de Nueva Zelandia, Jose Luis Lagrange 103,10th Floor, Colonia Los Morales Polanco Mexico DF 11510. ☎ (5) 281 5486. Fax: (5) 281 5212.

US: Avenida Reforma 7–01, Zona 10, Guatemala City. ☎ 331 1541/55. Fax: 334 8477. Website: http://usembassy.state.gov/guatemala/

Guatemalan embassies/consulates at home:

Australia: contact the Mexican embassy/consulate: 14 Perth Avenue, Yarralumla ACT 2600. ☎ (02) 6273 3963/05. Fax: (02) 6273 1190.

Canada: Suite 1010, 120 Albert Street, Ottawa, Ontario K1P 5G4. ☎ (613) 233 7237/188. Fax: (613) 233 0135. Email: embguate@webruler.ca

Ireland: represented by the Guatemalan embassy/ consulate in the UK: 13 Fawcett Street, London SW10 9HN. ☎ (0171) 351 3042 or 349 0346. Fax: (0171) 376 5708. Email: 101740.3655@compuserve.com

NZ: contact the Mexican embassy/consulate: Level 8, GRE House, 111–115 Custom House Quay, Wellington. ☎ (04) 472 5555/6. Fax: (04) 472 5800.

South Africa: contact the Mexican embassy/consulate: Southern Life Plaza, 2 Schoeman and Festival Street, Hatfield, Pretoria. ☎ (012) 342 5190.

UK: 13 Fawcett Street, London SW10 9HN. ☎ (020) 7351 3042 or 349 0346. Fax: (020) 7376 5708. Email: 101740.3655@compuserve.com

US: 2220 R Street, NW, Washington DC 20008. ☎ (202) 745 4952. Fax: (202) 745 1908. Email: embaguat@sysnet.net

Accommodation:

Continental 12 Calle 6–10, Zona 1, Guatemala City. ☎ 230 5814.

Lessing House 12 Calle 4–35, Zona 1, Guatemala City. ☎ 251 3891.

Poste restante:

Central Post Office 7 Avenida, 12C, Zona 1, Guatemala City.

Mexico ✈

(–6 to –8hrs GMT) **Capital:** Mexico City

☎ **Country: 52**, Mexico City: **5**   💲 Mexican nuevo peso

When you're flying into Mexico City, the second largest city in the world, don't panic. It's noisy, dirty, fast and lively, but that's because there's nearly a hundred million people next to you. Head for the Zocalo or Alameda areas for a bit of peace and quiet, some cool cafés and shops, and the odd museum or two. The nightlife around the Zona Rosa area is frenetic and should keep you up into the early hours. Cheap rooms are found to the south of Zocalo. Outside the capital there are loads of fantastic beaches along the Pacific coast; try Puerto Vallanta and the Yucatan Peninsula for some of the best. Acapulco still has the same image as it used to. It's one of the most 'fun' places in the country. Head to Baja California for a bit of the old-wilderness trekking and some more beach activity if you still haven't had enough. Aztec-ruin-wise, you have the pick of the Yucatan sites. Wherever you go in Mexico, take the utmost care with yourself and your belongings. Buses are a better way to travel than train in Mexico, they're fast and usually air-conditioned – but the distances can be huge. Flying is pretty pricey.

👁 Chichen Itza with Kukulcan's Pyramid and the Temple of Warriors, Chihuahua al Pacifico Railway, Mexico City's urban sprawl, Oaxaca, Palenque, San Cristobel de las Casas, Sierra de la Leguna in Baja California, Taxco, Teotihuacan – the Aztec capital, Tula, Tulum and its sand-beach setting, Uxmal, and the Yucatan Peninsula.

Weather:
In the mountains and plateau regions it's cooler than the burning heat of the coastal lowland. The rainy season is from June to October. Mexico is generally hot and sunny throughout the year.

Languages:
Spanish and over fifty indigenous languages. English is also widely spoken.

Religion:
Predominantly Roman Catholic; a Protestant minority.

Money:
Mexican nuevo peso = 100 cents.
Cirrus: good for ATMs.
Maestro: limited for ATMs.
MasterCard: good for retail, excellent for ATMs.
Traveller's cheques: US dollars.
Visa: excellent for retail, good for ATMs.

Living costs:
The tourist areas, such as the cities and the coastal resorts, charge more – making your daily budget about $20 per day for board and food, with entrance fees

CENTRAL AMERICA

and travel on top. You'll find places off the beaten track are a lot less expensive.

Visas:

Passports should be valid for a minimum of six months from your date of arrival. Visas are usually required, so check requirements before you go. If you get it wrong you risk a heavy fine and deportation.

Electricity:

110V, 60Hz

ADDRESS BOOK

Amex Campos Eliseos 204, Local 5 Col Polanco, Mexico City. ☎ (5) 281 1111.

Acapulco Convention and Visitors Bureau / Oficina de Convenciones y Visitantes de Acapulco

Ave. Costera Miguel Aleman No.3111, Fracc. Costa Azul, Suites 204-205, Acapulco, GRO 39850 Mexico.

☎ (7) 484-8555 Fax: (7) 484-8134

Email: cvb@acapulco-cvb.org

Website: http://www.acapulco-cvb.org/

STA Mundo Joven Travel Shop, Av Insurgentes Sur 1510, Local DCP 03920, Mexico City DF.

☎ (5) 661 3233/662 1488. Fax: (5) 663 1556.

Your embassy/consulate in Mexico:

Australian: Ruben Dario 55, Col. Polanco, Mexico DF 11560. ☎ (5) 395 9988. Fax: (5) 395 7870.

British: Lerma 71, Col Cuauhtemoc, Mexico City 06500. ☎ (5) 207 2089/2149. Fax: (5) 207 7672/2530.

Email: buzon1@mail.embajadabritanica.com.mx

Website: http://www.embajadabritanica.com.mx/

Canadian: Apartado Postal 105–05, Mexico City, 11560. ☎ (5) 724 7900. Fax: (5) 724 7980.

Email: embassy@canada.org.mx

Website: http://www.canada.org.mx/

Irish: Cda. Boulevard Avila Camacho 76-3, Col. Lomas de Chapultepec, C.P. 11000. ☎ (5) 520 5803.

Fax: (5) 520 5892. Email: embajada@irlands.org.mx

NZ: Embajada de Nueva Zelandia, Jose Luis Lagrange 103,10th Floor, Colonia Los Morales Polanco Mexico DF 11510. ☎ (5) 281 5486. Fax: (5) 281 5212.

Email: kiwimexico@compuserve.com.mx

US: Paseo de la Reforma 305, Colonia Cuauhtemoc, Mexico City 06500. ☎ (5) 09 9100. Fax: (5) 511-9980.

Website: http://www.usembassy-mexico.gov/

Health:

A yellow fever certificate is required if you're travelling from infected areas. Cholera (a major risk), dengue fever, hepatitis, malaria (in rural areas), polio, rabies, tetanus and typhoid.

Air pollution in Mexico City is extremely high between December and May.

Mexican embassies/consulates at home:

Australia: 14 Perth Avenue, Yarralumla ACT 2600. ☎ (02) 6273 3963/05. Fax: (02) 6273 1190.

Canada: 45 O'Connor Street, 1500 Ottawa, Ontario K1P 1A4. ☎ (613) 233 8988. Fax: (613) 235 9123.

Ireland: 42 Ailesbury Road, Dublin 4. ☎ (01) 260 0699.

NZ: Level 8, GRE House, 111–115 Custom House Quay, Wellington. ☎ (04) 472 5555/6.

Fax: (04) 472 5800.

South Africa: Southern Life Plaza, 2 Schoeman and Festival Street, Hatfield, Pretoria. ☎ (012) 342 5190.

UK: 42 Hertford Street, London W1Y 7TF.

☎ (020) 7499 8586.

US: 1911 Pennsylvania Avenue, NW, Washington DC 20006. ☎ (202) 728 1600.

Website: http://www.embassyofmexico.org/

Accommodation:

Mexico Hostels Andador Palmeras, Ave., Uxmal Supermanzana 23, Manzana 8, No. 30, Cancun.

☎ 699 3825. Fax: 962 8028.

Email: info@mexicohostels.com

Website: http://www.mexicohostels.com

Hostel Home: Tabasco #303, Colonia Roma, Mexico City. ☎ 55 11 16 83. Fax: 55 11 16 83

Email: wmaster@hostelhome.com.mx

Fuerte Bambu Kilometro 6, Carretera Tialtizapan, Morelos. ☎: (73) 12 44 12. Fax: (73) 12 76 10

Email: hostellingmexico@remaj.com

Poste restante:

Send letters to: Lista de Correos [in any town].

Mexico – Collect letters from: Window 6, Main Floor of Central Office, Mexico City.

Argentina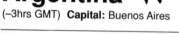

(−3hrs GMT) **Capital:** Buenos Aires

☎ **Country: 54**, Buenos Aires: 1 💲 Argentinian peso

If you know your tango from your cha-cha-cha, then you're ready for Argentina. Buenos Aires (BA) is a cool city with trendy places for posing and some cheap places to sleep. Congresso is the cheapest region to stay in, while the areas around La Boca, San Telmo and Lavalle are best for bargain eats. If you need an essential tan top-up, the beach at Mar del Plata is a mere 200 miles away (which is relatively near, in the eighth largest country on the planet). The area north of the capital, towards Santa Fe has great national parks, especially the huge Lihue Calel. Further west you'll stumble across the mighty Andes, where you can trek, ski and climb to your heart's content. The provinces of Mendoza and Salta are both good for hill-based antics, such as climbing and mountain biking, while in Patagonia, there are national parks galore (try the Parque Nacional Los Glaciares in the Santa Cruz province), and all are definitely worth exploring for some of the best natural scenery and wildlife in the world. Argentina is BIG...so travel is both time-consuming and, unfortunately, pretty expensive by either rail or road.

👁 The beach at Mar del Plata, Buenos Aires nightlife, Iguazu Falls, Moreno Glacier in the Parque Nacional Los Glaciares, the Pampas, skiing in the Cordoba highlands, and Torres del Paine.

Weather:
Northern Argentina is hot and humid during the summer months (from November to March). Central and eastern areas are warm and rainy in the summer and milder in the winter. The south and west are generally sunny and dry.

Languages:
Spanish, with a number of indigenous dialects.

Religion:
Predominantly Roman Catholic; Protestant and Jewish minorities.

Money:
Argentine peso = 100 centavos.
Cirrus: limited for ATMs.
Maestro: very limited for ATMs.
MasterCard: good for retail, limited for ATMs.
Traveller's cheques: US dollars (larger towns only).
Visa: fair for retail, limited for ATMs.

Living costs:
Prices vary between rural areas and cities. It can be expensive, especially by South American standards, so allow up to $30 per day for food, travel and board.

Visas:

Tourists don't need visas for stays of up to three months – it's possible to extend visas for a further three months. All visitors must demonstrate that they have sufficient funds for their stay.

Electricity:

220V, 50Hz. Older buildings use two-pin round plugs, but newer buildings usually have the three-pin flat type.

Health:

Cholera, gastroenteritis, hepatitis A and B, intestinal parasitosis, malaria (rural and lowland areas), polio, rabies, typhoid and yellow fever.

ADDRESS BOOK

Amex Plaza San Martin Arenales 707, 1061 Buenos Aires. ☎ (1) 312 9472.

Asociación Argentina de Agencias de Viajes y Turismo Viamonte 640, Piso 10, 1053 Buenos Aires. ☎ (1) 322 2804. Fax (1) 322 9641. Email: aaavet@tournet.com.ar

Secretaría de Turismo de la Nación Calle Suipacha 1111, Piso 21, 1368 Buenos Aires. ☎ (1) 312 5621. Fax: (1) 313 6834.

STA Travel Asatej, Florida 835, Piso 3. Off 320, 1005 Buenos Aires. ☎ 313 5208. Fax: (1) 311 6840.

Your embassy/consulate in Argentina:

Australian: Villanueva 1400, 1426 Buenos Aires. ☎ (1) 777 6580/5. Fax (1) 772 3349. Email: carolina.patron.costas@dfat.gov.au Website: http://www.australia.org.ar

British: Luis Agote 2412/52, 1425 Buenos Aires. ☎ (1) 4803 2222. Fax: (1) 4803 1731.

Canadian: Tagle 2828, 1425 Buenos Aires. ☎ (1) 4805 3032. Fax: (1) 4806 1209. Website: http://www.dfait-maeci.gc.ca/bairs/ Email: bairs@dfait-maeci.gc.ca Website: http://www.dfait-maeci.gc.ca/bairs/

Irish: Suipacha 1380, 2nd Floor, 1011 Buenos Aires. ☎ (1) 325 8588. Fax: (1) 325 7572.

NZ: Echeverria, 2140 Buenos Aires. ☎ (1) 787 0593. Fax: (1) 787 0593.

South African: MT de Alvear 590, Piso 8, Buenos Aires. ☎ (1) 317 2900. Fax: (1) 317 2951. Email: saemba@sicoar.com Website: http://www.sicoar.com/saemba/

US: Colombia 4300, 1425 Buenos Aires. ☎ (1) 4777 4533. Fax: (1) 4511 4997. Website: http://usembassy.state.gov/posts/ar1/wwwh0100.html

Argentine embassies/consulates at home:

Australia: Level 1, Suite 102, MLC Tower, Woden ACT 2606. ☎ (02) 6282 4855. Fax: (02) 6285 3062. Website: http://www.consarsydney.org.au/

Canada: Suite 5840, 1 First Canadian Place, Toronto, Ontario M5X 1K2. ☎ (416) 955 9075. Fax: (416) 955 0868. Website: http://www.consargtoro.org

NZ: PO Box 5430, Lambton Quay, Wellington. ☎ (04) 499 1802. Fax (04) 499 3644.

Ireland: represented by the Argentine embassy/consulate in the UK: 65 Brooke Street, London W1Y 1YE. ☎ (0171) 318 1300. Fax: (0171) 318 1301.

South Africa: Jan Smuts Building, 158 Jan Smuts Avenue, Johannesburg. ☎ (011) 442 4428.

UK: 65 Brooke Street, London W1Y 1YE. ☎ (020) 7318 1300. Fax: (020) 7318 1301. Website: http://easyweb.easynet.co.uk/~argentineembassy2/homepage/

US: 1600 New Hampshire Avenue, NW, Washington DC 20009. ☎ (202) 939 6400–3. Fax: (202) 332 3171. Website: http://emb-eeuu.mrecic.gov.ar/

Accommodation:

Buenos Aires Hostel Calle Brasil 675, Buenos Aires. ☎ (1) 362 9133.

Isla Martin Garcia Hostel Almirante Brown 85, Isla Martin Garcia, Provincia de Buenos Aires. ☎ (315) 24546.

National Hotel Association Tucuman 1610, 1050 Buenos Aires. ☎ (1) 372 7275. Fax: (1) 371 5108.

Poste restante:

Send letters to: c/o Correo Argentinos, Sarmiento y L. N. Alem, Buenos Aires. **Collect letters from:** 1st Floor, Correo Argentinos, Sarmiento y L. N. Alem, Buenos Aires.

Brazil ✈

(–3hrs in East; –5hrs GMT in far west) **Capital:** Brasília

☎ **Country: 55**, Brasília: 61, Rio de Janeiro: 21, São Paulo: 11 💲 Real

Braaazil!!! Party time! Head to Rio de Janeiro for the best of the action. You've seen it on TV, so get down to the beach and do your thang…as long as you're built like a god (or goddess). The most popular beach is Copacobana, but Ipenema beach is far more hip. In the middle of the city is the huge Corcovado Peak, topped with a towering statue of Jesus – and a fab view. The cheap areas to eat and sleep are Gloria, Calete and Flamengo, but take care of yourself and your belongings.

And then there's the Amazon – unfortunately a bit of a tourist trap these days. Manaus is the place to head for, to catch a boat trip. More advisable is a trip to the Pantanal, a huge area of wetlands with loads of wildlife to photograph.

The main hang-out for hippy types is Jericoacoara, just up the coast from Fortaleza. Cool. Brazil is huge, so if you want to get around quickly it means flying, but if you're hard up, the buses are cheap, in good condition and go to all the major cities. The trains are few and far between and infrequent but if you've got the time, a lovely way to travel.

👁 Beaches at Salvador da Bahia, the Corcovado and Sugar Loaf mountains, Mardi Gras Carnival, Iguacu Falls, Olinda, Pantanal, Parque Nacional da Serra da Chapada dos Veadeiros, Rio's beaches, and the Teatro Amazonas at Manaus.

Weather:

The Amazon Basin has an equatorial climate with high temperatures and rain spread throughout the year. The rest of Brazil (the plateau area) has more varied temperatures, with rain mainly from October to April. The north-east is the driest, and the south has hot summers and cold winters.

Languages:

Portuguese. French, German, Italian and English are also spoken in the most visited areas.

Religion:

Roman Catholic.

Money:

Real = 100 centavos.

Cirrus: not accepted.

Maestro: not accepted.

MasterCard: good for retail, no ATMs available.

Traveller's cheques: US dollars.

Visa: fair for retail and ATMs.

Living costs:

If you avoid the deluxe hotels in the south, you can survive on about $20 a day for food, bed and travel – but that's the cheapest it'll get.

Visas:

Visa required for Australians, New Zealanders and North Americans. British and Irish tourists do not require visas for visits under ninety days. No visa is required for South Africans.

Electricity:

220V, 60Hz (Brasília); 100V, 60Hz (Rio and São Paulo). two-pin plugs.

Health:

A yellow fever certificate is required if you're travelling from infected areas. Bilharzia, chagas' disease, dengue fever, malaria (some rural areas), meningitis, rabies and yellow fever.

ADDRESS BOOK

Amex Buriti Turismo Ltda, Cls 402 Bloco A Lojas 27/33, CEP 70236–510 Brasília. ☎ (61) 225 2686.
Brazilian Tourist Office SCN/ EMBRATUR Office (Rio de Janeiro) Rua Uruguaiana, 174, 8º Andar – Centro, Rio de Janeiro/RJ, CEP: 20050-092.
☎ (21) 509 6017 tourist information/ 509 6720 administration. Fax: (21) 509 7381.
Website: http://www.embratur.gov.br/

Your embassy/consulate in Brazil:
Australian: Shis QI09 Conjunto 16, Casa 01 CEP 70469–900, Brasília. ☎ (61) 248 5569.
Fax: (61) 248 1066.
British: Setor de Embaixadas Sul, Quadra 801, Conjunto K, CEP 70.408–900, Brasília.
☎ (61) 225 2710. Fax: (61) 225 1777.
Email: britemb@nutecnet.com
Website: http://www.reinounido.org.br
Canadian: Ses, Avenida das Nações, Quadra 803, Lote 16, 70410–900 Brasília DF.
☎ (61) 321 2171. Fax: (61) 321 4529.
Email: brsla@dfait-maeci.gc.ca
Website: http://www.dfait-maeci.gc.ca/brazil/brasilia/bsa-menu-e.html
Irish: Av Paulista 2006-5, São Paulo 01310, Brasília.
☎ (11) 287 6362. Fax: (11) 842 0587.
NZ: Al. Campinas 579, 15th floor, Cerqueira Cesar. 01404-000, São Paulo. ☎ (11) 288 0307.
Fax: (11) 288 0560.
South African: Ses Avenida das Nações, Quadra 801, Lote 6, CEP 70406–900 Brasília DF. ☎ (61) 312 9500.
Fax: (61) 322 8491. Email: saemb@tba.com.br
Website: http://www.africadosul-consp.org.br/

US: Unit 3500, Avenida das Nações, CEP 70403–900 Brasília DF. ☎ (61) 321 7272. Fax: (61) 225 9136.
Website: http://www.embaixada-americana.org.br/

Brazilian embassies/consulates at home:
Australia: 19 Forster Crescent, Yarralumla ACT 2600.
☎ (02) 273 2372/3/4. Fax: (02) 273 2375.
Canada: 450 Wilbrod Street Ottawa, Ontario K1N 6M8. ☎ (613) 237 1090. Fax: (613) 237 6144.
Ireland: contact the Argentine embassy/consulate in the UK: 32 Green Street, London W1Y 4AT.
☎ (0171) 499 0877. Fax: (0171) 839 8958.
NZ: 2 Lammermoor Drive, Saint Heliers, Auckland 5.
☎ (09) 528 9783. Fax: (09) 521 2227.
South Africa: 201 Leyds Street, Arcadia, Pretoria.
☎ (012) 341 1720. Fax: (012) 253670.
UK: 32 Green Street, London W1Y 4AT.
☎ (020) 7499 0877. Fax: (020) 7839 8958.
US: 3006 Massachusetts Avenue, NW, Washington DC 20008. ☎ (202) 238 2700. Fax: (202) 238 2827.
Website: http://www.brasil.emb.nw.dc.us/

Accommodation:
AJ Arraial do Cabo Rua Joaquim Nabuco 23, Arraial do Cabo, Rio de Janeiro 20910–000.
☎ (21) 224 4904. Fax: (21) 252 2383.
Youth Hostel Pousada Albergue Avenida 7 de Setembro, 1783 Alcobaca Beach, Bahia 2932101.
☎ (55) 293 2077.

Poste restante:
Send letters to: [name], Posta Restante, Rua Primeiro de Março, Rio de Janeiro.

Chile ✈

(−4hrs GMT) **Capital:** Santiago

☎ **Country: 56**, Santiago: 2 💲 Chilean peso

The capital, Santiago, is a mega metropolis that's surprisingly beautiful, with lots of parks, plazas and boulevards to show off. The whole city is watched over by a gigantic statue of the Virgin Mary sitting on top of the peak of Cerro San Cristobal. If you're on a budget, you'll probably be staying in the Terminal de Buses Norte area, not exactly renowned for elegance. Nicer is Valparaíso, which also has the excellent beaches of Viña del Mar close by. However, the reason you came to Chile is because the scenery is so amazing that you'll be blown away. The mighty Andes run the whole length of the country with a narrow coastal strip squeezed in beside the Pacific. It has a huge number of National Parks on offer, depending on whether you like it hot (north) or freezing (south). In the north, Parque Nacional Lauca will give you some of the most wonderful flora and fauna to be found, plus massive lakes and volcanoes (which, hopefully, are pretty inert). To the south, try Parque Nacional Torres del Paine. Filled with glaciers, waterfalls and forests, who could ask for more, except maybe another sweater? The bus service in Chile is superb and internal flights are low-cost. If you get a travel pass, you could find it a bit of a bargain.

👁 Atacama Desert, Chuquicamata copper mine, Easter Island, Elqui Valley wine-growing area, glaciers and fjords, horseriding, Lake District, Lake Titicaca, San Rafael Glacier and Torres del Paine.

Weather:

In the Andes, it's cold and dry in the north, and cold and wet in the south. The north coast is dry, hot and cloudy; central areas are hot and sunny during summer (from November to March); and the south is the wettest region. It *never* rains in the Atacama Desert!

Languages:

Spanish and indigenous languages – including Aymara, Mapuche and Rapa Nui. English is often spoken.

Religion:

Roman Catholic; a Protestant minority.

Money:

Chilean peso = 100 centavos.
Cirrus: good for ATMs.
Maestro: not accepted.
MasterCard: fair for retail, good for ATMs.
Traveller's cheques: US dollars (these need to be exchanged before midday).
Visa: fair for retail, good for ATMs.

SOUTH AMERICA

Living costs:

Not as inexpensive as it used to be, but still cheaper than Argentina, Europe and the USA. You can survive on about $20 per day for food and board.

Visas:

Passports must be valid for six months after the end of your trip. There's a ninety-day entry permit (rather than a visa), which is renewable for a further ninety days. US nationals must pay $20 for the permit.

Electricity:

220V, 50Hz. three-pin plugs.

Health:

Chagas' disease, cholera, hepatitis A, meningococcal meningitis, polio, rabies, tetanus and typhoid.
Heavy air pollution in Santiago.

ADDRESS BOOK

Amex Turismo Cocha, Avenida El Bosque Norte 0430, Santiago. ☎ (2) 230 1000.
Chile National Tourism Board of Chile SERNATUR
Providencia 1550, P.O. Box 14082, Santiago, Chile.
☎ (2) 696 7141. Fax: (2) 696 0981.
Email: info@sernatur.cl.
Website: http://www.sernatur.cl/

Your embassy/consulate in Chile:

Australian: 420 Gertrudis Echenique Las Condes, Correo 10, Las Condes, Santiago. ☎ (2) 208 1707.
Fax: (2) 228 5065. Email: austemb@entelchile.net
British: Avenida El Bosque Norte 0125, Casilla 72–D, Santiago 9. ☎ (2) 70 4100. Fax: (2) 335 5988.
Email: embsan@britemb.cl
Canadian: Edificio World Trade Centre, 12th Floor, Torre Norte, Nueva Tajamar 481, Santiago.
☎ (2) 362 9660. Fax: (2) 362 9663.
Website: http://www.dfait-maeci.gc.ca/santiago/
Irish: Isidora Goyenechea 3162 Piso 8, Oficina 801, Las Condes, Santiago. ☎ (2) 245 6616.
Fax: (2) 245 6636. Email: aylwin@netline.cl
NZ: El Golf 99, Oficina 703, (Casilla 112, Correo), Las Condes, Santiago. ☎ (2) 290 9802. Fax: (2) 207 2333.
Email: nzembassychile@adsl.tie.cl
South African: Avenida 11 de Septienbre 2353, Piso 16, Providencia, Santiago. ☎ (2) 231 2862.
Website: http://www.embajada-sudafrica.cl/
US: Avenida Andrés Bello 2800, Santiago.
☎ (2) 232 2600. Fax: (2) 330 3710.
Website: http://www.usembassy.cl/contents-en.htm

Chilean embassies/consulates at home:

Australia: 10 Culgoa Circuit, O'Malley, Canberra, 2606 ACT. ☎ (02) 6286 2430.
Email: echileau@dynamite.com.au
Website: http://www.netinfo.com.au/chile/
Canada: Suite 710, 1010 Sherbrooke Street West, Montréal, Québec H3A 2R7. ☎ (514) 499 0405.
Fax: (514) 499 8914. Email: cgmontca@total.net
Ireland: represented by the Chilean embassy in the UK: 12 Devonshire Street, London W1N 2DS.
☎ (0171) 580 6392. Fax: (0171) 436 5204.
NZ: 1–3 Willeston Street, 7th Floor, Willis Corroon House, Wellington. ☎ (04) 471 6270.
Fax: (04) 472 5324.
UK: 12 Devonshire Street, London W1N 2DS.
☎ (020) 7580 6392. Fax: (020) 7436 5204.
US: 1732 Massachusetts Avenue, NW, Washington DC 20036. ☎ (202) 785 1746. Fax: (202) 887 5579.

Accommodation:

Hi–Santiago Cienfuegos 151, Santiago. ☎ (2) 671 8532.
Fax: (2) 672 8880. Email: histgoch@entelchile.net
HI–Antofagasta Arturo Prat 749, Antofagasta.
☎ (55) 225 162.
Residencial Urmeneta Urmeneta 290, Puerto Montt.
☎ (65) 253262.

Poste restante:

Send letters to: [name], Post Office, Plaza de Armas, Santiago.
Collect letters from: Hall of Central Post Office, Plaza de Armas, Santiago.

Peru ✈

(−6hrs GMT) **Capital:** Lima

☎ **Country: 51**, Lima: 1   💲 Nuevo sol

Peru has some of the finest natural scenery in South America, plus some fantastic ruins. In Lima, stick to the centre of town for the cheapest rooms. Markets are superbly hectic, Polvos Azules is one of the best. The area around Mira Flores is for shopping, feeding and boogie-ing. Heading down the coast, you'll come to Pisco, a haven for travellers taking in the wildlife of the Islas Ballestas. Stepping back into a previous world can be done at a number of groovy locations. Heading for the Andes, be sure to relax a while on Lake Titicaca's calm waters and acclimatise to the altitude before hitting Cuzco, the centre of the Inca Empire. Cuzco has ruins a-plenty: Coricancha, Sacsayhuaman, Qenko and Puca Pucara are some of the hardest to pronounce! Nearby is Machu Picchu, the lost city of the Incas. Forget the tourist coach, put on those boots and walk the 20-mile Inca Trail to this awesome sight. Then return to Cuzco by train. Wildlife-wise, head for Iquitos for a delve into the Amazonian jungle basin. The buses are a good bet for long distances, and internal flights aren't that expensive.

👁 Aguas Calientes, Arequipa, Colca Canyon, Cuzco, Iquitos, Inca Trail, Islas Ballestas, Lake Titicaca, Machu Picchu, Nazca, Pisco, Puno, Sacsayhuaman ruins and Taquile Island.

Weather:

The coast is hot and dry all year, with low cloud and fog. The mountains have variable daily temperature ranges, and a rainy season from October to April. The Amazonian basin has a tropical climate and year-round rains.

Languages:

Spanish, Quechua and Aymará. English is spoken in most major tourist areas.

Religion:

Predominantly Roman Catholic.

Money:

Nuevo sol = 100 centimos.

Cirrus: not accepted.

Maestro: not accepted.

MasterCard: limited for retail, no ATMs available.

Traveller's cheques: US dollars (exchanged in Lima).

Visa: no retail availability, limited for ATMs.

SOUTH AMERICA

Living costs:
Tourist areas and cities are more expensive than rural areas. In Lima, it's about $20 per day for food and board. It's slightly more costly than neighbouring countries.

Visas:
Visas are not required for visits up to ninety days.

Electricity:
220V, 60Hz

Health:
A yellow fever certificate is required if you're travelling from infected areas. Cholera, hepatitis, malaria (in rural low-land areas), rabies, tuberculosis and typhoid. The yellow fever vaccination is essential if you plan to visit the eastern slopes of the Andes or the Amazonian Basin.

ADDRESS BOOK
Amex Lima Tours SA, Belen 1040, Lima 1.
☎ (1) 424 5110.
Promperu – Commission for the Promotion of Peru
Edificio MITINCI piso 13, Calle Uno oeste No. 50, Urb. Córpac – Lima 27. ☎ (1) 224 3279/3271/3395/3118. Fax: (1) 224-3323. Email: infoperu@promperu.gob.pe Website: http://www.peru.org.pe/
STA Intej, Avenida San Martin 240, Lima 4.
☎ (1) 477 4105/8264. Fax: (1) 448 1394.
Thomas Cook Viajes Laser SA, Avenida Benavides 1180 Miraflores, Lima 18. ☎ (1) 241 5567.

Your embassy/consulate in Peru:
Australian: Avenida Victor Andres Belaúnde 147, Via Principal 155, Edificio Real 3, Office 1301, San Isidro, Lima. ☎ (1) 222 8281. Fax: (1) 221 4996.
Email: richard.pillow@austrade.gov.au
British: Edificio El Pacifico Washington, Natalio Sanchez 125, Piso 12, Lima 100.
☎ (1) 433 4738. Fax: (1) 433 4735.
Email: britemb@terra.com.pe
Canada Calle Libertad 130, Miraflores, Lima.
☎ (1) 444 4015. Fax: (1) 444 4050.
Email: lima@dfait-maeci.gc.ca
Irish: Av. Angamos Oeste 340, Miraflores, Lima 18.
☎ (1) 446 3878. Fax: (1) 445 7673.
Email: mgrperu@terra.com.pe
NZ: Camino Real 390, Torre Central, Lima 27.
☎ (1) 442 1757. Fax: (1) 442 8671.
Email: 2012527@pol.com.pe
US: PO Box 1995, Avenida La Encalada cuadra 17, Lima 33. ☎ (1) 434 3000. Fax: (1) 434 3037.
Website: http://usembassy.state.gov/lima/

Peruvian embassies/consulates at home:
Australia: 43 Culgoa Circuit, O'Malley ACT 2606.
☎ (02) 6290 0922. Fax: (02) 6290 0924.
Canada: 130 Albert Street, Suite 1901 Ottawa, Ontario K1P 5G4. ☎ (613) 238 1777. Fax: (613) 232 3062.
Ireland: represented by the Peruvian embassy/consulate in the UK: 52 Sloane Street, London SW1X 9SP. ☎ (0171) 235 1917. Fax: (0171) 235 4463.
NZ: Level 8, Cigna House, 40 Mercer Street, Wellington. ☎ (04) 499 8087. Fax: (04) 499 8057.
South Africa: 202 Infotec Building, 1090 Arcadia Street, Hatfield, Pretoria. ☎ (012) 342 2390.
Fax: (012) 215944.
UK: 52 Sloane Street, London SW1X 9SP.
☎ (020) 7235 1917. Fax: (020) 7235 4463.
US: 1700 Massachusetts Avenue, NW, Washington DC 20036. ☎ (202) 833 9860. Fax: (202) 659 8124.
Email: lepruwash@aol.com

Accommodation:
HI–A.Turistico Juvenil Internacional Av. Casimiro Ulloa, 328 San Antonio Miraflores – Lima 18.
☎ (1) 446 5488. Fax: (1) 444 8187.
Email: hostell@terra.com.pe
HI–Nueva Espana Calle Antiquilla 106 Yanahuara Arequipa. ☎ (54) 252 941
Email: nueva_espagnaa@hotmail.com
HI Muyuna Amazon Lodge and Expeditions
Putumayo 163 - B, Iquitos - Loreto. ☎ (94) 242 858.
Fax: (1) 446 97834.
Email: muyuna@wayna.rcp.net.pe

Poste restante:
Central Post Office Pasaje Piura, near the Plaza de Armas, T 427–5592, Lima.

Venezuela ✈

(–4hrs GMT) **Capital:** Caracas

☎ **Country: 58**, Caracas: 2 💲 Bolivar

This is the place to come for diverse and stunning scenery. From mountains to beaches, it's pretty well all here. Caracas doesn't have much of its colonial roots left showing, but has transformed itself into an excellent modern capital. Night creatures should head to Las Mercedes, El Rosal or the La Floresta areas of the city. Must-sees in Venezuela are everywhere. The town of Canaima near Rio Carrao has some incredible waterfalls surrounding it, and nearby is the highest in the world, Angel Falls. You can get deep into the Amazon jungle on a river trip up the Orinoco – head to the town of Ayacucho to catch the boat. Western Venezuela has the Andes, for those inclined to trek. The town of Merida is a good base for some breathtakingly scenic trips up into the heights of Pico Bolivar on the world's longest, highest cable car. But if you just want to lie back and soak in the sun, Venezuela has about 1,600 miles of Caribbean coast for you to choose from: white sand, clear water and palm trees. Nice. Buses are definitely your best bet for travelling around, they're cheap and comfy and in plentiful supply.

👁 The Amazon, Angel Falls, Canaima, Caracas, Lake Maracaibo, Margarita Island, Morrocoy National Park, Orinoco River, Peninsula de Parguana, and Sierra Nevada de Merida in the Andes.

Weather:
The rainy season runs from May to December. The coast is hot, the Andes and the north coast are the driest areas, and the best time to go is between January and April.

Languages:
Spanish with over thirty indigenous Amerindian dialects. Also English, German, French and Portuguese.

Religion:
Roman Catholic; a tiny Protestant minority.

Money:
Bolivar = 100 centimos.
Cirrus: good for ATMs.
Maestro: limited for ATMs.
MasterCard: good for retail, fair for ATMs.
Traveller's cheques: US dollars.
Visa: fair for retail, good for ATMs.

Living costs:
Very cheap. You can spend only $10–15 dollars per day for food and a bed. Travel is a bargain too.

Visas:

Passports should be valid for at least six months. Visas aren't required for EU nationals – you receive a ninety-day tourist entry card issued by the air carrier when you show your tickets.

Electricity:

110V, 60Hz. American two-pin plugs.

Health:

A yellow fever certificate is not required, but a vaccination is recommended if you plan to travel outside urban areas. Cholera, dengue fever, hepatitis, malaria, polio and typhoid.

ADDRESS BOOK

Amex Turismo Consolidado Turisol CA, Avenida La Estancia, Centre Commercial Ccct, Nivel C–2, Cahuao, Caracas. ☎ (2) 959 1011.

Venezuelan Tourism Association Box 3010, Sausalito, CA 94966. ☎ (5) 331 0100. Email: vtajb@hotmail.com

STA IVI Tours Final Av. Ppal de Las Mercedes, Res. La Hacienda, Local 1-4-t PB, Caracas 1080. ☎ (2) 993 3930. Fax: (2) 992 9626.

Your embassy/consulate in Venezuela:

Australian: Quinta Yolanda, Avenida Luis Roche, Between the 6th and 7th transversals Altamira Apartado, Caracas. ☎ (2) 263 4033. Fax: (2) 261 3448.

British: Edificio Torre Las Mercedes, Piso 3, Avenida La Estancia Chuao, Caracas 1061.
☎ (2) 993 4111. Fax: (2) 993 9989.

Canadian: Aedificio Omni, 6 a Avda., entre 3a. y 5a. Transversal de Altamira, Caracas. ☎ (2) 264 0833. Fax: (2) 261 8741. Email: crcas@dfait-maeci.gc.ca Website: http://www.dfait-maeci.gc.ca/caracas/

Irish: Torre Alfa Penthouse, Avenida Principal Urbanizacion, Santa Sofia El Cafetal, Caracas. ☎ (2) 985 6659/4144. Fax: (2) 986 9709.

US: Calle F con Calle Suapure, Colinas de Valle Arriba, Caracas 1080. ☎ (2) 977 2011. Website: http://usembassy.state.gov/venezuela/

Venezuelan embassies/consulates at home:

Australia: 5 Culgoa Circuit, O'Malley ACT 2606. ☎ (2) 6290 2967/8. Fax: (2) 6290 2911.

Canada: 32 Range Road Ottawa, Ontario K1N 8J4. ☎ (613) 235 5151. Fax: (613) 235 3205.

Ireland: contact the Venezuelan embassy/consulate in the UK: 56 Grafton Way, London W1P 5LB. ☎ (020) 7387 6727. Fax: (020) 7383 3253. Website: http://www.demon.co.uk/emb-venuk/func.htm

UK: 56 Grafton Way, London W1P 5LB. ☎ (020) 7387 6727. Fax: (020) 7383 3253. Website: http://www.demon.co.uk/emb-venuk/func.htm

US: 1099 30th Street, NW, Washington DC 20007. ☎ (202) 342 2214. Fax: (202) 342 6820. Email: embavene@dgsys.com Website: http://www.embavenez-us.org

Accommodation:

Resd. La Hacienda Local 1-4T, Final Av. Ppal de las Mercedes, Apdo 80160. Caracas, 1080, Venezuela. ☎ (2) 933.60.82. Fax: (2) 992.96.26. Email: info@ividiomas.com Av. 20 entre calles 68 y 69, Centro Comercial las Tejas, Local 3-2 P.B. Maracaibo, Venezuela. ☎ (0261) 783.39.55. Fax: (0261) 783.02.46 Email: info-mcbo@ividiomas.com

Poste restante:

Central Post Office Urdaneta y Norte 4, near Plaza Bolívar, Caracas.

Cambodia ✈

(+7hrs GMT) **Capital:** Phnom Penh

☎ **Country: 855**, Phnom Penh: 23, Siem Reap: 63 $ Riel

Cambodia's still recovering from the devastating aftermath of Pol Pot's tyrannical regime (1975–79), but it's much safer to visit than it has been for many years. The situation, however, remains volatile and you should check with your embassy before you travel. If you want to play it safe, stick to the capital, Phnom Penh, and major sights such as the world-class temples at Angkor (go by air to Siem Reap).

The lively central market area of Phnom Penh is the best place for budget rooms, food and interesting stalls. Some sights just outside the capital, such as the Killing Fields of Choeung Ek (where 17,000 people were slaughtered) and the Memorial Stupa (with a display of 8,000 skulls of victims of the Khmer Rouge) are as chilling as they are unforgettable. Head south to the port of Sihanoukville for cool diving and snorkelling on the surrounding islands, as well as a couple of sweet beaches. If you're into trekking, go east to Ratanakiri Province, where you'll find waterfalls (such as Chaa Ong and Kinchaan) and plenty of wildlife.

Road travel outside the cities should be on National Routes 1 and 4, and it's best to avoid going anywhere after dark. Cambodia may be more stable now, but it's still off the standard tourist track, and there are risks of accidents on boats, and banditry in rural areas.

◉ Angkor Thom, Angkor Wat, Killing Fields of Choeung Ek, Ochatial Beach at Sihanoukville, Phnom Penh and the Silver Pagoda, and trekking around Ratanakari.

Weather:
Monsoon season is from May to October, when it's hot and wet. Throughout the year, temperatures are generally high – although winters in the north can be cold.

Languages:
Khmer, Chinese and Vietnamese. French and English are often spoken by the older and younger generations respectively.

Religion:
Theravada Buddhism; Muslim and Christian minorities.

Money:
Riel = 100 sen. Carry US dollars in cash.
Cirrus: not accepted.
Maestro: not accepted.
MasterCard: not accepted.
Traveller's cheques: not accepted.
Visa: not accepted.

Living costs:
Civil war means prices fluctuate. Generally speaking, budget about $10 per day for board and food.

Visas:

Everyone needs a visa and a passport valid for at least six months at time of entry. Visas valid for one month cost $20; up to three months $40; more than three months $60. Extensions may be granted by the Immigration Office in Phnom Penh. Visitors arriving by air can get a visa for up to thirty days on arrival at Pochentong International Airport, Phnom Penh or Siem Reap, Angkor. Make sure you know the current political situation, and check visa requirements before you go.

Electricity:

220V, 50Hz. Outside the capital, power is only available in the evenings.

Health:

A yellow fever certificate is required if you're travelling from infected areas. Cholera, hepatitis, malaria, typhoid and rabies. There are also landmines and a poor standard of hospital care. Water should be boiled, if not bottled.

ADDRESS BOOK

Amex Diethelm Travel (Cambodia) Limited, House 65, Street 240, PO Box 99, Phnom Penh. ☎ (23) 219 151. Fax: (23) 219 150.
Email: dtc@gncomtext.com
Ministry of Tourism Boulevard Preah Monivong, Corner Rue 232, Phnom Penh. ☎ (23) 362 085. Fax: (23) 426 364.

Your embassy/consulate in Cambodia:

Australian: Villa 11R, Senei Vannavaut Oum (Street 254) Daun Penh District, Phnom Penh.
☎ (23) 26 000. Fax: (23) 26 003.
Email: austemb@bigpond.com.kh
British: 29 Street 75, Phnom Penh. ☎ (23) 427 124. Fax: (23) 427 125. Email: Britemb@bigpond.com.kh
Canadian: #9, RV Senei Vannavaut Oum, Sangkat Chaktamouk, Khand Daun Penh, Phnom Penh.
☎ (23) 213 470. Fax: (23) 211 389.
Email: pnmpn@dfait-maeci.gc.ca
Irish: contact the British embassy: 29 Street 75, Phnom Penh. ☎ (23) 427 124. Fax: (23) 427 125.
NZ: contact the Australian embassy: Villa 11R, Senei Vannavaut Oum (St. 254) Daun Penh District, Phnom Penh. ☎ (23) 26000. Fax: (23) 26003.

US: 16, Street 228, Phnom Penh.
☎ (23) 216 436. Fax: (23) 216 437.
Website: http://usembassy.state.gov/cambodia/

Cambodian embassies/consulates at home:

Australia 5 Canterbury Court, Deakin, ACT 2600 Canberra. ☎ (02) 6273 1259.
UK: represented by the Cambodian embassy/consulate in France: 11 Avenue Charles Floquet, 75007 Paris. ☎ (1) 4065 0470.
US 4500 16th Street, NW, Washington DC 20011. ☎ (202) 726 7742. Fax: (202) 726 8381.
Email: cambodia@embassy.org

Accommodation:

Capitol Guesthouse 182 Street, Phnom Penh.
☎ (23) 364 104.
Hotel Indochine 144 Street, Phnom Penh.
☎ (23) 427 292.

Poste restante:

General Post Office 13 Street, Phnom Penh.

China ✈

(+8hrs GMT) **Capital:** Beijing

☎ **Country: 86**, Beijing: 10, Guangzhou: 20, Shanghai 21   💲 Yuan

This is one big country. Starting in Beijing, check out the Forbidden City, a vast maze of palaces. The Summer Gardens are also spectacular. Head off to Tiananmen Square, the centre point of the Cultural Revolution, and where pro-democracy demonstrators were cut down by the army in 1989. A perfectly preserved Chairman Mao is close by. A day trip away is the Great Wall, the Simatai area being one of the least touristy. Shanghai is a big pile of glitz, nightlife, shopping and frantic, colourful activity with some of the best food ever. Up north you've got the Mongolian grass plains. It's possible to get good tours, giving you a slice of authentic Mongolian life. Jilin is home to China's largest nature reserve, Changbaishan, where you can see tigers, forests, volcanoes, hot springs and all that jazz. Head south west to Yunnan province for beautiful scenery. Start with Tibet in the north (mega views of Mount Everest) and Chengdu in the Sichuan province – the home of the panda and the setting for *Wild Swans*. Moving south, you'll hit Dali, an incredibly chilled-out place with mountains and the Erhai Lake to blow you away. Sail the Yangzi river to view the incredible gorges before they're drowned by the dam. The transport is very good throughout the country, students can get discounted air fares and the superb train network goes everywhere. In cities, hire a bike and start pedalling.

👁 Army of Terracotta Warriors at Xi'an, Beijing's Forbidden City and Summer Palace, Dali, the Great Wall, Huashan mountain, Jiuzhaigou National Park, Kashgar and Turpan oases, Macan, Potala Palace in Lhasa, Tibet, and Yangshuo scenery.

Weather:

North China has extreme temperature variations: it's freezing in winter, and warm and dry in summer. Central areas are hot in summer and cold in winter, with the chance of cyclones from July to October. Southern areas are generally warmer, with rain throughout the year.

Languages:

Mandarin Chinese and Cantonese. English is sometimes spoken.

Religion:

Buddhist, Confucian, Daoist, Muslim, Protestant, Roman Catholic and Taoist.

Money:

Yuan = 10 chiao/jiao or 100 fen.
Cirrus: good for ATMs.
Maestro: not accepted.
MasterCard: fair for retail and ATMs.
Traveller's cheques: not accepted.
Visa: fair for retail and ATMs.

184

Living costs:

Tourists are charged more than locals. Keep in mind that prices vary between regions. In the east you could probably spend about $35 per day for food and lodgings, but the same might cost only $20 in the west.

Visas:

All nationalities require visas. Passports need to be valid a minimum of six months after the end of your stay.

Electricity:

220–240V, 50Hz. Plugs vary: you'll find the three- and two-pinned types.

Health:

A yellow fever certificate is required if you're travelling from infected areas. Cholera (west); dengue fever (south); malaria (south and the coast); and rabies and bilharzia (central Yangzi River basin). Immunisation is needed for cholera, hepatitis A and B, Japanese encephalitis, polio, rabies and typhoid. Diphtheria, tuberculosis and typhus are also present.

ADDRESS BOOK

Amex Guang Dong Star International Travel Co (Cits), Room 2444 Dong Fang Hotel, 120 Liu Hua Road, 510016 Guangzhou. ☎ (20) 8666 2427.

Gansu Provincial Tourism Administration
10, Nongmin Road, Lanzhou, Gansu.
Email: csr@chinasilkroad.com
Website: http://www.chinasilkroad.com/
STA 179 Huan Shi Xi Road, Guangzhou 510010.
☎ (20) 8667 1455. Fax: (20) 8667 7462.
Email: guangzhouhelp@statravel.com.cn

Your embassy/consulate in China:

Australian: 21 Dongzhimenwai Dajie, Beijing 100600.
☎ (10) 6532 2331–7. Fax: (10) 6532 4605/6718.
E-mail: webmaster@austemb.or.cn
Website: http://www.austemb.or.cn
British: 11 Guang Hua Lu, Jian Guo Men Wai, Beijing 100600. ☎ (10) 6532 1961/2/3/4. Fax: (10) 6532 1937.
Canadian: 19 Dong Zhi Men Wai Street, Chao Yang District, Beijing 100600. ☎ (10) 6532 3536.
Fax: (10) 6532 4072. Email: bejing@dfait-maeci.gc.ca
Website: http://www.dfait-maeci.gc.ca/china
Irish: 3 Ri Tan Donglu, Beijing 100600.
☎ (10) 6532 532 2914. Fax: (10) 6532 2168/6857.
Email: irishemb@info.ivol.cn.net
NZ: Ritan Dongerjie No 1, Chao Yang District, Beijing 100600. ☎ (10) 6532 2732/3/4. Fax: (10) 6532 4317.
Email: nzemb@eastnet.com.cn
US: 3 Xiushui Beijie, Beijing 100600.
☎ (10) 6532 3831. Fax: (10) 6532 6057.
Website: http://www.usembassy-china.org.cn/

Chinese embassies/consulates at home:

Australia: 15 Coronation Drive, Yarralumla ACT 2600.
☎ (02) 6273 4780. Fax: (02) 6273 4878.
Canada: 515 Saint Patrick Street, Ottawa, Ontario KIN 5H3. ☎ (613) 789 3434. Fax: (613) 789 1911.
Ireland: 40 Ailesbury Road, Dublin 4.
☎ (01) 269 1707.
NZ: 2–6 Glenmore Street, Wellington.
☎ (04) 472 1382/4. Fax: (04) 499 0419 or 472 1998.
South Africa: 972 Pretorius Street, Arcadia, Pretoria.
☎ (012) 342 4149.
UK: 31 Portland Place, London W1N 3AG.
☎ (020) 7636 5637.
US: 2300 Connecticut Avenue, NW, Washington DC 20008. ☎ (202) 328 2500. Fax: (202) 588 0032.
Email: webmaster@china-embassy.org
Website: http://www.china-embassy.org/

Accommodation:

HI–Jiangmen YH No. 86 Ti Zhong Road, Jiangmen City, Guangdong Province. ☎ 86 (750) 368 3908.
Fax: 86 (750) 3681908. Email: j.m.hostel@163.com
HI–Pu Jiang YH 15 Huang Pu Rd, Shanghai.
☎ (21) 6324 6388. Fax: (21) 6324 3179.
HI–Beiging International YH 9 Jian Guo Men Nei Da Jie, Beijing. ☎ (10) 6512 6688/6145/6146.
Fax: (10) 65229494. Email: BIH-YH@Sohu.com

Poste restante:

General Post Office Beijing.

Hong Kong ✈

(+8hrs GMT) **Capital:** Victoria

☎ **Hong Kong: 852** 〔$〕 Hong Kong dollar

Hong Kong (now part of China) is fast...and very expensive. It has shops, theatre, commerce, industry and a pace that would leave most places floundering. If you're thinking that the wealth and glamour are exaggerated, think again. Central Hong Kong is a mass of shops and offices all presented with that beehive atmosphere. Take a trip up Victoria Peak for an unrivalled view of the microcosm at work or, even better, at night. The beach at Repulse Bay is usually packed with bodies – skip to the area around Stanley for a far more relaxed atmosphere. The area of Kowloon has been made for tourists – and bars, clubs, shops, hotels and cafés all fight for your cash. If this is all a bit much, head for the New Territories, where it's possible to get away into some nature, have a quick hike along the coast and be rewarded by a dip in the warm waters. The outlying islands are becoming touristy, but they offer a far less frenetic pace and a more holiday feel. You've got more chance of learning Mandarin than getting to grips with the public transport system in Hong Kong – but it's cheap, fast and efficient, and wherever you end up, it'll look the same.

👁 Hong Kong skyline at night, jetfoil trip to Macau, outer islands, ride across Victoria Harbour on the Star Ferry, shopping in the Stanley Bazaar, Shek O Beach and Victoria Peak.

Weather:
It's very hot and sticky between June and August, when the heaviest rain falls. Spring and autumn are still pretty hot. Winters can be cold. The streets feel more humid because there's very little open space.

Languages:
Cantonese, English and Mandarin.

Religion:
Buddhist, Confucian and Taoist; Christian and Muslim minorities.

Money:
Hong Kong dollar = 100 cents.
Cirrus: good for ATMs.
Maestro: not accepted.
MasterCard: excellent for retail and good for ATMs.
Traveller's cheques: £ sterling.
Visa: excellent for retail and ATMs.

Living costs:
Accommodation is expensive – allow about $30 per day. However food and transport are fairly cheap.

Visas:

British and Irish nationals do not need a visa. Australian, New Zealand, Canadian and US nationals do not need a visa for trips of less than one month. South Africans do need a visa. Passports must be valid for at least three months after the trip. You need to carry ID at all times as the police make random checks.

Electricity:

220V, 50Hz

Health:

Malaria (rural areas), polio and typhoid.

ADDRESS BOOK

Amex Ground Floor, New World Tower, 16–18 Queen's Road, Central, Hong Kong. ☎ 2811 1200.

Hong Kong Tourism Board 9-11/F Citicorp Centre, 18 Whitfield Road, North Point.

☎ 2807 6543/2806 0303.

Email: info@hktourismboard.com

Website: http://www.DiscoverHongKong.com

STA Sincerity Travel 1112 Argyle Centre, 688 Nathan Road, Kowloon, Hong Kong. ☎ 236 3392.

Fax: 2730 9407.

Your embassy/consulate in Hong Kong:

Australian: 23rd Floor, Harbour Centre, 25 Harbour Road, Wanchai, Hong Kong. ☎ 2827 8881.

Fax: 2827 6583. Website: http://www.australia.org.hk/

British: No 1 Supreme Court Road Central, Hong Kong. ☎ 2901 3000. Fax: 2901 3066.

Canadian: 8 Connaught Place, 11–14 Floors, 1 Exchange Square, Kowloon, Hong Kong.

☎ 2810 4321. Fax: 2810 6736.

Irish: 6th Floor, Chung Nam Building, 1 Lockhart Road, Wanchai, Hong Kong.

☎ 2527 4897. Fax: 2520 1833.

NZ: 3414 Jardine House Connaught Road, GPO Box 2790, Kowloon, Hong Kong. ☎ 2525 5044.

Fax: 2845 2915.

South African: 27th Floor, Sunning Plaza, 10 Hysan Avenue, Kowloon, Hong Kong. ☎ 2577 3279.

Fax: 2890 1975.

US: 26 Garden Road, Mid-Levels, Central, Hong Kong. ☎ 2523 9011. Fax: 2845 1598.

Website: http://www.usconsulate.org.hk/

Chinese embassies/consulates at home:

Australia: 15 Coronation Drive, Yarralumla ACT 2600. ☎ (02) 6273 4780. Fax: (02) 6273 4878.

Canada: 347 Bay Street, Suite 1100 Toronto, Ontario M5H 2R7. ☎ (416) 366 3594. Fax: (416) 366 1569.

Ireland: 40 Ailesbury Road, Dublin 4.

☎ (01) 269 1707.

NZ: 2–6 Glenmore Street, Wellington.

☎ (04) 472 1382/4. Fax: (04) 499 0419 or 472 1998.

South Africa: 972 Pretorius Street, Arcadia, Pretoria.

☎ (012) 342 4149.

UK: 31 Portland Place, London W1N 3AG.

☎ (020) 7636 5637.

US: 2300 Connecticut Avenue, NW, Washington DC 20008. ☎ (202) 328 2500. Fax: (202) 588 0032.

Email: webmaster@china-embassy.org

Website: http://www.china-embassy.org/

Accommodation:

HI–Jockey Club Mt. Davis YH (Formerly Ma Wui Hall), Top of Mt. Davis Path, off Victoria Road, Kennedy Town Island. ☎ 2817 5715.

YMCA International House 23 Waterloo Road, Yau Ma Tei, Kowloon. ☎ 2771 9111. Fax: 2771 5238.

Email: resvndept@ymcainthousehk.org

HI–Jockey Club Mong Tung Wan Yh Lantau Island.

☎ 984-1389.

Poste restante:

Send letters to:

[Name], c/o Poste Restante, GPO Hong Kong.

Collect letters from:

GPO Hong Kong, 2 Connaught Place, Connaught Road, Central, Hong Kong.

India ✈

(+5hrs 30mins GMT) **Capital:** New Delhi

☎ **Country: 91**, Bombay (Mumbai): 22, Calcutta: 33, New Delhi: 11 ⌇$⌇ Rupee

Once in New Delhi, head for the bazaars at Pahargani to meet other travellers and get a feel for the country. Things you shouldn't miss include Chandi Chowk, the main area of 'Old' Delhi, which is stuffed with activity, noise and stalls. In New Delhi, Connaught Place, the Spice Market on Khari Baoli and the Qutab Minar tower are worth checking out. New Delhi is the best base for visiting that wonder-of-the-world, the Taj Mahal at Agra, and for trips into the Himalayas, where you'll find superb and cheap skiing and trekking. Mumbai (formerly Bombay) is a mix of industry and old-style colonial kitsch, attracting both India's rich and poor. The nightlife at Chowpatty beach is an eclectic mix of festivities, whilst the days should be spent at the bazaars of Kalbadevi. Goa still has some good beaches with on-tap, spaced-out hippies. Head for the Andaman and Nicobar Islands in the Bay of Bengal for the best of the sand, sea and snorkelling. The only way to travel distances is by India's legendary train network. The long-distance buses provide a good service, whereas the local ones are farcical. Taxis or auto-rickshaws (for those with nerves of steel) are your best bet.

👁 Bangalore, Bombay (Mumbai) and the Gateway of India, Darjeeling and the tea plantations, Goa's beaches, Hyderabad, Jaipur, Kerala's coastal lagoons, markets in Mysore, New Dehli, Pushkar and Jaisalmer in Rajasthan, the Red Fort and Taj Mahal at Agra, sacred ghats (steps down to the Ganges river) of Varanasi, and Udaipur.

Weather:
It's hottest from April to June, and coolest from November to March. Between June and September, it's monsoon season in most regions.

Languages:
Hindi and English; thirteen other main languages including Urdu.

Religion:
Predominantly Hindu; also Muslim, Sikh, Christian, Buddhist and Jain.

Money:
Rupee = 100 paise.
Cirrus: not accepted.
Maestro: not accepted.
MasterCard: limited for retail, no ATMs available.
Traveller's cheques: £ sterling.
Visa: limited for retail, no ATMs available.

Living costs:
If you can cope without creature comforts, India's one of the cheapest places to stay. Allow $5 per day for food and board, and local travel costs almost nothing.

Visas:

Passports must be valid for at least six months from the date of entry. Visas for tourists usually last six months. These can be extended at your embassy or high commission.

Electricity:

220V, 50Hz. Round two- or three-pin plugs.

Health:

A yellow fever certificate is required if you're travelling from infected areas. Bubonic plague, cholera, dengue fever, dysentery, hepatitis B, malaria, meningitis (trekking areas only), polio, tick-borne relapsing fever and typhoid. The big cities have severe pollution.

ADDRESS BOOK

Amex Ashlin Travels, 64 Yashwant Place, Chanakyapuri, New Delhi 110021. ☎ (11) 607 927.

Government of India Tourist Office (GTI)
88 Janpath, New Delhi 110 001.
☎ (11) 332 0005/0008/0109/0266/0342.
Fax: (11) 3320342.
Email: newdelhi@tourisminindia.com

STA STIC Travels Pvt Limited, R907 New Rajinder Nagar, Janpath, New Delhi 110060. ☎(11) 332 5559/7909/7582/4789. Fax: (11) 371 2710.

Thomas Cook 717–718 International Trade Towers, Nehru Place, New Delhi 110 019. ☎(11) 642 3035.

Your embassy/consulate in India:

Australian: No, 1/50 G Shanti Path, Chanakyapuri, New Delhi 110021. ☎ (11) 688 8223. Fax: (11) 687 4126.
Website: http://www.ausgovindia.com/

British: Shanti Path, Chanakyapuri, New Delhi 110021. ☎ (11) 687 2161. Fax: (11) 687 2882.
Website: http://www.ukinindia.org

Canadian: 7/8 Shanti Path, Chanakyapuri, New Delhi 110021. ☎ (11) 687 6500. Fax: (11) 687 6579.
Email: delhi@dfait-maeci.gc.ca

Irish: 230 Jor Bagh, New Delhi 110003.
☎ (11) 462 6741. Fax: (11) 469 7053.
Email: ireland@ndf.vsnl.net.in

NZ: 50N Nyaya Marg, Chanakyapuri, New Delhi 110021. ☎ (11) 688 3170. Fax: (11) 688 3165.

South African: B18 Basant Amag Basant Bisel, New Delhi 57. ☎ (11) 614 9412.

US: Shanti Path, Chanakyapuri, New Delhi 110021.
☎ (11) 688 9033. Fax: (11) 419 0017.
Email: vn1@pd.state.gov
Website: http://usembassy.state.gov/posts/in1/

Indian embassies/consulates at home:

Australia: 3–5 Moonah Place, Yarralumla ACT 2600.
☎ (02) 6273 3999/3774/3875. Fax: (02) 6273 1308.

Canada: 10 Springfield Road, Ottawa, Ontario K1M 1C9. ☎(613) 744 3751. Fax: (613) 744 0913.

NZ: 10th Floor, FAI House, 180 Molesworth Street, Wellington. ☎ (04) 473 6390/1. Fax: (04) 499 0665.

South Africa: 852 Schoeman Street, Arcadia, Pretoria. ☎ (012) 342 5392.

UK: India House, Aldwych, London WC2B 4NA.
☎ (020) 7836 8484.

US: 2107 Massachusetts Avenue, NW, Washington DC 20008. ☎ (202) 939 7000.
Website: http://www.indianembassy.org/

Accommodation:

HI–New Delhi International YH 5 Nyaya Marg, Chanakyapuri, New Delhi 110021. ☎ (11) 611 6285 or (11) 410 1246. Fax: (11) 611 3469.
Email: yhostel@del2.vsnl.net.in
Website: www.yhaindia.org

HI–Tirupati-Tirumala Near Reserve Police Quarters, M.R. Palle, Tirupati - 517502. ☎ (8574) 40300.

HI–Naharlagun Naharlagun, PO Naharlagun - 791110, Arunachal Pradesh. ☎ (3781) 4730.

Poste restante:

General Post Office Market Street, New Delhi.

Indesia ✈

(+7hrs GMT in Sumatra and Java; +9hrs GMT in Malaku) **Capital:** Jakarta

☎ **Country: 62**, Bali: 361, Jakarta: 21   〔$〕Rupiah

On Sumatra, head for Berastagi and Bukittinggi if you want to hook up with trekkers. Gunung National Park and the culture of the Karo Batak people are also good pulling reasons. On Java, the town of Yogyakarta has temple appeal, or head to Bandung to chill out. Indonesia boasts a good couple of thousand islands with great beaches and crystal clear waters. Make your way to Krakatau islands for some spectacular volcanic scenery. Pulau Seribu and Karimunjawa have the best of the beaches, and chartering boats is easy. On the island of Bali, Lavina has the most tourists – but when you see the beaches you'll know why. If you want to be cultured, head for Pejeng near Ubud, while Bali Barat National Park has some stunning coastal scenery and coral. Lombok is a top tip if you don't want to meet anyone. The main urban areas are Ampenan (cheap accommodation) and Sweta (travel links and excellent markets). Best of all are the Gili Islands where heaven meets earth. They're pretty quiet, the people are friendly and the beaches...wow! Getting around Indonesia isn't hard, there are enough ferries and private boats to island-hop for the rest of your life.

👁 Bandung Malang and Yogyakarta on Java, Bukittinggi, Gili Islands off Lombok, Gunung Leuser National Park and Padang on Sumatra, Irian Jaya, Kalimantan, Maluku, Nusa Tenggara, Sulawesi, Ubud in Bali, and the volcanoes of Flores.

Weather:

Hot and wet – the model tropical monsoon climate. The rainy season is from December to March, but it's generally wet throughout the year. The driest season is from June to September.

Languages:

Bahasa Indonesia (plus many variations); also English and Dutch.

Religion:

Predominantly Muslim; Buddhism, Hindu and Roman Catholic minorities.

Money:

Rupiah = 100 sen.

Cirrus: not accepted.

Maestro: not accepted.

MasterCard: limited for retail, no ATMs available.

Traveller's cheques: £ sterling.

Visa: limited for retail, no ATMs available.

Living costs:

The exchange rate varies. Tourist resorts are more expensive than elsewhere for accommodation.

190

Visas:

Passports should be valid for at least six months from the date of entry. Nationals of several countries can stay for up to sixty days without a visa. Requirements are subject to change, so check before you go.

Electricity:

110V, 50Hz (some regional variation).

Health:

A yellow fever certificate is required if travelling from infected areas. Dengue fever, giardiasis, hepatitis, Japanese encephalitis, malaria, paratyphoid, rabies and typhoid.

ADDRESS BOOK

Amex Pacto Limited Tour and Travel, c/o Lagoon Tower, Hilton International, Jalang Jend Gatot Subroto, PO Box 2563, Jakarta 10002. ☎ (21) 5705 8000.
Direktorat Jenderal Pariwistat Indonesia (Directorate-General of Tourism) 16/19 Jalan Medan Merdeka-Barat, Jakarta 10110. ☎ (21) 386 0934. Fax: (21) 386 0828.
STA Menara BDN Building, 11th Floor Jalan Kebon Sirih No. 83, Jakarta Pusat 10340. ☎(21) 230 0336. Fax: (21) 230 2021.

Further Information:

Indonesia Tourist Promotion Office 3–4 Hanover Street, London W1R 9HH. ☎ (0171) 493 0030. Fax: (0171) 493 1747. Email: itpo@hotmail.com Website: http://www.visit-indonesia.com

Your embassy/consulate in Indonesia:

Australian: Jl. H.R. Rasuna Said Kav. C15-16, Kuningan, Jakarta Selatan,12940.
☎ (21) 2550 5555. Fax: (21) 522 7101.
Website: http://www.austembjak.or.id/
British: Jalan MH Thamrin 75, Jakarta 10310.
☎ (21) 315 6264. Fax: (21) 314 1824.
Website: http://www.british-emb-jakarta.or.id/
Canadian: 5th Floor, Wisma Metropolitan, Jalan Jenderal Sudirman, Jakarta 12920.
☎ (21) 525 0709. Fax: (21) 571 2251.
Email: jkrta@dfait-maeci.gc.ca
Irish: c/o Jakarta International School, JL Terogong Raya No. 33, Jakarta 12430. ☎ (21) 768 5142. Fax: (21) 750 3644.
NZ: 23rd floor, Jln. Jend Sudirman Kav, 44–46, Jakarta, 10210. ☎ (21) 570 9460. Fax: (21) 570 9457. Email: nzembjak@cbn.net.id

South African: Suite 705, 7th Floor Wisma GKBI Suite 705 JL Jend, Sudirman No. 28, Jakarta 10210.
☎ (21) 574 0660. Fax: (21) 574 0661.
Website: http://www.saembassy-jakarta.or.id/
US: JL Merdeka Selatan 4–5, Jakarta 10110.
☎ (21) 344 2211. Fax: (21) 350 8466.
Website: http://www.usembassyjakarta.org/

Indonesian embassies/consulates at home:

Australia: 8 Darwin Avenue, Yarralumla ACT 2600.
☎ (02) 6250 8600. Fax: (02) 6273 6017.
Canada: 287 MacLaren Street Ottawa, Ontario K2P 0L9. ☎ (613) 236 7403. Fax: (613) 563 2858.
Ireland: represented by the Indonesian embassy/ consulate in the UK: 38 Grosvenor Square, London W1X 9AD. ☎ (0171) 499 7661. Fax: (0171) 491 4993.
NZ: 70 Glen Road, Kelburn, Wellington.
☎(04) 475 8697/8/9. Fax: (04) 475 9374.
South Africa: 968 Pretorius Street, Arcadia, Pretoria.
☎ (012) 342 3356.
UK: 38 Grosvenor Square, London W1X 9AD.
☎ (020) 7499 7661. Fax: (020) 7491 4993.
US: 2020 Massachusetts Avenue, NW, Washington DC 20036. ☎ (202) 775 5200.

Accommodation:

Bali-Panji Sakti YH Seririt, St PO Box 127 Code Pos 81, Singaraja, Bali. ☎ (361) 21349.
Delima YH Jl Jaksa 5, Jakarta (central). ☎ (21) 337026.
Vagabnd YH Jl Prawirotaman MG III 589, JL Sisingamangaraja 28B, Yogyakarta, Central Java.
☎ (274) 371207. Fax: (274) 371207.

Poste restante:

General Post Office Jakarta.
General Post Office Kuta, Bali.

Japan ✈

(+9hrs GMT) **Capital:** Tokyo

☎ **Country: 81**, Kyoto: 75, Tokyo: 3 💲 Yen

Japan is synonymous with industrious efficiency, and this is the image you'll get in Tokyo. It's an incredibly energetic city full of tiny houses, shops, shops and...shops. The Ginza area has the highest profile, with the classiest establishments, but head for Asakusa for a more authentic Japanese experience. Don't worry, it's still jammed with shops and boutiques selling everything you could ever want. Entertainment-wise, head for the Shinjuku area where the streets contain all forms of nightlife, bars, theatres and surprisingly cheap, if minuscule, accommodation. About sixty miles away is Mount Fuji – the most scenic image of Japan – and it's definitely worth a visit if you need a break from the hectic pace of Tokyo. The city of Kyoto is where to head for your old-style culture and to catch up with that all-important meditation. Skiing is superb on the island of Honshu and water babies should head for Okinawa for the diving. Outdoors freaks will also enjoy the national parks, complete with waterfalls, hot springs and the odd volcano. Travel in Japan must be done by train, a ride on the 160mph bullet is mandatory for anyone who visits. Rail passes make it a pretty cheap option, too.

👁 Bullet train ride, Daisetsuzan National Park, Hiroshima and the A-bomb museum, Iriomote-jima Island, Kagoshima, Kamakura with the 13th-century statue of Buddha, Kyoto, Mount Aso, Mount Fuji, Nijo Castle, Nikko and the impressive Tosho-gu Shrine, Shikotsu-Toya National Park and Tokyo.

Weather:

The north can get pretty cold and wet from October to April, and expect snow in the mountains. The south is a lot milder, getting quite hot between June and September. This is also when the rains fall. Typhoons may occur between September and October.

Languages:

Japanese. Some English may be spoken in the main cities.

Religion:

Shinto Buddhist; Buddhist and Christian minorities.

Money:

Yen.

Cirrus: fair for ATMs.

Maestro: not accepted.

MasterCard: excellent for retail and fair for ATMs.

Traveller's cheques: £ sterling or Yen.

Visa: good for retail and fair for ATMs (some Visa ATMs are valid for Japanese-issued cards only).

Living costs:

The cost of living is very high. If you travel very little and don't buy anything, then allow about $35 per day.

Visas:

Australians and South Africans need a visa. UK, Irish, US, Canadian and NZ nationals can stay for up to ninety days without one. Requirements are subject to change so check before you go.

Electricity:

100V, 50Hz (Tokyo and east Japan), 60Hz (west Japan).

Health:

Japanese encephalitis, paragonimiasis, polio and typhoid.

ADDRESS BOOK

Amex 4–30–16, Ogikubo, Suginami–Ku, Tokyo 16701. ☎ (3) 3220 6200.

Information and Public Relations Division, Overseas Promotion Department 2–10–1, Yuraku-cho, Chiyoda-ku, Tokyo 100–0006. ☎ (3) 3216 1902. Fax: (3) 3216 1846. Email: jnto@jnto.go.jp">jnto@jnto.go.jp Website: http://www.jnto.go.jp

STA 1st Floor, Star Plaza Aoyama Building, 1-10-3 Shibuya, Shibuya-Ku, Tokyo 150-0002. ☎ (3) 5485 8380. Fax: (3) 5485 8373. Email: shibuya@statravel.co.uk

Tourist Information Center (JNTO) Tokyo B1F, Tokyo International Forum 351, Marunouchi, Chiyoda-ku, Tokyo 100–0005. ☎ (3) 3201 3331. Fax: (3) 3201 3347. Email: jnto@jnto.go.jp Website: http://www.jnto.go.jp

Your embassy/consulate in Japan

Australian: 2–1–14 Mita Minato-ku, Tokyo 108. ☎ (3) 5232 4111. Fax: (3) 5232 4149. Website: http://www.australia.or.jp/home.html

British: 1 Ichiban-cho Chiyoda-ku, Tokyo 102-8381. ☎ (3) 5211 1100. Fax: (3) 5275 0346. Website: http://www.uknow.or.jp/

Canadian: 3–38 Akasaka, 7-Chome, Minanto-ku, Tokyo 107-8503. ☎ (3) 5412 6200. Fax: (3) 5412 6303. Website: http://www.dfait-maeci.gc.ca/ni-ka/menu-e.asp

Irish: Ireland House 5F, 2–10–7 Kojimachi, Chiyoda–ku, Tokyo 102. ☎ (3) 3263 0695. Fax: (3) 3265 2275.

NZ: 20–40 Kamiyama-cho-Shibuya-ku, Tokyo 150-0047. ☎ (3) 3467 2271. Fax: (3) 3467 2278 Website: http://www.nzembassy.com/japan

South African: 414, Zenkyoren Building 2–7–9 Hirakawa-cho Chiyoda-ku, Tokyo, 102. ☎ (3) 3265 3366. Fax: (3) 3261 1108. Website: http://sunsite.sut.ac.jp/embassy/jasanet/

US: 10–5, Akasaka 1-Chome, Minato-ku, Tokyo 107-8420. ☎ (3) 3224 5000. Fax: (3) 3505 1862. Website: http://usembassy.state.gov/tokyo/

Japanese embassies/consulates at home:

Australia: 112 Empire Circuit, Yarralumla ACT 2600. ☎ (02) 6273 3244. Fax: (02) 6273 1848.

Canada: 255 Sussex Drive Ottawa, Ontario K1N 9E6. ☎ (613) 241 8541. Fax: (613) 241 2232.

Ireland: Nutley Building, Merrion Centre, Nutley Lane, Dublin 4. ☎ (01) 269 4244/033. Fax: (01) 260 1285.

NZ: Norwich Insurance House, 3 Hunter Street, Wellington. ☎ (04) 473 1540. Fax: (04) 471 2951.

South Africa: 2nd Floor, Sanlam Building, Festival and Arcadia Street, Hatfield, Pretoria. ☎ (012) 342 2100. Fax: (012) 251 695.

UK: 101 Piccadilly, London W1V 9FN. ☎ (020) 7465 6500.

US: 2520 Massachusetts Avenue, NW, Washington DC 20008. ☎ (202) 238 6700. Fax: (202) 328 2187.

Accommodation:

Bali–Panji Sakti YH Seririt St PO Box 127 Code Pos 81, Singaraja, Bali. ☎ (361) 21349.

Delima YH Jl Jaksa 5, Jakarta (central). ☎ (21) 337026.

Vagabond YH Jl Prawirotaman MG III 589, JL Sisingamangaraja 28B, Yogyakarta, Central Java. ☎ (274) 371207. Fax: (274) 371207.

Poste restante:

Tokyo International Post Office, 2–3–3 Otemachi, Chiyoda-ku, Tokyo. ☎ (3) 3241 4891.

Laos

(+7hrs GMT) **Capital:** Vientiane

☎ **Country: 856**, Vientiane: 21   💲 Laotian new kip

Laos has hardly been touched by western travellers, and is therefore the best place to get a look at the real Southeast Asia. Over half is covered in beautiful forest and the Annamite Mountains will keep trekkers happy. It's sparsely populated, so what it lacks in bustling activity, it makes up for in traditional experiences. Vientiane has the lion's share of the markets and temples. The Morning Market is one of the best, replaced at night by the Dong Palan Night Market, it has good nosh. The accommodation's cheap and there are a good number of guesthouses starting to pop up. The ancient capital, Luang Prabang, is definitely worth checking out too. The mountainous border with Vietnam is perfect for some trekking, and it's easy to find guides at the local towns. The Bolaven Plateau in the south is dotted with tribal villages and fantastic waterfalls, such as Taat Lo, where you can do that 'swim in a natural pool' thing. The central feature in Laos is the Mekong River, which runs the length of the country. It's useful to travel down, as the roads are pretty shabby and the transport is rough, to say the least.

👁 Annamite Mountains, Bolaven Plateau, Kuang Si waterfalls, Luang Prabang, Mekong River, Muang Sing morning market, Pak Ou caves, Plain of Jars, and Vientiane.

Weather:

May to October is the rainy season, and also has the highest temperatures. The rest of the year it's dry, but still very hot and tropical. However, you'll find cooler weather in the highlands.

Languages:

Lao and French.

Religion:

Predominantly Buddhist; an Animist minority.

Money:

Laotian new kip = 100 cents.
Cirrus: not accepted.
Maestro: not accepted.
MasterCard: not accepted.
Traveller's cheques: US dollars or £ sterling.
Visa: not accepted.
Take US dollars in cash.

Living costs:

Laos is a poor country and local goods are cheap.
Prices in the capital are slightly more expensive than

elsewhere, but you'll still be hard-pushed to find a good room costing over $5–10. The price of food and drink is minimal.

Visas:

It's better to organise a visa before you travel to Laos, but it's possible to get one at the airport when you arrive (lasts fifteen days). If you're coming from Thailand, get a visa from a travel agency in Bangkok, as it's much easier than going through the embassy.

Electricity:

220V, 50Hz

Health:

A yellow fever certificate is required if you're travelling from infected areas. Cholera, dengue fever, hepatitis, Japanese encephalitis, malaria, rabies and typhoid.

ADDRESS BOOK

National Tourism Authority of Laos PDR
PO Box 3556, Vientiane, Laos PDR.
☎ (21) 2248. Fax: (21) 2769
Website: http://visit-laos.com/

Your embassy/consulate in Laos:
Australian: Rue J. Nehru, Quartier Phone Xay, Vientiane. ☎ (41) 3602/5. Fax: (41) 3613.
British: PO Box 6626 Vientiane. ☎ (21) 413 606. Fax: (21) 41 3607. Email: btolaos@loxinfo.co.th
Canadian: Contact the embassy in Thailand.
Irish: Contact the British embassy: PO Box 6626 Vientiane. ☎ (21) 413 606. Fax: (21) 413 607. Email: btolaos@loxinfo.co.th
US: 19 Rue Bartholomie, Vientiane.
☎ (21) 2581/2/5. Fax: (21) 2584.
Website: http://usembassy.state.gov/laos/

Laotian embassies/consulates at home:
Australia: 1 Dalman Crescent, O'Malley ACT 2606.
☎ (02) 6286 4595. Fax: (02) 6290 1910.

Canada: represented by the Laotian embassy/consulate in the US: 2222 S Street, NW, Washington DC 20008. ☎ (202) 332 6416. Fax: (202) 332 4923.
UK: Contact the embassy in France: 74 Avenue Raymond Poincare, 75116 Paris. ☎ (161) 4553 0298. Fax: (161) 4727 5789.
US: 2222 S Street, NW, Washington DC 20008.
☎ (202) 332 6416. Fax: (202) 332 4923.

Accommodation:
Ministry of Information and Culture (MIC) Guest House 67 Thanon Manthatulat, Vientiane.
☎ (21) 2362.
Vanvisa Guest House Ban Wat That, nr the Mekong River, Vientiane. ☎ (21) 2925.

Poste restante:
Post, Telephone and Telegraph (PTT) Office Corner of Thanon Lan Xang and Thanon Khu Vieng, opposite Talaat Sao, Laos.

Malaysia ✈

(+8 hrs GMT) **Capital:** Kuala Lumpur

☎ **Country: 60**, Kuala Lumpur: 3 💲 Ringgit

The peninsular area of Malaysia is where you'll find the most tourist-geared activities. On the west coast is the capital, Kuala Lumpur, which is a lively mix of economic activity and colonial and Asian tradition. Chinatown has all the frantic activity you could wish for. A travellers' paradise. The Golden Triangle is KL's economic pride and great for shopping. For trekking along jungle walks, head inland to the Cameron Highlands. The islands of Pulau Pangkor and Panang are perfect for beach therapy, while the eastern city of Kota Bahru has some excellent night markets. Further down the east coast, the Perhentian Islands and Cherating are ideal for hooking up with other travellers and doing some serious snorkelling. East Malaysia offers beautiful national parks, untouched jungle and idyllic off-shore islands begging to be explored. Good domestic airlines cover most of the major cities, an average flight being RM100 to get from one end of the peninsula to the other. The bus system in Peninsular Malaysia is excellent for covering big distances with reasonable fares (approx RM25 for a ten-hour journey). The train system is also of a good standard, but isn't as widespread. Taxi-sharing is a great and cheap way to get around, if there are enough of you.

👁 Cameron Highlands, Cherating, Kota Bharu, Kuala Lumpur, Kuching and Sarawak, Melaka, Mount Kinabalu in Sabah, Penang Island and Georgetown, Pulau Langkawi, and Tioman Island.

Weather:
It's extremely hot all year round. The west coast's wettest month is August, and there's a rainy season on the east coast with monsoons from November to January. The hill stations in the centre of Peninsular Malaysia are a welcome relief from the 90% humidity of coastal areas.

Languages:
Malay; many people speak English.

Religion:
Predominantly Muslim; Buddhist, Hindu and Christian.

Money:
Ringgit = 100 sen.
Cirrus: excellent for ATMs.
Maestro: limited for ATMs.
MasterCard: excellent for retail, good for ATMs.
Traveller's cheques: US dollars or sterling (accepted in banks, hotels and department stores).
Visa: good for retail and ATMs.

Living costs:

It starts as cheap as $3.50 for a good meal and a dorm room. Standard hotel rooms cost around $5, and a full dinner is about $3.

Visas:

Passport must be valid for at least six months from the date of entry, and you must have sufficient funds for your stay. Visas are needed for visits longer than two months (or longer than three months for UK, Irish and US nationals). Women over six months pregnant may be refused entry; it may also be difficult to enter the country if you look scruffy and dirty, so clean up before you arrive if you've been sleeping rough.

Electricity:

220V, 50Hz. Square three-pin plugs like those in Britain.

Health:

A yellow fever certificate is required if you're travelling from infected areas. Cholera, malaria (east and high-lands), polio and typhoid.

ADDRESS BOOK

Amex Travel Office 18th Floor, The Weld, Jalan Raja, Chulan, Kuala Lumpur 50200. ☎ (3) 213 0007.

Sarawak Tourism Board 6th and 7th Floors, Bangunan Yayasan Sarawak, Jalan Masjid, 93400 Kuching, Sarawak, Malaysia. ☎ (82) 423 600. Fax: (82) 416 700. Email: stb@sarawaktourism.com
Website: http://www.sarawaktourism.com/

STA Travel Lot 506, 5th Floor Plaza Magnum, 55100 Kuala Lumpur. ☎ (3) 248 9800. Fax: (3) 243 3046.

Your embassy/consulate in Malaysia:

Australian: 6 Jalan Yap Kwan Seng, Kuala Lumpur 50450. ☎ (3) 242 3122. Fax: (3) 241 5773.
Website: http://www.jaring.my/austcomm/

Canadian: Plaza OSK, 7th and 15th Floors, 172 Jalan Ampang, 50450 Kuala Lumpur. ☎ (3) 261 2000. Fax: (3) 261 3428. E-mail: klmpr@dfait-maeci.gc.ca
Website: http://www.dfait-maeci.gc.ca/kualalumpur

British: 185 Jalan Ampang, 50450 Kuala Lumpur. ☎ (3) 248 2122. Fax: (3) 244 9692.
Website: http://www.britain.org.my/

Irish: Ireland House, Amp Walk, 218 Jalan Ampang, 50450 Kuala Lumpur. ☎ (3) 2161 2963.
Fax: (3) 2161 3427 Email: ireland@po.jaring.my.

NZ: 21st Floor, Menara IMC, 8 Jalan Sultan Ismail, 50250 Kuala Lumpur. ☎ (3) 238 2533.
Fax: (3) 238 0387. Email: nzhckl@pc.jaring.my

South African: 12 Lorong Titiwangsa 12, Taman Tasik Titiwangsa, Setapak, Kuala Lumpur. ☎ (3) 424 4456.

US: 376 Jalan Tun Razak, 50400 Kuala Lumpur. ☎ (3) 268 5000.
Website: http://usembassymalaysia.org.my/

Malaysian embassies/consulates at home:

Australia: 7 Perth Avenue, Yarralumla, Canberra, ACT 2600. ☎ (02) 6273 1543.

Canada: 60 Boteler Street, Ottawa, Ontario K1N 8Y7. ☎ (613) 241 5182.

Ireland: represented by the Malaysian embassy/consulate in the UK: 45–46 Belgrade Square, London SW1X 8QT. ☎ (0171) 235 8033.

NZ: 10 Washington Avenue, Brooklyn, Wellington. ☎ (04) 385 2439.

South Africa: 1007 Schoeman Street, Arcadia, Pretoria 0083. ☎ (012) 342 5990.

UK: 45–46 Belgrave Square, London SW1X 8QT. ☎ (020) 7235 8033.

Accommodation:

HI - Kuala Lumpur International YH 21 Jalan Kampung Attap, 50460 Kuala Lumpur. ☎ (3) 22736870/71. Fax: (3) 22741115. Email: myha@pd.jaring.my

Borneo Hostel P.M.M. Box 141, Miri Morsjaya, MIRI Sarawak, Borneo. ☎ 85 482449. Fax: 7092 131068. Email: mikerich@borneo-holidays.com

Golden Plaza Jalan Petaling {China Town}, 106 First Floor, Kuala Lumpur, 50000. ☎ (60) 20268559. Fax: (60) 20268559. Email: goldenplazakl@hotmail.com

Poste restante:

General Post Office Kuala Lumpur.

Nepal ✈

(+5hrs 45mins GMT) **Capital:** Kathmandu

☎ **Country: 977**, Kathmandu: 1 💲 Nepalese rupee

If you've come to Nepal to do anything but trek, you're in the wrong place. In Kathmandu, head for the Thamel area, and in particular Freak Street, for the best accommodation bargains and any nightlife that may be wandering around. All your trekking needs can be taken care of from here, and the prices are pretty low. Before moving on, it's well worth checking out the nearby medieval towns of Patan and Bhaktapur. Both are stuffed with temples and atmosphere, and feel like Kathmandu did before the smog arrived in the 1990s. Before you're all templed out – make time for Swayambhunath, known as the Monkey Temple, for reasons that will become apparent...Then head for the hills to tackle the Himalayas – the most amazing mountain range in the world. From Kathmandu, you can strike out on the excellent Helambu or Langtang trails. Alternatively, head for Pokhara. This relaxed, lakeside town is the starting point for longer treks, such as the Annapurna Sanctury and Everest Base Camp trails. There's good rafting and kayaking available near Kathmandu on the Trisuli River, but if you don't spend most of your time halfway up a mountain, either breathless from the view or the lack of oxygen – you've wasted your trip.

👁 Bhaktapur, Bodhnath Temple, Everest Base Camp, Helambu, Jomsom, Kathmandu, Langtang, Patan, Pokhara, Swayambhunath Temple, trekking on trails such as Annapurna, whitewater rafting on the Trisuli River.

Weather:

It rains heavily between June and October – the months when it is also hottest. November to February it's dry and generally mild, except for the valley temperatures in the Himalayas which are much colder than elsewhere.

Languages:

Nepali; also Maithir and Bhojpuri.

Religion:

Predominantly Hindu and Buddhist; a Muslim minority.

Money:

Nepalese rupee = 100 paisa.

Cirrus: not accepted.

Maestro: not accepted.

MasterCard: very limited for retail, no ATMs available.

Traveller's cheques: US dollars or £ sterling (accepted in banks and major hotels).

Visa: very limited for retail, no ATMs available.

Living costs:

Nepal is pretty cheap so allow $15 per day for food and board. Organised trekking is more costly and will push your daily budget up by another $10 a day.

Visas:

Tourist visas are issued for up to thirty days and can be extended to a maximum of three months.

Electricity:

220V, 50Hz (when available).

Health:

A yellow fever certificate is required if you're travelling from infected areas. Hepatitis A, malaria (in low-lying areas only), meningococcal meningitis (the Kathmandu Valley region) and typhoid.

ADDRESS BOOK

Amex Yeti Travels, Hotel Mayalu, Jamal Tole, Durbar Marg (PO Box 76), Kathmandu. ☎ (977) 227 635.
Nepal Tourism Board Tourist Service Center, PO Box 11018, Bhrikuti Mandap. ☎ 256229 or 256909. Fax: 256910. Email: info@ntb.wlink.com.np
STA Student Travel and Tours, Air House (PO Box 4701), Maitighar, Kathmandu. ☎ (1) 262 452/486/563/730. Fax: (1) 262 848.
Thomas Cook Natraj Tours and Travel Ltd, PO Box 495, Ghantagher, Kamaladi, Kathmandu. ☎ (1) 249 811.

Your embassy/consulate in Nepal:

Australian: Bansbari, Kathmandu. ☎ (1) 413 076/566. Fax: (1) 417 533.
British: Lainchaur, (PO Box 106), Kathmandu. ☎ (1) 410 583 or 411 281. Fax: (1) 411 789. Email: britemb@wlink.com.np
Irish: represented by the Irish embassy/consulate in India: 13 Jor Bagh, New Delhi 110003. ☎ (11) 461 7435/5485. Fax: (11) 469 7053.
NZ: Dilli Bazar (PO Box 224), Kathmandu. ☎ (1) 412 436. Fax: (1) 414 750.
US: Pani Pokhari, Kathmandu. ☎ (1) 411 179. Fax: (1) 419 963.

Nepalese embassies/consulates at home:

Canada: contact the Indian embassy/consulate: 10 Springfield Road, Ottawa, Ontario K1M 1C9. ☎ (613) 744 3751. Fax: (613) 744 0913.
NZ: 278a Remuera Road, Auckland 5. ☎ (09) 520 3169. Fax: (09) 520 7847.
UK: 12a Kensington Palace Gardens, London W8 4QU. ☎ (020) 7229 1594 or 7229 6231. Fax: (020) 7792 9861. Email: rnelondon@compuserve.com
US: 2131 Leroy Place, NW, Washington DC 20008. ☎ (202) 667 4550.

Accommodation:

Hotel Millennium P.O. Box 10752, Thamel, Kathmandu. ☎ (1) 249 579. Fax: (1) 264 106 Email: millennium@wlink.com.np
Kathmandu Guest House Thamel, Kathmandu. ☎ 41362.
Dhangadhi YH Kailali District, Dhangadhi.

Poste restante:

General Post Office Kathmandu.

Pakistan ✈

(+5hrs GMT) **Capital:** Islamabad

☎ **Country: 92**, Karachi: 21, Islamabad: 51   💲 Pakistani rupee

Bypass modern Islamabad if you can, and head for its ancient twin, Rawalpindi. Lahore is another must, with more bazaars, temples, narrow streets, stalls and 'Why the hell did I buy that?' items than you would think possible. Lahore is also one of the country's more relaxed places to hang out. Heading north into the mountains, you come to Peshawar, with more shop-till-you-drop markets. The town of Gilgit is your best bet for a base – it's possible to arrange most types of trek from here. Popular ones are Nanga Parbat and Balistan (if you fancy trying the second highest mountain in the world, K2). You can also take a spectacular flight from Gilgit to Skardu. The Karakoram Highway and the Khyber Pass are more northern destinations, where you'll find plenty of other travellers, hippies and serious hikers. Further hiking possibilities are available along the irrigation channels of the Hunza Valley, which also happens to be where those unsulphured apricots come from. For insatiable toughies, there's whitewater rafting along the River Indus too. The best way to travel is by bus – they go everywhere – and hopefully arrive too, if you're lucky. In towns there are tons of taxis and auto-rickshaws.

👁 Chitral, Cholistan, Gilgit, Hanna Lake, Hunza, Khyber Pass, Lahore, Lal Suhanra National Park, Peshawar, Quetta, Rawalpindi, the Swat Valley, Urak Valley, Ziarat.

Weather:

From July to September it is monsoon season and that means humid, hot and soggy – especially in the hills. Between October and February it's much drier, and cooled by sea breezes. The summer months (from April to July) are blistering.

Languages:

Urdu and English; also Punjabi, Sindhi, and various regional dialects.

Religion:

Predominantly Sunni Muslim; Shi'a Muslim minority.

Money:

Pakistan rupee = 100 paisa.

Cirrus: not accepted.

Maestro: not accepted.

MasterCard: limited for retail, no ATMs available.

Traveller's cheques: US dollars (accepted in banks, upmarket hotels and major shops).

Visa: not accepted.

Electricity:

220V, 50Hz. Round two- or three-pin plugs.

Living costs:

At a push, you can spend up to $10–20 a day and live like a king. If you want to save money you can find a bed for as little as $2 a night. Shop at markets, and the cost of food is negligible.

Visas:

Passports should be valid for a minimum of six months from your date of arrival. Visas are required – check with the embassy before you travel.

Health:

A yellow fever certificate is required if you're travelling from infected areas. Cholera, dengue fever, hepatitis A, Japanese encephalitis (only in rural areas), malaria, polio and rabies.

ADDRESS BOOK

Amex Ali Plaza, 1–E, Blue Area (PO Box 91), Islamabad. ☎ (51) 272 425–32.

Pakistan Tourism Development Corporation 2nd Floor, 22/A Saeed Plaza, Jinnah Avenue, Blue Area, P.O. Box 1465, Islamabad 44000.
☎ (51) 287 7039. Fax: (51) 227 4507.
Email: tourism@isb.comsats.net.pk
Alternate email: ptl@isb.comsats.net.pk

Thomas Cook Travel Waljis Pvt Limited, 10 Khyaban E Suhrawardy Waljis Building (PO Box 1088), Islamabad. ☎ (51) 270 745–8.

Your embassy/consulate in Pakistan:

Australian: Plot 17 Sector G4/4 Diplomatic Enclave No. 2 (PO Box 1046), Islamabad. ☎ (51) 214 902. Fax: (51) 214 763.

British: Diplomatic Enclave Ramna 5 (PO Box 1122), Islamabad. ☎ (51) 822 131/5. Fax: (51) 823 439.
Website: http://britainonline.org.pk/

Canadian: Diplomatic Enclave, Sector G-5, Islamabad.
☎ (51) 279 100. Fax: (51) 823 466.
Email: isbad@dfait-maeci.gc.ca

Irish: represented by the embassy in Iran: Avenue Mirdamad, 10 Khlaban Razane Shomall, Tehran 19166. ☎ (98) (21) 222 7872.

NZ: 74/1a, Lalazar, Moulvi, Tamizuddin Khan Road, Karachi. ☎ (21) 561 0198. Fax: (21) 561 0959.

US: Diplomatic Enclave, Ramna 5, Islamabad.
☎ (51) 208 000. Fax: (51) 276 427.
Email: fuwad@pd.state.gov
Website: http://usembassy.state.gov/posts/pk1/ wwwhusis.html

Pakistani embassies/consulates at home:

Australia: 4 Timbarra Crescent, O'Malley ACT 2606.
☎ (02) 6290 1676. Fax: (02) 6290 1073.

Canada: 4881 Yonge Street, Suite 810 Willowdale, Ontario M2N 5X3. ☎ (416) 250 1255.
Fax: (416) 250 1321.

South Africa: 35 Marais Street, Brooklyn, Pretoria.
☎ (012) 461 080.

UK: 36 Lowndes Square, London SW1X 9JN.
☎ (020) 7664 9200.

US: 2315 Massachusetts Avenue, NW, Washington DC 20008. ☎ (202) 939 6200.
Email: info@pakistan-embassy.com
Website: http://www.pakistan-embassy.com

Accommodation:

HI–Islamabad Adjoining Akhabar Market Aabpata, Shaheed-e-Millat Rd. Sector G-6/4, Islamabad.
☎ (51) 826899. Fax: (51) 826417.

HI–Peshawar Plot No 37 Block B/ 1, Phase V Hayatabad, Peshawar. ☎ 813581.

HI–Lahore 110-B-3 Gulberg-III, near Firdaus Market, Lahore. ☎ 878201.

Poste restante:

General post offices in Lahore, Karachi and Rawalpindi.

Singapore ✈

(+8hrs GMT) **Capital:** Singapore City

☎ **Country: 65** ⌧ Singapore dollar

Base your stay in Singapore in the Chinatown area, where you'll find the cheapest accommodation. The majority of Singapore is given over to shopping – if you can't get it here, then there's no chance anywhere else. Little India, Chinatown and Arab Street are areas where you'll find more authentic Asian flavours, and they're a lot easier on your pocket. The city-state's main attraction is Sentosa Island, a conglomeration of parks, museums, aquariums, rides, beaches and walks. Also worth a visit is Jurong Town, home to the beautiful Chinese and Japanese Gardens and a bizarre theme park called Haw Par Villa, based on traditional Chinese culture. No visit would be complete without a Singapore Sling at Raffles Hotel. One of the best known marks of colonialism, it still retains the feel of the empire-crazy days. There are some excellent beaches on the surrounding islands. Bukit Timah Nature Reserve has the majority of Singapore's flora, while the zoo is the place to see fauna in good condition. Pulau Ubin to the north and the Lazarus Islands to the south are the best for swimming, snorkelling and just wandering around for as long as your cash lasts.

👁 Arab Street for shopping, boat trip on the Singapore River, Bukit Timah Hill, Chinatown, the Gateway Building, Jurong Town, Little India's thriving community, the night safari in Singapore Zoo and Raffles Hotel.

Weather:
It's hot, wet, sticky and humid all year round. The wettest months are between November and January, when showers can be sudden.

Languages:
Mandarin Chinese, Malay, Tamil and English.

Religion:
Confucian, Taoist, Buddhist, Muslim, Christian and Hindu.

Money:
Singapore dollar = 100 cents.
Cirrus: excellent for ATMs.
Maestro: not accepted.
MasterCard: good for retail, excellent for ATMs.
Traveller's cheques: £ sterling.
Visa: good for retail, excellent for ATMs.

Living costs:
It's easy to blow your entire budget in Singapore. If you're very careful, you can get by on about $10–20 for food and board per day. Save money by buying

food from vendors (and try haggling). You'll also be able to find some cheap hostels.

Visas:

Passports should be valid for a minimum of six months from your date of arrival. You also need suffient funds for the trip's duration. Everyone needs a fourteen-day social visit pass which is issued on arrival and may be extended for three months. Women more than six months pregnant must arrange a pass prior to arrival.

Requirements are subject to change, so check before you go.

Electricity:

220–240V, 50Hz. Flat three-pin plugs.

Health:

Cholera, polio and typhoid. Dehydration is also a risk.

ADDRESS BOOK

Amex 300 Beach RTd, The Concourse, 18/F Singapore 199555. ☎ 299 8133.
Singapore Tourism Board Tourism Court, 1 Orchard Spring Lane, Singapore 247729. ☎ 6736 6622. Fax: 636-9423. Email: stb_sog@stb.gov.sg
STA 2–17 Orchard Parade Hotel, 1 Tanglin Road, Singapore 247905. ☎ 737 7188. Fax: 737 2591.

Your embassy/consulate in Singapore:

Australian: 25 Napier Road, Tanglin 9124 Singapore. ☎ 737 9311. Website: http://www.aushighcom.org.sg/
British: Tanglin Road, Singapore 247919.
☎ 473 9333. Fax: 474 1958.
Email: brit_hc@pacific.net.sg
Website: http://www.britain.org.sg
Canadian: 80 Anson Road, 14th and 15th Floors, IBM Towers, Singapore 079907. ☎ 325 3200.
Fax: 325 3296. Email: spore@dfait-maeci.gc.ca
Irish: 541 Orchard Road, Liat Towers, 8th Floor, Singapore, 238881. ☎ 238 7616. Fax: 238 7615.
Email: ireland@magix.com.sq
South African: 15th Floor Odeon Towers, 331 North Bridge Road, Singapore,188720.
☎ 339 3319. Fax: 337 0196.
Website: http://web.singnet.com.sg/~satrade2/.
US: 27 Napier Road, Singapore 258508. ☎ 476 9100.
Fax: 476 9340.
Website: http://www.usembassysingapore.org.sg/

Singaporean embassies/consulates at home:

Australia: 17 Forster Crescent, Yarralumla ACT 2600.
☎ (02) 6273 3944. Fax: (02) 6273 3260.

Canada: represented by the Singaporean embassy/consulate in the US: 3501 International Place, NW, Washington DC 20008. ☎ (202) 537 3100.
Website: http://www.gov.sg
Ireland: represented by the Singaporean embassy/consulate in the UK: 9 Wilton Crescent, London SW1X 8SA. ☎ (0171) 245 0273.
Fax: (0171) 245 6583.
Email: schlondon@singcomm.demon.co.uk
NZ: 17 Kabul Street, Khandallah, Wellington.
☎ (04) 479 2076/7. Fax: (04) 479 2315.
South Africa: 173 Beckett Street, Arcadia, Pretoria.
☎ (012) 343 437/4.
UK: 9 Wilton Crescent, London SW1X 8SA.
☎ (020) 7245 0273. Fax: (020) 7245 6583.
Email: schlondon@singcomm.demon.co.uk
US: 3501 International Place, NW, Washington DC 20008. ☎ (202) 537 3100.
Website: http://www.gov.sg

Accommodation:

Fragrance Hotel-Emerald No. 20 Lorong 6 Geylang, 399174, Singapore. ☎ (65) 841 2455.
Fax: (65) 841 0211.
Email: contact@fragrancehotel.com
Lee Boarding House 46-52, Bencoolean Street, #07-52 Pony Mansion, Singapore 189629. ☎ (65) 338-3149.
Fax: (65) 338-6509.

Poste restante:

General Post Office Fullerton Road, Singapore.

Thailand

(+7hrs GMT) **Capital:** Bangkok

☎ **Country: 66**, Bangkok: 2 　💲 Baht

Flying into Bangkok, head first for the Khao San Road. This is where you'll find other travellers and the cheapest guesthouses in Bangkok. The floating markets, numerous wats (temples) and a huge golden statue of Buddha are all within easy reach. It's fast, sweaty and noisy, but you didn't come here to relax, did you? The northern city of Chiang Mai is a 12-hour train or bus journey away. Head for the Moon Meuang Road area for the best of the budget guesthouses. Chiang Mai, and Chiang Rai further north, are the starting points for treks (often pretty touristy) into the foothills of the Himalayas. The islands of Ko Tao, Ko Pha-Ngan and Koh Samui, off the east coast, are the places to do some serious relaxing and partying. The smallest, Ko Tao, is excellent for diving and is the least busy. Ko Pha-Ngan is infamous for its monthly full-moon parties on the southeastern Hat Rin Nok beach. The largest and most popular of these islands is Koh Samui. It's good fun and very sociable, with lots of travellers. The atmosphere on these islands is chilled and friendly, so just sunbathe, dive, relax and party.

👁 Ayuthaya's 18th-century ruins, Bangkok's Grand Palace and Wat Po temple complex, Chiang Mai's night market, Ko Pha-Ngan, Koh Samui, and Wat Traimit with its solid gold statue of Buddha.

Weather:

Hot and humid in April, followed with monsoons from May to November. It's cooler and drier (and much more pleasant to visit) from November to March.

Languages:

Thai; English, Malay and Chinese.

Religion:

Buddhist; Muslim minority.

Money:

Baht = 100 satang.

Cirrus: fair for ATMs.

Maestro: not accepted.

MasterCard: good for retail, fair for ATMs.

Traveller's cheques: US dollars or £ sterling (accepted in major hotels and shops).

Visa: fair for retail, good for ATMs.

Living costs:

You can get by on about $10 per day for food and board. The cost of living is cheaper outside Bangkok.

Visas:

Passports should be valid for a minimum of six months from your date of arrival. If you're staying for under thirty days, you don't need a visa. A tourist visa lasts for sixty days and costs $15. For longer stays (up to ninety days) there's a non-immigrant visa – apply from your home country, it costs around $20. Requirements are subject to change so check before you go.

Electricity:

220V, 50Hz. A variety of plugs are used.

Health:

A yellow fever certificate is required if you're travelling from an infected area. Cholera, dengue fever, diphtheria, dysentery, Japanese encephalitis, hepatitis A and B, malaria, polio, tetanus and typhoid. The Australian, UK and US embassies have lists of English-speaking doctors.

ADDRESS BOOK

Amex Sea Tours Co Ltd, Suite 88–92, 8/F Payatati Road, Rajthavee, Bangkok 10400. ☎ (2) 216 5934–36.
STA Wall Street Tower Bldg, Room 1406, 33 Surawong Road, Bangrak, Bangkok 10500.
☎ (2) 236 0262. Fax: (2) 237 6006.
Thomas Cook Turismo Thai, Building 511, Soi 6, Sri Ayuthaya Road, Bangkok 10400. ☎ (2) 642 4504/5.
Tourism Authority of Thailand Le Concorde Building, 202 Ratchadaphisek Road, Huai Khwang, Bangkok 10310. ☎ (2) 694 1222. Fax: (2) 6941372.
Email: center@tat.or.th. Website: http://www.tat.or.th/thai/

Your embassy/consulate in Thailand:
Australian: 37 South Sathon Road, Bangkok 10120.
☎ (2) 287 2680. Fax: (2) 287 2029.
Website: http://www.austembassy.or.th/
British: Wireless Road, Bangkok 10330.
☎ (2) 253 0191–9. Fax: (2) 255 6051.
Website: http://www.britishemb.or.th/
Canadian: 990 Rama IV, Abdulrahim Place, Bangrak, Bangkok 10500. ☎ (2) 636 0540. Fax: (2) 636 0566.
Website: http://www.dfait-maeci.gc.ca/bangkok
Irish: represented by the embassy/consulate in Malaysia: Rooms 1527–1529, Shangri-La-Hotel, 11 Jalan Sultan Ismail, 50250 Kuala Lumpur.
☎ (3) 232 2388. Fax: (3) 234 3510.
NZ: M Thai Tower, 14th Floor, All Seasons Place,87 Wireless Road , Bangkok 10330. ☎ (2) 254 2530.
Fax: (2) 253 9045. E-mail: nzembbkk@loxinfo.co.th
South African: represented by the embassy/consulate in Malaysia: 12 Lorong Titiwangsa 12, Taman Tasik, Titiwangsa, Setapak, Kuala Lumpur. ☎ (3) 424 4456.

US: 95 Wireless Road, Bangkok 10330.
☎ (2) 252 5040–9 or 252 5171–9. Fax: (2) 254 2990.
Website: http://www.usa.or.th/

Thai embassies/consulates at home:
Australia: 111 Empire Circuit, Yarralumla ACT 2600.
☎ (02) 6273 1149. Fax: (02) 6273 1518.
Canada: 180 Island Park Drive, Ottawa, Ontario KIY OA2. ☎ (613) 722 4444. Fax: (613) 722 6624.
Ireland: represented by the Thai embassy/consulate in the UK: 29 Queen's Gate, London SW7 5JB.
☎ (020) 7589 0173.
NZ: 2 Cook Street, Karori, Wellington.
☎ (04) 476 8618/9. Fax: (04) 476 3677.
South Africa: 840 Church Street, Eastwood, Pretoria.
☎ (012) 342 4516.
UK: 29/30 Queen's Gate, London SW7 5JB.
☎ (020) 7589 2944. Fax: (020) 7823 9695.
US: 1024 Wisconsin Avenue, NW, Suite 401, Washington DC 20007. ☎ (202) 944 3600.
Fax: (202) 944 3611. Website: http://www.thaiembdc.org/

Accommodation
HI–Bangkok International Hostel 25/2 Phitsanulok Rd, Sisao Theves, Dusit, Bangkok 10300.
☎ (2) 281 0361/282 0950. Fax: (2) 281 6834.
Viengtai Hotel 42 Tanee Road, Banglampu, Bangkok 10200, Thailand. ☎ (2) 280-5434-45. Fax: (2) 281 8153.
7 Holder Guest House 216/2-3 Khao San Road, Banglimpoo, Bangkok, 10200. ☎ 281 3682/281 3683.

Poste restante:
Main GPO Charoen Krung Road, Bangkok.

Vietnam ✈

(+7hrs GMT) **Capital:** Hanoi

☎ **Country: 84**, Hanoi: 4, Ho Chi Minh City: 8   💲 Dông

You've seen the films, now experience the country. Ho Chi Minh City is packed with market traders, boasts a cool nightlife (the best is in the Mac Thai Buoi street area) and has remnants of Vietnam's colonial past. Head for the western end of District 1, around Pham Ngu Lao Street for the cheapest rooms. The beaches south east of Ho Chi Mihn City and near the Gulf of Thailand are made for lazing on. With over 3,000 islands, Halong Bay has more beaches than you could shake a stick at. Halong City West is a place to take things easy and soak up the ambience. Jungle freaks should check out Cuc Phong National Park. Hanoi is pretty, posh and has a few excellent cafés. There are a number of stark reminders of the Vietnam War, such as the network of tunnels built by the Viet Cong. Those at Cu Chi and Vinh Moc give a realistic experience of what it must have been like. Overland travel is time-consuming and less than comfy. Steer clear of buses to minimise stress. A good way to see the country is on the Reunification Express Train that runs from Ho Chi Minh City to Hanoi.

👁 Boat tour of Ha Long Bay, Central Highlands, Da Lat, Hanoi, Ha Tien, Ho Chi Minh City, Hoi An, Hué, Mekong Delta, Nha Trang, Red River Delta, Sam Mountain, and Sapa.

Weather:

It's hot all year round. Dry, except for the monsoon season from May to October.

Languages:

Vietnamese, French, Chinese, English and local dialects.

Religion:

Predominantly Buddhist; Muslim, Confucian, Taoist, Hoa Hao, Christian and Caodaist minorities.

Money:

Dông = 100 hao.

Cirrus: not accepted.

Maestro: not accepted.

MasterCard: not accepted.

Traveller's cheques: not recommended.

Visa: no retail availability, *very* limited for ATMs.

Take cash in US dollars.

Living costs:

Vietnam is good for cheap hostels and guesthouses, so you shouldn't spend much over $5–10 a night on accommodation. Food is cheap, especially if you love noodles. Travel is also a bargain. You can budget for about $15–20 a day all in.

Visas:

Passports should be valid for a minimum of one month from your date of arrival. Visas are necessary for any stay longer than 24 hours. They last one month and can be extended at a price. Requirements are subject to change, so check before you go.

Electricity:

110–220V, 50Hz

Health:

A yellow fever certificate is required if you're travelling from infected areas. Bilharzia, cholera, dengue fever, hepatitis, Japanese encephalitis, malaria, plague, polio, rabies, tuberculosis, schistosomiasis and typhoid.

ADDRESS BOOK

Your embassy/consulate in Vietnam:

Australian: The Landmark, 5B Duong Ton Duc Thang, District 1, Ho Chi Minh City. ☎ (8) 829 6035. Fax: (8) 829 6031.

British: 31 Hai Ba Trung, Hanoi. ☎ (4) 825 2510. Fax: (4) 826 5762. Email: behanoi@fpt.vn Website: http://www.uk-vietnam.org/

Canadian: 31 Hung Vuong Street, Hanoi. ☎ (4) 823 5500. Fax: (4) 823 5333. Email: hanoi@dfait-maeci.gc.ca

NZ: 32 Hang Bai Street, Hanoi. ☎ (4) 241 481. Fax: (4) 241 480. Email: nzembhan@fpt.vn

US: 7 Lang Ha Road, Hanoi. ☎ (4) 843 1500. Fax: (4) 843 1510. Website: http://usembassy.state.gov/vietnam/

Vietnamese embassies/consulates at home:

Australia: 6 Timbarra Crescent, O'Malley ACT 2606. ☎ (02) 6286 6059. Fax: (02) 6286 4534.

Canada: 226 Maclaren Street, Ottawa, Ontario K2P OL9. ☎ (613) 236 0772. Fax: (613) 236 2704.

UK: 12–14 Victoria Road, London W8 5RD. ☎ (020) 7937 1912.

US: 734 15th Street, NW, Suite 400, Washington DC 20005. ☎ (202) 638 3800. Email: vietnamembassy@msn.com Website: http://www.vietnamembassy-usa.org/

Accommodation:

Hotel 211 211 Pham Ngu Lao St., District 1, Ho Chi Minh City. ☎ 836 7353/836 0047. Email: hotelduy@hotmail.com Website: www.1saigon.net/hotel211

New Tong Dan 17 Tong Dan Street, Hanoi. ☎ 825 2219 or 826 5328. Fax: 825 5354. Email: tongdanhotel@hn.vnn.vn

3 Ky Chinh-Thang Hotel 3 Ly Chinh Thang Str., Dist. 3, Ho Chi Minh City. ☎ 844 5313. Fax: 844 5887.

Poste restante:

General Post Office 75 Pho Dinh Tien Hoang, Hanoi.

Israel ✈

(+2hrs GMT) **Capital:** Jerusalem

☎ **Country: 972,** Tel Aviv: 3, Jerusalem: 2 💲 New Israeli shekel

If you've got any interest in religion or history, then you'll be pretty happy in Israel. The Old City area of Jerusalem with its Christian, Jewish and Muslim quarters, is well worth wandering around. The New City and East Jerusalem are more upbeat and are perfect for lounging over a coffee and having a quick peek in the shops. It's a living, working city, not just a historical landmark. Next on the tour is Galilee, which is where Jesus of Nazareth spent most of his life. It's a beautiful area, with lovely green forests and valleys. Then trot on down to Bethlehem to the huge Church of the Nativity, supposedly built on the spot where Mary gave birth. Tel Aviv is a much-needed modern contrast to all the 2,000 years of history. It's good fun with some great bars and a lively atmosphere. Also, don't miss your chance to imitate a block of wood – go for one of those famous floats on the Dead Sea. There's more fertile land around here, and you can check out the Ein Gedi oasis for a bit of therapeutic chill-out time. Buses are superb in Israel – cheap, comfy and fast. Don't bother with the trains, they're all a bit dishevelled.

👁 Bethlehem – where a silver star marks the birthplace of Christ, Dead Sea, Dome of the Rock, Jerusalem's Old City with the Church of the Holy Sepulchre, Nazareth, Red Sea, River Jordan, Safed, Sea of Galilee, Tel Aviv (Jaffa), Western (Wailing) Wall, and the Yad Vashem Holocaust Memorial in the New City.

Weather:

Between April and November, the south is very hot and very dry. There's a chance of rain and bearable heat the rest of the year. The north is slightly cooler and gets heavier rain from December to March.

Languages:

Hebrew and Arabic. English is spoken in major tourist centres.

Religion:

Predominantly Jewish; Muslim and Christian minorities.

Money:

New Israeli shekel = 100 new agorot.
Cirrus: good for ATMs (at the three main airports).
Maestro: fair for retail and banks, good for ATMs.
MasterCard: good for retail and ATMs.
Traveller's cheques: US dollars.
Visa: good for retail and ATMs.

Living costs:

Street food is amazingly cheap, only about $3 per day, and a room will cost less than $8 per night. Entrance fees and tours can be costly.

Visas:

Passports should be valid for a minimum of six months from your date of arrival. EU nationals can stay in Israel for three months without a visa. Try not to get your passport stamped – or ask for it to be stamped on a separate piece of paper – it can create difficulties on entering Arab countries.

Electricity:

220V, 50Hz. three-pin plugs.

Health:

Polio, typhoid and rabies.

ADDRESS BOOK

Ministry of Tourism PO Box 1018, Mevo Hamatmid 4, Jerusalem. ☎ (2) 675 4811. Fax: (2) 623 3686. Website: http://www.infotour.co.il
STA ISSTA 128 Ben Yehuda Street, Tel Aviv 63401. ☎ (3) 524 6322. Fax: (3) 524 6324.

Your embassy/consulate in Israel:

Australian: Beit Europa, 4th Floor, 37 Shaul Hamelech Boulevard, Tel Aviv 64928. ☎ (3) 695 0451.
Fax: (3) 696 8404. Email: aussie@inter.net.il
Website: http://www.australianembassy.org.il/
British: 192 Hayarkon Street, Tel Aviv 63405.
☎ (3) 725 1222. Fax: (3) 524 3313.
Website: http://www.britemb.org.il/
Canadian: 3 Nirim Street, 4th Floor, Tel Aviv 67060.
☎ (3) 636 3300. Fax: (3) 636 3380.
Email: taviv@dfait-maeci.gc.ca
Website: http://www.dfait-maeci.gc.ca/telaviv/
Irish: The Tower, 17th Floor, 3 Daniel Frisch Street, Tel Aviv 63573. ☎ (3) 696 4166. Fax: (3) 696 4160.
Email: telaviv@iveagh.irlgov.ie
South African: 15th floor, Dizengoff Centre, Dizengoff Street, Tel Aviv 64332. ☎ (3) 525 2566.
Fax: (3) 525 3236. Email: saemtel@isdn.net.il
Website: http://www.safis.co.il/
US: 1 Ben Yehuda Street, POB 26180, Tel Aviv 63903.
☎ (2) 625 5755. Fax: (2) 510 3828.
Email: webmaster@usembassy-israel.org.il
Website: http://www.usembassy-israel.org.il/

Israeli embassies/consulates at home:

Australia: 6 Turrana Street, Yarralumla ACT 2600.
☎ (02) 6273 1309. Fax: (02) 6273 4273.
Canada: 50 O'Connor Street, Suite 1005, Ottawa, Ontario K1P 6L2. ☎ (613) 567 6450.
Fax: (613) 237 8865.
Ireland: Carrisbrook House, 122 Pembroke Road, Dublin 4. ☎ (01) 668 0303. Fax: (01) 668 0418.
Email: embisrael@iol.ie
NZ: 13th Floor, DB Tower, 111 The Terrace (PO Box 2171), Wellington. ☎ (04) 472 2362.
Fax: (04) 499 0632.
South Africa: 3rd Floor, Dashing Centre, 339 Hatfield Street, Hatfield, Pretoria. ☎ (012) 342 2693.
UK: 2 Palace Gate, London W8 4QB.
☎ (020) 7957 9500.
US: 3514 International Drive, NW, Washington DC 20008. ☎ (202) 364 5500. Fax: (202) 364 5423.
Email: ask@israelemb.org
Website: http://www.israelemb.org/

Accommodation:

HI–Bayit Vagan (Waterman-Weiss) 8 HaPisga St., Beit VaGan, Jerusalem. ☎ (02) 642 3366.
Fax: (02) 642 3362. Email: betbg@zahav.net.il
HI–Massada D.N. Dead Sea 86935. ☎ (08) 658 4349.
Fax: (08) 658 4650. Email: massada@iyha.org.il
HI–Tiberias "Meyouchas" 2 Jordan St., POB 81, Tiberias 14100. ☎ (04) 672 1775. Fax: (04) 6720372.
Email: tiberias@iyha.org.il

Poste restante:

General Post Office Jerusalem.
General Post Office 170 Ibngvirol Street, Tel Aviv.

Turkey ✈

(+2hrs GMT) **Capital:** Ankara

☎ **Country: 90**, Ankara: 312, Istanbul: 212 💲 Turkish lira

How bazaar! Turkey is very friendly with a lot to pack in. Istanbul is the capital as far as history and culture are concerned. Top of the sights are Topkapi Palace, Aya Sofya (Church of the Divine) and the Blue Mosque – all very impressive. Take time to trawl the markets and bazaars, and you won't be disappointed. The Grand Bazaar is a bit of a tourist festival so try Uzuncars Caddesi or Istiklal Caddesi to get weighed down with souvenirs. Cheap places to rest your head are in the Sultanahmet area of the old city. However if you want really ancient buildings, head to Ephesus, the jewel in Turkey's historical crown. It's very glam and well worth a browse. The South Aegean resort of Bodrum is the perfect antidote to all this culture and history. A self-proclaimed party town, with some of the best swimming and snorkelling in the country, don't expect to get much sleep. You can beach-hop along the Mediterranean coast by dolmus, the very convenient system of shared mini-bus. Make sure you catch Patara's incredible long, sandy beach. Head inland to Cappadocia for some mind-bending rock formations. The long distances are best covered by the cheap and reliable bus network.

👁 Antalya, Bodrum's outdoor disco scene, boat trip on the Bosphorus, Cappadocia, Celçuk, Dalyan's turtle beach, Ephesus, Göreme, Kalkan, Kas for restaurants and nightlife, mosques and markets in Istanbul, Pammukale's hillside scenery, and Patara Beach.

Weather:

Coastal areas have hot summers and mild winters. Inland it's hot and dry from June to September; the rest of the year it's much colder.

Languages:

Turkish and Kurdish. English, French and German may be spoken.

Religion:

Predominantly Muslim; Christian minority.

Money:

Turkish lira = 100 kurus.
Cirrus: good for ATMs.
Maestro: limited for ATMs.
MasterCard: good for retail and ATMs.
Traveller's cheques: £ sterling.
Visa: good for retail and ATMs.

Living costs:

For good value, eat from the vendors and stay in hostels – you'll spend about $15 per day.

Visas:

UK and Irish nationals must obtain a visa on entry for about $16. Nationals of the US need a visa valid for three months. Other nationals don't need a visa. Passports should be valid for six months or one year from your date of arrival, depending respectively whether your visa was issued on arrival or by the Turkish Consulate.

ADDRESS BOOK

Amex Turk Ekspress, Cinnah Caddesi 9/4 Cankaya, Ankara. ☎ (312) 467 7369.

Ministry of Tourism Ismet Inönü Bulvar 5, Bahçelievler, Ankara. ☎ (312) 212 8300.
Fax: (312) 212 8391.
Email: turizm.bilgi.islem@fim.net.tr
Website: http://www.turkey.org/turkey

Thomas Cook Setur Cumhuriyet Caddesi No. 107, Elmadag, Istanbul 80230. ☎ 212 230 0336.

Your embassy/consulate in Turkey:

Australian: 83 Nenehatun Caddesi, Gaziosmanpasa, Ankara 06700. ☎ (312) 446 1180–87.
Fax: (312) 446 1188.
Website: http://www.embaustralia.org.tr/

British: Sehit Ersan Caddesi 46/A, Cankaya, Ankara. ☎ (312) 468 6230/42. Fax: (312) 468 6643.
Email: britembank@ankara.mail.fco.gov.uk
Website: http://www.britishembassy.org.tr

Canadian: 75 Nenehaeun Caddesi, Gaziosmanpasa, 06700 Ankara. ☎ (312) 436 1275.
Fax: (312) 446 4437. Email: ankra@dfait-maeci.gc.ca
Website: http://www.dfait-maeci.gc.ca/ankara/

Irish: Ugur Mumcu Caddesi, MNG Binasi, B Bloc, Kat 3, Gaziosmanpasa, Ankara 06700.
☎ (312) 446 6172. Fax: (312) 446 8061.
Email: ireland@superonline.com

NZ: Level 4, Iran Caddesi 13 Kavaklidere, 06700 Ankara. ☎ (312) 467 9054/6/8. Fax: (312) 467 9013.
Email: newzealand@superonline.com

South African: 27 Filistin Caddesi, Gaziosmanpasa, Ankara. ☎ (312) 446 4056. Fax: (312) 446 6434.
Email: saemb@ada.net.tr
Website: http://www.southafrica.org.tr/

US: Atatürk Bulvar 110, Kavaklidere, 06100 Ankara.
☎ (312) 468 6110. Fax: (312) 467 0019.
Website: http://www.usis-ankara.org.tr/

Electricity:

220V, 50 Hz

Health:

Cholera, malaria, polio, rabies and typhoid.

Turkish embassies/consulates at home:

Australia: 60 Mugga Way, Red Hill ACT 2603.
☎ (02) 6295 0227/8. Fax: (02) 6239 6592.

Canada: 197 Wurtemburg, Ottawa, Ontario KIN 8L9.
☎ (613) 789 4044. Fax: (613) 789 3442.

Ireland: 11 Clyde Road, Dubin 4. ☎ (01) 668 5240.

NZ: 15–17 Murphy Street, Thorndon, Wellington.
☎ (04) 472 1292.

South Africa: 1067 Church Street, Hatfield, Pretoria.
☎ (012) 342 6053.

UK: 43 Belgrave Square, London SW1X 8PA.
☎ (020) 7393 0202. Fax: (020) 7393 0066.
Email: turkish.embassy@virgin.net
Website: http://www.mfa.gov.tr

US: 1714 Massachusetts Avenue, NW, Washington DC 20036. ☎ (202) 659 8200. Fax: (202) 659 0744.
Website: http://www.turkey.org/turkey/

Accommodation:

HI–Yucelt Interyouth Hostel Caferiye Sok. No 6/1 34400 Sultanahmet, Istanbul 34400.
☎ (212) 513 6150.
Fax: (212) 512 7628. Email: info@yucelthostel.com

Cordial House Hotel and Hostel Divanyolu Cad. Peykhane Sok. 29, Cemberlitas, Istanbul 34400.
☎ (212) 518 0576. Fax: (212) 516 4108.
Email: cordial@dominet.in.com.tr
Web: http://www.cordialhouse.com

Mavi Deniz Hostel and Backpackers On the beach front, Oludeniz, Fethiye, Mugla. ☎ (535) 777 2084.
Fax: (252) 617 0559. Email: info@mavidenizcamp.com

Poste restante:

Send letters to: [name; with surname underlined], c/o Poste Restante, Büyük PTT, Yeni Postane Sokak, Sirkeci, Istanbul.

Collect letters from: Yeni Postane Sokak, Sirkeci, Istanbul.

Czech Republic ✈

(+1hr GMT) **Capital:** Prague

☎ **Country: 42**, Prague: 2   [$] Czech koruna

Prague, apart from being overrun by tourists, is still a beautiful city to visit. The incredible range of architectural styles comes from over 900 years of building, making the city one of Europe's most enjoyable to explore. For culture freaks, check out any of the capital's prolific theatres, operas, museums or galleries, all a short amble away from the heart of the city. Head straight for the Nove Mesto and Smichov areas for the cheapest rooms. Outside Prague there are a plethora of pretty old towns and cities, such as Kutna Hora, and Karlovy, which offer visitors a step back in time. Hiking, climbing, trekking, skiing and any other ways you can think of to punish your body are available to those who venture into the rich and varied rural areas of the country. Hikers should head to the Sumava area in the south west of Bohemia, whilst the Krkonose mountains in the north offer the best and cheapest downhill skiing. The bus and train services are easily adequate for travelling around, buses being slightly more expensive. Road networks are also good. Prague's tram system is not to be missed.

👁 Caves of Moravsky Kras and Punkevni – best seen by boat tour, Karlovy Vary, Krivoklat castle and forest, Krkonose mountains for winter skiing, Kutna Hora with St Barbara's Cathedral, Prague's Charles Bridge, Wenceslas Cathedral and Castle, and Sumava National Park.

Weather:

Warm, wet and mild in the summer. Temperatures are freezing in the winter, and it can also be very windy.

Languages:

Czech; Slovak, German, Russian and English are also spoken.

Religion:

Roman Catholic; Protestant minority.

Money:

Czech koruna or crown = 100 hellers.

Cirrus: fair for ATMs.

Maestro: limited for ATMs.

MasterCard: limited for retail and fair for ATMs.

Traveller's cheques: US dollars, £ sterling or euros.

Visa: very limited for retail, limited for ATMs.

Living costs:

Allow $15 per day for a cheap hostel and food. Prague is more expensive than the rest of the country. Prices are increasing as the tourist trade expands, but it's still cheaper than elsewhere in western Europe.

Visas:

Passports must be valid for at least eight months at the time of application. Visas are required by nationals of Australia, South Africa and the US. Nationals of New Zealand don't require visas for visits under three months; nationals of the UK, Ireland and Canada don't need visas for visits under six months.

Electricity:

220V, 50 Hz

Health:

Encephalitis and lyme disease.

ADDRESS BOOK

Amex Vaclavske Namesti 56, Prague 11000.
☎ (2) 3312 2301.
Czech Tourist Authority Vinohradska 46, Praha 2.
☎ (2) 2158 0411. Email: visitczech@cccr-cta.cz
GTS International Ve Smeckach 27, Prague 1 11000.
☎ (2) 2223 1623. Fax: (2) 5731 1454.
STA Travel Agency Lesser SRO, Karmelitska 24, 11800 Prague. ☎ (2) 530 545/195. Fax: (2) 539 175.

Your embassy/consulate in the Czech Republic:

Australian: Na Orechovce 38, 16000 Prague 6.
☎ (2) 2431 0743/0071. Fax: (2) 311 9531.
British: Thunovska 14, 118 00, Prague 1.
☎ (2) 5753 0278. Fax: (2) 5753 0285.
Email: info@britain.cz Website: http://www.britain.cz/
Canadian: Mickiewiczova 6, Prague 12533.
☎ (2) 7210 1800. Fax: (2) 7210 1890.
Email: prgue@dfait-maeci.gc.ca
Website: http://www.dfait-maeci.gc.ca/~prague/
Irish: Velvyslanectvi Irska, Trziste 13, 11800 Prague 1.
☎ (2) 5753 0061. Fax: (2) 5753 1387.
NZ: Dykova 19, 10100 Prague 10. ☎ (2) 2251 4672.
Fax: (2) 2425 4640.
South African: Velvyslanectví Jihoafrické Republiky Ruská 65, 10000 Prague 10. ☎ (2) 6731 1114.
Fax: (2) 6731 1395.
US: Trziste 15 Mala Strana, Prague 1.
☎ (2) 5732 0663. Website: http://www.usis.cz/

Czech embassies/consulates at home:

Australia: 38 Culgoa Circuit, O'Malley ACT 2606.
☎ (02) 6290 1386/0010. Fax: (02) 6290 0006.
Canada: 50 Sussex Drive Ottawa, Ontario K1N 6Z6.
☎ (613) 562 3875. Fax: (613) 562 3878.
Ireland: contact the Czech embassy in the UK: 25 Kensington Palace Gardens, London W8.
☎ (020) 7243 1115. Fax: (020) 7727 9654.
NZ: 11 Queen Street, Wainuiomata, Wellington.
☎ (04) 564 9055. Fax: (04) 564 9022.
South Africa: 936 Pretorius Street, Arcadia, Pretoria.
☎ (012) 342 3477. Fax: (012) 432 033.
UK: 25 Kensington Palace Gardens, London W8.
☎ (020) 7243 1115. Fax: (020) 7727 9654.
US: 3900 Spring of Freedom Street, NW, Washington DC 20008. ☎ (202) 274 9100. Fax: (202) 966 8540.
Email: washington@embassy.mzv.cz
Website: http://www.czech.cz/washington/

Accommodation:

Arpacay Hostel Radlicka 13, Prague 150 00.
☎ (2) 5155 1441. Email: prague@arpacayhostel.com
Website: http://www.arpacayhostel.com
Hotel Advantage Sokolska 11-13, Prague 12000.
☎ (2) 2491 4062/ Fax: (2) 2491 4067.
Email: advantage@jsc.cz
Website: http://advantage.jsc.cz
HI–BRNO Ubytovna Interservis, Lomena 38, Brno - Komarov, 61700. ☎ (5) 331 111.

Poste restante:

Main Post Office Jindrisska 14, Prague.
☎ (2) 2422 8856.

Denmark ✈

(+1hr GMT) **Capital:** Copenhagen

☎ **Country: 45**   💲 Danish krone

Copenhagen is a great place to chill out. All the main sites are relatively close together, and within easy reach of the city centre, which remains pretty untouched by modern life. The cheapest accommodation is to be found to the west of the Central Station. In Nyhavn there are some fine cafés and restaurants – but if you're scrimping, Strøget is the best place for cheap eats, while you watch street performers entertain the passers-by. Norrebro and Christianshavn have an excellent up-beat atmosphere where you'll meet most of the younger Danes. Århus, on the east coast, is a hub of entertainment and activity, with some of Jutland's best culture thrown in. Danes are addicted to cycling, with trails all across the country. If you've got the time and inclination, they are one of the best and cheapest ways to see the country. If you think you're hard enough, the northern shores of Jutland have some beautiful beaches, but if you like things a little warmer, the southern islands around the Smålandshavet area are for you. Denmark has a fast and reliable train service which is good value, combined with an adequate local bus service.

👁 Aerø island, Århus's music scene, Christiansø island, Copenhagen's Tivoli Gardens' amusement park, Egeskov Castle, Funen Island, Jutland's islands, Louisiana Museum of Modern Art at Humlebaek, North Zealand's villages and coast, and the town of Skagen.

Weather:
Cold winters (February is the coldest month) and warm summers (from June to August). There's the possibility of rain all year round.

Languages:
Danish; English, German and French are widely spoken.

Religion:
Evangelical Lutheran; Roman Catholic minority.

Money:
Danish krone = 100 øre.
Cirrus: fair for ATMs.
Maestro: limited for ATMs.
MasterCard: limited for retail and good for ATMs.
Traveller's cheques: £ sterling.
Visa: limited for retail and good for ATMs.

Living costs:
Scandinavia is expensive by most European standards. Allow about $30 per day for food and board. If you go in the summer, try camping to cut your costs.

Visas:

Passports should be valid for two months from your date of arrival. Nationals of South Africa and the USA require visas. Requirements may be subject to change, so check before you go.

Electricity:

220V, 50Hz. Continental two-pin plugs.

Health:

No major health risks.

ADDRESS BOOK

Amex: Amagertov 18 (Strøget), 1160 Copenhagen
☎ 3312 2301.
Danmarks Turistrad Vesterbrogade 6 D, 1620
København V. ☎ 3311 1415. Fax: 3393 1416.
Email: dt@dt.dk
STA Fiolstraede 18, 1171 Copenhagen.
☎ 3314 1501. Fax: 3373 4050
Email: copenhagen@statravel.dk

Your embassy/consulate in Denmark:

Australian: 21, Kristianiagade, Copenhagen DK 2100.
☎ 3526 2244/071. Fax: 3543 2218.
British: Kastelsvej 36/38/40, Copenhagen DK 2100.
☎ 3526 4600. Fax: 3544 5293.
Email: brit-emb@post6.tele.dk
Website: http://www.britishembassy.dk
Canadian: Kr. Bernikowsgade 1, Copenhagen
DK 1105. ☎ 3348 3200. Fax: 3348 3220.
Email: copen@dfait-maeci.gc.ca
Website: http://www.canada.dk/
South African: 8, Gammel Vartovvej, Hellerup 2900.
☎ 3118 0155.
US: 24, Dag Hammerskjölds Allé, Copenhagen
DK 2100. ☎ 3142 3144.
Website: http://www.usembassy.dk/

Danish embassies/consulates at home:

Australia: 15 Hunter Street, Yarralumla ACT 2600.
☎ (02) 6273 2195/6. Fax: (02) 6273 3864.
Canada: 47 Clarence Street, Suite 450, Ottawa,
Ontario K1N 9K1. ☎ (613) 234 0704.
Fax: (613) 234 7368. Email: danemb@cyberus.ca

Ireland: 121 Saint Stephen's Green, Dublin 2.
☎ (01) 475 6404/5.
NZ: c/o Morrison Morpeth House, 105–109 The Terrace,
Wellington. ☎ (04) 472 0020. Fax: (04) 472 7017.
South Africa: 8th Floor, Sanlam Centre, cnr Andries
and Pretorius Street, Pretoria. ☎ (012) 322 0595.
Fax: (012) 797 1789.
UK: Danish Embassy, 55 Sloane Street, London SW1X
9SR. ☎ (020) 7333 0200. Fax: (020) 7333 0270.
US: 3200 Whitehaven Street, NW, Washington DC
20008. ☎ (202) 234 4300. Fax: (202) 328 1470.
Email: ambadane@erols.com
Website: http://www.denmarkemb.org/

Accommodation:

Copenhagen Sleep-In Blegdamsvej 132, 2100-
Copenhagen. ☎ 3526 5059. Fax: 3543 5058.
Email: copenhagen@sleep-in.dk
Website: http://www.citysleep-in.dk
HI–Danhostel Copenhagen Bellahoj Herbergvejen 8,
2700 Brønshøj. ☎ 3828 9715. Fax: 3889 0210.
Email: bellahoej@danhostel.dk
City Sleep-in Havnegade 20, 8000 C. - Århus.
☎ 8619 2055. Fax: 8619 1811.
Email: sleep-in@citysleep-in.dk
Website: http://www.citysleep-in.dk

Poste restante:

All post offices offer poste restante.

France ✈

(+1hr GMT) **Capital:** Paris

☎ **Country 33**, Paris: 1   💲 Euro

Paris is crammed with enough attractions to keep you going for a month: not only galleries, museums and architecture, but all those obligatory romantic side streets and pavement cafés, too. Things that demand to be seen include the Eiffel Tower (naturally), the Louvre (home of the *Mona Lisa* and the *Venus de Milo*), Notre-Dame Cathedral, the Pompidou Centre (modern art, including Picasso), and the Musée d'Orsay (Impressionist paintings, and sculptures by Rodin). There are also loads of excellent street and flea markets to while away the hours and francs. The Alps and Pyrenees offer some of the best skiing, hiking and climbing in Europe. France also has some great bits of coast for sunbathing and swimming, including cool Cannes and, of course, St Tropez on the Med, while the best of the west has to be Biarritz. It's worth travelling along the coastlines for some less popular (and cheaper) areas. Inland, you'll find studenty places like Aix-en-Provence. Car hire isn't cheap and travelling any distance is best done on the train network. Buses are usually cheaper but take a while. There are metros and tram systems in the larger cities, so getting around isn't a problem. A cheap alternative is camping, as sites are prolific throughout France.

👁 Aix-en-Provence, the Alps, the Atlantic coast, Avignon, Brittany, the Côte d'Azur, EuroDisney, Loire Valley castles, Mont-St-Michel, Nice, Notre-Dame for its Gothic arches, Paris, Pont du Gard, the Pyrenees, Versailles and vineyards.

Weather:

The north is warm in the summer and cool in the winter; generally mild, but with the possibility of rain throughout the year. The south has a warmer Mediterranean climate with hot and dry summers. Mountain areas are generally cold and dry.

Languages:

French; also Flemish, Alsacian, Breton, Basque, Catalan, Provençal and Corsican. English is spoken in major tourist centres.

Religion:

Predominantly Roman Catholic; Protestant minority.

Money:

Euro = 100 cents.
Cirrus: good for ATMs.
Maestro: limited for ATMs.
MasterCard: good for retail and excellent for ATMs.
Traveller's cheques: £ sterling or euros.
Visa: good for retail and excellent for ATMs.

Living costs:

Allow $30 per day for food and board. Cities and tourist centres are more expensive than other areas, but student discounts are quite common.

Visas:

Passports should be valid for three months after your date of arrival. Nationals of South Africa need a visa which is valid for ninety days.

Electricity:

220V, 50Hz. two-pin plugs.

Health:

No major health risks.

ADDRESS BOOK

Amex 11 Rue Scribe, Paris 75009. ☎ (1) 4777 7707.

Direction du Tourisme 2 Rue Linois, 75740 Paris. ☎ (1) 4437 3600. Fax: (1) 4437 3636. Website: http://www.tourisme.gouv.fr

Maison de la France (Tourist Information Agency) 20 Avenue de l'Opéra, 75001 Paris. ☎ (1) 4296 7000. Fax: (1) 4296 7071. Email: admin@france.com

STA Voyages Wasteels, 11 Rue Dupuytren 75006 Paris. ☎ (1) 4325 5835. Fax: (1) 4325 4625.

Thomas Cook Gare d'Austerlitz, 55 Quai d'Austerlitz, Paris 75013. ☎ (1) 5360 1297.

Your embassy/consulate in France:

Australian: 4 Rue Jean Rey, Paris 75015. ☎ (1) 4059 3300. Fax: (1) 4059 3310. Website: http://www.austgov.fr/

British: 35 Rue du Faubourg, St. Honoré, Paris 75383. ☎ (1) 4451 3100. Fax: (1) 4451 3288. Website: http://www.amb-grandebretagne.fr/

Canadian: 35 Avenue Montaigne, Paris 75008. ☎ (1) 4443 2900. Fax: (1) 4443 2999. Email: paris@dfait-maeci.gc.ca Website: http://www.dfait-maeci.gc.ca/paris/

Irish: 4 Rue Rude, Paris 75116. ☎ (1) 4417 6700. Fax: (1) 4417 6760. Email: irembparis@wanadoo.fr Website: http://www.irlande-tourisme.fr/home/

NZ: 7 ter, Rue Léonard de Vinci, Paris 75116. ☎ (1) 4501 4343. Fax: (1) 4501 2639. Email: nzembassy.paris@wanadoo.fr

South African: 59 Quai d'Orsay, Paris 75343. ☎ (1) 5359 2323. Fax: (1) 5359 2368. Email: info@afriquesud.net Website: http://www.afriquesud.net/

US: 2 Avenue Gabriel, Paris 75008. ☎ (1) 4312 2222. Fax: (1) 4266 9783. Website: http://www.amb-usa.fr/

French embassies/consulates at home:

Australia: 6 Perth Avenue, Yarralumla ACT 2600. ☎ (02) 6216 0100. Fax: (02) 6216 0127.

Canada: 42 Sussex Drive, Ottawa, Ontario K1M 2C9. ☎ (613) 789 1795. Fax: (613) 789 3484.

Ireland: 36 Ailesbury Road, Dublin 4. ☎ (01) 260 1666.

NZ: Willis Corroon House, 1–3 Willeston Street, Wellington. ☎ (04) 472 0200. Fax: (04) 472 5887.

South Africa: 35th Floor, Carlton, Commissioner Street, Johannesburg. ☎ (011) 331 3468. Fax: (011) 231 575.

UK: 58 Knightsbridge, London SW1X 7JT. ☎ (020) 7201 1000.

US: 4101 Reservoir Road, NW, Washington DC 20007. ☎ (202) 944 6000. Fax: (202) 944 6072. Website: http://www.info-france-usa.org/

Accommodation:

HI–Auberge "Jules Ferry" 8, bd Jules Ferry, 75011 Paris. ☎ (1) 4357 5560. Fax: (1) 4314 8209.

HI–Auberge de Jeunesse Route Forestière du Mont-Alban, 06300 Nice. ☎ (4) 9389 2364. Fax: (4) 9204 0310.

HI–Residence "Port Beaulieu" 9, bd Vincent Gâche, 44200 Nantes. ☎ (2) 4012 2400. Fax: (2) 5182 0005.

Poste restante:

Paris-Louvre Post Office 52 Rue de Louvre, Paris 75001. ☎ (1) 4028 2000.

Germany ✈

(+1hr GMT) **Capital:** Berlin

☎ **Country 49**, Berlin: 30, Cologne: 221, Munich: 89 💲 Euro

German cities such as Berlin and Munich have a fine cultural and artistic legacy coupled with a social scene unlike anything else on earth. In Berlin, the site of the Berlin Wall is where to head for the best of the clubs and bars. The Brandenburg Gate, a centrepoint of the wall's history, is a fearsome piece of architecture. There are some beautiful buildings dotted throughout the city, such as the Kaiser-Wilhelm-Gedächtnis-Kirche and Dahlem Museum complex. Both are a well-needed respite to the industrious feel of the city. And if you happen to arrive in June, the annual Love Parade will be in full swing. Munich is relaxed, with a more western European feel to it. It's impossible to escape the *Bierkellers* (not that you'd want to) and there are various museums and gardens to wander around. Frankfurt is home to the Stadel Museum and the Museum of Modern Art, which are both must-sees if you're of that persuasion. Outdoor activities centre around excellent hiking trails and skiing in the Black Forest, the Harz Mountains and the Bavarian Alps. Getting around is easy, both the road, and especially the rail, networks are excellent.

👁 Bavarian Alps, Berlin and the Brandenburg Gate, the Black Forest for scenic walks, Frankfurt, Harz Mountains, Heidelberg's castle ruins, Lübeck for medieval buildings, Munich, and Tübingen.

Weather:
The north coast has warm and sunny summers but the winters can be bitter. Inland the summers are temperate with moderate rain and the winters are fairly cold, especially in the Bavarian Alps.

Languages:
German. English and French are often spoken.

Religion:
Protestant and Roman Catholic.

Money:
Euro = 100 cents.
Cirrus: excellent for ATMs.
Maestro: very limited for ATMs.
MasterCard: good for retail and excellent for ATMs.
Traveller's cheques: £ sterling or euros.
Visa: good for retail and excellent for ATMs.

Living costs:
Allow about $30 per day for food and board. Travelling (especially long distances) is costly. Eastern Germany is still slightly cheaper than the west of the country.

Visas:

Passports should be valid for three months from your intended date of arrival. If you travel without a return ticket, you must be able to show sufficient funds for your trip. South Africans need a visa, which is valid for up to ninety days. Requirements are subject to change, so check before you go.

ADDRESS BOOK

Amex Mullerstrasse 176, Berlin 13353.
☎ (30) 462 3072.
German National Tourist Office/Deutsche Zentrale für Tourismus (DZT) Beethovenstrasse 69, 60325 Frankfurt am Main. ☎ (69) 974 640. Fax: (69) 751 903.
Website: http://www.germany-tourism.de
STA Goethestrasse 73, Berlin 10625.
☎ (30) 311 0950. Fax: (30) 313 0948.
Email: berlin.goeth@statravel.de
Thomas Cook Reiseburo Im Metro-Markt, Beilsteiner Strasse 120, Berlin 12681. ☎ (30) 543 78460.

Your embassy/consulate in Germany:

Australian: Godesberger Allee 105-107, Bonn 53175.
☎ (228) 81030. Fax: (228) 8103130.
Website: http://www.australian-embassy.de/
British: Unter den Linden 32-34, Berlin 10117.
☎ (30) 2018 4159. Fax: (30) 2018 4137.
Website: http://www.britbot.de/
Canadian: Friedrichstrasse 95, Berlin 10117.
☎ (30) 203 120. Fax: (30) 203 125.
Email: brlin@dfait-maeci.gc.ca
Website: http://www.dfait-maeci.gc.ca/~bonn/
Irish: Friedrichstrasse 200, Berlin 10117.
☎ (30) 220 720. Fax: (30) 220 72299.
NZ: Friedrichstrasse 60, Berlin 10117.
☎ (30) 206 210. Fax: (30) 2062 1114.
Email: nzemb@t-online.de
South African: Friedrichstrasse 60, Berlin 10117.
☎ (30) 220 730. Email: botschaft@suedafrika.org
Website: http://www.suedafrika.org/
US: Deichmanns Aue 29, Bonn D-53170
☎ (228) 3391. Fax: (228) 339 2663.
Website: http://www.usembassy.de/

Electricity:

220V, 50Hz

Health:

Rabies.

German embassies/consulates at home:

Australia: 119 Empire Circuit, Yarralumla ACT 2600.
☎ (02) 6270 1911. Fax: (02) 6270 1951.
Canada: 275 Slater Street, 14th Floor, Ottawa, Ontario K1P 5H9. ☎ (613) 232 1101. Fax: (613) 594 9330.
Ireland: 31 Trimleston Avenue, Booterstown, Co. Dublin. ☎ (01) 269 3011.
NZ: 90-92 Hobson Street, Thorndon, Wellington.
☎ (04) 473 6063/4. Fax: (04) 473 6069.
South Africa: Consulate General, 74 Queen Victoria Street, Cape Town. ☎ (021) 242 410.
Fax: (021) 344 3854.
UK: 23 Belgrave Square, London SW1X 8PZ.
☎ (020) 7235 5033.
US: 4645 Reservoir Road, NW, Washington DC 20007.
☎ (202) 298 4000. Fax: (202) 298 4249.
Website: http://www.germany-info.org/

Accommodation:

HI–JH Berlin International Kluckstr. 3, 10785 Berlin.
☎ (30) 261 1097. Fax: (30) 265 0383.
Email: jh-berlin@jugendherberge.de
HI - JH München - Neuhausen Wendl-Dietrich-Str. 20, 80634 Munich. ☎ (89) 131156. Fax: (89) 167 8745.
Email: jhmuenchen@djh-bayern.de
HI - JH Bonn-Venusberg / Kulturjugendherberge Haager Weg 42, 53127 Bonn. ☎ (02) 2828 9970.
Fax: (02) 28289 9714. Email: jh-bonn@djh-rheinland.de

Poste restante:

Central Post Office Handjirystrasse 34–63, Berlin 12159. ☎ (30) 850 820.
Central Post Office 1 Bahnhofplatz, Munich.
☎ (89) 5388 2732.

Great Britain ✈

(GMT) **Capital:** London

☎ **Country: 44**, London: 020   💲 Pound sterling

Central London's got some unmissable sights: architecture, museums and galleries as well as Piccadilly Circus and Buckingham Palace. Not far from the centre are pleasures a lot of tourists don't bother with. Camden Town and Notting Hill (home to an excellent carnival) have incredible atmospheres both day (markets a go-go) and night (bars to die for). In the West End, Soho and Covent Garden are your best bet for shopping and cafés. An hour away, on the south coast, Brighton has a very chilled, happy scene. For something a little more sedate, try the historic towns of Bath, Oxford, York and Cambridge. Countryside-wise, the Lake District and the North Yorkshire Moors are both good if you're in need of contemplative isolation, while Scotland has more breathtaking scenery than it knows what to do with. The city of Edinburgh is incredibly beautiful – take a trip along Prince's Street at night and gawp up at the castle. Or head off to Wales and check the capital buzz in Cardiff before venturing into the wilderness of the Brecon Beacons or Snowdonia. Britain has a comprehensive transport system, but stick to the National Express coaches if you've got the time and you're watching your pennies.

👁 Bath, Brighton, Cambridge, Cornwall's beaches, the Cotswolds, Edinburgh, Hadrian's Wall, the Lake District, London, Manchester's club scene, Oxford, the Scottish highlands, islands and lochs, Stratford-upon-Avon, Welsh mountains, Windsor Castle and York.

Weather:

Most of the UK has warm summers and mild winters, with the chance of rain all year round. There are regional variations: the south is warmer than the north, and the west is wetter than the east. Mountain areas in Scotland, Wales and the north of England can be extremely cold.

Languages:

English, Welsh, Scottish and Gaelic.

Religion:

Anglican; also Methodist, Baptist, Roman Catholic, Presbyterian and Muslim.

Money:

Pound sterling = 100 pence.
Cirrus: good for ATMs.
Maestro: good for ATMs.
MasterCard: excellent for retail and ATMs.
Traveller's cheques: £ sterling.
Visa: excellent for retail and ATMs.

Living costs:

London is pretty expensive – allow at least $15–20 per night for a hostel, and about $5–10 per day for food. Entrance fees and travel are costly. Outside the capital, the cost of living is cheaper, averaging about three-quarters of the price.

Visas:

Passports should be valid for a minimum of six months from your date of entry. Visas are not required for nationals of Australia, Canada, US and Japan.

Electricity:

240V, 50Hz. Square three-pin plugs.

Health:

No major health risks.

ADDRESS BOOK

Amex 102 Victoria Street, London SW1E 5JL.
☎ (020) 7828 7411.
English Tourist Board Thames Tower, Black's Road, Hammersmith, London W6 9EL. ☎ 0800 192 192 (free call in England).
Website: http://www.travelengland.org.uk/
The Belfast Welcome Centre 35 Donegal Place, Belfast, Co. Antrim, Northern Ireland BT1 5AD.
☎ (28) 9024 6609. Fax: (28) 9031 2424.
Website: http://www.gotobelfast.com
Visit Scotland 23 Ravelston Terrace, Edinburgh, Scotland EH4 3TP. ☎ (131) 332 2433.
Fax: (131) 343-1513. Email: info@visitscotland.com
Wales Tourist Board Brunel House, 2 Fitzalan Road, Cardiff CF24 OUY. ☎ (29) 2049 9909.
Fax: (29) 2048 5031. Website: http://www.visitwales.com
STA 85 Shaftesbury Avenue, London W1V 7AD.
☎ (020) 7361 6129. Fax: (020) 7983 9570.
Email: enquiries@statravel.co.uk.

Your embassy/consulate in Great Britain:
Australian: Australia House, The Strand, London WC2B 4LA. ☎ (020) 7379 4334. Fax: (020) 7240 5333.
Website: http://www.australia.org.uk/
Canadian: 1 Grosvenor Square, London W1X 0AB.
☎ (020) 7258 6600. Fax: (020) 7258 6333.
Website: http://www.canada.org.uk/
Irish: 17 Grosvenor Place, London SWIX 7HR.
☎ (020) 7235 2171. Fax: (020) 7245 6961.
Email: ir.embassy@lineone.net
NZ: New Zealand House, The Haymarket, London SW1Y 4TQ. ☎ (020) 7930 8422. Fax: (020) 7839 4580.
South African: South Africa House, Trafalgar Square, London WC2N 5DP. ☎ (020) 7451 7299.
Fax: (020) 7451 7284.
Website: http://www.southafricahouse.com

US: 24 Grosvenor Square, London W1A 1AE.
☎ (020) 7499 9000. Fax: (020) 7894 0699.
Website: http://www.usembassy.org.uk/

British embassies/consulates at home:
Australia: Commonwealth Avenue, Yarralumla ACT 2600. ☎ (61) 6270 6666. Fax: (61) 6273 3236.
Website: http://www.uk.emb.gov.au/
Canada: 80 Elgin Street, Ottawa, Ontario K1P 5K7.
☎ (613) 237 1530. Fax: (613) 237 6537.
Website: http://www.britain-in-canada.org/
Ireland: 29 Merrion Road, Dublin 4. (01) 205 3700.
Fax: (01) 205 3893. Email: bembassy@internet-ireland.ie
NZ: 44 Hill Street, Wellington 1.
☎ (04) 472 6049 or 495 0889. Fax: (04) 471 1974.
Website: http://www.brithighcomm.org.nz/
South Africa: 19th Floor, Sanlam Centre, Jeppe and Von Wielligh Steet, Johannesburg.
☎ (011) 337 8940. Fax: (011) 253670.
US: 3100 Massachusetts Avenue, NW, Washington DC 20008. ☎ (202) 588 6500. Fax: (202) 588 7870. Website: http://www.britainusa.com/bis/embassy/embassy.stm

Accommodation:
YHA–Earls Court–London 38 Bolton Gardens, London SW5 0AQ. ☎ (020) 7373 7083.
Fax: (020) 7835 2034. Email: earlscourt@yha.org.uk
Belfast International Hostel 22-32 Donegal Road, Belfast. ☎ (028) 90315435. Fax: (028) 90439699
Edinburgh Bruntfield YH 7 Bruntsfield Crescent, Edinburgh. EH10 4EZ. ☎ (0131)- 447 2994.

Poste restante:
Send letters to: [name], 'Poste Restante', Post Office, 24–28 William IV Street, London WC2N 4DL.
☎ (020) 7930 9580.

Greece ✈

(+2hrs GMT) **Capital:** Athens

☎ **Country: 30**, Athens: 1   💲 Euro

Greece's past can out-rank anyone's. Start the classical tour with Athens and the Parthenon, Acropolis and Erechtheion. Greece's southern peninsula, called the Peloponnese, is stuffed with antiquity. Major sites include Olympia (yes, original home to those games!), Delphi and Mycenae. Trekking is popular in the barren hilly landscape, especially in the northern Pindos Mountains. The other main attraction is the thousands of islands. Paleohora in the south west of Crete is where you'll find many a backpacker. Crete also has the amazing site of Knossos, where you can admire Minoan culture in all its glory, and the 12-mile long Samaria Gorge, if you're really feeling energetic. The Cycladic islands of Sikinos, Anafi and Naxos, to the east of Crete, are less visited as are Lipsi and Tilos, located just off the coast of Turkey. The beaches on all these islands are superb – as is the snorkelling – and if you avoid the hordes, they're pretty near paradise. Gavdos Island, south of Crete, is well off the beaten track and staying with the locals makes it a cheap and authentic taste of Greece. The cheapest skiing in Europe is available if you head to Mount Parnassos near Delphi.

👁 The Aegean islands, Athens and the Acropolis, Corfu, Crete, the Cycladic islands, Delphi's ruined shrine, island-hopping, the Mani, the Peloponnese, and the Pindos Mountains.

Weather:
The south is hot and sunny in the summer, with little rain; cooler but mild in the winter. Temperatures are lower in the north, and the winter is much colder.

Languages:
Greek. English, German, Italian and French are sometimes spoken in tourist centres.

Religion:
Greek Orthodox; Muslim and Roman Catholic minorities.

Money:
Euro = 100 cents.
Cirrus: good for ATMs.
Maestro: limited for ATMs.
MasterCard: fair for retail and good for ATMs.
Traveller's cheques: £ sterling or euros.
Visa: good for retail and ATMs.

Living costs:
Budget $20 per day for food and board. Tourist centres are cheap by European standards.

Visas:

Passports should be valid for six months from your date of arrival. Visas are not required for stays under three months.

Electricity:

220V, 50Hz

Health:

A yellow fever certificate is required if you're travelling from infected areas. Rabies.

ADDRESS BOOK

Amex 2 Hermou Street, Syntagma Square, Athens 10225. ☎ (1) 324 4976.

Greek/Hellenic National Tourism Organisation/ Ellinikos Organismos Tourismou (EOT) 2, Amerikis Street, 105 64 Athens, Greece. ☎ (1) 327 1300/2 Email: info@gnto.gr Website: http://www.gnto.gr/

STA ISYTS, 11 Nikis Street, 1st Floor, Near Syntagma Square, Athens 10557. ☎ (1) 322 1267 or 323 3767. Fax: (1) 322 1531.

Thomas Cook Diners World Travel SA, 180 Kifissias Avenue, Psychiko, Athens 15231. ☎ (1) 687 5890. Fax: (1) 687 9530.

Your embassy/consulate in Greece:

Australian: 37 Dimitriou Soutsou Street, Ambelokipi, Athens 11510. ☎ (1) 644 7303. Fax: (1) 646 6595. Website: http://www.ausemb.gr/

British: 1 Ploutarchou Street, Athens 10675.

☎ (1) 727 7600. Fax: (1) 727 2722.

Email: britania@hol.gr

Website: http://www.british-embassy.gr/

Canadian: 4 I. Gennadiou Street, Athens.

☎ (1) 727 3400. Fax: (1) 727 3480.

Email: athns@dfait-maeci.gc.ca

Irish: 7 Leoforos Vasileos, Konstantinou, Athens.

☎ (1) 723 2771. Fax: (1) 729 3383.

NZ: 268 Kifissias Avenue, 15232 Halandri, Athens.

☎ (1) 687 4700. Fax: (1) 687 4444.

Email: costa.cotsilinis@gr.pwcglobal.com

South African: 60 Kipshias, Psychiko, Athens.

☎ (1) 689 53309. Fax: (1) 680 6640.

Email: embassy@southafrica.gr

Website: http://www.southafrica.gr/

US: 91 Vassilissis Sophias, Athens. ☎ (1) 721 2951. Website: http://www.usisathens.gr/

Greek embassies/consulates at home:

Australia: 9 Turrana Street, Yarralumla ACT 2600.

☎ (02) 6273 3011 Fax: (02) 6273 2620.

Canada: 76–80 MacLaren Street, Ottawa, Ontario K2P 0K6. ☎ (613) 238 6271. Fax: (613) 238 5676.

Ireland: 1 Upper Pembrook Street, Dublin 2.

☎ (01) 676 7254.

NZ: 10th Floor, 57 Willeston Street, Wellington.

☎ (04) 473 7775/6. Fax: (04) 473 7441.

South Africa: 995 Pretorius Street, Hatfield, Pretoria.

☎ (012) 437 351.

UK: 1a Holland Park, London W11 3TG.

☎ (020) 7229 3850.

US: 2221 Massachusetts Avenue, NW, Washington DC 20008. ☎ (202) 939 5800.

Website: http://www.greekembassy.org/

Accommodation:

Hostel Aphrodite 12 Einardou Street, Victoria Square, Athens 10440. ☎ (1) 881 0589. Fax: (1) 881 6574.

Delphi Hostel 31 Appollonos St, Delphi.

☎ (265) 82268.

Purple Pig Star Camping Los Kyclades, Mylapotas Beach 84001. ☎ (286) 91302. Fax: (286) 91612.

Email: purplepigios@hotmail.com

Poste restante:

Main Post Office Syntagma Square, Athens.

Hungary

(+1hr GMT) **Capital:** Budapest

☎ **Country: 36**, Budapest: 1   💲 Forint

The country is firmly centred around its capital, Budapest, which is a lot quieter and more relaxed than many other European cities. The Castle District, Old Town and Obuda areas are where you'll find most of the life and tourist attractions or, if you're trying to be romantic, how about a moonlit swagger along the Danube? Relaxing in one of the numerous spas is highly recommended – try a massage and swim in the fabulous surroundings of the Art Deco Gelert Hotel. Follow this by a night out in the cool cafés and bars. You'll find the cheapest beds in the Buda and Pest areas, either side of the Danube, east and west of the centre. Outside Budapest, there are lots of old towns to explore, such as Pécs and Eger. Located in the south east corner of the country is the Hortobagy National Park (if bird-watching is your thing) and to the north the mountain ranges offer excellent trekking. Travelling in Hungary is cheap and easy, the vast bus networks cover even the remotest areas. Buses, trolley buses and trams mean that getting around the major cities is a cheap and easy experience.

👁 Budapest, cycling by the Danube, Eger for amazing architecture, the outdoor pool in City Park, Pécs with its mosques and synagogue, turn-of-the-century coffee houses – such as Café Gerbeaud in Budapest – and underground caves in the Bukk Hills.

Weather:

From May to August the weather is hot. Temperatures plunge during the winter and you can expect snow. Rain falls throughout the year.

Languages:

Hungarian. German is widely spoken.

Religion:

Roman Catholic and Calvinist.

Money:

Forint = 100 fillér.

Cirrus: good for ATMs.

Maestro: limited for ATMs.

MasterCard: limited for retail, good for ATMs.

Traveller's cheques: £ sterling.

Visa: limited for retail, good for ATMs.

Living costs:

Hostels are quite widespread, allow about $8-10 per night for a decent quality one. Food and travel are pretty cheap. Overall, budget for about $12–15 a day.

Visas:

Passports should be valid for six months from your date of arrival. Requirements are subject to change, so check before you go.

Electricity:

220V, 50Hz

Health:

Rabies.

ADDRESS BOOK

Amex deak Ferenc u/0, H–1052 Budapest.
☎ (1) 214 6446.

Hungarian National Tourist Office (HNTO) Margi Körút 85, H–1024 Budapest. ☎ (1) 355 1133. Fax: (1) 375 3819. Email: htbudapest@hungarytourism.hu Website: http://www.hungarytourism.hu

Ministry of Economic Affairs (Tourism Field) V. Honvéd u/13–15, H–1880 Budapest. ☎ (1) 302 2355. Fax: (1) 302 2355. Email: webmaster@ikm.hu Website: http://www.ikm.iif.hu

STA Express Travel, Zoltan u/10, H–1054 Budapest.
☎ (1) 311 9898. Fax: (1) 311 6418.

Tourinform (HNTO) Sütö-u/2, H–1052 Budapest.
☎ (1) 317 9800. Fax: (1) 317 9578.
Email: tourinform@mail.hungarytourism.hu
Website: http://www.hungarytourism.hu

Your embassy/consulate in Hungary:

Australia: Kiralyhago Ter 8–10, H–1126 Budapest.
☎ (1) 201 8899/568/567. Fax: (1) 201 9792.
Email: ausembbp@mail.datanet.hu
Website: http://www.ausembbp.hu/

Ireland: Szabadság tér 7–9, H–1054 Budapest.
☎ (1) 302 9600/1. Fax: (1) 302 9599.
Email: iremb@elender.hu

NZ: Terèzkrt. 38, H–1066 Budapest.
☎ (1) 175 4908. Fax: (1) 175 4908.
Email: nzconsul@mail.matav.hu

UK: Harmincad u/6, H–1051 Budapest.
☎ (1) 266 2888. Fax: (1) 266 0907.
Email: info@britemb.hu
Website: http://www.britishembassy.hu/

US: Szabadság tér 12, H–1054 Budapest.
☎ (1) 267 4400. Fax: (1) 269 9326.
Website: http://www.usis.hu/emb.htm

Hungarian embassies/consulates at home:

Australian: 17 Beale Crescent, Deakin ACT 2600.
☎ (02) 6282 3226/2555. Fax: (02) 6285 3012.

British: 35 Eaton Place, London SW1X 8BY.
☎ (020) 7235 5218. Fax: (020) 7823 1348.

Canadian: 299 Waverly Street, Ottawa, Ontario K2P 0V9. ☎ (613) 230 2717. Fax: (613) 232 7560.

NZ: 151 Orangi Kaupapa Road, Wellington.
☎ (04) 475 8574. Fax: (04) 475 8574.

South African: 959 Arcadia Street, Arcadia, Pretoria.
☎ (012) 433 030. Fax: (012) 641 547.

US: 3910 Shoemaker Street, NW, Washington DC 20008. ☎ (202) 362 6730. Fax: (202) 686 6412.
Website: http://www.hungaryemb.org/

Accommodation:

Travellers Hostel Hill YHA XI. District Ménesi út 5., Budapest. ☎ (1) 413 2065. Fax: (1) 321 4851

Travellers Hostel Schonherz YHA XI. district Irinyi u. 42., Budapest. ☎ (1) 413 2065. Fax: (1) 321 4851.

Travellers Hostel Universias XI. District Irinyi u. 42., Budapest. ☎ (1) 413 2065. Fax: (1) 321 4851.

Poste restante:

Main Post Office: Nyuguti Station, VI Nyugati tér, Budapest.

Ireland ✈

(GMT) **Capital:** Dublin

☎ **Country: 353**, Dublin: 1   💲 Euro

Dublin is a beautiful and friendly city, with some stunning architecture, and inspiring museums and galleries. It's mandatory to visit as many pubs as possible in your time here and you'll find the locals more than welcoming. Areas you might want to while away your hours in are the streets around Temple Bar (good restaurants, shops and bars) and Saint Stephen's Green (a beautiful sculptured garden in the heart of Dublin). The cheapest accommodation is bunched around O'Connell Street, located north of the River Liffey. Head northwest to the city of Galway and check out its great nightlife and club scene. Then on to Connemara to see the best of Ireland's rural beauty. Walking around these areas is an exercise in desolation, finding yourself surrounded by nothing but mountains, valleys and green, green, green. The Aran Islands offer a more barren landscape. With no tourist cars allowed on the islands, the way to get about is by bicycle. Public transport in Ireland is sporadic, and, in the winter, practically non-existent. Hiring a car is the best way to see the remote and beautiful places in Ireland (if you've got the cash), but there's still plenty to do if you stay on the beaten track.

👁 The Aran Islands, the Burren, Connemara, Cork, Dingle Peninsula, Dublin, Galway, Kenmare, Kerry, Kilkenny, Stone Age passage graves at Newgrange and Knowth, River Shannon, Wexford, Wicklow Mountains.

Weather:
Mild weather with rain throughout the year. Go between June and September for the warmest and driest weather. Winter months are cooler.

Languages:
English and Gaelic.

Religion:
Roman Catholic; Protestant minority.

Money:
Euro = 100 cents.
Cirrus: good for ATMs.
Maestro: not accepted.
MasterCard: good for retail and ATMs.
Traveller's cheques: £ sterling or euros.
Visa: good for retail and ATMs.

Living costs:

More expensive than you'd expect – about $20 per day for basic food and board. Hostels are of a good standard, but camp sites offer a cheaper alternative.

Visas:

Visas aren't required.

Electricity:

220V, 50Hz. Three-pin square plugs.

Health:

No major health risks.

ADDRESS BOOK

Amex 116 Grafton Street, Dublin 2. ☎ (1) 677 2874.
Irish Tourist Board (Bord Fáilte Eireann) Baggot Street Bridge, Dublin 2. ☎ (1) 602 4000. Fax: (1) 602 4100. Website: http://www.ireland.travel.ie
STA Trinity College Students Union, House 6, Trinity College, Dublin 2. ☎ (1) 677 5076. Fax: (1) 677 7957.
Thomas Cook 118 Grafton Street, Dublin 2. ☎ (1) 677 1721.

Your embassy/consulate in Ireland:

Australian: Fitzwilton House, Wilton Terrace, Dublin 2. ☎ (1) 676 1517. Fax: (1) 678 5185.
Email: services@australianembassy.ie
Website: http://www.australianembassy.ie/
British: 29 Merrion Road, Ballsbridge, Dublin 4. ☎ (1) 205 3700. Fax: (1) 205 3893.
Email: bembassy@internet-ireland.ie
Canadian: 65/68 St Stephen's Green, Dublin 2. ☎ (1) 478 1988. Fax: (1) 478 1285.
Email: dubln@dfait-maeci.gc.ca
NZ: 37 Leeson Park, Dublin 6. ☎ (1) 660 4233. Fax: (1) 660 4228. Email: nzconsul@indigo.ie
South African: 2nd Floor, Alexandra House, Earlsfort Centre, Earlsfort Terrace, Dubin 2. ☎ (01) 661 5553. Fax: (1) 661 5590.
US: 42 Elgin Road, Ballsbridge, Dublin 4. ☎ (1) 668 8777. Fax: (1) 668 9946.
Email: webmaster@usemb.ie
Website: http://www.usembassy.ie/

Irish embassies/consulates at home:

Australia: 20 Arkana Street, Yarralumla ACT 2600. ☎ (02) 6273 3022. Fax: (02) 6273 3741.
Email: irishemb@computech.com.au
Canada: 287 MacLaren Street, Ottawa, Ontario K2P 0L9. ☎ (613) 236 7403. Fax: (613) 563 2858.
NZ: 6th Floor, 18 Shortland Street, Auckland. ☎ (09) 302 2867. Fax: (09) 302 2420.
South Africa: First Floor, Sothern Life Plaza,1059 Schoeman Street (Corner Festival Street), Arcadia 0083. ☎ (012) 342 5062.
UK: 17 Grosvenor Place, London SW1X 7HR. ☎ (020) 7235 2171. Fax: (020) 7245 6961.
Email: ir.embassy@lineone.net
US: 2234 Massachusetts Avenue, NW, Washington DC 20008. ☎ (202) 462 3939. Fax: (202) 232 5993.
Email: embirlus@aol.com
Website: http://www.irelandemb.org/

Accommodation:

Oliver St. John Gogorty 12-21 Anglesea Str., Temple Bar, Dublin. ☎ (1) 671 1822. Fax: (1) 671 7637.
Email: olivergogarty@hotmail.com
Mountgrange Hostel Ashbrook, Dennehy's Cross, Cork. ☎ (21) 946 585. Fax: (21) 541 177.
Email: mgrange@iol.ie
Barnacles Quay Street House 10 Quay Str., Galway, Co. Galway. ☎ (91) 588 644. Fax: (91) 588 644.
Email: qshostel@barnacles.iol.ie

Poste restante:

General Post Office O'Connell Street, Dublin 1. ☎ (1) 705 7000. Letters are kept for three months, packets/parcels for two weeks.

Italy ✈

(+1hr GMT) **Capital:** Rome

☎ **Country: 39**, Florence: 55, Milan: 2, Naples: 81, Rome: 6, Venice: 42 💲 Euro

It doesn't matter where you go in Italy, you're going to be in constant awe of art, architecture, landscape, beaches, history, food, weather, religion, shops...or just the prices. Rome, Florence, Verona and Venice are all at the forefront where beauty is concerned. Rome is home to the Forum, which, in turn, encapsulates the Coliseum. The Palatine Hills hold more architectural amazements in greener surroundings. The smallest state in the world, Vatican City, is cocooned inside this incredible city. Rome and Milan are the liveliest places, with excellent nightlife and shop-till-your-pocket-drops opportunities. Florence (leave plenty of time to queue for the Uffizi Gallery) and Venice are slower-paced, both being concentrated enough to walk around. Florence has a wonder of the Renaissance world on every corner, while Venice's picturesque canals and architecture are even more romantic than you could've imagined. If this isn't enough, Italy also has mountains, islands and the hippest of beach resorts. Sicily and Sardinia are the places for sun-seekers, while the Dolomites, up in the north, have excellent year-round skiing. Train and bus networks offer good, standard travel – it's really just a question of exactly how long you can afford to stay.

👁 The Amalfi Coast with its lemon groves, the Dolomites, the Lakes (including Lake Maggiore and Lake Garda), Lucca, Milan, Pompeii, Rome, San Giminiano, Sardinia's beaches, Sicily, Sienna, Tuscany, Venice and the canals, Verona, and Vesuvius.

Weather:
The north is cooler than the south, and the Alps are cold and snowy between October and May. The south is warmer, especially from June to September when it's hot, sunny and dry.

Languages:
Italian. German and French are sometimes spoken in tourist centres.

Religion:
Roman Catholic; Protestant minority.

Money:
Euro = 100 cents.
Cirrus: good for ATMs.
Maestro: limited for ATMs.
MasterCard: excellent for retail, good for ATMs.
Traveller's cheques: £ sterling or euros.
Visa: good for retail, fair for ATMs.

Living costs:
This is expensive – especially in the tourist centres. Even if you stay in hostels and make your own food

you need to allow about $30 per day. If you buy a coffee, it's more expensive to sit outside than inside the café.

Visas:

South African nationals must obtain a visa.

Electricity:

220V, 50Hz. Two-pin, round-pronged plugs.

Health:

Rabies.

ADDRESS BOOK

Amex Piazza di Spagna 38, Rome 00187.
☎ (6) 67641.

Italian Tourist Office/Ente Nazionale Italiano per il Turismo (ENIT) Via Marghera 2, Rome 00185.
☎ (6) 49711. Fax: (6) 446 3379/9907.
Email: sedecentrale@enit.it

STA Viaggi Wasteels, Via Milazzo 8/C, Rome 00185.
☎ (6) 445 6679. Fax: (6) 445 6685.

Your embassy/consulate in Italy:

Australian: Via Alessandria 215, Rome 00198.
☎ (6) 852 721. Fax: (6) 8527 2300.
Email: info@australian-embassy.it
Website: http://www.australian-embassy.it/
British: Via XX Settembre 80a, Rome 00390.
☎ (6) 482 5551. Fax: (6) 487 3324
Email: info@rome.mail.fco.gov.uk
Website: http://www.britain.it/
Canadian: Via GB De Rossi 27, Rome.
☎ (6) 445 981. Fax: (6) 4459 8750.
Email: rome@dfait-maeci.gc.ca
Website: http://www.canada.it/
Irish: Piazza di Campitelli 3, Rome 00186.
☎ (6) 697 9121. Fax: (6) 679 2354.
NZ: Via Zara 28, Rome 00198. ☎ (6) 441 7171.
Fax: (6) 440 2984. Email: nzemb.rom@flashnet.it
South African: Via Tanaro 14/16, Rome.
☎ (6) 841 9794. Email: ua003135@fnc.net
Website: http://www.flashnet.it/users/ua003135/
US: Via Veneto 119/a, Rome 00187.
☎ (6) 46741. Fax: (6) 488 2672.
Website: http://www.usis.it/

Italian embassies/consulates at home:

Australia: 12 Grey Street, Deakin ACT 2600.
☎ (02) 6273 3333. Fax: (02) 6273 4223.
Canada: 275 Slater Street, 21st Floor, Ottawa, Ontario K1P 5H9. ☎ (613) 232 2401. Fax: (613) 233 1484.
Ireland: 63 Northumberland Road, Dublin 4.
☎ (01) 660 1774.
NZ: 34 Grant Road, Thorndon (PO Box 463), Wellington. ☎ (04) 473 5339. Fax: (04) 472 7255.
South Africa: 796 George Avenue, Arcadia, Pretoria.
☎ (012) 435 541. Fax: (012) 241 256.
UK: 4 Grosvenor Square, London W1Y 2EH.
☎ (020) 7312 2200.
US: 1601 Fuller Street, NW, Washington DC 20009.
☎ (202) 328 5500. Fax: (202) 462 3605.
Website: http://www.italyemb.nw.dc. us/italy/index.html

Accommodation:

Rome Lazio «Foro Italico-A.F.Pessina» Youth Hostel
Viale delle Olimpiadi 61, 00194 Roma.
☎ (06) 323 6267. Fax: (0)6 324 2613.
Naples Campania «Mergellina» Youth Hostel
Salita della Grotta, a Piedigrotta 23, 80122 Napolina.
☎ (81) 761 2346/1215. Fax: (81) 761 2391.
Florence Tuscany «Europa-Villa Camerata» Youth Hostel Viale Augusto Righi 2/4, 50137 Firenze.
☎ (55) 601 451. Fax: (55) 610300.

Poste restante:

Central Post Office Via Della, Mercedez 96, Rome 00187.

Netherlands ✈

(+1hr GMT) **Capitals:** Amsterdam, The Hague

☎ **Country: 31**, Amsterdam: **20**, The Hague: **70**, Rotterdam: **10** 💲 Euro

Amsterdam is well used to travellers. With such an excellent mix of cultures and people, the atmosphere for visitors is one of the best in Europe. The nightlife is superb, plus the liberalism creates one of the most chilled-out cities you're likely to encounter. If you do indulge in a bit of therapeutic smoking, make sure you're in a designated coffee shop. Museums, such as the Rijksmuseum, the Van Gogh Museum and the Stedelijk Museum, offer some of the world's great masterpieces. A trip on the canals that meander through the city provides a lazy way to soak up its fine architecture. Head for The Hague and you are within a tram ride of Scheveningen, which sports miles of beaches, bars, and restaurants. The area known as the Ranstad is home to the bulb fields, best visited between March and May for a total sensory overload experience. A fantastic network of cycle tracks connects most parts of the Netherlands and hiring a bicycle couldn't be easier. Pick one up at a railway station. Around the country there are adequate camping facilities to lessen the burden on your pocket. A rail pass is also advised if you're going to do much long-distance moving around.

👁 Amsterdam: Anne Frank's House, canal trips, Rijksmuseum with Rembrandt's famous '*Nightwatch*', and the Van Gogh Museum; bulb fields, cycling, Delft with its blue-and-white pottery, Haarlem museum for Dutch paintings, The Hague, the university town of Leiden, and Utrecht.

Weather:
A mild climate, with the possibilty of rain throughout the year. Expect cold weather between December and February. Summers are generally warm, but can be changeable.

Languages:
Dutch. English is widely spoken.

Religion:
Roman Catholic and Protestant.

Money:
Euro = 100 cents.
Cirrus: good for ATMs.
Maestro: not accepted.
MasterCard: good for retail and ATMs.
Traveller's cheques: £ sterling or euros.
Visa: good for retail, limited for ATMs.

Living costs:
At a push, you can probably eat and sleep in Holland for about $25 per day. Entrance fees can be

expensive. Hire a bike instead of public transport to keep overall costs down.

Visas:

Passports should be valid for three months from your intended date of arrival. South African nationals require a visa.

Electricity:

220V, 50Hz.

Health:

No major health risks.

ADDRESS BOOK

Amex Van Baerlestraat 39, Amsterdam 1071.
☎ (20) 673 8550.
Nederlands Bureau voor Toerisme PO Box 458, Leidschendam 2260 MG. ☎ (70) 370 5705.
Fax: (70) 320 1654. Email: info@nbt.nl
STA NBBS Reizen Weteringschans 28 D SG, Amsterdam 1017. ☎ (20) 620 5071.
Fax: (71) 522 7243.
Thomas Cook 31a Leidseplein, Amsterdam 1017 PS.
☎ (20) 626 7000.

Your embassy/consulate in the Netherlands:

Australian: Carnegielaan 4, 2517 KH, The Hague.
☎ (70) 310 8200. Fax: (70) 310 7863.
Website: http://www.australian-embassy.nl/
British: Lange Voorhout 10, 2514 ED, The Hague.
☎ (70) 427 0427. Fax: (70) 427 0345.
Website: http://www.britain.nl/
Canadian: Sophialaan 7, 2514 JP, The Hague.
☎ (70) 311 1600. Fax: (70) 311 1620.
Email: hague@dfait-maeci.gc.ca
Website: http://www.dfait-maeci.gc.ca/~thehague/
Irish: Dr. Kuyperstraat 9, 2514 BA, The Hague.
☎ (70) 363 0993/4. Fax: (70) 361 7604.
Email: irish-embassy@demon.nl
NZ: Carnegielaan 10, 2517 KH, The Hague.
☎ (70) 346 9324. Fax: (70) 363 2983.
South African: Wassenaarseweg 40, 2596 CJ, The Hague. ☎ (70) 392 4501. Fax: (7) 346 0669.
Email: info@zuidafrika.nl
Website: http://www.zuidafrika.nl/
US: Lange Voorhout 102, 2514 EJ, The Hague.
☎ (70) 310 9209. Website: http://www.usemb.nl/

Dutch embassies/consulates at home:

Australia: 120 Empire Circuit, Yarralumla ACT 2600.
☎ (02) 6273 3111/386/089/899. Fax: (02) 6273 3206.
Canada: 350 Albert Street, Suite 2020, Ottawa, Ontario K1R 1A4. ☎ (613) 237 5030.
Fax: (613) 237 6471.
Ireland: 160 Merrion Road, Dublin 4.
☎ (01) 269 3444.
NZ: Investment Centre, cnr Ballance and Featherston Streets (PO Box 840), Wellington.
☎ (04) 473 8652. Fax: (04) 471 2923.
South Africa: 825 Arcadia Street, Aradia, Pretoria.
☎ (012) 344 3910. Fax: (012) 215 660.
UK: 38 Hyde Park Gate, London SW7 5DP. ☎ (020) 7584 5040.
US: 4200 Linnean Avenue, NW, Washington DC 20008. ☎ (202) 244 5300. Fax: (202) 362 3430.
Website: http://www.netherlands-embassy.org/

Accommodation:

NJHC City Hostel Stadsoelen Kloveniersburgwal 97, 1011 KB Amsterdam. ☎ (20) 624 6832.
Fax: (20) 639 1035. Email: stadsdoelen@njhc.org
NJHC Hostel de Dousberg Dousbergweg 4, 6216 GC Maastricht. ☎ (43) 346 6777. Fax: (43) 346 6755.
Email: maastricht@njhc.org
NJHC City Hostel Rotterdam Rochussenstraat 107-109, 3015 EH Rotterdam. ☎ (10) 436 5763
Fax: (10) 436 5569. Email: rotterdam@njhc.org

Poste restante:

Hoofdpostkantoor PTT Singel 250–256, Amsterdam.
☎ (20) 556 3311.

Norway

(+1hr GMT) **Capital:** Oslo

☎ **Country:** 47   💲 Norwegian krone

It's gonna be c-c-cold, but Norway's sights more than compensate for the temperature. If you want to climb, ski, hike or just be left breathless by nature, Norway is the place to be. The coastline is made up of gigantic fjords and surrounded by off-shore islands, while the interior mostly consists of spectacular mountains and glaciers. The best way to see as much as possible is to take the train from Oslo to Bergen, which cuts across the southern end of the country. The capital, Oslo, has a few historical attractions, especially the Bygdoy peninsula, with its own Viking ships. The city of Bergen is the best place to base yourself to visit the fjords and glaciers on the western coast. In particular, check out Sogenfjord, Hardangerfjord, the Jostedalsbreen glacier and the waterfalls at Geirangerfjord. The national park at Jotunheimen has many fantastic trails, again all surrounded by beautiful scenery. Head north to be overwhelmed by the Northern Lights. Internal flights are frequent, and offer a comprehensive service. Bus routes are pretty good, but the extent of the train system leaves a lot to be desired. Getting around towns is easy, as most of them have efficient public transport systems.

👁 Akerhus Castle in Oslo, Bergen for medieval roots, fjords – Geirangerfjord, Nordfjord and Romsdalfjord, Jotunheimen National Park, Northern Lights, spectacular glaciers, and the city of Tromsø, inside the Arctic circle.

Weather:

The west coast is the warmest and wettest part of Norway. Oslo is extremely cold in winter (from December to February). The highest chance of rain is between July and September. The land of the midnight sun in summer, the downside of which is very long nights in winter.

Languages:

Norwegian. English is widely spoken.

Religion:

Evangelical Lutheran.

Money:

Norwegian krone = 100 øre.

Cirrus: good for ATMs.

Maestro: good for ATMs.

MasterCard: fair for retail and ATMs.

Traveller's cheques: US dollars or £ sterling.

Visa: fair for retail and excellent for ATMs.

Living costs:

Scandinavia is expensive – about $35 per day for food and board. Travel and enjoying yourself cost extra.

Visas:

Passports should be valid for two months from your intended date of arrival. South African nationals need a visa which is valid for three months.

Electricity:

220V, 50–60Hz. Continental two-pin plugs.

Health:

No major health risks.

ADDRESS BOOK

Amex Fridtjof Nansens Pl 6, 509 Sentrum, Oslo.
☎ 2298 3730.
Norwegian Tourist Board (Nortra) PO Box 2893 Solli, Drammensveien 40, Oslo 0230.
☎ 2292 5200. Fax: 2256 0505.
Email: norway@ntr.no Website: http://www.ntr.no
STA Karl Johans gt 8, Oslo 0154.
☎ 8155 9905. Fax: 2247 4360.
Email: oslo@statravel.no

Your embassy/consulate in Norway:

Australian: Jernbanetorget 2, Oslo.
☎ 2241 4433. Fax: 2242 2683.
Email: australian.consulate@online.no
British: Thomas Heftyesgate 8, Oslo 0244.
☎ 2255 2400. Fax: 2255 1041.
Website: http://home.sol.no/britemb/
Canadian: Wergelandsveien 7, Oslo 0244.
☎ 2299 5300. Fax: 2299 5301.
Email: oslo@dfait-maeci.gc.ca
Irish: c/o Radisson SAS Scandinavia Hotel, Holbergsgate 30, Oslo 0166.
☎ 2220 4370. Fax: 2220 4371.
Email: hibernia@online.no
NZ: Billingstadsletta 19B, Asker, Oslo 2.
☎ 6677 5330. Fax: 6677 5331.
South African: Drammensveien 88c, Oslo 0244.
☎ 2244 7910. Fax: 2244 3975.
US: Drammensveien 18, Oslo 0244. ☎ 2244 8550.
Fax: 2244 0436. Email: oslo@usis.no
Website: http://www.usa.no/

Norwegian embassies/consulates at home:

Australia: 17 Hunter Street, Yarralumla ACT 2600.
☎ (02) 6273 3444. Fax: (02) 6273 3669.
Canada: 2600 South Sheridan Way, Mississauga, Ontario L5J 2M4. ☎ (905) 822 2339.
Fax: (905) 855 1450.
Ireland: 69 Saint Stephen's Green, Dublin 2.
☎ (01) 478 3133.
NZ: 61 Molesworth Street, Wellington.
☎ (04) 471 2503. Fax: (04) 472 8023.
South Africa: 7th Floor, Sancardia Bld, 524 Church Street, Arcadia, Pretoria. ☎ (012) 323 4790.
UK: 25 Belgrave Square, London SW1X 8QD.
☎ (020) 7235 7151.
US: 2720 34th Street, NW, Washington DC 20008.
☎ (202) 333 6000.
Website: http://www.norway.org/

Accommodation:

HI–Oslo Vandrerhjem IMI Staffeldsgt. 4 (Inng./ Entrance Linstowgt.), 0166 Oslo. ☎ 6988 1900.
Fax: 6988 4104. Email: imisommerhotel@hotmail.com
HI–Oslo Vandrerhjem LBM - Ekeberg Kongsvn. 82, P.b. 23, 1109 Oslo. ☎ 2274 1890. Fax: 2274 7505.
Email: delf.vandre@frikirken.no
HI–Trondheim Vandrerhjem Rosenbourg
Weidemannsvei 41, 7043 Trondheim. Tel: ☎ 7387 4450
Fax: 7387 4455. Host: Per Ingvald Karlsen

Poste restante:

Main Post Office Biskop Gunerus Gate 14, Oslo 0020.

Portugal ✈

(GMT) **Capital:** Lisbon

☎ **Country: 351**, Lisbon: 1 💲 Euro

Hot weather, nice beaches, rural beauty, fantastic food...so get out to Portugal now. The capital, Lisbon, is a friendly mix of cultural sights and old-style attractions. The Baixa and Alfama districts are festooned with colourful market activity and craft stalls, and worth exploring in full. There are also a number of museums to drool over, or if you want something a little more upbeat try a local soccer match or rock concert. Food and accommodation are comparatively cheap, and the nightlife combines some of Europe's premier clubs, discos and jazz bars. While in the area, a visit to the amazing site of Sintra is an absolute must. The southern coast has the best of the weather and beaches, especially around Lagos (if you don't mind the hordes). The area known as the Algarve has a plentiful supply of amazing beaches and some of the best swimming in Europe. Other worthwhile havens include the nearby port of Sagres, which is both cheaper and quieter and also the town of Monchique, which is so laid back it's practically horizontal. Inland to the north, there are national parks, such as Peneda-Gerês and the Douro Valley, which offer trails and horse riding.

👁 The Algarve's beaches, Douro Valley, Évora, Lisbon for atmosphere, Peneda-Gerês National Park, the port of Lagos, and Sintra's palaces.

Weather:
Mediterranean climate with hot summers and mild winters. Most rain falls in the mountainous north. The Algarve region in the south is hot and dry.

Languages:
Portuguese.

Religion:
Roman Catholic; Protestant minority.

Money:
Euro = 100 cents.
Cirrus: excellent for ATMs.
Maestro: fair for ATMs.
MasterCard: good for retail, excellent for ATMs.
Traveller's cheques: £ sterling or euros.
Visa: good for retail, excellent for ATMs.

Living costs:

Portugal is one of Europe's bargains. Allow $15 per day for food and accommodation. Outside the major tourist areas, it's even cheaper.

Visas:

Passports valid for three months are required by all. Nationals from Australia, Canada, New Zealand and the USA don't need visas for visits under three months.

Electricity:

220V, 50Hz. Continental, round two-pin plugs.

Health:

A yellow fever certificate is required if you're travelling to the Azores or Madeira from infected areas.

ADDRESS BOOK

Amex Top Tours, Avenida Duque De Loule 108, Lisbon 1050. ☎ (1) 315 5881.

Turismo de Lisboa / Lisbon Visitors and Convention Bureau ☎ (1) 031 2737. Fax: (1) 031 28 99. Email: atl@atl-turismolisboa.pt Web site: http://www.atl-turismolisboa.pt/

STA Wasteels Viagens, Rua dos Cominhos ole Ferro N90, Lisbon 1100. ☎ (1) 886 9793. Fax: (1) 886 9797.

Thomas Cook Star Viagens SA, Travessa Escola Araujo 31, Lisbon 1110. ☎ (1) 314 2425.

Your embassy/consulate in Portugal:

Australian: Rua Marques de Sáda Bandeira 8, 10D Lisbon 1300. ☎ (1) 353 0750.

British: Rua de São Bernardo 33, Lisbon 1200. ☎ (1) 392 4000. Fax: (1) 392 4183.

Canadian: Avenida da Liberdade 198–200, Lisbon 1269. ☎ (1) 316 4600. Fax: (1) 316 4691. Email: lsbon@dfait-maeci.gc.ca Website: http://www.dfait-maeci.gc.ca/lisbon/

Irish: Rua da Imprensa à Estrela 1–4, Lisbon 1200. ☎ (1) 392 9440. Fax: (1) 397 7363.

NZ: Av. Antonio Augusta de Aguiar, 9th floor, Lisbon 1097. ☎ (1) 350 9690. Fax: (1) 572 004. Email: gassint@unicre.pt

South African: Avenida Luís Bivar 10a, Lisbon 1050. ☎ (1) 353 5041. Fax: (1) 353 5713.

US: Avenida das Forcas Armadas, Lisbon. ☎ (1) 727 3300. Fax: (1) 726 9109. Email: ref@american-embassy.pt Website: http://www.american-embassy.pt/

Portuguese embassies/consulates at home:

Australia: 23 Culgoa Circuit, O'Malley ACT 2606. ☎ (02) 6290 1733. Fax: (02) 6290 1957.

Canada: 645 Island Park, Ottawa, Ontario K1Y 0B8. ☎ (613) 729 0883. Fax: (613) 729 4236.

Ireland: Knocksinna House, Knocksinna, Foxrock, Dublin 18. ☎ (01) 289 4416.

NZ: 61 Molesworth Street, Wellington. ☎ (04) 472 1677. Fax: (04) 472 8023.

SA: Diamond Corner Building, 68 Eloff Street, Johannesburg. ☎ (012) 323 6540. Fax (012) 241454.

UK: 11 Belgrave Square, London SW1X 8PP. ☎ (020) 7235 5331.

US: 2125 Kalorama Road, NW, Washington DC 20008. ☎ (202) 328 8610. Fax: (202) 462 3726. Website: http://www.portugal.org/geninfo/ missions/states.html

Accommodation:

Pousade de Juventude de Lisboa Rua Andrade Corvo 46, Lisboa 1000. ☎ (1) 353 2696. Fax: (1) 353 2696.

Rua Rodrigues Lobo 98 Porto 4000. ☎ (2) 606 5535. Fax: (2) 606 5535.

R. Dr Sousa Martins 40 Vila Real de Santo Antonio, (Algarve) 8900. ☎ (81) 44565. Fax: (81) 44565.

Poste restante:

Correios Centrais Restauradores, Lisbon.

Russia ✈

(+3hrs GMT in Moscow) **Capital:** Moscow

☎ **Country: 7**, Moscow: 095, Vladivostok: 4237 💲 Rouble

It's big, it's very, very big. Moscow's landmarks, such as Red Square, the Kremlin and St Basil's Cathedral are nothing short of breathtaking and are all easy to reach on foot. Chill out (literally) in Gorky Park and see Lenin's tomb. Travel by Metro is a must, just to see the chandeliers. Another must is the train to St Petersburg, dubbed 'The Venice of the North'. The incredible Winter Palace, forming part of the State Hermitage Museum, is a lesson in grandeur. Also worth checking out are the Summer Palace and the Beloselsky-Belozersky Palace. The old cultural and political capital of Russia, Novgorod, also overflows with fine Russian artefacts. And on the banks of the river Volga, Volgograd has a fine collection of museums and monuments to World War II. If you fancy seeing the whole of Russia in six days, hop on the Trans-Siberian Express. Take extreme care as muggings on the train are common. When you alight at Vladivostok, check out the Far East Maritime Reserve for some of the wildest wildlife, including tigers and bears. Trekkers should head to the Caucasus or the Kola Peninsula for a taste of barren beauty. Skiing can be enjoyed at Mount Elbrus, Europe's highest peak.

👁 Black Sea, boat trip on River Volga, Caucasus Mountains, Kola Peninsula, Moscow, Mount Elbrus, the old town of Novgorod, St Petersburg, Trans-Siberian Express, and Volgograd.

Weather:
Winters in Russia (from December to February) are severe, especially in Siberia, whereas summers are generally quite warm. Spring and autumn are brief temperate periods between these two extremes.

Languages:
Russian. English, French or Geman are sometimes spoken.

Religion:
Russian Orthodox, Muslim, Animist.

Money:
Rouble = 100 kopeks.
Cirrus: fair for ATMs.
Maestro: very limited for ATMs.
MasterCard: very limited for retail, limited for ATMs.
Traveller's cheques: US dollars.
Visa: no retail availability, very limited for ATMs.

Living costs:
Budget about $30 per day for food, travel and a bed.

Visas:

Requirements are subject to change so check before you go. All travellers are advised to contact the nearest Russian Embassy or Consulate for up-to-date details. You need to carry ID at all times.

Electricity:

220V, 50Hz.

ADDRESS BOOK

Amex 21a Sadovaya-Kudrinskaya, Moscow 103001. ☎(095) 755 9000.
Intourist 13/1 Milyutinsky Per, Moscow 101000. ☎ (095) 923 8575 or (095) 232 2424. Fax: (095) 234 3778. Email: info@intourist.ru Website: //www.intourist.ru/Eng/s_bureau.htm
STA Sta Travel, 9 Baltiyskaya, 3rd Floor, Moscow 125178. ☎ (095) 797 9555. Fax: (095) 797 9554.
Thomas Cook Travel House, Tournee Petroverigskii Pereulok 4, Moscow 101912. ☎ (095) 928 9980.

Your embassy/consulate in Russia:

Australian: 13 Kropotkinsky Pereulok, Moscow ☎ (095) 956 6070/5. Fax: (095) 956 6170. Website: http://www.australianembassy.ru/
British: Sofiiskaya Naberezhnaya 14, Moscow 109072. ☎ (503) 956 7200. Fax: (503) 956 7440. Email: britembppas@glas.apc.org Website: http://www.britemb.msk.ru/
Canadian: 23 Starkonyushenny Pereulok, Moscow. ☎ (095) 956 6666. Fax: (095) 232-9948. Email: mosco@dfait-maeci.gc.ca
Irish: Grokholski Pereulok 5, Moscow 129010. ☎ (095) 937 5911. Fax: (095) 975 2066.
NZ: 44 Ulitsa Povarskaya (formerly Vorovskovo), Moscow 121069. ☎ (095) 956 3579/80. Fax: (095) 956 3583. Email: nzembmos@glasnet.ru Website: http://www.nzembassy.msk.ru/
US: 19/23 Novinsky Blvd, 121099 Moscow. ☎(095) 252 2451/59. Fax: (095) 956 4261. Email: consulmo@state.gov Website: http://usembassy.state.gov/moscow/

Russian embassies/consulates at home:

Australia: 78 Canberra Avenue, Griffith ACT 2603. ☎ (02) 6295 9033. Fax: (02) 6295 1847.
Ireland: 186 Orwell Road, Dublin 6. ☎ (01) 492 2048.
NZ: 57 Messines Road, Karori, Wellington. ☎ (04) 476 6113. Fax: (04) 476 3843.
South Africa: 316 Brooke Street, Menlo Park, Pretoria. ☎(012) 432 731. Fax: (012) 418 3656.
UK: 5 Kensington Palace Gardens, London W8 4QG. ☎ (020) 7229 8027.
US: 2650 Wisconsin Avenue, NW, Washington DC 20007. ☎ (202) 298 5700. Fax: (202) 298 5749. Website: http://www.russianembassy.org

Accommodation:

HI–G&R Hostel Asia Zelenodolskaya str. 3/2, 15th floor, Moscow 109377. ☎ (095) 378 0001. Fax: (095) 378 2866. Email: hostelasia@mtu-net.ru Website: http://www.hostels-trains.ru
Hostel Tramp Bld. 7, 17/2 Selskohozyaistvennaya ul., Metro, Moscow 129226. ☎ (095) 551 2876. Fax: (095) 551 2876. Email: info@hostelling.ru Website: http://www.hostelling.ru
HI–St Petersburg International Hostel St. Petersburg, 3rd Sovetskaya, 28, Lappeenranta, Finland ☎ (812) 329 8018. Fax: (812) 329 8019. Email: ryh@ryh.ru

Poste restante:

Central Post Office 33 Varshavskoe Shosse, Moscow 113105.

Health:

Cholera, polio, rabies and typhoid.

Spain ✈

(+1hr GMT) **Capital:** Madrid

☎ **Country: 34**, Barcelona: 93, Madrid: 91 〔$〕 Euro

Spain, country of sandy beaches, hot weather and beautiful and lively cities. The capital, Madrid, has some of Spain's best nightlife and museums. There's an amazing amount of art to keep you culturally topped up, plus markets and nightclubs galore, all of which are frantic with activity. Sports-wise, there's soccer or bullfighting, depending on your taste. Accommodation isn't a problem...but the heat may well be. The Spanish coasts are knee-deep in sun-worshippers during the summer, but cities such as Barcelona (east) and San Sebastian (north) are both worth visiting. Inland, Spain offers great skiing in the shape of the Sierra Nevada, the Pyrenees and the Sierra de Guadarrama just above Madrid. It's cheap, so take advantage. The interior of Spain is well worth exploring, mixing sun-drenched countryside with traditional and not-too-touristy towns, such as Toledo and Segovia. The southern city of Seville has a hip scene, and if you have the time, Ibiza is worth a jaunt. Apart from its notorious nightlife, it boasts some great beaches. The buses are a lot cheaper and more comprehensive than Spain's train system and, unless you can afford to fly, the best way to travel around the country.

👁 The Alhambra Palace at Granada, Barcelona, Cadiz, Cordoba, Guggenheim Museum at Bilbao, Ibiza, Madrid, Mallorca, Mediterranean beaches, Pyrenees, San Sebastian, Segovia, Seville, Sierra Nevada, and Toledo.

Weather:
Best visited between April and September, when it's hot and dry. The south is hot all year, but milder between October and May. The north is cool and rainy from October to March, and fairly dry at other times.

Languages:
Castillan Spanish; also Catalan, Galician and Basque.

Religion:
Roman Catholic.

Money:
Euro = 100 cents.
Cirrus: good for ATMs.
Maestro: good for ATMs.
MasterCard: excellent for retail and ATMs.
Traveller's cheques: £ sterling or euros.
Visa: excellent for retail and ATMs.

Living costs:
There are plenty of hostels in all the major resorts, and food is pretty cheap as well. Long-distance travel is

expensive, so avoid it if possible. Overall, to sleep and eat, budget for about $20 a day.

Visas:

South African visitors need a visa. Other nationals can stay up to ninety days as a tourist without a visa. Requirements are subject to change so check before you go.

Electricity:

220V, 50Hz. Round two-pin plugs.

Health:

Rabies.

ADDRESS BOOK

Amex Plaza De Las Cortes 2, Madrid 28014.
☎ (91) 322 5225/5.
STA Barcelo Viajes Princesa 3, Madrid 28008.
☎ (91) 559 1819. Fax: (91) 559 1325.
Thomas Cook Ambassador Tours, Leganitos 47, 8 Ed Compost, Madrid 28013. ☎ (91) 540 1550.
Fax: (91) 559 0046.

Your embassy/consulate in Spain:

Australian: Pza Descubridor Diego de Ordás, 3 (Santa Engracia, 120) Madrid 28003.
☎ (91) 441 9300. Fax: (91) 442 5362.
Email: information@embaustralia.es
Website: http://www.embaustralia.es/
British: Calle de Fernando, El Santo 16, Madrid 28010. ☎ (91) 319 0200. Fax: (91) 700 8272.
Canadian: Núñez de Balboa 35, Madrid 28001.
☎ (91) 423 3250. Fax: (91) 423 3251.
Email: mdrid@dfait-maeci.gc.ca
Website: http://www.canada-es.org/
Irish: Ireland House, Paseo de la Castellana 46-4, Madrid 28046. ☎ (1) 436 4093. Fax: (1) 435 1677.
Email: embajada.irlanda@ran.es
NZ: 3rd Floor, Plaza de La Lealtad 2, Madrid 28014.
☎ (91) 523 0226. Fax: (91) 523 0171.
South African: Claudio Coello 91, Madrid 28071.
☎ (91) 435 6688.
US: Serrano, 75, Madrid 28006. ☎ (91) 587 2200.
Fax: (91) 587 2303. Website: http://www.embusa.es/

Spanish embassies/consulates at home:

Australia: PO Box 9076, Deakin, ACT 2600.
☎ (02) 6273 3555. Fax: (02) 6723 3918.
Canada: 350 Sparks Street, Suite 802, Ottawa, Ontario K1R 7S8. ☎ (613) 237 2193.
Fax: (613) 236 9246.
Ireland: 17a Merlyn Park, Dublin 4. ☎ (01) 269 1640.
NZ: PO Box 71, Papakura, Auckland. ☎ (09) 299 6019. Fax: (09) 298 9986.
South Africa: 169 Pine Street, Arcadia, Pretoria.
☎ (012) 344 3875.
UK: 24 Belgrave Square, London SW1X 8QA.
☎ (020) 7235 5555. Fax: (020) 7224 6409.
US: 2375 Pennsylvania Avenue, NW, Washington DC 20037. ☎ (202) 452 0100. Fax: (202) 833 5670.
Website: http://www.spainemb.org/information/

Accommodation:

Alberg La Cuitat C/Ca L'Alegre de Dalt 66, C/Marti 121, Barcelona 08024. ☎ (93) 213 0300.
Fax: (93) 219 3695. Email: laciutat@nnhotels.es
Website: http://laciutat.nnhotels.es
Hostel Lorenzo Infantas n 263, Madrid.
☎ (91) 521 3057. Fax: (91) 532 7978.
Email: hostallorenzo@wanadoo.es
HI–Albergue Juvenil "Salamanca" c/ Escoto, 13-15, Salamanca 37008. ☎ (923) 269 141.
Fax: (923) 214 227.
Email: esterra@mmteam.disbumad.es

Poste restante:

Lista de Correos, Plaza de la Cibeles, Madrid.

Sweden ✈

(+1hr GMT) **Capital:** Stockholm

☎ **Country: 46**, Gothenburg: 31, Stockholm: 8 💲 Swedish krona

The expense of visiting Sweden may put you off, but if you can afford it, its beautiful scenic landscape of lakes, glaciers and pine forests make the trip worthwhile. Stockholm, especially the medieval old town, is a labyrinth of streets and lanes. To the east of the city is the island of Djurgarden, seemingly made up of nothing but gardens and museums. Un-hectic, to say the least. The city centre has many hostels offering rooms at pretty good prices. The real beauty of Sweden, particularly in the summer, lies in its countryside. The northern area is almost totally made up of forest and lakes; the national parks of Sareks, Stora Sjofallets and Padjelanta all display amazing scenery above the Arctic Circle but be warned, trekking is hard work up here. The village of Jokkmokk is nearby and should not be missed. You've got about 100,000 lakes to chose from in Sweden, so it would be hard to avoid visiting one – Vänern and Vättern lying south west of Stockholm are the grandest. Gothenburg on the west coast is definitely worth a look, for its excellent amusement park if not its beauty. There's also the islands of Oland and Gotland off the west coast if you want sandy beaches and high temperatures. The train service is one of the best and buses take up the rest of the slack. Both are a great way to take in the scenery.

👁 Cross-country skiing, Gothenburg, Gotland's bars and beaches, Jokkmokk, Lake Vänern, Lake Vättern, Liseberg amusement park, Oland's countryside, Sareks National Park, Skansen open-air museum, Stockholm archipelago, Stockholm city, and Visby.

Weather:
North is sunny between April and November with daylight for much of the time, and a temperate climate. The rest of the year it's bitterly cold, and either wet or snowy. The south has the same climate with less rain.

Languages:
Swedish, but English is also widely spoken.

Religion:
Evangelical Lutheran.

Money:
Swedish krona = 100 øre.
Cirrus: good for ATMs.
Maestro: very limited for ATMs.
MasterCard: good for retail and ATMs.
Traveller's cheques: £ sterling.
Visa: good for retail and ATMs.

Living costs:
Sweden is 're-mortgage your house for a coffee' territory, so be careful. If you stay in hostels and self-cater, then allow about $30–40 per day.

Visas:

Visas aren't required.

Electricity:

220V, 50Hz. Two-pin plugs.

Health:

No major health risks.

ADDRESS BOOK

Amex Birger Jarlsgatan 1 (PO Box 1761), Stockholm 1187 ☎ (8) 679 5200.

STA 30 Kungsgatan, 11135 Stockholm.
☎ (8) 5452 6666. Fax: (8) 5452 5848.
Email: stockholm@statravel.se

Swedish Tourist Federation (Svenska Turistföreningen) PO Box 25, Stureplan 4C, Stockholm 10120. ☎ (8) 463 2100. Fax: (8) 678 1958.
Email: info@stfturist.se
Website: http://www.stfturist.se

Swedish Travel and Tourism Council PO Box 3030, Stockholm 10361. ☎ (8) 725 5500. Fax: (8) 725 5531.
Email: info@swetourism.se
Website: http://www.swetourism.se

Your embassy/consulate in Sweden:

Australian: Sergels Torg 12, Stockholm 10386.
☎ (8) 613 2900. Fax: (8) 247 414.
Website: http://www.austemb.se/www.austemb.se/

British: Skarpogatan 6–8 (PO Box 27819), Stockholm 11593. ☎ (8) 671 9000. Fax: (8) 661 9766.
Website: http://www.britishembassy.com/

Canadian: Tegelbacken 4, 7th Floor, Stockholm 10323. ☎ (8) 453 3000. Fax: (8) 242 491.
Email: stkhm@dfait-maeci.gc.ca
Website: http://www.canadaemb.se/

Irish: Ostermalmsgatan 97, Stockholm 100 55.
☎ (8) 661 8005. Fax: (8) 660 1353.
Email: irish.embassy@swipnet.se

NZ: Nybrogatan 34, Stockholm S–114 39.
☎ (8) 611 2625. Fax: (8) 611 3551.
Email: mifr@gaddaek.dahl.se

South African: Linnègatan 76, Stockholm 11523.
☎ (8) 243 950. Fax: (8) 660 7136.
Website: http://www.southafricanemb.se/

US: Dag Hammarskolds 31, Stockholm 11589.
☎ (8) 783 5300. Fax: (8) 661 1964.
Email: webmaster@usemb.se
Website: http://www.usis.usemb.se/

Swedish embassies/consulates at home:

Australia: 5 Turrana Street, Yarralumla ACT 2600.
☎ (02) 6270 2700. Fax: (02) 6270 2755.

Canada: 2 Bloor Street West, Suite 1504, Toronto, Ontario M4W 3E2. ☎ (416) 963 8768.
Fax: (416) 923 8809.

Ireland: Sun Alliance House, Dublin 2.
☎ (01) 671 5822.

NZ: Vogel Building, 13th Floor, Aitken Street, Wellington. ☎ (04) 499 9895. Fax: (04) 473 7430.

South Africa: 9th Floor, Old Mutual Building, 167 Andries Street, Pretoria. ☎ (12) 321 1050.

UK: 11 Montagu Place, London W1H 1RT.
☎ (020) 7724 3101.

US: 1501 M Street, NW, Washington DC 20005.
☎ (202) 467 2600. Fax: (202) 467 2656.
Website: http://www.swedenemb.org/

Accommodation:

STF/HI Youth Hostel Bogesund/Vaxholm
185 93 Vaxholm, Stockholm. ☎ (8) 5413 2240.
Fax: (8) 5413 2240.

STF/HI Youth Hostel Kiruna Bergmästaregatan 7, Mitt i City, 981 33 Kiruna. ☎ (980) 17195
Fax: (980) 84142.

Poste restante:

Central Post Office Stockholm 1.

Switzerland ✈

(+1hr GMT) **Capital:** Bern

☎ **Country: 41**, Bern: 31, Geneva: 22, Zürich: 1 〔$〕 Swiss franc

The main reasons you'll want to visit Switzerland are the outstanding landscape and cool towns, such as Zürich and Geneva. The reason you'll leave is because you're broke. Zürich was definitely built with good looks in mind, located on the northern shores of Lake Zürich (perfect for sunbathing, swimming and taking in the beauty) and combines the style and elegance of the pedestrianised old town with excellent nightlife (head for the Niederdorfstrasse area). It's a lovely city to chill out in, with a few budget hostels on the outskirts of the city centre. Geneva is on the shores of another beautiful lake. If you want to visit yodelling country and breathe in the clear mountain air, the Jungfrau region near Interlaken should suit you well. The mountainous scenery is spellbinding and there are loads of cable cars and railways to get you to scenic vantage points. The west of the country is home to the Jura Mountains which are less popular but easily as awe-inspiring. Switzerland is renowned for skiing, but it comes at a price. Public transport is excellent: trains, buses, trams, cable cars, you name it – they're comfortable and go wherever you want.

👁 Bernese Oberland, Geneva, Hinter Dorf, Jungfrau, Jura Mountains, Lake Geneva, Lake Zürich, Matterhorn, Zermatt, and Zürich.

Weather:

North of the Alps the summer months are warm, and the winters are dry, cool and foggy. The north east mountainous regions are the coldest, and get bitter from December to February. South of the Alps, it's milder with hot summers.

Languages:

German, French and Italian.

Religion:

Roman Catholic and Protestant.

Money:

Swiss franc = 100 rappen or centimes.

Cirrus: excellent for ATMs.

Maestro: very limited for ATMs.

MasterCard: good for retail, excellent for ATMs.

Traveller's cheques: £ sterling or Swiss francs.

Visa: good for retail, fair for ATMs.

Living costs:

There are quite a few hostels to choose from and they are not too expensive. Allow about $25 per day for food, board and travel.

Visas:

Passports valid for six months from the date of arrival are required by all.

Electricity:

220V, 50Hz.

Health:

No major health risks.

ADDRESS BOOK

Amex 7–Seas Travel Ltd, 83 Kramgrasse, Bern 7.
☎ (31) 327 7777.
STA SSR Travel, 40 Baeckerstrasse, CH–8004 Zürich.
☎ (1) 323 6554. Fax: (1) 323 6557.
Switzerland Tourism 7 Tödistrasse, CH–8027 Zürich.
☎ (1) 288 1111. Fax: (1) 288 1205.
Email: postoffice@switzerlandtourism.ch
Website: http://www.myswitzerland.com/

Your embassy/consulate in Switzerland:
Australian: 29 Alpenstrasse, CH–3006 Bern.
☎ (31) 351 0143–46. Fax: (31) 352 1234.
Website: http://www.australia.ch/~australi/
British: 50 Thunstrasse, CH–3005 Bern.
☎ (31) 359 7700. Fax: (31) 359 7701.
Email: Information@british-embassy-berne.ch
Website: http://www.british-embassy-berne.ch/
Canadian: 88 Kirchenfeldstrasse, CH–3005 Bern.
☎ (31) 357 3200. Fax: (31) 357 3210.
Email: bern@dfait-maeci.gc.ca
Website: http://www.canada-ambassade.ch/
Irish: 68 Kirchenfeldstrasse, CH–3005 Bern.
☎ (31) 352 1442/3. Fax: (31) 352 1455.
NZ: 28a Chemin des Fins, 1218 Grand Saconnex,
CH–1211, Geneva. ☎ (22) 929 0350.
Fax: (22) 929 0374. Email: mission.nz@itu.ch
US: 95 Jubilaeumsstrasse, CH–3001 Bern.
☎ (31) 357 7011. Fax: (31) 357 7344.
Website: http://www.us-embassy.ch/

Swiss embassies/consulates at home:
Australia: 7 Melbourne Avenue, Forrest ACT 2603.
☎ (02) 6273 3977. Fax: (02) 6273 3428.
Canada: 5 Malborough Avenue, Ottawa, Ontario K1N
8E6. ☎ (613) 235 1837. Fax: (613) 563 1394.
Ireland: Ailesbury Road, Dublin 4. ☎ (01) 269 2515.
NZ: Panama House, 22 Panama Street, Wellington.
☎ (04) 472 1593/4. Fax: (04) 499 6302.
South Africa: Cradock Heights, 21 Cradock Avenue,
Rosebank, Johannesburg. ☎ (011) 442 7500.
Fax: (011) 436 707.
UK: 16–18 Montagu Place, London W1H 2BQ.
☎ (020) 7616 6000. Fax: (020) 7724 7001.
Email: Vertretung@Lon.rep.admin.ch
Website: http://www.swissembassy.org.uk
US: 2900 Cathedral Avenue, NW, Washington DC
20008. ☎ (202) 745 7900. Fax: (202) 387 2564.
Website: http://www.swissemb.org/

Accommodation:
HI–YH Bern Weihergasse 4, CH–3005 Bern.
☎ (31) 311 6316. Fax: (31) 312 5240.
Email: bern@youthhostel.ch
HI–YH St. Moritz Stille, Via Surpunt 60, CH-7500 St.
☎ (81) 833 3969. Fax: (81) 833 8046.
Email: st.moritz@youthhostel.ch
HI–YH Klosters "Soldanella", Talstrasse 73, CH-7250
Klosters. ☎ (81) 422 1316. Fax: (81) 422 5209.
Email: klosters@youthhostel.ch

Poste restante:
Post Schanzenpost CH–3003 Bern.
☎ (31) 386 4810.

Australia ✈

(east +10hrs; west +8hrs GMT) **Capital:** Canberra

☎ **Country: 61**, Canberra: 6, Perth: 8, Sydney: 2 💲 Australian dollar

It's rather large and there's lots of space...and sun...and coastline! Sydney Harbour's fab setting is best appreciated by boat. Further into the city, check out The Rocks, the oldest part of town. The cheapest place to stay is the Kings Cross area, which is easily accessible by bus from the airport. If you want to say you've done it all, which you probably will, don't forget to visit the ultimate surfers' paradise, Bondi Beach. Otherwise, hip and happening Perth, capital of Western Australia, is surrounded by some of Oz's coolest beaches: Peppermint Grove, Como, Swanbourne, Scarborough and Fremantle are the cream of the crop. Another top attraction has to be the whale-watching trips into the Antarctic Ocean. For a taste of the Outback, head for Darwin and Kakadu National Park – this is real Crocodile Dundee country where you can experience an unforgettable bush trip (although grub-eating is strictly optional). The Northern Territories is also home to the world's most famous slab of red rock – Uluru, better known as Ayers Rock. And then there's the breathtaking Great Barrier Reef which meanders down the entire coast of Queensland, taking in more than 600 islands. Lady Elizabeth, Heron or Great Keppel islands are good for watersports, and have the most affordable accommodation. Other places that are well worth a look are Cairns, Brisbane and Frazer Island.

👁 Alice Springs, Ayers Rock (Uluru), Blue Mountains, Bondi Beach, Cairns, Darwin and Kakadu National Park, Great Barrier Reef, Melbourne, Perth, skiing in the Australian Alps, Sydney Harbour and Opera House, vineyards of NSW, whale-watching.

Weather:
Central regions are very dry, but it can get cold at night – especially from April to September. Monsoons affect the north between November and March, and it stays hot all year round. The south is very hot, reaching the highest temperatures from November to March.

Languages:
English.

Religion:
Predominantly Protestant; Roman Catholic minority.

Money:
Australian dollar = 100 cents.
Cirrus: excellent for ATMs.
Maestro: limited for ATMs.
MasterCard: excellent for retail and ATMs.
Traveller's cheques: £ sterling or Australian dollars.
Visa: excellent for retail, good for ATMs.

AUSTRALASIA AND THE PACIFIC ISLANDS

Living costs:

For your food and board, budget about $15–20 per day. But because it's such a huge country, travelling isn't cheap. (Breakfast $4; hostels/backpackers $8–14 per night.)

Visas:

Everyone (except nationals of New Zealand) needs a visa: six-month tourist visas are $22; visas under three months are free.

Electricity:

240–250V, 50Hz. Unique three-pin plugs (adaptor needed).

Health:

A yellow fever vaccination is required if you're travelling from infected areas.

ADDRESS BOOK

Amex 92 Pitt Street, Sydney NSW 2000.
☎ (2) 9239 0666.
Australian Tourist Commission Level 4, 80 William Street, Woolloomooloo, Sydney NSW 2011.
☎ (2) 9360 1111. Fax: (2) 9331 6469.
Website: http://www.aussie.net.au
STA Travel 100 James Street Northbridge, Perth WA 6003. ☎ (9) 227 7569. Fax: (9) 227 5572.
Email: ames@statravel.com.au
STA Travel 79 Oxford Street, Darlinghurst, NSW 2010.
☎ (2) 9361 4966. Fax: (2) 9361 4620.
Email: darlinghurst@statravel.com.au

Your embassy/consulate in Australia:

British: Commonwealth Avenue, Yarralumla ACT 2600. ☎ (2) 270 6666. Fax: (2) 270 6653.
Website: http://www.uk.emb.gov.au/
Canadian: Level 5, Quay West, 111 Harrington Street, Sydney NSW 2000. ☎ (2) 364 3050. Fax: (2) 364 4099.
Website: http://www.dfait-maeci.gc.ca/australia/
Irish: 20 Arkana Street, Yarralumla ACT 2600.
☎ (2) 273 3022/3201. Fax: (2) 273 3741.
Email: irishemb@computech.com.au
NZ: Commonwealth Avenue, Canberra ACT 2600.
☎ (2) 270 4211. Fax: (2) 273 3194.
Email: nzhccba@dynamite.com.au
South African: cnr of State Circle and Rhodes Place, Yarralumla ACT 2600. ☎ (2) 273 2424.
Fax: (2) 273 3543. Email: info@rsa.emb.gov.au
Website: http://www.rsa.emb.gov.au/
US: Moonah Place, Yarralumla ACT 2600.
☎ (2) 214 5600. Fax: (2) 214 5970.
Website: http://usembassy-australia.state.gov/embassy/

Australian embassies/consulates at home:

Canada: World Trade Centre Complex, Suite 602-999 Canada Place, Vancouver BC. ☎ (604) 684 1177.
Fax: (604) 684 1856. Website: http://www.ahc-ottawa.org/
Ireland: 2nd Floor, Fitzwilton House, Wilton Terrace, Dublin 2. ☎ (01) 676 1517. Fax: (1) 668 5266.
Website: http://www.australianembassy.ie/
NZ: 8th Floor, Union House, 32-38 Quay Street, Aukland. ☎ (9) 303 2429. Fax: (9) 377 0798.
South Africa: 214th Floor, BP Centre, Thibault Square, Cape Town 8001. ☎ (21) 419 5425-9.
Fax: (21) 419 7345. Website:
http://www.australia.co.za/
UK: Australia House, Strand, London WC2B 4LA.
☎ (020) 7379 4334. Fax: (020) 7240 5333.
Website: http://www.australia.org.uk/
US: 1601 Massachusetts Avenue NW, Washington DC 20036. ☎ (202) 797 3000. Fax: (202) 797 3168.
Website: http://www. austemb.org/

Accommodation:

Sydney Central YHA 11 Rawson Place, Sydney 2000.
☎ (02) 9281 9111. Fax: (02) 9281 9199.
Email: sydcentral@yhansw.org.au
Bondi Beachouse YHA Cnr Fletcher and Dellview Street, Bondi Beach 2027. ☎ (02) 9365 2088.
Fax: (02) 9365 2177. Email: bondi@intercoast.com.au
YHA on the Esplanade 93 The Esplanade, Cairns 4870. ☎ (07) 4031 1919. Fax: (07) 4031 4381.
Email: cairnsesplanade@yhaqld.org

Poste restante:

General Post Office 159 Pitt Street, Sydney NSW 2000. ☎ (2) 9230 7236.

Cook Islands ✈

(−10hrs GMT) **Capital:** Avarua

☎ **Cook Islands: 682** 💲 New Zealand dollar (interchangeable with the Cook Islands dollar)

If heaven on earth exists, the Cook Islands must have the copyright. These fifteen Pacific islands have some of the world's best beaches and ocean waters on offer. Rarotonga, the largest island, packs in both excellent beaches and a lush mountainous inland area. If you fancy a good view, hike up to Raemaru, located behind the capital, Avarua. Head south for Wigmore's Falls if you care to dive into the kind of oasis seen only in *The Blue Lagoon*. The island of Aitutaki is less popular with tourists, but is well worth checking out for its northern lagoon, with over twenty small islands, coral, clear sea and bright fish. The island of Atiu is pretty tourist-free and, again, has those beautiful beaches. Activitiy-wise, there are a couple of good hikes on Rarotonga. Buses offer good transport on the bigger islands, and there are loads of cars, 4WDs and motorbikes for hire. Getting between the islands is fastest by plane, and there are some good deals to be had. Travel to the outer islands is a little more sporadic, so be prepared to wait a couple of days for a return trip.

👁 Atiu, Aitutaki, Raemaru, Rarotonga, and Wigmore's Falls.

Weather:
Hot throughout the year, with the highest rainfall between November and April.

Languages:
Cook Islands Maori. English is widely spoken.

Religion:
Cook Islands Christian Church, Roman Catholic, Latter Day Saint, Seventh Day Adventists and Assembly of God.

Money:
New Zealand dollar/Cook Islands dollar = 100 cents.
Cirrus: not accepted.
Maestro: not accepted.
MasterCard: limited for retail, no ATMs available.
Traveller's cheques: £ sterling.
Visa: limited for retail, no ATMs available.

Living costs:
The tourist centres are usually expensive. If you cut down on your travel and scout around, allow about $20 per day for food and board.

Visas:

Passports should be valid for six months from your date of arrival. Visas aren't required by visitors for tourist visits under one month. You need onward or return tickets, proof of accommodation and sufficient funds.

Electricity:

240V, 50Hz.

Health:

Polio and typhoid.

ADDRESS BOOK

Cook Islands Tourist Accommodation Council (CITAC) PO Box 45, Rarotonga. ☎ 22020. Fax: 22021
Cook Islands Tourism Corporation PO Box 14, Rarotonga, Cook Islands. ☎ 29435 or 29436. Fax: 21435. Email: tourism@cookislands.gov.ck
Website: http://www.cook-islands.com

Any problems while in the Cook Islands contact the New Zealand High Commission:
1st Floor, Philatelic Bureau Building Takuvaine Road Avarua, Rarotonga. ☎ 22201. Fax: 21241.
Otherwise all representation is via your embassy/ consulate in New Zealand.

Your embassy/consulate in New Zealand:
Australian: 8th Floor Union House, 32–38 Quay Street, Auckland. ☎ (9) 303 2429. Fax: (9) 377 0798.
British: 44 Hill Street, Wellington 1.
☎ (4) 472 6049. Fax: (4) 473 4982 or 471 1974.
Website: http://www.brithighcomm.org.nz
Email: bhc.wel@xtra.co.nz
Website: http://www.brithighcomm.org.nz/
Canadian: 3rd Floor, 61 Molesworth Street, Thorndon, Wellington. ☎ (4) 473 9577. Fax: (4) 471 2082.
Email: wlgtn@dfait-maeci.gc.ca
Website: http://www.dfait-maeci.gc.ca/newzealand/
Irish: 6th Floor, 18 Shortland Street, Auckland 1.
☎ (9) 302 2867. Fax: (9) 302 2420.
South African: cnr of State Circle and Rhodes Place, Yarralumla ACT 2600. ☎ (2) 273 2424.
Fax: (2) 273 3543. Email: info@rsa.emb.gov.au
Website: http://www.rsa.emb.gov.au/
US: 29 Fitzherbert Terrace, Thorndon, Wellington.
☎ (4) 472 2068.
Website: http://usembassy.state.gov/wellington/

New Zealand embassies/consulates at home:
Australia: Commonwealth Avenue, Yarralumla ACT 2600. ☎ (02) 6270 4211. Fax: (02) 6273 3194.
Email: nzhccba@dynamite.com.au
Canada: Metropolitan House (suite 727), 99 Bank Street, Ottawa. ☎ (613) 238 5991.
Fax: (613) 238 5707. Email: nzhcott@istar.com
Website: http://www.nzhcottawa.org/
Ireland: 37 Leeson Park, Dublin. ☎ (1) 660 4233.
Fax: (1) 660 4228. Email: nzconsul@indigo.ie
South Africa: 1110 Arcadia Street, Arcadia, Pretoria.
☎ (012) 342 8656/7. Fax: (012) 342 8640.
Email: nzhc@global.co.za
UK: New Zealand House, 80 Haymarket, London SW1Y 4TQ. ☎ (020) 7973 0366. Fax: (020) 7839 4580.
US: 37 Observatory Circle, Washington DC 20008.
☎ (202) 328 4848. Fax: (202) 667 5227.
Email: nz@nzemb.org Website: http://www.nzemb.org/

Further information:
Tourism Council for the South Pacific 203 Sheen Lane, London SW14 8LE. ☎ (020) 8876 1938.
Fax: (020) 8878 9876. Email: UK@interface-tourism.com

Accommodation:
Are Renga Backpacker Hostel Box 223, Arorangi, Rarotonga, Cook Islands. ☎ (682) 20 050.
Email: arerenga@oyster.net.ck
Cook Islands Lodges Box 3050, Arorangi, Rarotonga, Cook Islands. ☎/Fax: (682) 24-303.
Email: cilodges@yahoo.com
Ariana Hostel PO Box 925, Rarotonga, Cook Islands.
☎/Fax: (682) 20521. Email: bobh@ariana.co.ck

Poste restante:
Central Post Office, Avarua, Rarotonga, Cook Islands.

Fiji ✈

(+12hrs GMT) **Capital:** Suva

☎ **Country: 679** 〔$〕Fiji dollar

The 800 islands that go to make up Fiji offer travellers probably the warmest welcome in the Pacific, with a great mix of European, Indian and Pacific cultures. Don't plan on doing too much whilst you're here, the most frenetic pastime being surfing off the coast of the Mamanuca group of islands. This is also a good place to hook up with travellers. There is some beautiful aquatic scenery, in the shape of lagoons, reefs, and white sand beaches, most of which offer excellent diving and snorkelling. Most people fly into Nadi Airport, on the main island of Viti Levu. Head for the town of Nadi, the tourist centre of Fiji. This is a great place to base yourself, as it has loads of tourist-geared accommodation and services. The capital, Suva, is more urbanised, but the waterfront markets are exotic to say the least. Inland, you can trek, horse-ride, river-raft or just enjoy the friendliness of the locals. They've managed to keep their traditions, whilst accommodating tourism. The bus and ferry services in Fiji offer excellent coverage and are cheap, making travel easy and enjoyable.

◉ Lau Group, Mamanuca Group, Nausori Highlands, Suva's market, Vanau Levu, Suva on Viti Levu and Rabi.

Weather:
Hot and humid all year round. The rainy season is from December to April, and it's wettest on the eastern sides of the islands. Fiji is also located in a cyclone path.

Languages:
English, Fijian and Hindi.

Religion:
Methodist and Hindu; Roman Catholic and Muslim minorities.

Money:
Fiji dollar = 100 cents.
Cirrus: not accepted.
Maestro: not accepted.
MasterCard: very limited for retail, no ATMs available.
Traveller's cheques: £ sterling.
Visa: very limited for retail, limited for ATMs.

Living costs:

It's pretty expensive – you can just get by on $30 per day for food and board, but that's without doing anything. If you enter Fiji on a package deal, you may well find that some of your activities work out cheaper.

Visas:

Passports should be valid for six months from your date of arrival. South African nationals need a visa: issued for thirty days and possibly extended for up to six months.

Electricity:

240V, 50Hz.

Health:

A yellow fever certificate is required if you're travelling from infected areas. Dengue fever, polio and typhoid.

ADDRESS BOOK

Amex Tapa International Ltd, 4th Floor, Anz House, 25 Victoria Parade, Suva. ☎ 302 333.

Fiji Visitors Bureau G.P.O. Box 92, Thomson Street, Suva, Fiji Islands. ☎ 302 433. Fax: 300 986. Email: infodesk@fijifvb.gov.fj. Website: http://www.BulaFiji.com

Ministry of Tourism and Civil Aviation PO Box 1260, 1st Floor, Sabrina Building, Victoria Parade, Suva. ☎ 312 788. Fax: 302 060.

STA Rosie the Travel Service, Nadi Airport, Suva. ☎ 722 755. Fax: 722 607/790 460.

Thomas Cook 7 Kusum Centre, Main Street, Nadi. ☎ 703 110.

Tourism Council of the South Pacific Street Level, 3 Victoria Parade, Suva. Fax: 301 995. Website: http://www.tcsp.com

Your embassy/consulate in Fiji:

Australian: 37 Princes Street, Suva. ☎ 382 211. Fax: 382 065. Email: austembassy@is.com.fj Website: http://www.austhighcomm.org.fj

British: Victoria House, 47 Gladstone Road, Suva. ☎ 311 033. Fax: 301 406. Email: ukchancery@is.com.fj Website: http://www.ukinthepacific.bhc.org.fj

Canadian: PO Box 10690, Nadi Airport. ☎ 721 936. Fax: 750 666.

NZ: Reserve Bank of Fiji Building, Pratt Street, Suva. ☎ 311 422. Fax: 300 842. Email: nzhc@is.com.fj

US: 31 Loftus Street, Suva. ☎ 314 466. Fax: 300 081. Email: usembsuva@is.com.fj Website: http://www.amembassy-fiji.gov/

Fijian embassies/consulates at home:

Australia: 19 Beale Crescent, Deakin ACT 2600. ☎ (02) 6260 5115. Fax: (02) 6260 5105.

Canada: 130 Slater, Suite 750, Ottawa, Ontario K1P 6E2. ☎ (613) 233 9252. Fax: (613) 594 8705.

Ireland: represented by the embassy/consulate in the UK: 34 Hyde Park Gate, London SW7 5DN. ☎ (020) 7584 3661. Fax: (020) 7584 2838. Email: fijirepuk@compuserve.com

NZ: 31 Pipitea Street, Thorndon, Wellington. ☎ (04) 473 5401/2. Fax: (04) 499 1011.

UK: 34 Hyde Park Gate, London SW7 5DN. ☎ (020) 7584 3661. Fax: (020) 7584 2838. Email: fijirepuk@compuserve.com

US: 2233 Wisconsin Avenue, NW, Suite 240, Washington DC 20007. ☎ (202) 337 8320. Fax: (202) 337 1996. Email: fijiemb@earthlink.net

Accommodation:

Tubakula Beah Bungalows PO Box 2, Sigatoka, Coral Coast, Suva 0000. ☎ (679) 500097. Fax: (679) 500201. Email: tubakula@fiji4less.com Website: http://www.Fiji4Less.com/tuba.html

Goodtime Inn P.O. Box 377, Queens Road, Martinar, Nadi. ☎ (679) 725-610. Fax: (679) 725-610 Email: goodtimeinnfiji@hotmail.com

Poste restante:

Main Post Office Suva, Fiji.

Hawaii ✈

(−10hrs GMT) **Capital:** Honolulu

□HONOLULU

☎ **Hawaii: 808**   💲US dollar

Despite a bad 1970s cop show, the islands that go to make up Hawaii are all pretty cool. Oahu, home to the capital, Honolulu, is very tourist-orientated. Famous beaches, such as Waikiki and Sunset beach, are crowded, but it's still easy to find your own little mecca. Inland, the peak of Diamond Head is worth the hike for some fine views of the island. If surfing's your bag, then you're in the right place – the north shore offers the raddest waves. The island of Kaui, to the west, is the place for tropical flora on a huge scale. There are also some secluded beaches, such as Polihale. Travelling types should head for Secret Beach, which is the place to chill in Hawaii. Maui has even more perfect Pacific beaches. West Maui is for tourists, so it's best left well alone. The rest is perfect for exploring the rainforests, surfing, or just lazing around. Hawaii Volcanoes National Park has scenery ranging from desert through rainforest, mountains, volcanoes and more beaches, for good measure. There's a good network of inter-island flights and ferries, and Oahu has a decent bus service. Bikes are also available for hire.

👁 Hawaii Volcanoes National Park, Kauai, Kihola Bay, Na Pali Coast, Oahu, Secret Beach, and Waimea Canyon.

Weather:
Hot temperatures all year round, with a rainy season from December to March. Mountainous regions can get pretty blustery. There may be cyclones between May and November.

Languages:
English and pidgin.

Religion:
Predominantly Catholic; Buddhist, Hindu, Taoist, Jewish and Muslim minorities.

Money:
US dollar = 100 cents.
Cirrus: excellent for ATMs.
Maestro: not accepted.
MasterCard: good for retail, excellent for ATMs.
Traveller's cheques: US dollars.
Visa: good for retail and ATMs.

Living costs:

Not as expensive as you might expect. You can get a decent day's food for about $10, and a cheap room for $10–15 per night. Travel may be a little more expensive – so stay put.

Visas:

As Hawaii is part of the USA, visa requirements are the same as for the US. Visas aren't required for EU nationals on visits under ninety days. Nationals of non-EU countries should check with the embassy or consulate before travelling.

Electricity:

110–120V, 60Hz.

Health:

Leptospirosis. Watch out for sunburn and jellyfish.

ADDRESS BOOK

Amex Commerce Tower, Suite 104, 1440 Kapiolani Blvd, Honolulu 96814. ☎ 946 7741.
Hawaii Visitors and Convention Bureau 2270 Kalakaua Ave., Suite 801, Honolulu, HI 96815.
☎ (808) 923 1811or (800) 353 5846 toll-free in USA. Fax: (808) 922 8991.
Website: http://www.visit.hawaii.org/

Your embassy/consulate in the US:

Australian: 1601 Massachusetts Avenue, NW, Washington DC 20036. ☎ (202) 797 3000.
Fax: (202) 797 3168. Website: http://www.austemb.org/
British: 3100 Massachusetts Avenue, NW, Washington DC 20008. ☎ (202) 588 6500. Fax: (202) 588 7850.
Website: http://www.britainusa.com/bis/embassy.stm
Canadian: 501 Pennsylvania Avenue, NW, Washington DC 20001. ☎ (202) 682 1740. Fax: (202) 682 7726.
Website: http://www.cdnemb-washdc.org/
Irish: 2234 Massachusetts Avenue, NW, Washington DC 20008. ☎ (202) 462 3939. Fax: (202) 232 5993.
Website: http://www.irelandemb.org/
NZ: 37 Observatory Circle, NW, Washington DC 20008. ☎ (202) 328 4848. Fax: (202) 667 5227.
Website: http://www.nzemb.org/
South African: 3051 Massachusetts Avenue, NW, Washington DC 20008. ☎ (202) 232 4400.
Fax: (202) 265 1607. Website: http://www.southafrica.net/

US embassies/consulates at home:

Australia: Moonah Place Yarralumla ACT 2600.
☎ (06) 270 5970. Fax: (06) 270 5970.
Website: http://usembassy-australia.state.gov/embassy

Canada: 100 Wellington Street, Ottawa, Ontario K1P 5T1. ☎ (613) 238 4470.
Website: http://www.usembassycanada.gov/
Ireland: 42 Elgin Road, Dublin 4. ☎ (01) 668 8777.
Fax: (01) 668 9946. Website: http://www.usembassy.ie/
NZ: 29 Fitzherbert Terrace, Thorndon, Wellington.
☎ (04) 472 2068. Website:
http://usembassy.state.gov/wellington/
South Africa: 877 Pretorius Street, Pretoria 0001.
☎ (012) 342 1048. Fax: (012) 342 2244.
Website: http://usembassy.state.gov/pretoria/
UK: 24 Grosvenor Square, London W1A 1AE.
☎ (020) 7499 9000. Fax: (020) 7894 0699
Website: http://www.usembassy.org.uk

Accommodation:

Hokondo Waikiki Beachside Hotel and Hostel
2556 Lemon Road. B101, Honolulu, HI 96815.
☎ (808) 923 9566. Fax: (808) 923 7525.
Email: Hokondo@aol.com
Website: http://www.hokondo.com
Brecks on the Beach Hostel (OAHU) 59-043 Huelo Street, Sunset Beach, HI 96712. ☎ (808) 638 7873.
Fax: (808) 373 9196. Email: brecks2000@yahoo.com
Arnotts' Lodge and Hiking Adventures 98 Apapane, Hilo, (Big Island), HI 96720. ☎ (808) 969 7097.
Email: info@arnottslodge.com
Website: http://www.arnottslodge.com

Further information:

Website: www.gohawaii.com

Poste restante:

General Post Office Honolulu, Hawaii.

New Zealand ✈

(+12hrs GMT) **Capital:** Wellington

☎ **Country: 64**, Auckland: 9, Wellington: 4 💲 New Zealand dollar

Auckland, on the North Island, is a cool city to hang out in. From here, you can branch out to Great Barrier Island, Hauraki Gulf and the North Cape for great beaches and crystal clear water. On the west coast, the area around Taranaki, has awesome scenery, including Tongariro National Park. For water-based activities, head out to the Bay of Plenty and the East Cape area, and check out Ninety Mile Beach. The capital, Wellington, has a lively scene, with good food and cheap accommodation around the Mount Victoria area. A ferry ride gets you onto the South Island. The town of Picton is a scenic starting point. Around here, and the areas of Nelson and Blenheim are where to watch whales and swim with dolphins. A trek in Mount Cook National Park's incredible scenery will leave you speechless. For those with a death wish, head either for the West Coast Glaciers (for white-water rafting and canoeing) or Queenstown (bungee-jumping, rafting, jet boats and river rapids to name but a few). There's also a great range of picturesque lakes to choose from here. Around Lake Te Anau you should be able to find some nice, cheap rooms.

👁 Auckland, bungee-jump at Queenstown, Christchurch, Egmont National Park, glaciers at Westland National Park, Marlborough Sounds, Mount Cook National Park, Otago Peninsula, Rotorua for Maori culture, Tongariro National Park, Waitomo Caves, and Wellington.

Weather:

North Island is mild between April and September, with no extremes of temperature and a fair chance of rain throughout the year. It gets pretty hot in summer from December to March. South Island is cooler, with cold winters and a greater chance of rain and snow.

Languagess:

English and Maori.

Religion:

Anglican and Roman Catholic.

Money:

New Zealand dollar = 100 cents.

Cirrus: good for ATMs.

Maestro: not accepted.

MasterCard: good for retail and ATMs.

Traveller's cheques: £ sterling or Australian dollars.

Visa: good for retail, excellent for ATMs.

Living costs:

It's an inexpensive country, with lots geared towards people travelling. Hostels and cheap food are easy to find – budget about $20 per day.

Visas:

Passports should be valid for six months from your intended date of arrival. Visas are not required.

Electricity:

230–240V, 50Hz.

Health:

No major health risks; tetanus booster is recommended.

ADDRESS BOOK

Amex 280–292 Lambton Quay, Wellington.
☎ (4) 473 7766.
New Zealand Tourism Board Fletcher Challenge House, 89 The Terrace, Wellington. ☎ (4) 472 8860. Fax: (4) 478 1736. Email: enquiries@nztb.govt.nz Website: http://www.nztb.govt.nz
Tourism New Zealand 147 Victoria Street, PO Box 91 893, Auckland. ☎ (9) 914 4780. Fax: (9) 914 4789.
STA 130 Cuba Street, Wellington. ☎ (4) 385 0561. Fax: ☎ (4) 385 8170. Email: cuba@statravel.co.nz

Your embassy/consulate in New Zealand:

Australian: 8th Floor Union House, 32–38 Quay Street, Auckland. ☎ (9) 303 2429. Fax: (9) 377 0798.
British: 44 Hill Street, Wellington 1.
☎ (4) 472 6049. Fax: (4) 473 4982 or 471 1974.
Website: http://www.brithighcomm.org.nz
Email: bhc.wel@xtra.co.nz
Website: http://www.brithighcomm.org.nz/
Canadian: 3rd Floor, 61 Molesworth Street, Thorndon, Wellington. ☎ (4) 473 9577. Fax: (4) 471 2082.
Email: wlgtn@dfait-maeci.gc.ca
Website: http://www.dfait-maeci.gc.ca/newzealand/
Irish: 6th Floor, 18 Shortland Street, Auckland 1.
☎ (9) 302 2867. Fax: (9) 302 2420.
South African: cnr of State Circle and Rhodes Place, Yarralumla ACT 2600. ☎ (2) 273 2424.
Fax: (2) 273 3543. Email: info@rsa.emb.gov.au
Website: http://www.rsa.emb.gov.au/
US: 29 Fitzherbert Terrace, Thorndon, Wellington.
☎ (4) 472 2068.
Website: http://usembassy.state.gov/wellington/

New Zealand embassies/consulates at home:

Australia: Commonwealth Avenue, Yarralumla ACT 2600. ☎ (02) 6270 4211. Fax: (02) 6273 3194.
Email: nzhccba@dynamite.com.au
Canada: Metropolitan House (suite 727), 99 Bank Street, Ottawa. ☎ (613) 238 5991.
Fax: (613) 238 5707. Email: nzhcott@istar.com
Website: http://www.nzhcottawa.org/
Ireland: 37 Leeson Park, Dublin. ☎ (1) 660 4233.
Fax: (1) 660 4228. Email: nzconsul@indigo.ie
South Africa: 1110 Arcadia Street, Arcadia, Pretoria.
☎ (012) 342 8656/7. Fax: (012) 342 8640.
Email: nzhc@global.co.za
UK: New Zealand House, 80 Haymarket, London SW1Y 4TQ. ☎ (020) 7973 0366. Fax: (020) 7839 4580.
US: 37 Observatory Circle, Washington DC 20008.
☎ (202) 328 4848. Fax: (202) 667 5227.
Email: nz@nzemb.org Website: http://www.nzemb.org/

Accommodation:

HI–Auckland International YHA 5 Turner Street, Auckland, North Island. ☎ (9) 302 8200.
Fax: (9) 302 8205. Email: yhaakint@yha.org.nz
Wellington City YHA 292 Wakefield St (cnr Cambridge Tce), Wellington, North Island.
☎ (04) 801 7280. Fax: (04) 801 7278/
Email: yhawgtn@yha.org.nz
Christchurch City Central YHA 273 Manchester Street, Christchurch, South Island. ☎ (03) 379 9535.
Fax: (03) 379 9537. Email: yhachch@yha.org.nz

Poste restante:

Capital Post Shop 7–27 Waterloo Quay (PO Box 196), Wellington.

Egypt ✈

(+2hrs GMT) **Capital:** Cairo

☎ **Country: 20**, Cairo: 2   💲 Egyptian pound

It's pyramids, it's sand and some of the best diving you could ever imagine. Cairo is a weird mix of the 20th century trying to crowbar its way into history. The cheapest accommodation is towards the Midan Orabi and Midan Tulaat Haib areas in Cairo's centre. Nip out to Giza and take a look at the Great Pyramids and the Sphinx. There are some really cheap rooms around here. Further down the Nile Delta is the town of Luxor and the Valley of the Kings, a collection of ancient monuments and tombs that will definitely take your breath away. Built upon the edge of Lake Nasser, Aswan is where the Nile is at its best. For the desert experience, catch a bus from Cairo and head for the Dakhla Oasis. The town of Mut is a good base. The Red Sea coast has great beaches and diving. If you want more of a hippy hang out, head to Dahbab, near the Israeli border. It's a bit cheesy now, but very cheap. Egypt has good but crowded public transport; buses will take you to any of the major places and also the desert oases.

👁 Abu Simbel for stunning figures of Rameses II, Aswan, Cairo's buzz, Giza and the Pyramids, Hurghadaldfu, Luxor, the Red Sea coastline, River Nile, Temple of Karnak, and the Valley of the Kings.

Weather:

Very hot from April to November, peaking in July and August. During winter, it's dry with cool nights. Expect winds from the Sahara in April.

Languages:

Arabic; English and French are widely spoken.

Religion:

Muslim.

Money:

Egyptian pound = 100 piastres.

Cirrus: not accepted.

Maestro: not accepted.

MasterCard: limited for retail, no ATMs available.

Traveller's cheques: £ sterling.

Visa: very limited for retail and ATMs.

Living costs:

Food off the streets costs next to nothing – you could eat well for about $2 per day and you can find board for as little as $5 per night. Costs rise when you start to see the sites, as these are pretty pricey.

Visas:

Passports should be valid for six months from your date of arrival. Visas are also necessary for everyone (except nationals of South Africa visiting for less than ninety days).

Electricity:

220V, 50Hz.

Health:

A yellow fever certificate is required if you're travelling from infected areas. Cholera, malaria (not in Cairo or Alexandria), polio, rabies and typhoid.

ADDRESS BOOK

Amex 15 Kasr El Nil Street, Cairo. ☎ (2) 747991–6.

Egyptian Youth Travel Bureau 7 Dr. Abdel Hamid Saiid St Maarouf, Cairo. ☎ (2) 577 9773.
Fax: (2) 579 1953.

Egyptian Tourist Authority
Misr Travel Tower, Abbassia Square, Cairo.
☎ (2) 285 4509 or 284 1970. Fax: (2) 285 4363.
Website: http://touregypt.net/

Thomas Cook Cairo International Airport Travel Office, Cairo. ☎ (2) 244 3149.

Your embassy/consulate in Egypt:

Australian: World Trade Centre, 11th Floor, Corniche El Nil Boulac, Cairo. ☎ (2) 575 0444.
Fax: (2) 578 1638.

British: Ahmed Ragheb Street, Garden City, Cairo.
☎ (2) 354 0850/8. Fax: (2) 354 3065.

Canadian: Arab International Bank Building, 5 Midan El Saraya el Kobra, Garden City, Cairo.
☎ (2) 354 3110. Fax: (2) 356 3548.
Email: cairo@dfait-maeci.gc.ca

Irish: 3 Abu El Fida Street, 7th Floor, Zamalek, Cairo.
☎ (2) 340 8264/8547/4653. Fax: (2) 341 2863.
Email: irishemb@rite.com

South African: 21–23, Giza Street, 18th Floor, Giza.
☎ (2) 571 7238.

US: 5 Latin America Street, Garden City, Cairo.
☎ (2) 355 7371. Fax: (2) 357 3200.
Website: http://www.usis.egnet.net/

Egyptian embassies/consulates at home:

Australia: 1 Darwin Avenue, Yarralumla ACT 2600.
☎ (02) 6273 4437/8. Fax: (02) 6273 4279.

Canada: 454 Laurier Avenue East Ottawa, Ontario K1N 6R3. ☎ (613) 234 4931. Fax: (613) 234 9347.

Ireland: 12 Clyde Road, Ballsbridge, Dublin 4.
☎ (01) 660 6566.

South Africa: 270 Bourke Street, Muckleneuk, Pretoria. ☎ (012) 343 1590/1.

UK: 26 South Street, London W1Y 6DD.
☎ (020) 7499 2401. Fax: (020) 7355 3568.

US: 3521 International Court, NW, Washington DC 20008. ☎ (202) 895 5400 or 966 6342.
Fax: (202) 244/5131.

Accommodation:

HI–Cairo International Youth Hostel 135 Abdel Aziz Al Saoud St, El Manial, Kobri El Gamaa (University Bridge), Cairo. ☎ (2) 364 0729 or 362 4593.
Fax: (2) 368 4107.

HI–Alexandria Hostel 32 Port Said Street, Shatbi, Raml, Alexandria. ☎ 597 5459. Fax: 596 4759.

HI–Luxor 16 Maabad El Karnark Street, Luxor.
☎ 372 139. Fax: 372 139.

Poste restante:

General Post Office Attabba Square, Cairo.

Kenya ✈

(+3hrs GMT) **Capital:** Nairobi

☎ **Country: 254**, Nairobi: 2   💲 Kenyan shilling

If you want to see wild animals with big teeth, then Kenya's certainly the place. Nairobi has some lively markets and cafés that have sprung up in the centre of the town. This is also where you'll find the cheapest of the accommodation – but be alert and watch out for muggers. The older town of Mombasa is a tropical sweatbox, though it does have some excellent beaches to cool off on. Visit the island of Lamu for more of a relaxed and Swahili-induced cultural atmosphere – there's also great diving and snorkelling off its coast. Head west of Nairobi for the town of Narok and the game parks. You'll discover lions, elephants, giraffes and all the rest of the Serengeti gang. For more of a rainforest feel, there's the Kakamega Park and also the Amboseli, where the bull elephants have some of the largest tusks in the land. Kenya really is the home of the safari, so take full advantage of nature at its grandest. The Rift Valley's national parks are worth checking on the wildlife front, too. Although somewhat dilapidated, the Kenyan train service provides a much better service than the buses do. Flights should also be checked out, they can be amazingly cheap.

👁 Kakamega and Amboseli National Parks, Lamu Island, Masai Mara National Reserve, Mount Kenya, the Rift Valley and Lakes Naivasha and Nakuru, Watamu Marine Park, Mount Elgon, Hell's Gate National Park, Njorowa Gorge and views of Mount Kilimanjaro.

Weather:

Avoid safaris during the rains – these fall from April to June and October to November. The coast is hot and humid, inland is more temperate, and the north east is hot and dry.

Languages:

English, Swahili and Kikuyu.

Religion:

Predominantly Protestant; Roman Catholic, indigenous beliefs and Muslim minorities.

Money:

Kenyan shilling = 100 cents.

Cirrus: not accepted.

Maestro: not accepted.

MasterCard: limited for retail, no ATMs available.

Traveller's cheques: US dollars or £ sterling.

Visa: limited for retail, very limited for ATMs.

Living costs:

You can live cheaply if you want to go for the rustic experience. A bed for a night and a full stomach will cost you about $15 per day. If you want to go on safari, it'll be more costly – about $30–40 a day.

Visas:

Irish nationals do not need a visa for trips of less than thirty days. South Africans do not need a visa for travel of up to three months. Other nationals require visas.

Electricity:

220–2440, 50Hz. UK-type three-pin plugs.

Health:

A yellow fever certificate is required if you're travelling from infected areas. Cholera, hepatitis, malaria (except in Nairobi and high-altitude areas), meningitis, Rift Valley fever, typhoid, and yellow fever.

ADDRESS BOOK

Amex Express Travel Group, Bruce House, Standard Street, Nairobi. ☎ 334 722/33.
Kenya Tourism Foundation Lenana Road, PO Box 51351, Nairobi. ☎ (2) 716 244/5. Fax: (2) 716 246. http://www.kenyatourism.org/

Your embassy/consulate in Kenya

Australian: PO Box 39341, Riverside Drive (400 metres off Chiromo Road), Nairobi. ☎ (2) 445 034/9. Fax: (2) 444 617.
Irish: PO Box 30659, O' Washika Road, Lavington, Nairobi. ☎ (2) 578 043. Fax: (2) 578 043.
British: PO Box 30465, Upper Hill Road, Nairobi. ☎ (2) 714 699. Fax: (2) 719 082.
Email: bhcinfo@africaonline.co.ke
Canadian: Comcraft House, Hailé Sélassie Avenue, Nairobi. ☎ (2) 214804. Fax: (2) 226987.
Email: nrobi@dfait-maeci.gc.ca
NZ: Minet ICDC Insurance, 3rd Floor, Minet House, Nyerere Road, Nairobi. ☎ (2) 722 467. Fax: (2) 722 556.
US: Barclays Plaza, Loita Street, Nairobi. ☎ (2) 537 800. Fax: (2) 537 810.
Email: usis@usis.africaonline.co.ke
Website: http://usembassy.state.gov/nairobi/

Kenyan embassies/consulates at home:

Australia: Level 6, QBE Building, 33/35 Ainslie Avenue, Canberra ACT 2601. ☎ (02) 6247 4788/22. Fax: (02) 6257 6613.
Canada: 255 Sussex Drive, Ottawa, Ontario K1N 9E6. ☎ (613) 241 8541. Fax: (613) 241 2232.
Ireland: represented by the embassy in the UK: 45 Portland Place, London W1N 4AF. ☎ (020) 7636 2371. Fax: (020) 7323 6717.
South Africa: 302 Brooks Street, Menlo Park, Pretoria. ☎ (012) 342 5066.
UK: 45 Portland Place, London W1N 4AF. ☎ (020) 7636 2371 Fax: (020) 7323 6717.
US: 2249 R. Street, NW, Washington DC 20008. ☎ (202) 387 6101. Fax: (202) 462 3829.
Email: KLQY53A@Prodigy.com
Website: http://www.embassyofkenya.com/

Accommodation

HI–Nairobi Hostel Ralph Bunche Rd, PO Box 48661, Nairobi. ☎ 723 012 or 721 765.
HI–Kanamai Holiday and Youth Centre PO Box 46, Mombasa, Kikambala. ☎ (0125) 32442 or 32101.

Poste restante:

Kenyan Post and Telecommunications Corporation PO Box 30210, Nairobi.

Morocco ✈

(GMT) **Capital:** Rabat

☎ **Country: 212**, Rabat: 7 💲 Moroccan dirham

Morocco is an excellent place to start the African experience. The cities offer open markets selling carpets, spices, crafts and lots and lots of leather. You've also got excellent beaches and amazingly scenic mountain treks. Rabat is still pretty tourist-free, with some good open air markets and cheap accommodation around the Jardins Triangle de Vue. It's got a cool European feel and it's easy to find a good café to chill in. Marrakesh is well worth a visit if you want an incredibly hectic market town. You're going to get hassled by the traders, but it's all part of the fun. If you want a bit of scenic splendour head to the Todra Gorge area at the end of the High Atlas Mountains. The town of Tinerhir makes a good base for exploring this beautiful valley area. The High Atlas Mountains are home to some good trekking routes, and a two-day shimmy up Jebel Toubkal rewards you with fantastic views of the whole region. Beach-inclined individuals should head to Essaouira, where it's easy to hook up with other travellers. Trains and buses in Morocco are excellent ways to see the country. Both networks are cheap, comprehensive and reliable.

👁 Treks in the Atlas Mountains, a camel ride in the Erg Chebbi desert, Dadès Valley, Drâa Valley, Essaouira, Fès's medina, Jebel Sarhro, Jebel Toubkal, Marrakesh, Meknès, Tafraoute, Tangier, Taroudannt, Todra Gorge and Ziz Gorges.

Weather:

It's hot and dry in the south, especially between June and October, but the nights get cold. November to March on the coast is the wettest time, but the temperatures are still pretty high all year.

Languages:

Arabic. English is generally understood in the north.

Religion:

Muslim.

Money:

Moroccan dirham = 100 centimes.
Cirrus: limited for ATMs.
Maestro: not accepted.
MasterCard: fair for retail, limited for ATMs.
Traveller's cheques: Euros or £ sterling.
Visa: no retail availability, limited for ATMs.

Living costs:

The travel, beds and food are all cheap – allow about $10–15 per day.

Visas:

Nationals of South Africa need a visa. Other visitors don't require a visa and are usually issued with a ninety day stamp on entry.

Electricity:

110–120V, 50Hz.

Health:

Malaria (rural areas), polio and typhoid.

ADDRESS BOOK

Amex Voyages Schwartz SA, 112 Avenue Prince Moulay Abdellah, Casablanca. ☎ (2) 222 947.
Office National Marocain de Tourisme 31 Rue Oued Fès, Angle Avenue Abtal, Agdal, Rabat.
☎ (7) 681 5310–3. Fax: (7) 773 774.
Email: admin@tourisminmorocco.com
Website: http://www.tourism-in-morocco.com
Thomas Cook Menara Tours, Tour Atlas, 6th Floor, 57 Place Zaltaga, Casablanca 20000. ☎ (2) 307 607.

Your embassy/consulate in Morocco:

Australian: contact the Australian embassy/consulate in France: 4 Rue Jean Ray, Paris 75015. ☎ (1) 4059 3300. Fax: (1) 4059 3310.
British: 17 Boulevard de la Tour Hassan (BP 45), Rabat ☎ (7) 720 905/6. Fax: (7) 704 532.
Canadian: 13 Bis, Rue Jaafar As-Sadik, Rabat-Agdal.
☎ (7) 672 880. Fax: (7) 627 187.
Email: rabat@dfait-maeci.gc.ca
South African: 34 rue des Saadiens, Hassan.
☎ (7) 706 760. Fax: (7) 706 756.
US: 8, Boulevard Moulay Youssef, Casablanca.
☎ (2) 264 550. Fax: (2) 204 127.
Email: iorabat@pd.state.gov
Website: http://www.usembassy-morocco.org.ma/

Moroccan embassies/consulates at home:

Canada: 38 Range Road, Ottawa, Ontario K1N 8J4.
☎ (613) 236 7391. Fax: (613) 236 6164.
Ireland: 53 Raglan Road, Ballsbridge, Dublin 4.
☎ (01) 660 9449.
NZ: c/o Agrimat (NZ) Limited, PO Box 9925, Auckland.
☎ (09) 520 4129. Fax: (09) 520 5661.
South Africa: 799 Schoeman Street, Arcadia, Pretoria.
☎ (012) 343 0230.
UK: 49 Queen's Gate Gardens, London SW7 5NE.
☎ (020) 7581 5001. Fax: (020) 7225 3862.
US: 1601 21st Street, NW, Washington DC 20009.
☎ (202) 462 7979. Fax: (202) 265 0161.
Email: sifamausa@trident.net

Accommodation:

HI–Casablanca YH 6 Place Abmed Al Bidaoui, Ville Ancienne, Casablanca. ☎ (2) 22055. Fax: (2) 295587.
Email: casa_hostel@caramail.com
HI–Rue el Jahed Quartier Industriel, Marrakech.
☎ (44) 7713 32831

Poste restante:

Central Post Office Boulevard de Paris, cnr Avenue Hassan II, Casablanca.

South Africa

(+2hrs GMT) **Capital:** Pretoria

☎ **Country: 27**, Cape Town: 21, Pretoria: 12　💲 Rand

In northern and central South Africa there are amazing game reserves, the most famous being the Kruger National Park. This has all the big game and is large enough for you to lose other tourists. On the east coast, you'll find Durban a good place to stay at the start of the 'Garden Route'. North of the city has the best beaches, Umhlanga Rocks being a good starting point. Head south for some amazing surf spots – Jeffrey's Bay is world-renowned. Further south you'll find the Wild Coast – rugged, untamed and scenic. Follow the Garden Route and you'll come across some untouched beaches before arriving at Cape Town. Here, the Victoria and Albert Waterfront is popular, but also check out Clifton beach – it's très chic. Cape Town also has a cool nightlife scene. Take a cable car up Table Mountain to enjoy incredible views. The west coast of South Africa is where scuba divers head, plus there are some large dolphin and whale populations for all to enjoy. Public transport is less than reliable, and not always comfortable. The Blue Train, which runs from Johannesburg to Cape Town, is the mega-expensive train ride of a lifetime. Treat yourself to a short section, if you can afford it.

👁 Blue Train ride, the Cape of Good Hope, Cape Town, Drakensberg, Durban, Jeffrey's Bay, Kalahari Gemsbok National Park, Kruger National Park for wildlife, Orange River trip, Port St Johns, Royal Natal National Park, Shipwreck Hiking Trail, and Umhlanga Rocks.

Weather:

Warm, temperate and dry climate. Cape Town is cold and wet in winter (June to September), Durban is more sub-tropical. The best time to visit is during the summer from February to April.

Languages:

English, Afrikaans and indigenous dialects.

Religion:

Dutch Reform Church, Zion Christan Church, Roman Catholic, Methodist, Nededuitsch, Hervormde, Hindu and Muslim.

Money:

Rand = 100 cents.

Cirrus: fair for ATMs.

Maestro: not accepted.

MasterCard: excellent for retail, fair for ATMs.

Traveller's cheques: £ sterling.

Visa: excellent for retail and for ATMs.

Living costs:

If you look out for cheap hostels (from about $9 per night) and bargain food, South Africa can be fairly inexpensive. However tourist attractions and city taxis are pricey.

Visas:

Passports should be valid for six months beyond your intended date of arrival. No visas are required for visits up to ninety days.

Electricity:

220–230V; 250V (Pretoria).

Health:

A yellow fever certificate is required if you're travelling from infected areas. Malaria (low lying northern and eastern areas), polio and typhoid.

ADDRESS BOOK

Amex 288 Van Der Walt Street, Pretoria.
☎ (12) 322 2620.
South African Tourism Board (SATOUR) 442 Rigel Avenue South, Erasmusrand, Pretoria 0181.
☎ (12) 347 0600. Fax: (12) 347 8753.
Email: satour@icon.co.za
South African Tourism 61, rue la Boëtie, 75008 Paris.
☎ (1) 45 61 01 97. Fax: (1) 45 61 01 96.
STA 31 Riebeek Street, Cape Town 8000.
☎ (21) 418 6570. Fax: (21) 418 4689.
Email: capetown@statravel.co.za

Your embassy/consulate in South Africa:

Australian: 14th Floor, BP Centre, Thibault Square, Cape Town 8001. ☎ (21) 419 5425. Fax: (21) 419 7345.
Website: http://www.australia.co.za/
British: 91 Parliament Street, Cape Town 8001.
☎ (21) 461 7220. Fax: (21) 461 0017.
Email: britain@icon.co.za
Canadian: 1103 Arcadia Street, Hatfield 0083, Pretoria. ☎ (12) 422 3000. Fax: (12) 422 3052.
Email: pret@dfait-maeci.gc.ca
Website: http://www.canada.co.za/
Irish: First Floor, Sothern Life Plaza, 1059 Schoeman Street (Corner Festival Street), Arcadia 0083, Pretoria.
☎ (12) 342 5062. Fax: (12) 342 4752.
Email: pretoria@iveagh.irlgov.ie
US: 877 Pretorius St, Pretoria. ☎ (12) 342 1048.
Fax: (12) 342 2244.
Website: http://usembassy.state.gov/pretoria/

South African embassies/consulates at home:

Australia: cnr State Circle and Rhodes Place, Yarralumla ACT 2600 ☎ (02) 6273 2424.
Fax: (02) 6273 3543. Email: info@rsa.emb.gov.au
Website: http://www.rsa.emb.gov.au/
Canada: 15 Sussex Drive, Ottawa, Ontario K1M 1M8.
☎ (613) 744 0330. Fax: (613) 741 1639.
Email: rsafrica@sympatico.ca
Website: http://www.docuweb.ca/SouthAfrica/
Ireland: 2nd Floor, Alexandra House, Earlsfort Centre, Earlsfort Terrace, Dublin 2. ☎ (01) 661 5553.
Fax: (1) 661 5590.
NZ: PO Box 71, Papakura, Auckland. ☎ (09) 299 6019. Fax: (09) 298 9986.
UK: South Africa House, Trafalgar Square, London WC2N 5DP. ☎ (020) 7451 7299. Fax: (020) 7451 7284.
Website: http://www.southafricahouse.com
US: 3051 Massachusetts Avenue, NW, Washington DC 20008. ☎ (202) 232 4400. Fax: (202) 265 1607.
Email: safrica@southafrica.net
Website: http://www.southafrica.net/

Accommodation:

HI–Airport Backpackers 3 Mohawk Street, Rhodesfield, Kempton Park, Johannesburg.
☎ (11) 394 0485. Fax: (11) 394 0485.
Website: http://home.mweb.co.za/ai/airbackp/
HI–OVC Cape Town 230 Long Street, Cape Town
☎ (21) 424 6800. Fax: (21) 423 4870.
Website: www.ovc.co.za
HI–Tekweni 169 Ninth Avenue, Morningside, Durban, 4001. ☎ (31) 303 433. Fax: (31) 303 4369.
Website: www.tekweniecotours.co.za

Poste restante:

Available at main post offices: Parliament Street, Cape Town, Jeppe Street, Johannesburg.

The Virgin Traveller

Accommodation

You will stay in all sorts of accommodation, from 'backpackers' (the cool circuit name for hostels), youth hostels, hotels, motels, houses, camp sites, airport floors etc. Some will be amazing, some will be...ermm...crap!

Things to bear in mind
● If you hear of a good place, note it down and go there – reputations spread for a reason...likewise, other travellers will soon tell you if they stayed in a place that smells worse than a slaughter-house.

● If you arrive at the same time as a festival, national event, or my birthday, most places will be full – so ring and book a bed with a credit card. A lot of places will pick you up from the train/bus station or airport and will also drop you back there when you leave.

When you arrive at the 'backpackers' have a quick look around before you decide to stay...or book for one night and then make a decision in the morning. If they're full, ask them what you should do, as they'll know of other places.

Make sure there is someone there who can show you around
● Is there a safe for your valuables?
● Where is the clean linen? kitchen? washing machine? (are they free?)
● Are the dorms single-sex or mixed?
● Are meals provided? (Are they free?) – where and when are they served?
● What are the rooms like? – can you see one?

A few things to look for:
● Does the price you've been quoted match the tariff at reception?
● Does this include breakfast? Are there any other hidden costs?
● Can the windows be secured for safety, but opened in an emergency?
● Are there emergency exits, and can you use them?
● Are there smoke detectors?

Beware: blocking off emergency exits to get more beds in happens...what if the whole place catches fire? Also, with the horrific Childers Hostel fire in mind, bars on the windows are great for stopping thieves from getting in, but become a death-trap in the event of an emergency. Please take these last two points extremely seriously, and let us know if you see any bad places you feel backpackers should boycott (email us at info@gapyear.com).

What they should provide

- A good map of the area.
- A good noticeboard with everything that's happening.
- Organised trips, car hire and everything else you need (all the best deals).

Basically, good vibes about places travel well on the backpacker grape-vine. Good 'backpackers' will give you an overview of everything in the area and leave you to make up your own mind. The bad ones are generally run by people with 'vested interests' – channelling you into activities run by their family and friends.

In most 'backpackers' there are no rules. The rules are that you are a polite, civilised human being, who respects the property and others. The best places normally run themselves. Don't abuse this, as you'll stick out as the asshole and may be asked to leave…in shame. Some hostels can be like detention camps, with notes everywhere telling you what you can or can't use/touch (including members of the opposite sex!). Rules like 'be in by…' are a pain, and I once stayed in a place where they closed the hostel during the day!! If there is an **'honesty system'** operating with the bar (a fridge full of beer…help yourself and note it down) don't abuse it. It's great to have a bit of trust and be treated like an adult, so don't let yourself or others down.

What else is out there?

The International Youth Hostel Federation has over 5,000 youth hostels worldwide. Their international computerised reservation system means you can book from anywhere in the world. These are the 'safe' ones…a fraction more expensive, but I haven't seen a bad one yet. There's a selection listed in the *Top Fifty Destinations* for a secure first night.

For further info **www.iyhf.org**

YMCA / YWCA and the Salvation Army are around in North America, Europe, the Middle East and Far East. When I was hitching in Canada the Salvation Army helped me out of a dodgy situation…they'll always find you a bed if in need. Next time they're collecting in town, pop some pennies in.

Hostel searches: www.hostels.com – a hostel search engine. Always worth a look. **hostelworld.com** or head to **gapyear.com** for a comprehensive search and booking service.

Universities and colleges. Good for cheap food, hooking up with other travellers/students/decent nightlife, and for cheap accommodation ('I'm a student from England' works wonders).

Camp grounds – even if you don't have a tent, many have tents or cabins of their own. Waking up to a forest or beach on a sunny morning is pure class.

The Golden Rule: If a place is exceptionally good, or incredibly bad, <u>tell everyone</u>. The backpacker trail works by word of mouth – the only way to stamp out the guys who rip us all off. It's your duty to your fellow travellers!

Been to a great hostel? Let others know in our 'Hostelwatch' on **gapyear.com** – and warn us about the crap ones, too!

Backpacks

See *How to...pack* for more in-depth information.

Your backpack is your home – you'll soon appreciate this. Stories about people planting drugs in your bag are more myth than legend, as you tend to keep a close eye on your stuff. Look after your pack, and it'll look after you. They double as seats when you wait for buses, and as sponges in monsoon rain – when you get absolutely soaked! Wet passport, traveller's cheques and pants? – *'they said it was waterproof!'* Get a chain to secure it to the bed, seats, railings etc.

Day bag
Spread your cash and cards between this and your major pack...then if someone does do a runner with one, you have something to fall back on. Thieves will go through the top and outside pockets first – think about it.

Money belt
My passport, documents and all valuables live here. Easy to snatch in a second, so pay attention and keep an eye on it at all times. Subtly worn under your clothes for best security. Neck purses are OK but again, if worn outside, sort of say 'MUG ME!'

Hiding money and valuables
In your pack – buried in 'the smelly pants' compartment where not even the Special Forces would dare to go!
Whilst out and about – in your socks or pants works really well. Tubigrip (the elastic bandage) worn on your thigh or arm can store and conceal cash (impossible to spot – but can get hot and sweaty). A wallet with a loop that you can attach to your belt will stop pickpockets.
At night – in the bottom of your sleeping bag or in your pillowcase.

The general rule
Feel at risk? Carry only small amounts of cash around with you in a dummy wallet (see *How to...organise your finances*).

Safety / protection
Why not take a brief self-defence course in the run-up to your trip (this may worry parents)...and I'm talking to the lads as well here. You may think you're hard, but I'll show you a 2ft ninja who may disagree. Basic self-defence is not for knocking out a 16-stone robber with a blunt spoon, but knowing how to manoeuvre him off balance to give you time to rip your bag away and run...

Protecting yourself and keeping safe boils down to common sense. Your 'sixth sense' will develop and mature as your trip progresses, helping you to avoid dodgy situations. Read *Being safe* for more suggestions.

Personal alarms (often called 'rape alarms' – which is why men never buy them)
When activated, these can alert others and scare off trouble. By having the main part of the alarm in your bag and the cord attached to your wrist, if your bag is snatched, the alarm will go off. The bag will probably be dropped as it draws too much attention. **Get one.**

Door alarm
Secure an alarm to the door at night (tape the main part of the alarm to the wall and the cord to the door) so if the door is opened in the middle of the night the alarm will sound. There are proper door alarms, protector pressure mats and wedges on the market.

Lock the door!
...if you are worried about the owners and/or other residents. Be aware: the staff have keys too, as may other previous residents. At night, leave the key in the door in case there is an emergency, such as a fire or explosive bowels! *If in doubt about a place, don't stay there.* There is also a keyless door lock (at **gapyearshop.com**) which lets you lock doors without a lock. Yes, really!

To lock your backpack
The 'Saklock' locks off the closing catch on your backpack so it can't be opened. You can also get a lockable luggage strap with a combination lock to go around your stuff.

Tourist information offices
Use for information on accommodation, travel passes and day-to-day stuff like the opening hours of businesses, galleries, museums and tourist attractions...and free maps to help you get around. They will tell you where to go and where not to go. Ask about discounts and departure taxes. *Best used in tandem with...*

Guide books
One of the things that really amazes people who have never travelled is this 'how do I get around?' idea. *'Do you really just turn up to a place without knowing where you are going to stay?'* Well...**yes!**

There are guide books on just about every country in the world. They cover transport, accommodation, where to go, where not to go, what to do, how to do it, and how much it will cost you...everything you need to know about the countries you are visiting – they often include maps too.

Decide which style you like and who you feel comfortable with. The leading travel guides for backpackers are:

Bradt Publications bradtpublications@compuserve.com
Footprint Handbooks www.footprint-handbook.co.uk
Lonely Planet www.lonelyplanet.com
Rough Guides www.roughguides.com
Trailblazer www.trailblazer-guides.com

If you go thousands of miles around the world, make sure you see it. Excuses like 'I didn't realise that it was there…' just don't cut the ice with me. **The combination of a guide book, fellow travellers, the hostel network and tourist information…and you've got it made.**

Transport

BUSES

- Take a sleeping bag and/or jumper and warm trousers on the bus, **as the air-conditioning can get cold** when the doors are shut (especially at night).
- **Where's your luggage?** I like to sit above the luggage compartment so that I can see that my backpack doesn't get off before I do! If in doubt, get off and keep an eye on it. If it's stored on the roof, secure it with a chain.
- **Sit close to the driver to prevent hassle**, far enough from the front (accident impact zone) to be safe, and not hidden at the back where you are vulnerable to dodgy locals.
- **How to sleep on a bus?** Try sliding down the seat and putting your knees up on the seat in front – a nice comfortable curled position.

TRAINS

- **Most capital cities have more than one railway station.** Are you heading for the right one? Hostel staff or tourist information centres can help with complex bookings and reservations…or write it all down for you.
- **Beware of trains that split**…you could be left in the station, or suddenly find yourself on your way to the wrong part of the country!
- **Tables** are good for resting your head and sleeping on, for reading, writing, eating and subtly securing your day bag to.
- **Sleeping on trains.** In Russia I took a train from Moscow to Perm, a fourteen-hour overnight journey. I'd heard about sleeper-train attacks and was a bit wary, but as I was with my Russian girlfriend and her dad, I thought I'd be OK. It was the demonstration of how to use the pepper gas I was to hide under my pillow that made me rethink! The journey was fine, but be aware that, should you choose first class or an upgraded sleeper, you could be targeted simply because you are there. Cramped in with the hoards gives you safety in numbers. Valuables in your sleeping bag + dummy wallet to hand = no worries.

Trains and buses
- Next to the window puts you out of reach of hassle and thieves.
- Clothes and/or a towel are perfect for a pillow.
- Make sure you're on the right side for the best views of any passing sights.
- In hot countries avoid sitting on the sunny side of the bus unless you know that the views are going to be spectacular…then it's worth dying for!
- Ear-plugs, eye-shades and Walkmans are essential for not being disturbed, and for getting a good night's sleep (annoying person next to you?…on they go). All three together can make you vulnerable – so beware.

- Toilets – make sure you don't end up inside one, finding it to be the only place with a bit of legroom! Take your own toilet paper and go early (...because there is always one!)
- **Never, ever get off, go for a snack or to the toilet, without taking your valuables with you.** Asking someone to 'watch them for you' may not be good enough.

FLIGHTS ✈

Courier flights

This is a great way to get a really cheap flight – become a courier for the day. Simply turn up at the airport, pick up a package (people still ask me if it's safe!...no, it's a bomb!)... take it on to the plane, hand it over to the staff who will meet you when you land, and you get flights at dead-cheap prices. All you have to do is to dress up smartly, and book the flight early (as they are quite a popular form of transport!). The only disadvantages are that you have to abide by the rules, some only giving you a week overseas, others a fortnight, and there is generally only one courier seat per flight (so you won't be able to go with a friend). But you get the usual baggage allowance, so why not?

For more information contact: British Airways Travel Shop, Room E328, 3rd Floor, E Block, Cranebank, S551, Heathrow Airport, Hounslow TW6 2JA.

Overbooked flights...

Get to the front of the queue and offer to give your seat up. Basically the airline has over-booked the plane. They have, say, 400 seats and 410 people waiting to get on.

What to do?

Offer your seat up in return for compensation – there's a fine line, so play the game. It has been known for backpackers to be put up in five-star hotels for the night, all expenses paid, and flown back first class. I've been there twice, but only got a business class seat and a big fat voucher for another flight! If they are desperate, hold out for a good deal and, if you stay overnight, ensure they cover phone calls, meals, and taxis to and from the airport. Yes it is a bit mercenary, but if it isn't you, it'll be someone else.

Jet lag

(See **Health**). My tip – when you arrive, force yourself to stay up until 10–11pm (grit your teeth if necessary), then go to bed, set your alarm and **get up and do things**...your body will adjust. If you are young and fit, it shouldn't really affect you – mind over matter. Nuff said.

TAXIS 🚗

Beware of being charged 'tourist prices' (the hostels will tell you the rate). Agree the price in advance and only hand the money over when you arrive – be sure to have small change with you. Many taxi drivers are also touts, taking travellers to hostels owned by their family or friends, but if you find a good one, why not negotiate a tour of the city for the day/afternoon, so you can see the sights in your own time and at a reasonable rate?

Street level

Restaurants

Tipping…is expected in many countries. Read the guides and check with other travellers and locals ('what's the norm?'). In the States it is considered rude not to tip, so get it right. But watch out for places which automatically include a service charge and then expect a tip too.

- Always eat in busy restaurants…they are obviously the good ones.
- Where's the night life? Ask young locals, bar staff, waiters etc.
- Cheap eats can be found in student areas – take your ISIC card with you.

Tourist rates

You will have to pay them in some places. In Moscow my Russian girlfriend would pay four or five times less than me…even though I was heavily disguised as a Russian…with my bobble hat and rosy cheeks! Saying that though, in some of the poorer countries, why shouldn't we pay a bit extra? We pay no taxes to maintain these places…

Locals

It is easy to see others as tourists in your country, yet impossible to see how you are viewed by the locals in the country you are visiting. You may think that you are acting with exemplary behaviour, being a shining ambassador for your country, yet all the locals may see is the western guy who came two months ago, was rude, disruptive, disrespectful and, in short, an unwelcome visitor. Likewise, when you leave, a whole string of people will be following you. Be a considerate traveller.

Arriving in countries like India, you may be overwhelmed by touts and a crush of people after your trade. There are a lot of misconceptions when East meets West and rich meets poor. You will automatically be seen as wealthy. You may be uneasy with this, but then you do possess comparative wealth afforded to you purely by where you popped up into this world! Be thankful for this, and appreciate where you come from.

For a local to get you into his taxi or accommodation, to buy his souvenirs, his food or anything else he has to sell…is a good day. They may be able to charge double because an extra few rupees to you won't be noticed. They know this, which is why the touts want your trade. What may seem to you to be public disorder, and more scrummaging than an England v Wales rugby match, is purely them trying to get your business. Don't panic, you'll be fine. Just beware that pickpockets may use this as a great opportunity.

If you're with a friend, get your belongings on the ground where you can see them all and get the other person to do the haggling. If you are by yourself move yourself to the edge of the melee, get your backpack on the ground and sit on it. Chill out. Watch what is going on. If you're still surrounded by touts and salesmen, make like you're not interested and they'll soon lose interest. When you're ready, approach one and start to make a deal…they'll soon keep the others away! Be nice, be polite, be firm, be confident, be relaxed, be chilled…be yourself and smile.

Police

There are a number of countries where the police abuse their position and can't always be trusted. From the stories I've heard…the rule seems to be, **'when you go to them, you're fine, *when they come to you, trouble starts'*.**

Bogus police are easily dealt with, by asking to be taken to the police station or the embassy and having the matter dealt with properly.

The rules are simple :
- Get in touch with your embassy as quick as you can.
- Try not to get put in handcuffs, you're powerless to do anything.
- Act poor. You are a backpacker, you have no money.
- If in a 'dodgy' country, take the photocopies of all your stuff out with you. If someone wants to see your passport, show them the copies. If that's not good enough, take them back to the hostel where everything else is…and where there will be others around who can help you out. You could of course tell them that your passport and other things are at the embassy, which is why you have the photocopies.

Discounts and cheap tickets
As a student, you should be able to get discounts anywhere. My motto is:

'If you don't ask, you don't get!'…it's as simple as that!

Make sure you get an International Student Identity Card (ISIC) – through most student travel outlets, student unions etc or through **www.istc.org** as proof of student ID. There are loads of fakes going around (bought in Thailand for next-to-nothing so under 21-year-olds can drink in the US!), so occasionally it won't be accepted. Any card with the word 'student' on is good…no one will understand what it is anyway! ISIC is recognised worldwide and will give you access to loads of discounts around. **You need one, so get one and always ask about discounts.**

Tickets
- **Cheap airline tickets** for sale on noticeboards? Leave well alone – they have someone else's name on them. A great way to lose cash.
- **Most travel passes and tickets can be bought in bulk** – 'carnets' of ten or more tickets to go on public transport in the cities – sell spares to other travellers.

Sending things home
- Are they going to send it?
- They could send something of lesser value and quality. Avoid this by getting their name, address, phone number and all contact details. Also mention your 'friend who lives nearby' who can sort out any problems.

Borders

Be patient, polite and smile. A good, clean-cut photo on your passport will help, as will a smart, clean appearance. Have enough money, evidence of inoculations, six months on your passport and a ticket out of there.

PIN numbers

PIN numbers are an arse to remember...here's an interesting idea for you to think about:

Mr Villos, 12 Beelas Gardens, Knutsford, Kent KN3 8UH
Tel: (01974) 624 7734

This would be an entry in my diary for my Visa PIN number (the last four digits of the telephone number 7734). Clever eh? Mastercard under 'M' (Matthew Morten), American Express under 'A' (Helen Arlington). Simple.

Out and about

BEACHES

...are great. Some of the beaches in Thailand, Fiji and Indonesia were amazing, drenched with palms, fishing boats and coconut shells. Sound good? They are. A few words of warning. The sand, when the sun is high, can burn your feet. The midday sun may well help you tan, but it is also the time when the rays are at their most harmful and you are more likely to burn.

Swimming

When I was in Oz, a young British guy dived straight into a sandbank on Bondi beach and broke his neck. It happens regularly. I'm led to believe that he's now paralysed and wheelchair-bound. A reason for good insurance cover...see Max's bit on *Insurance*.

Rip tides

We've all seen *Baywatch* and know the score right? Wrong. When I got caught in a 'rip', it was terrifying. Luckily I remembered to swim across it and not against it. What exactly is it? Basically it is when the tide drags you out to sea at an alarming rate. Relax, you should pop out of the end of it, and then swim in. If there are lifeguards around, try and signal to them. People only drown in them because they try and swim against them and wear themselves out. Keep calm.

Jelly fish

Can sting. Can kill. Find out when the 'seasons' are and take it seriously.

MAPS

Maps of the country are great, and carry loads of extra information. Try bookshops or tourist information centres. *Encarta*, the world atlas on computer, is also worth having a look at – it may help you plan your route, and it also tells you a bit about culture, history, shows you slides, etc.

MOPEDS, BIKES, ETC

If you're going to come off anything at speed whilst you're away, it'll be one of these. Be careful when you hire these things. Are you insured? Really? Check for the size of engine you're allowed to ride. What condition are the bikes in? Don't take risks!

PHOTOGRAPHY

Great photos are worth a million memories, and are the best things you'll bring back with you. Sadly, I didn't. Mates of mine have returned with sensational photos, I have just memories. Why? I have always relied on a basic camera, which had given me good photos. Unfortunately, when two opportunities presented themselves to me...both within a week of each other on Vancouver Island (a pod of killer whales swimming around the boat, and finding myself four feet from a baby bear)...all I got was a collection of black dots and a blurred photo of what looked like a dog. Since then, I have vowed to get a decent camera. And have I? Not yet!...

So what camera?

Get one with auto-focus. If you can afford it, buy one with a built-in zoom lens. If you are a serious photographer, or are going somewhere where you are guaranteed of getting some great shots, eg. African game reserves, why not invest in a really good camera with a separate zoom lens? (This can also double as a pair of binoculars.)

Disposable / waterproof cameras

These are a great laugh, ideal for beach parties, trekking, or snorkelling the Great Barrier Reef (the waterproof ones that is!). They aren't particularly expensive, especially if shared between a group – sharing the cost of the camera and of producing ten sets of prints...works out really cheaply. The waterproof ones can't go scuba-diving, as the pressure breaks them after three metres...however, most of the coral can be accessed in shallow water, so there should be no problem there.

Film type?

You need to be covered for both sunny and cloudy conditions. 200 ASA does the job OK, 400 ASA is even better, is slightly more expensive, but the quality of photo is definitely worth it. Kodak's Advantix system (where you can adjust the camera with the flick of a switch, swapping between wide-angled and normal photos) is quite cool, especially if under a waterfall, or in a jeep surrounded by a family of cheetahs.

Film developing – where to get it done?

Overseas or back at home? Doing it as you go along means you can enjoy your photos, write on the back, put them into folders, and keep swallowing what is a costly process bit by bit. The only problem is that it's expensive and you have to carry bulky piccies with you. They may also get damp and damaged. So, do you send the films back? We did.

But what if the parcel gets lost?…all your photos, gone. Uncensored photos developed by mum? However, if OK, your parents can see that you're alive and all limbed-up! It also saves you money!

The solution?
If you carry films with you, keep them in their little plastic containers and wrap them, 'snake-like', in plastic or freezer bags. **If you get them developed**, send one parcel with the photos, and a separate envelope with the negatives. The best idea is to send them home. You won't realise this until they are nicked or damaged in some way.

The most important thing is to keep track of the people's names, and the places you have been to. Try and sit down for a weekend and organise the whole lot. I never have. Mine are now all mixed up in a massive pile…I can't remember who is who, where we met, or anything. I have also lost my two best photos. Learn from my mistake and get this sorted!

Taking photos
We are happy to take photos of anything that moves, but what if a bunch of tourists stuck their cameras in **your** face, snapping away like an underfed crocodile? In many places locals believe it takes their spirit away, so you won't be thanked! Photograph the police/army and you could be arrested, have your film taken out and destroyed, or your camera smashed. It's been known to be called 'spying', so if officials or locals say 'no', don't push it, you'll only lose your film, your camera or worse. Respect people you photograph. Have a chat and check they're OK with it, and **always** be polite. Failure to do so could mean the UN would have to be called, plus a few divers to retrieve the camera from the bottom of the river! Be wary of those who offer to take your photo for you…as they may indulge themselves a little and take the camera as well. Unless you have the acceleration of a Porshe 911 turbo and the apprehending skills of the Special Forces, then you can kiss your camera goodbye!

Cameras can also be snatched if worn on your belt or hung around your neck or shoulder. Be sensible. Either keep it in your pocket (if it's a small camera), or tightly wrapped around your hand. Don't ever put it down, as thieves will wait for this moment to make a grab for it.

Final points
- If it's a valuable camera, make sure that it's insured.
- Keep your camera in a sealed bag so no dust, water etc can get in – but be careful of condensation.
- Any major problems, let the experts sort it out – in the dark. I didn't once…

THE BACK SECTION

I've been referring to this all the way through the book...and here it is. Fill it in and leave it at home for your parents...all the crucial info they are going to need while you're away...

Also, take a photocopy with you and keep it in your backpack – you never know when you're going to need it.

The trip ✕

Destination	Arrival date	Flight number	Departure date

Notes

BACK SECTION

Important numbers

	Serial numbers, dates issued, emergency numbers...put all relevant information down.	Notes
Passport		
Driving licence		
Flight tickets		
Insurance policy		
Spectacles/contact lenses		
Camera		
Walkman		
Mobile phone		
Email address		
Voicemail number		

Traveller's cheques

Number	Amount	Number	Amount	Number	Amount

Contact details

Date	Country, City, Address, Name of Accommodation, Room...	Telephone, Fax, Email

Emergency numbers

Western Union-Money Transfer	☎ 0800 833 833
Money Gram-Money Transfer	☎ 0800 894 887
Lost credit cards	☎
	☎
	☎
	☎
	☎
	☎

Photocopies and receipts

We both have photocopies of...	You have receipts of...

Notes

Final week diary – things to do

---

7 days to go
Date

---

6 days to go
Date

---

5 days to go
Date

---

4 days to go
Date

BACK SECTION

3 days to go
Date

2 days to go
Date

1 day to go
Date

...you're off

Now give this to your parents or someone you trust.

Acknowledgements

There are many people who I would like to thank for all their hard work, tolerance and downright kindness over the past couple of years.

My management / advisor / 'are you wearing clean pants' second mum Anne James. Thank you. My thanks also to **Alison Davies** who has gone way beyond the call of duty – a classy chick! **The team at Virgin:** The big cheese/John Peel-lookalike **Rob Shreeve** for having faith in me; **Louise Cavanagh** as the original editor and **Carolyn Thorne** for taking up the mantle and doing such a sterling job. **Kefi** and **Jamie** for making it happen. **Dominic Cooper**, who initially put it all together – and **Peter Cooling** for the last stage to final copy.

The guys at Oxygen for their faith, support and amazing working atmosphere. All those who have put me up on their couches – **Tim, Steve and John, brother Rob, Nicky, Steve 'Taffy Sheepmaster' Evans and Lynn. The boys from Ipswich and 179 Cemetery Road** – you now know why you haven't seen me for months. Cheers, lads! **Mr and Mrs Martin** for your guidance on behalf of all the worried mums and dads out there and **Scottish Susan and Jane**, my dieticians, for the healthy bits! **Cockney Paul and Dr Claire** for all their support and advice, and **Katie Miller, Lynds, Dan and Flips** for all being there when I couldn't be arsed to go on. **Finnoooola**, for organising me and finally, last but not least, the shaven-headed South African, **Jez**, for his hard graft and superb biltong.

Contributors

Richard Mortimer – [How to...use the internet]
I've known Richard for years, and he's just finished an 18-month round-the-world trip with another mate, Steve. On their travels we all kept up with their exploits via email, making him the perfect writer for this section. Thanks for your help and advice fella.

David Parker – [Travelling with diabetes]
Anyone who can walk across Australia must be a nutcase, but to do it in world-record time – fair play. All respect to you mate, and a shining example to everyone (especially other diabetics) that you really can achieve anything if you put your mind to it.

Max Andrews – [Drugs, Etiquette, Insurance]
I knew Max at University in Manchester when he had crazy hair. He travelled the world with Simon (nickname 'Fresh' – the first fresher to throw up!). The questions they had spurred me on to help other first-time travellers. Max is now completing his MA in Investigative Journalism at Nottingham Trent University. He is already published in magazines such as *FHM*.

Helena Sampson – [Girl Solo]
...is my cousin. She has been there, done that, and was one of my reasons for going travelling. She's travelled all over the world on her own, with friends, and with the occasional bloke! She's also lovely. Thanks cuzz!

Alex Scott and Claire Fogg – [researchers – *Top Fifty Destinations*]
...and I thought researchers were boring! Thanks for all the hours, late nights, library trips, web 'surfing' and coffee drinking.

Travel Health
Many thanks to Paul Goodyer and the team at Nomad Travel Store for giving us such a great Travel Health section.

Index